Short Cases, History Taking and Communication Skills for the Paediatric Membership

2nd edition

Simon J Bedwani
MBBS MRCPCH

Christopher J R Anderson
MBChB MRCPCH

R Mark Beattie
BSc MBBS FRCPCH MRCP

PasTest
Dedicated to your success

© 2008 PASTEST LTD
Egerton Court
Parkgate Estate
Knutsford
Cheshire
WA16 8DX
Telephone: 01565 752000

A percentage of the material was previously published in *Short Cases for the Paediatric Membership* (1901198251)

First edition 1999
Reprinted with revisions 2004
Reprinted 2005
Second edition 2008
Reprinted 2009

ISBN: 1905635 419
       978 1905635 412

A catalogue record for this book is available from the British Library.

The information contained within this book was obtained by the authors from reliable sources. However, while every effort has been made to ensure its accuracy, no responsibility for loss, damage or injury occasioned to any person acting or refraining from action as a result of information contained herein can be accepted by the publishers or authors.

PasTest Revision Books and Intensive Courses

PasTest has been established in the field of postgraduate medical education since 1972, providing revision books and intensive study courses for doctors preparing for their professional examinations.

Books and courses are available for the following specialties:
MRCGP, MRCP Parts 1 and 2, MRCPCH Parts 1 and 2, MRCS, MRCOG Parts 1 and 2, DRCOG, DCH, FRCA, Dentistry.

For further details contact:
PasTest, Freepost, Knutsford, Cheshire WA16 7BR
Tel: 01565 752000 Fax: 01565 650264
www.pastest.co.uk enquiries@pastest.co.uk

Text prepared by Saxon Graphics Ltd, Derby
Printed and bound in the UK by Athenaeum Press, Gateshead

Contributors to Second Edition

Simon J Bedwani
MBBS MRCPCH

Paediatric Specialist Registrar, Paediatric Medical Unit, Southampton General Hospital, Southampton

Christopher J R Anderson
MBChB MRCPCH

Paediatric Specialist Registrar, Paediatric Medical Unit, Southampton General Hospital, Southampton

R Mark Beattie
BSc MBBS FRCPCH MRCP

Consultant Paediatric Gastroenterologist, Paediatric Medical Unit, Southampton General Hospital, Southampton

The Publisher and Authors would also like to thank the following contributors to the 1st edition for their contribution:

Andrew T Clark
Consultant in Paediatric Allergy, Department of Allergy, Addenbrooke's NHS Trust, Cambridge

Anne Smith
Consultant Paediatrician, Department of Child Health, Northampton General Hospital, Northampton

CONTENTS

Introduction	vii
The MRCPCH Clinical Examination	ix
Part I History taking and management planning station	**1**
1 Introduction and suggested approach	3
2 Cases	9
3 Further scenarios	55
Part II The communication skills station	**79**
4 Introduction and suggested approach	81
5 Cases	87
6 Further scenarios	123
Part III Clinical stations	**139**
7 Short case preparation and technique	141
8 Cardiology	147
9 Gastroenterology and hepatology	199
10 Respiratory medicine	233
11 Neurology (including eye examination)	267
12 'Other' station	329
12.1 Haematology	333
12.2 Rheumatology	358
12.3 Dermatology	388
12.4 Endocrinology and growth	401
12.5 Nephrology	438
13 Child development	451
Index	487

INTRODUCTION

The structure of Paediatric training in the UK has changed, as has the format of the MRCPCH examination. What has not changed is the fact that the College examination is still a significant hurdle to the Paediatric trainee. This has necessitated revision of the highly successful previous edition of this text *Short Cases for the Paediatric Membership*. The revised book focuses on the learning needs of the new MRCPCH clinical examination. It is split into three parts – History Taking and Management Planning, Communication Skills and Short Case examination the Clinical Stations.

Part I – History Taking and Management Planning has been written by first giving practical tips and pointers on taking a good history and conducting oneself appropriately in this station. There then follow some in-depth examples of cases with the emphasis on how the good candidate might tailor their history to answer questions posed in the form of a referral letter, and also mock 'question and answer' sessions to reflect what happens when one is left with the examiners at the end of the station. There are additional cases that can be worked through by the candidate and used as practice questions.

Part II – Communication Skills is designed to help the candidate maximise their chances of doing well in this potentially tricky section of the exam. There are suggestions about how to practise for the station, templates helping you to deal with different categories of tasks and worked examples.

Part III – Clinical Stations has been split into sections as seen in the examination – Cardiovascular, Abdomen, Respiratory, Neurological, 'Other' (encompassing haematology, rheumatology, dermatology, endocrinology and growth and nephrology) and the Child

Development station. The text includes notes on examination technique, useful background information and summaries of cases that have been seen in recent exams.

We do not cover the video station anywhere in this book. This station tends to assess examination and management of acutely unwell children who could not easily be brought along to the short case station. The conditions seen reflect those that a paediatrician would encounter on call or on the wards, and your exposure to hospital paediatrics will be a good preparation. Currently, candidates are sent a CD-ROM with practice scenarios for the video station by the College when they are allocated their examination date and location.

This book has been put together by authors who between them have had experience of teaching on membership courses, writing previous PasTest books and also helping to run the examinations when the format changed in 2004 to the more OSCE-orientated style. Much of the advice in this book comes from direct experience of recruiting appropriate patients, briefing candidates, looking after both patients and candidates during the examination and listening to candidate feedback about cases and scenarios encountered.

It is not a textbook of paediatrics or indeed a textbook on clinical skills but contains as much useful information as possible with the aim of helping the candidate pass the exam. There is also the acknowledgement that the candidate does not want to waste time looking for information that is superfluous or out of date. The principles outlined in this book are also designed to be applicable on the wards and in outpatient clinics, where every day there are tests in our ability to take a focused history, examine patients and communicate with those around us.

We have carefully and conscientiously endeavoured to provide information in this book which is considered correct and up to date at the time of writing. Our aim is to summarise what we consider to be current practice in a helpful way. It is a medical professional's duty, however, to check their own practice with a variety of sources, including college or local hospital guidelines, policies and procedures as well as peer-reviewed literature.

We hope you find the book helpful.

Simon J Bedwani, Christopher J R Anderson, R Mark Beattie
2008

THE MRCPCH CLINICAL EXAMINATION

The clinical examination was radically changed in 2004 to better reflect the skills required to partake in 'middle-grade' rotas and training. The current OSCE-style format means that the candidate is observed throughout the examination by a total of at least 9 different examiners, with mark sheets based on definable, reproducible criteria.

The aim of the examination is to assess whether the candidate has the necessary **all-round skills** that would be expected of a new Specialist Registrar.

The RCPCH website (www.rcpch.ac.uk/Examinations/MRCPCH-Clinical) contains excellent information and links for candidates, including examples of questions and mark sheets. What follows below is a synopsis of the examination with some tips on how to cope on the day.

A clearly defined **circuit** is set up which includes the following stations:

History taking and management planning (22 min)
A test of your ability to take a focused history and discuss a management plan.

Communication skills (two stations; 9 min each)
Primarily a test of good communication but background knowledge does help.

Clinical video station (22 min)

This tests recognition of acute symptoms and signs, many of which cannot be tested in the short cases. Conditions such as severe croup and meningococcal disease are examples. A CD-ROM sent out by the College will contain a practice run. The video station will not be mentioned again as it is beyond the scope of this book to provide more detail about this part of the examination.

Clinical stations (six stations; 9 min each)

A series of 'short cases' testing physical examination skills, interpretation of findings and knowledge around the case in general.

You can start at any point on the circuit. There are 4-min breaks between each station with the entire examination lasting 152 min. Candidates can see the circuit diagram on the RCPCH website and should be shown around their examination circuit on arrival at the exam centre. It is vital to concentrate on the route that is particular to your centre, and be mindful of the location of toilets, water, etc. Although there will be people there to direct you to the next station, it helps you to concentrate if you can smoothly make your own way there. The format and length of the exam mean it can be physically as well as mentally taxing. A good sleep the night before, a decent meal before the exam and stops for drinks during the circuit all sound obvious but can easily be ignored by the nervous candidate!

> **Look after yourself before and during this examination and pay attention to your briefing.**

Another point to make based on observations of candidates is that they have been asked to produce their mark sheet for the examiner at the start of the station but have left it outside the room on a chair. This means they have had to exit the room, pick it up and re-enter. This is mildly embarrassing but moreover breaks concentration and feels like a 'bad start' when you are nervous.

We hope that if you have prepared thoroughly and followed the advice given to you by your colleagues, patients, parents and by ourselves, you will have ironed out any uncertainties or bad habits.

You will then pass!

PART I

History taking and management planning station

INTRODUCTION AND SUGGESTED APPROACH

The aim of this station is to assess your ability to take a focused history and then summarise back to the examiner the main issues pertinent to the case.

A management plan must then be formulated. This station closely reflects an outpatient or ward review setting, in keeping with the philosophy of the exam. Children could have a new diagnosis or complaint, or you may be asked to address a specific problem in a child with a known diagnosis. You will never be asked to examine a patient but may be given additional information, eg results of investigations.

You will be given instructions that provide information about your role and these are often in the form of a referral letter. The parents and child will also have been briefed; in many cases the clinical scenario or at least the child's background problem is real. In some cases a role player, health care professional or member of the public may be used.

The 22-min station is divided into 13 min with the patient (with a 2-min warning) and 9 min alone with the examiner to discuss the case. The 2-min preparation time prior to the station is of crucial importance as it gives you time to gather your thoughts about the case. After all, nobody would want to ask a new patient into clinic without having read the referral letter thoroughly! Candidates have been seen to take a toilet break at this stage and have less time to prepare for the station. Try to avoid this unless it is really necessary – you need to give yourself the best chance possible.

The Royal College of Paediatrics and Child Health (RCPCH) Anchor Statements for Expected Standard/Clear Pass demonstrate that three key areas are assessed: **Conduct of interview** (ie your behaviours and attitude), **History taking** and **Interpretation/management planning**. These can be found at www.rcpch.ac.uk/Examinations/MRCPCH-Clinical/MRCPCH-Clinical-Structure and are summarised below.

1.1 CONDUCT OF INTERVIEW

○ Greet parents and child appropriately and introduce yourself
○ Clarify your role and agree aims and objectives
○ Maintain appropriate eye contact/body language throughout
○ Remain attentive throughout; give verbal and non – verbal signs to that effect
○ Make sure you are fully understood by patients, parents and examiner
○ Be confident yet empathetic
○ Patient and parent(s) should be at ease with you

You may feel that all of the above behaviours apply to you in a work setting but how many times have you been observed? What feedback have you received from Consultants, peers, nursing staff, parents and children? A little reflection will not go amiss when planning for this section of the examination. The day of the exam is not the best time to discover that you actually talk with your hand over your mouth or look at the floor when you are anxious! The greeting is all-important, as are your clarity of speech, eye contact and general approach throughout this station.

1.2 HISTORY TAKING

Doing this well involves:

○ Phrasing questions clearly and making sure they are not all 'closed'
○ Avoiding medical phrases that may not be understood by patient/parent

○ Allowing patient/parent time to speak – this takes conscious effort in the stress of an exam setting
○ Developing a problem list as you go on
○ Exploring the main problems fully, including psychological, social and family issues as these may be what you are asked about
○ Ensuring your history is focused to getting maximum information
○ Exploring feelings of the patient and parents
○ Concisely summarising parent/child history

ALL THIS NEEDS PRACTICE

Practising your history-taking skills will reap dividends in the exam and will reveal any faults that may have become ingrained over the years. It is particularly important to let parents/patients speak, as this will reveal many issues without your having to ask. The skilled interviewer knows when to use open and closed questions and to interject politely when sufficient information has been required in order to move on and explore another area.

Just like the Clinical Section, you will need to get used to being scrutinised while you perform the task in hand. If you have performed a few Mini Clinical Examinations (CEXs) you will already be used to being watched while taking a history. What were your strengths and weaknesses in those situations? If you haven't done this before get your colleagues to observe and comment on your performance.

1.3 INTERPRETATION AND MANAGEMENT PLANNING

○ Summarise the case to the examiner – it is very important to be able to summarise a case succinctly without going through every detail again; this will get your 9 min with the examiner off to a good start and boost confidence. Look at your previous entries in clinical notes to see how often you write a brief impression or summary of a case as well as a sensible differential diagnosis – getting used to doing this will help in the exam and improve your performance on ward rounds
○ Demonstrate a good understanding of different problems raised in the history

○ Discuss the differential diagnosis listing the most likely first – not some rare differential, especially if you cannot talk about the condition you have just blurted out!

○ Outline the essential points in the management; be sensible and pragmatic, ie do not suggest any experimental or controversial treatments unless asked about them directly. There are many national guidelines on the management of a range of conditions that are referenced in this book where it is felt appropriate

○ Ensure that your management is appropriate and effective and addresses patient/parent concerns that have been raised in the history

○ Discuss referral to other agencies and be aware of providing further contact information, eg parent groups/respite – this is often forgotten or done poorly

A thorough knowledge of the medical and psychosocial aspects of many chronic conditions is essential. It is essential that you practise on the wards with colleagues and also attend outpatient clinics to see for yourself what the main issues and agendas are for families affected by a child's illness. Try to list them for each condition – they may not match the problems you will read about in many standard texts.

SUGGESTED APPROACH

The following is a suggested template that you can apply to most cases and will be used in the six full examples that follow in Chapter 2. You still need to be fluid in your approach as things may take an unexpected turn.

1.4 PREPARATION TIME – 2 MIN

Read the candidate information and the task itself (often a referral letter) thoroughly, including the background information. There may be clues as to which avenue to take in the consultation. Imagine yourself in this role and setting. Try to think of an opening line after you have greeted the parent and child. What are the main issues you wish to clarify about this case? What possible agendas might the parent have, eg concern about a treatment? Try to put yourself in their position for a moment; what would be worrying you most as a parent? You are allowed to make notes and bring them in with you.

1.5 CONSULTATION – 13 MIN

First 9 min

Introduce yourself, explain your role. Ensure that the patient and parent are comfortable and at ease.

Outline the aims and objectives of the consultation – best done by initially referring to the letter.

Proceed to take a focused history using the template below but homing in on the most important problems. **This may mean that you cannot cover all of the headings below – try not to feel too uncomfortable about this.**

Remember, the RCPCH guidance notes stipulate that this 'is not a test of the ability to take a comprehensive history'

○ History of presenting problem(s) – including descriptions of symptoms and what has been done so far
○ Birth history, neonatal history
○ Previous childhood illnesses (if chronic illness, how this was diagnosed and when)/GP visits/hospital admissions/professionals involved so far
○ Development
○ Immunisations (including extra immunisations, eg influenza for ex-premature with chronic lung disease)
○ Drug history – remember to include doses and compliance
○ Allergies – if so get description of what happens
○ Social and family history – try to explore any problems such as one-parent family, partner away most of time, siblings with same problem, etc. Explore support systems that the family might have in place. Are you actually talking to the parent who knows the child's illness best?

Last 4 min

The bell will ring signifying that there are 4 min remaining with the parents and child. At this stage you should be thinking of exploring any concerns, expectations and feelings that have not come out of this consultation so far. Do you feel there is an agenda that has not been covered?

It is useful to ask such questions as:

○ **What is your biggest worry?**
○ **Are you concerned about any diagnosis in particular?**
○ **Is there anything else you would like to tell me/ask me?**
○ **Is there anything you haven't understood?**

When you feel that the consultation has come to a close you should summarise the main points back to the parent and child as appropriate.

1.6 REFLECTION – WHILE PARENT AND CHILD ARE SHOWN OUT OF THE ROOM

Do not panic; try to develop a problem-orientated summary of the key facts/issues of the case. Do not reflect on the information that you could have gathered but didn't – be positive.

1.7 THE 9 MIN WITH THE EXAMINER

Summarise the case, including the main issues covered in the history. Come up with responses to potential issues, a differential diagnosis, investigations and management plan. Suggest contacts for the family and/or outline how you would refer the patient to other agencies.

2

CASES

CONTENTS

2.1 Case one: Cystic fibrosis – respiratory deterioration
Notes on some important clinical problems in cystic fibrosis
Notes on management of cystic fibrosis

2.2 Case two: Asthma – poorly controlled
Notes on management of asthma

2.3 Case three: Ex-premature baby with recurrent wheeze
Notes on problems faced by ex-premature babies

2.4 Case four: Recurrent abdominal pain
Notes on recurrent abdominal pain

2.5 Case five: Cerebral palsy
Notes on management of cerebral palsy

2.6 Case six: Nephrotic syndrome – relapse
Notes on nephrotic syndrome

Full example scenarios (including suggestions for summaries and For each of the six full scenarios you are given a **role**, a **setting** and a **task**. There will be some **background information** also. Remember that the examiner will be given information on some key features in the medical and social history that you will be expected to elicit. The first case includes initial instructions that would be similar to the candidate instructions seen on the examination sheet. See the example question on the RCPCH website, www.rcpch.ac.uk/Examinations/MRCPCH-Clinical. It is good practice to familiarise yourself with the timekeeping instructions in the box. These are not given for the other five full examples to avoid unnecessary repetition. A template for how you might approach the history is given, along with some information that a good candidate would elicit from the history and the examiner will have to hand. Note that some of the information is not specific to that condition but is very relevant – especially the social situations covered.

Some notes on management pertaining to the scenario in particular (using a question and answer format) are then provided. These are followed by additional notes on the condition/presentation, as there are of course many possible scenarios for a given condition.

A further 12 examples of scenarios you may encounter are also given in Chapter 3, along with more concise guidance about the most important information to elicit, and key management points. These can be practised as full scenarios with colleagues. For further examples see also the RCPCH webpage referenced in the introduction and click on the PDF file, Guide Notes for Candidates.

2.1 CASE ONE: CYSTIC FIBROSIS –
RESPIRATORY DETERIORATION

○ Take a focused history having read the scenario below
○ The subject/role player may ask you questions
○ When the consultation has finished the examiner will discuss
   your management plan with you

Timing:
*Total time provided for this station is **22–min**.*

There are 2 min before you are called in to read this sheet and prepare yourself. A bell will signal the start of the station and you will be invited into the examination room – take your instruction sheet with you.

*You will have **13 min** in total with the patient; a warning will be issued when you have **4 min** left to complete your history*

*You will then have **9 min alone** with the examiner to discuss your management plan.*

You may take notes.
You will not be asked to examine the patient.

Role

You are the Specialist Trainee

Setting

Cubicle on the Children's Ward

You are talking to

Craig, a 10-year-old boy, and his mother

Task

Take a focused history, aiming to explore the problem indicated as you would in the clinical situation. You may answer questions that the subject (role player) may pose to you. After the consultation the examiner will focus on your management planning.

Dear Dr...

Re: Craig S

This boy, who is 10 years old, whose family are visiting the area for the half-term and who has cystic fibrosis, has become very chesty over the last few days. He was last seen in his usual clinic 6 weeks ago for his annual review. He is colonised with *Pseudomonas*. On examination he has a temperature of 38.2°C, and on chest examination has polyphonic wheeze and coarse expiratory crackles at the right base. I would be grateful if you could assess him and I do wonder whether he needs admission.

Yours sincerely,

Dr S Smith

General Practitioner

Background information

Craig has been seen regularly in his usual cystic fibrosis clinic at City Hospital and has had very few admissions as an emergency. He has not attended any other hospital before now.

Any other information

Your examination findings are the same as Dr Smith's.
Craig is thin (0.4th centile).

Preparation time (2 min): initial thoughts

Once you have read the question, concentrate on remembering the child's name and coming up with an appropriate greeting to him and his mother. What issues can you see between the lines already? In this case the family are not used to this particular hospital and might feel less confident than they normally would.

Consultation

Introduction. Clarify role, agree aims and objectives.

Remember to include the patient as much as possible in the consultation, which is sometimes difficult when the parents talk freely and you are nervous.

History

- ○ When did Craig become chesty?
- ○ What are the main symptoms? Ask about fevers, malaise, wheeze
- ○ Triggers if wheezy episodes
- ○ Exercise tolerance at moment
- ○ Normal exercise tolerance, background health
- ○ Results of last lung function tests
- ○ Results of last sputum sample or cough swab. Any details re colonisation or antibiotic resistance?
- ○ Number of hospital admissions/year – elective and emergency
- ○ Respiratory paediatrician involved. How was Craig diagnosed?
- ○ Other health professionals involved, eg physiotherapist, dietician
- ○ Birth and neonatal history – *brief enquiry in this case*
- ○ Any other medical problems? Has Craig been gaining weight along 0.4th centile or is he losing weight? Ask about stool frequency. Has the dose of pancreatic enzyme supplementation needed adjusting recently?
- ○ Immunisations, especially for *Pneumococcus*
- ○ Drug history. Any problems with compliance?
- ○ Allergies
- ○ Family and social history

Warning bell rings; you have 4 min left with Craig and his mother. You have gathered the following information so far:

Craig has had a cough for the last 5 days, which has gradually worsened in frequency. He has become productive of green sputum and developed a fever today. He has had many wheezy episodes in the past 3 months for which he has taken 5 puffs of salbutamol to good effect. He is more wheezy at the moment. He can still run around but only for 10 or 15 min; he needs a sit down at this point.

He was diagnosed with cystic fibrosis as a neonate having had meconium ileus which necessitated surgery on day 10 of life.

There have been many elective admissions for antibiotics over the years, which have needed to be more frequent. He had an implantable venous access system (Port-A-Cath®) inserted 6 months ago. On his last clinic visit lung function had deteriorated and sputum was colonised with *Pseudomonas*. He has always been close to the 0.4th centile. He is not nasogastrically fed overnight.

Medications: oral ciprofloxacin, multivitamins, Creon® pancreatic enzyme supplements.

Craig lives with his parents and 4-year-old brother, who is fit and well. This is their first holiday with Craig for 3 years as they have been worried about being too far from their local hospital.

Questions to ask at this point:

○ Who is Craig's Consultant?
○ Who is looking after Craig's brother and where are you all staying at the moment?
○ Is there anything that you would like to ask me? Remember to address this to both Craig and his mother
○ Have you any other concerns that we have not covered?

It transpires that Craig's mother was extremely anxious about coming away with him, as he has not had such a good year. They are staying with his aunt who is currently looking after Craig's brother. The father is back home at work; they do not have their own transport to the hospital and needed a lift from the aunt. His mother is additionally concerned as they forgot his PEP mask (Positive Expiratory Pressure device used as part of the daily physiotherapy routine to aid clearance of secretions) whilst packing for their holiday and she feels this is the cause of this deterioration.

You verify the main points and summarise the history. There are no further questions from Craig or his mother.

The bell rings and you are left with the examiner.

Discussion with examiner (9 min)

Would you please summarise this case?

I saw Craig, who is 10 years old and has a respiratory exacerbation of cystic fibrosis. He is visiting the area and is normally looked after by Dr Jones in City Hospital. He is colonised with *Pseudomonas* and his respiratory function has been deteriorating recently. He has also developed an episodic wheeze.

How would you manage this child's current exacerbation?

Points to cover here are:

○ Hospital admission, saturation monitoring, oxygen as needed
○ Investigations: cough swab or sputum sample, blood cultures and inflammatory markers, peak flow, lung function tests if available
○ Find out results of last cough swab/sputum from tertiary centre. This can be done by contacting the cystic fibrosis team. When was last chest X-ray? Have tests for *Aspergillosis* been done recently?
○ Treatment with i.v. antibiotics such as ceftazidime and gentamicin.
○ DNAse
○ Physiotherapy twice a day; liaise with department and give them a summary of Craig's history

Craig's mother wants to go back to the City Hospital as soon as possible. She wants to see the cystic fibrosis team, and her other child goes back to school in 2 days. What do you tell her?

… that you will liaise with your Consultant and the cystic fibrosis team to try to transfer Craig back to City Hospital. This does depend on finding him a cubicle. He will be here overnight at least and the cystic fibrosis team are aware of our management plan.

Notes on some important clinical problems in cystic fibrosis

Respiratory

○ Almost all deaths in cystic fibrosis patients are due to pulmonary disease. As well as bacterial colonisation and infection, cor pulmonale and allergic bronchopulmonary aspergillosis (ABPA) need to be considered
○ Cor pulmonale can develop in the second decade secondary to severe lung disease; it is recognised by a raised jugular venous

pressure, hepatomegaly and oedema. Mean survival subsequently is 8 months
○ ABPA occurs in up to 10% of patients: wheeze, eosinophilia, raised specific IgE and IgG and/or positive sputum culture for *Aspergillus*
○ Asthma: up to 20% of patients have atopic asthma

Gastrointestinal/hepatic

○ Pancreatic insufficiency with resultant malabsorption in 85% of patients – resultant failure to thrive, steatorrhoea
○ Meconium ileus is the presenting feature for 15% of patients
○ Distal intestinal obstruction syndrome (DIOS) or meconium ileus equivalent occurs in older children (20%), presenting as cramping abdominal pains and a palpable mass in the right iliac fossa. Remember that such masses may form the apex of an intussusception
○ Rectal prolapse occurs in up to 20% (toddler presentation) and is caused by a combination of steatorrhoea and coughing. It usually resolves on starting pancreatic replacement therapy
○ Patients may present in the neonatal period with obstructive jaundice due to inspissated bile
○ Chronic liver disease occurs mainly in teenage children (around 20%); some can develop focal biliary cirrhosis and 2% of these progress to multilobular cirrhosis with portal hypertension and oesophageal varices

Endocrine

○ Insulin-dependent diabetes occurs in 7% of patients (mainly over 10 years), secondary to pancreatic fibrosis. Best diagnosed by oral glucose tolerance test in patients with cystic fibrosis. It can be easily controlled with insulin, and diabetic ketoacidosis is rare. However, as patients survive longer, evidence of microangiopathy is now emerging

Metabolic

○ Salt deficiency state, especially in summer months (loss through sweat) resulting in hyponatraemic, hypochloraemic metabolic alkalosis. Potentially major problem in active young patients who still rely on parents for drinks

Genitourinary

○ Azoospermia and thus male infertility

Notes on management of cystic fibrosis

Emphasis is on multidisciplinary outpatient-based management, involving medical staff, physiotherapist, dietician, community nurses, social workers and psychologist as required. Annual specialist review advised. Please also refer to British Thoracic Society (BTS) website at www.brit-thoracic.org.uk

Physiotherapy

Percussion and vibration techniques are used to loosen mucus, and gravity is used to drain it. Ideally 20 min twice a day for life. Normally performed by chest percussion head down over a foam wedge.

Forced expiratory technique, performing 'huffs' from medium to low lung volume, aids clearance. Alternatively, the patient may use breaths through a positive expiratory pressure (PEP) mask followed by coughing. A regular exercise programme is beneficial and along with physiotherapy has been shown to improve lung function.

Optimise nutrition

Patients with cystic fibrosis suffer because they have increased metabolic demands, malabsorption and poor appetites. Assessing and optimising nutritional status is one of the most important factors in managing a patient with cystic fibrosis as this is strongly correlated with the severity of pulmonary disease. Patients should have their height and weight plotted on centile charts every 3 months; if there is concern triceps and subscapular skinfold thickness can be measured with callipers and compared to normal values.

Patients should consult a dietician to receive a high-calorie, high-protein diet. This can be supplemented by high-calorie drinks. Overnight nasogastric feeds are an alternative as the appetite is often poor, and eventually patients with severe weight loss may benefit from overnight gastrostomy feeds. **Vitamin A, D and E supplementation** is necessary as these are fat soluble. Plasma concentrations should be measured at the annual review.

Pancreatic enzyme supplementation

Most need **pancreatic enzyme supplements** (pancreatin) in pH-sensitive polymer capsules. The dose is titrated against growth and steatorrhoea. Capsules with a high lipase concentration have been shown to cause colonic strictures.

Antibiotics

Used to reduce colonisation and treat acute chest infections.

Colonisation is usually with *Staphylococcus* and *Haemophilus* in infants and *Pseudomonas* in older children. **Flucloxacillin** is used either prophylactically from diagnosis or long-term after colonisation. **Nebulised tobramycin/colomycin** can be used in *Pseudomonas* colonisation; this has been shown to improve lung function.

Some centres advocate a 2-week course of intravenous antibiotics every 3 months in colonised individuals.

Acute infections are treated as they arise. Organisms can normally be predicted from previous cough swabs/sputum samples or isolated. Oral (**ciprofloxacin**) or intravenous (**ceftazidime/piperacillin** plus an **aminoglycoside** such as **gentamicin**) therapy can be started as appropriate. Patients have altered pharmacokinetics and so higher doses are used for longer duration. *Burkholderia cepacia* is a highly resistant Gram-negative organism that can spread from patient to patient. Some patients with *Burkholderia* infection can develop a life-threatening septicaemia. **Meropenem** is often used for this infection.

DNase

DNase has been available since 1992 as recombinant human DNase. Acts to digest viscous DNA derived from inflammatory cells in bronchial exudates. Most can expect a 10% increase in forced expiratory volume in 1 s (FEV_1) in the first week. Warn patients that it can make them hoarse.

Treatment of co-existent conditions/complications

- Asthma – at least 20% have atopic asthma
- ABPA – high-dose corticosteroids
- Constipation

○ DIOS – laxatives and hydration if mild, through to Gastrografin®
  or even surgical treatment
○ Liver disease – ursodeoxycholic acid used in patients with raised
  transaminases or early ultrasound features of liver disease
○ Cor pulmonale – heart lung transplant (adults with cystic fibrosis
  have 70% survival at 1 year, 40% at 5 years)

Separation of patients in clinic settings

This is done to reduce spread of harmful organisms such as
Burkholderia cepacia.

Gene therapy

Using vectors such as liposomes or replication-deficient adenovirus to
transfer normal cystic fibrosis transmembrane conductance regulator
(CFTR) into host cells. Still in early stages.

2.2 CASE TWO: ASTHMA – POORLY CONTROLLED

Role

You are the Specialist Trainee

Setting

Outpatient clinic

You are talking to

Adam, a 12-year-old boy with asthma, and his mother

Dear Dr...

Re Adam J

This 12-year-old boy has attended my surgery 5 times in the last 3 months with moderate exacerbations of his asthma. He has recently moved house and the family thinks this is the reason for his symptoms. His last attendance resulted in me doubling his flixotide to 100 micrograms, 1 puff twice a day. I have not started any other medications. I would be grateful for your help as he is going through many repeat prescriptions of salbutamol.

Yours sincerely,

Dr D McCann,

General Practitioner

Background information

Takes occasional cetirizine for hayfever.

Any other information

Weight and height on 50th centile.

Preparation time (2 min): initial thoughts

You should already be thinking of focusing your history to elicit the reasons for Adam's recurrent attendances to the GP.

Consultation

Introduction. Clarify role, agree aims and objectives.

Remember to ask **Adam** about his symptoms. Children very often reveal additional triggers of their asthma if allowed to talk by their parents and history taker!

History

○ When diagnosed
○ Number of GP and hospital visits in last year. Known to asthma nurse in GP practice?
○ Number of visits for repeat prescriptions of beta-agonist
○ Number of steroid courses in last year
○ Worst attack and level of treatment needed, eg high dependency unit (HDU) and intravenous (i.v.) salbutamol
○ Description of the last few attacks; related to chest infections?
○ Best peak flow – is a diary kept?
○ Triggers – cover parental smoking, pets, hayfever, house dust mite, recent house move
○ Any skin prick tests performed previously
○ Other atopic features? May have (had) eczema, food allergy
○ Birth history, relevant past medical history, breast or bottle fed – *brief enquiry*
○ Medications (previous and current), means of delivery and compliance issues
○ Family history of asthma/atopy in general
○ Social history – details of housing, type of flooring, furnishing, pets, measures to reduce house dust mite numbers

Warning bell rings; you have 4 min left with Adam and his mother. You have gathered the following information so far:

Adam was diagnosed at 6 years of age following admission to hospital for severe wheeze requiring admission to the HDU and IV salbutamol. He has also been seen by a previous GP for viral-induced wheeze and eczema between the ages of 1 and 2 years. In retrospect his mother thinks he had some mild exercise-induced symptoms before this first admission. He was seen in clinic for a couple of years then discharged as he was stable on 100 µg flixotide per day. He has not been given any other medications. He has been worse in the last few weeks, taking his salbutamol two to three times a day. He has required four courses of prednisolone in the past 5 weeks. Adam is becoming more independent and is taking the flixotide without supervision. The family have moved house recently and there is a lot of building work. His father is quite stressed and has taken to smoking again; he had given up for a few years after Adam's first admission.

Questions to ask now:

○ How exactly is he taking his flixotide? Does he use a spacer?
○ Ask Adam about compliance. If you phrase this question correctly you will get an honest answer. For example, asking '*do you take your flixotide Adam?*' will result in '*Yes*'. Asking the same patient, '*Adam, do you ever forget to take your flixotide? Lots of people do when they are in a rush*' will also result in a '*Yes*'! Then gently ask how often he misses it. After using this approach I once got the answer, '*Actually, the flixotide is still in its box*'
○ Explore parental knowledge about inhaled steroids and risk factors for worsening asthma such as parental smoking (if time)

Adam tells you that he has been missing all his morning doses of flixotide recently because he has started walking to his new school; he has to set off earlier and he finds it hard to remember when he is in a rush. Besides, he doesn't notice any obvious benefits when he takes his flixotide – the salbutamol is better. When he remembers, he takes his flixotide using an Easibreathe®.

You verify the main points and summarise the history. There are no further questions from Adam or his mother.

The bell rings and you are left with the examiner.

Discussion with examiner (9 min)

Would you please summarise this case?

Adam is a 12–year-old boy with a long history of asthma and past history of eczema. One of his exacerbations 6 years ago required i.v. salbutamol on HDU. His control has worsened recently and this co-incides with poorer compliance to his inhaled steroids and recent cigarette smoke exposure.

What other reasons might there be for poor response to his current asthma therapy?

Mention the recent house move and building work and the fact that the Easibreathe® device may not suit him. He may also need additional medication.

How would you manage this boy now?

Cover the following:

○ Educate parent and child about the importance of taking inhaled steroids regularly and their mechanisms of action. Mother will have to supervise for a while longer. You could tell him to take it before he brushes his teeth morning and night
○ Check inhaler technique. Large volume spacer would be more appropriate for flixotide especially while control is not as good (see NICE guidelines at www.nice.org.uk)
○ Encourage use of peak flow diary; make sure there is an action plan for future attacks. Ask to plot his predicted peak flow for height
○ Address paternal smoking; ask GP to help in your clinic letter if necessary
○ Optimise management of hayfever in season
○ Leave other medications as they are and review in a few weeks; they may have an effect if taken regularly. If control still poor then can double flixotide to 200 μg/day. Review again with peak flow diary in a few weeks; if control still poor and he is compliant add in a long-acting beta-agonist or leukotriene receptor agonist

Notes on management of asthma

The aims:

- ○ Control of symptoms (including nocturnal and exercise-induced)
- ○ Prevention of exacerbations
- ○ Achievement of normal physical activity and growth along with best possible lung function ... with **minimal side-effects**

General measures

Avoiding cigarette smoke is the most significant measure. There is no doubt that exposure to tobacco smoke in the home contributes to the severity of childhood asthma. You may be instructed to counsel a proxy parent about smoking – mention the risk to themselves and their child's health as well as offering appropriate support. This reflects the skills you will need in a ward or clinic situation. Remember that a significant percentage of older children smoke.

Weight reduction is recommended in obese patients (an increasing number) with asthma.

Measures to reduce house dust mite numbers such as damp dusting, mattress covers, changing carpeted bedroom floors to laminate flooring and washing/freezing toys may reduce symptoms in some patients.

Avoiding animal dander can be difficult for patients with current or even previous pets – even if dogs/cats are removed from a household, their dander will remain in significant quantities for 6 months or more.

People often forget to ask children and teenagers where else they go apart from their own home; grandmother's smoky flat and three cats may not feature in your social history but could be the reason for a deterioration.

Drug therapy

Keep up to date with joint British Thoracic Society (BTS) and Scottish Intercollegiate Guidelines Network (SIGN) guidelines. These were last revised April 2004 and can be found at www.sign.ac.uk/guidelines/index.html or at www.brit-thoracic. org.uk. Be aware of any changes by the time you take the exam; the latest *British National Formulary for Children* is also a useful reference

Acute attacks: inhaled or nebulised beta-2 agonists and oral steroids. More severe acute attacks are managed with intravenous **salbutamol, aminophylline, hydrocortisone** and in some instances **magnesium sulphate.** Ventilation is occasionally required

Long-term treatment – summary of BTS stepwise therapy as an aide-mémoire

- ○ **Step 1:** inhaled short-acting beta-agonist as required
- ○ **Step 2:** inhaled prophylactic steroids
  - Consider starting when symptomatic or *correctly and appropriately* using inhaled beta-2 agonists three times a week or more
  - Start at dose appropriate to the severity of disease (200–400 µg/day) and titrate to lowest dose at which effective control of asthma is maintained
  - The *device* selected for drug delivery is important and age specific
  - It is important to be familiar with all the inhaler and spacer devices and the most appropriate age to use them (see 'Summary of delivery devices' box)
  - The side-effects of inhaled steroids are a common concern to parents and clinicians; this is discussed on page 128
- ○ **Step 3:** add-on therapy. Should be considered if control is not achieved on escalating doses of inhaled steroid, having checked compliance, inhaler technique and triggers
  - *Long-acting beta-2 agonists* (LABA), eg **salmeterol**, are recommended in the *over-5s*, especially if there are exercise-induced symptoms. Note that they should not be used without inhaled corticosteroids. *Leukotriene receptor antagonists* (eg **montelukast**) may also be added in the over-5s and are used at Step 3 instead of LABA in 2- to 5-year-olds
- ○ **Step 4:** as Step 3 plus increase inhaled steroid in over-5s; refer to respiratory paediatrician if under 5 years old
- ○ **Step 5:** as Step 4 plus oral corticosteroid plus refer to respiratory paediatrician if have not already done so

SUMMARY OF DELIVERY DEVICES

More detailed notes on these devices from a practical point of view can be found in the Clinical section (page 243). Remember you may be asked to demonstrate their use

- Metered dose inhalers
- Spacer devices: Volumatic®/Babyhaler® + face mask
- Dry powder: Diskhaler®, Turbuhaler®, Accuhaler®, Rotahaler® (used rarely)
- Self-actuating with propellant: Autohaler®/Easibreathe®

Reasons for poor response to escalating asthma therapy

Remember these when assessing any asthmatic child:

- Poor inhaler technique or inappropriate device for that child
- Poor compliance to treatment regimen
- Poor understanding of disease management
- Emerging allergies/new environmental triggers, eg moved house, building work
- Stress; physical or psychological
- Wrong diagnosis

Summary of assessment of an asthmatic child ready for discharge

This may also be tested in the clinical station or even the communication station.

Remember to include the following points:

- Adjust the child's medication if appropriate – did under-treatment precipitate the admission, is the child's bronchodilator usage high suggesting poor control (contact GP – how many repeat prescriptions?) and is there a need to increase prophylactic medication?
- Check patient is stable on the medication they will receive at home; should not need bronchodilator more frequently than 4-hourly

○ Check inhaler/spacer and peak flow technique and adjust as necessary

○ Explain in basic terms the difference between bronchospasm and inflammation and the relevance of using a regular preventative steroid in that context

○ Provide a written action plan with clear instructions of what to do if the asthma worsens

○ Provide a peak flow diary

○ Give advice on avoiding precipitants

○ Write to the GP

○ Arrange community or asthma nurse to visit, eg if there are concerns over compliance

○ Arrange appropriate follow-up

Newer management strategies to be aware of – only mention if asked!

○ Intravenous magnesium sulphate in moderate to severe asthma (used in adults)

○ Monoclonal anti-IgE treatment

2.3   CASE THREE: EX-PREMATURE BABY WITH RECURRENT WHEEZE

Role

You are the Specialist Trainee in a District General Hospital

Setting

Outpatient clinic

You are talking to

Jess, mother of Samuel

Dear Dr...

Re: Samuel Adams

Thank you for seeing this 14-month-old boy with persistent cough and wheeze, unresponsive to salbutamol. He has a special care baby unit (SCBU) developmental follow-up clinic at City Hospital in 4 months but I would be grateful if you could see him before this. His mother has attended my surgery 4 times in the last 2 months.

He has mild respiratory distress but has never required hospital admission. He was born at 27 weeks' gestation and had a difficult first 2 weeks of life: he was ventilated for respiratory distress syndrome and had chronic lung disease. At first I thought he had bronchiolitis but this has persisted for a while and his mother is anxious.

Yours sincerely,

Dr Jefferies

General Practitioner

Background information

Weight and height on 9th centile.

Other information

Mother is a respiratory nurse on an adult ward in this hospital.

Preparation time (2 min): initial thoughts

You are going to need to take a detailed history of Samuel's symptoms as well as a neonatal history. His mother may have some ideas about what she thinks the problem might be.

Consultation

Introduction. Clarify role, agree aims and objectives.

History

○ Current symptoms – persistent or intermittent wheeze? Any days when there has not been a problem?
○ Did the problem start suddenly or gradually?
○ Associations with coughs, colds, etc
○ Presence or absence of fevers, other features indicating that illness is affecting baby such as poor feeding, weight loss
○ *Thorough birth and neonatal history – a template is given below for any case involving an ex- premature baby; it needs to be adapted for the situation*
  • Details of pregnancy (including maternal health, smoking)
  • Delivery/resuscitation
  • Respiratory management on SCBU and number of days in oxygen
  • Home oxygen required?
  • Go through checklist of other potential problems on SCBU, eg patent ductus arteriosus, interventricular haemorrhage, retinopathy of prematurity, feeding problems (length of time on total parenteral nutrition (TPN) if relevant), jaundice, sepsis. Make sure you address the respiratory problems in detail and do not explore these other issues to the detriment of finding out the cause of the wheeze

- Total length of time on SCBU
- Other medical problems/admissions. Always ask about eczema and food allergy in wheezy infants
- Feeding history, reflux symptoms?
- Developmental history (detail depends on the case)
- Medications (current and previous) and immunisations
- Consultant in charge/follow-up previously arranged

Warning bell rings; you have 4 min left with Samuel and his mother. You have gathered the following information so far:

Samuel was well until he developed a runny nose followed by a nasty cough and mild respiratory distress 2 months ago. Hospital admission was considered but his saturations were 97%, feeding was minimally affected and his mother was fairly confident she could manage him at home. His GP thought he had bronchiolitis. This cough and wheeze persisted for 3 weeks and the GP was visited a second time. Salbutamol was tried at this stage but did not work. There was a period of about a week when the cough and wheeze went away but then he started wheezing again. He had a runny nose at this time. Again, this lasted 2–3 weeks and he gradually got better. There has never been any stridor. In the past week it has happened again and his mother has visited the GP twice to discuss other treatments. She is concerned it may be reflux but no treatments have been started yet. You then asked about symptoms of reflux; there do not seem to be any present.

Samuel is thriving.

He was born at 27 weeks after his mother had an antepartum haemorrhage. He needed 2 weeks of ventilation and also blood and inotropes initially. He was in oxygen for nearly all of his 15-week admission. He was on TPN for 10 days and was given breast milk from day 2. Development is normal for corrected gestation.

Remaining 4 min:

You take a social history. There are no major issues; she and her husband also have a 4-year-old boy who has just started nursery. You also try to explore her concerns and give her some time to air them. She still feels that reflux might be a reason for these episodes of wheeze and is worried that his lungs will not recover from all the previous damage. You verify the main points and summarise the history. There are no further questions from Samuel's mother.

The bell rings and you are left with the examiner.

Discussion with examiner (9 min)

Would you summarise this case for me?

I saw Samuel, a 14-month-old boy born at 27 weeks' gestation so corrected to 11 months. His main problem on SCBU was respiratory distress syndrome (RDS) and chronic lung disease. His current problem is recurrent cough and wheeze, which started after an episode of bronchiolitis. He has had two other viral illnesses since then so has been wheezy most of the time.

What would you say to his mother ?

A first episode of bronchiolitis can leave a residual wheeze in any patient that can take a while to settle. This is especially true of ex-premature babies. It does not often respond to ipratropium bromide or salbutamol, but both are worth a trial. In this case it seems there was recovery between bouts of cough and wheeze; this was not apparent from the GP letter. The most likely cause (especially with the brother in nursery) is two or three separate viral lower respiratory tract infections (LRTIs) affecting small, hyper-reactive airways. Inhaled steroids are not usually warranted for this situation. I would advise that her child is seen by a doctor if he is acutely unwell with the wheeze or is failing to gain weight adequately.

What other causes would you consider in a persistently wheezy infant and how would you investigate them?

- Inhaled foreign body – inspiratory and expiratory chest X-ray
- Pertussis – pernasal swab
- True early asthma – demonstrable reversibility of symptoms, atopy, family history
- Cystic fibrosis – sweat test
- Congenital airway malformation – bronchoscopy

Wheeze that is persistent, frequent, associated with focal signs or occurs in the presence of *faltering growth* or signs of malabsorption warrants further investigation and follow-up.

Notes on problems faced by ex-premature babies

Families whose children are graduates from SCBU are often happy to help out in exams and are often already in contact with the hospital. It is therefore useful to brush up on all of the common problems that ex-premature babies may have faced and in particular which of these may still be affecting them. It is useful to attend your nearest SCBU follow-up clinic to see these issues first-hand, especially if it has been a while since your last neonatal job. Remember to answer the question as just one or two problems may be addressed in the task given.

You should be able to discuss the following with examiners and indeed parents, as these topics may also crop up in a communication scenario. They can all be found in standard neonatal texts.

Chronic lung disease

Prognosis is a common parental concern. Most babies with chronic lung disease can be weaned off oxygen before discharge. The rest need home oxygen setting up, which can delay discharge if not planned well in advance. The long-term respiratory function of ex-premature babies is often good, but do mention the importance of influenza and pneumococcal vaccines. Some patients can have problems with wheeze and are especially symptomatic during episodes of bronchiolitis; the illness can be more severe and the effects can last for longer than in full-term babies. Threshold for admission should therefore be lower.

Patent ductus arteriosus

Treatment is supportive but medical therapy (**indomethacin**) and occasionally surgical therapy will have been required. This is usually when a baby is unresponsive to indomethacin (one-third also relapse) and is ventilator dependent. Remember the risks of indomethacin – renal impairment and necrotising enterocolitis. **Ibuprofen** is increasingly being used and has fewer renal side-effects.

Feeding/nutrition

Total parenteral nutrition and its complications (extravasation injury, infection of long lines, conjugated hyperbilirubinaemia) are often a source of concern, as are difficulties in establishing feeds, poor weight gain and necrotising enterocolitis.

Periventricular haemorrhage and periventricular leukomalacia

Periventricular haemorrhage (PVH) remains a significant cause of morbidity in premature babies but its incidence has decreased with improvements in neonatal care. It is graded on ultrasound findings; the sequelae are due to destruction of the brain parenchyma or post-haemorrhagic hydrocephalus; some babies require a ventriculoperitoneal shunt.

Periventricular leukomalacia (PVL) is due to ischaemic damage in areas of the brain supplied by branches of the middle cerebral artery. This results in motor impairment (descending corticospinal tracts), which is variable in severity. Cortical blindness is another risk. Most babies with PVL will develop cerebral palsy, most commonly diplegic but occasionally quadriplegic.

Visual problems

May be due to retinopathy of prematurity (ROP), PVL or to direct cortical damage. Ask if laser treatment was required if the baby had ROP. This prevents blindness from retinal detachment but causes peripheral field defects. Patients are followed-up in SCBU and ophthalmology clinics.

Hearing problems

All SCBU graduates should have had a hearing test. If hearing is suboptimal ask about risk factors, ie aminoglycosides, jaundice, hypoxia, PVH and PVL. They will need follow-up, usually by a community paediatrician with a special interest in audiology or a consultant paediatric audiologist.

Developmental delay and learning difficulties

Although this may not be a major problem when correcting for prematurity, it is a huge concern for parents. There is a higher than normal incidence of learning difficulties even in more mature ex-prematures (eg 32 weeks' gestation), who appear normal at 2 years of age. A smooth transition between the neonatal follow-up clinic and child development clinics is required for infants whose development is a cause for concern.

2.4 CASE FOUR: RECURRENT ABDOMINAL PAIN

Role

You are the Specialist Trainee

Setting

Outpatient department

You are talking to

Mrs Oliver and her 9-year-old daughter Milly

Dear Dr...

Re: Milly Oliver

Thank you for seeing Milly, who is 9 years old and has complained of central abdominal pain on and off for the last 4 months. Her attacks are painful and she has been sent home from school on numerous occasions. Her brother Saul has constipation and I saw him 2 weeks ago. Mrs Oliver says that she has no concerns about Milly's bowel habits but is concerned at the amount of school she's missing. Examination today was normal. Although an organic cause is unlikely, I would be grateful if you could assess her to see if this needs investigating further.

Yours sincerely

Dr Lincoln

General Practitioner

Background information

Weight and height on 25th centile.

Preparation time (2 min): initial thoughts

You will need to focus your history very well; this may avoid unnecessary investigations. A good social history is required.

Consultation

Introduction. Clarify role, agree aims and objectives.

History

○ When did the pain start? Any obvious triggers?
○ Location, intensity, character and duration, time of day or night
○ Does pain wake her at night?
○ Exacerbating and relieving factors
○ Appetite, diet, satiety
○ Presence of nausea, emesis, reflux symptoms, urinary symptoms
○ Stool pattern, consistency, completeness of evacuation
○ Weight loss, growth delay, rash, joint or eye symptoms
○ Past medical history, focusing on relevant previous illnesses and gastrointestinal problems
○ Drug history, allergies (especially food allergies)
○ Family history of migraine, irritable bowel syndrome, inflammatory bowel disease
○ Social history: school, play, peer relationships, family dynamics

Warning bell rings; you have 4 min left with Milly and her mother. You have gathered the following information so far:

Milly began to get the pain over 4 months ago. This seemed to come 'out of nowhere'. Now occurs on most days and can last from 20 min to 2 hours. Paracetamol helps. Felt in the centre of her abdomen, 'near her belly button'. She does feel sick but has not vomited. She occasionally looks pale with these attacks. Her appetite is occasionally reduced. Bowels open once or twice daily and normal consistency according to her mother. Past medical history unremarkable, not on medication. Brother has constipation, mother has migraine.

Remaining 4 min

You take a social history and learn that Milly lives with her parents and brother. She has lived in the same house all her life. There do not seem to be any problems at school but she is a shy girl and 'a bit of a worrier'. Her father is in the army and is away for half the year. You ask Milly and her mother if there are any other concerns and are told that she has missed about 2 weeks worth of school in the past 2 months. Mrs Oliver is very concerned that this is Crohn's disease, which her sister has been battling for 4 years.

The bell rings and you are left with the examiner.

Discussion with examiner (9 min)

Would you summarise this case for me?

I saw Milly, who is 9 years old, with her mother. She has been suffering from recurrent bouts of central abdominal pain that have resulted in her missing 2 weeks worth of school in the last 2 months. She has not lost weight and has no obvious pointers to an organic cause in the history I obtained. There is however a family history of Crohn's disease.

What are pointers towards an organic cause?

Warning signs in chronic abdominal pain are:

- Very young child
- Pain well localised and further out from the umbilicus
- Vomiting
- Unexplained fever
- Change in bowel habit especially diarrhoea
- Nocturnal waking with pain
- Weight loss, blood in stool, perianal disease
- Poor growth
- Family history of coeliac disease or inflammatory bowel disease

What would your initial management be in this case?

Cover the following:

- Exclude commoner organic causes (especially as family history of inflammatory bowel disease): full blood count, inflammatory markers, liver function tests, coeliac screen, stool culture, urine for microscopy, culture and sensitivities (MC&S). If all are normal and there are no pointers to further investigation, then follow with a confident explanation that the most likely cause is functional abdominal pain, followed by an explanation of this term
- Show sympathy toward the child and family as the pain is very real. Advise that the child should try to attend school as much as possible

○ Simple analgesia when pain first comes on

What if these strategies do not work?

○ Referral to the Child and Adolescent Mental Health Team/psychologist to look further into family dynamics and hopefully come up with pain management techniques
○ Liaise with school (with parental consent) to explore any obvious barriers to school attendance

Notes on recurrent abdominal pain

There are plenty of children with long histories of abdominal pain who are well known to outpatient departments. They are often managed by multidisciplinary teams. They may well be invited to the exam for a session, to reflect the kind of patients that you will meet when you conduct outpatient clinics more regularly.

The majority of patients have *functional abdominal pain*. This means that there is no evidence of a pathological condition causing the pain. It is now believed that children with functional abdominal pain have abnormal bowel reactivity to physiologically and psychologically stressful stimuli.

Four categories of functional abdominal pain are described:

○ Functional dyspepsia – upper abdominal pain often related temporally to food
○ Irritable bowel syndrome – alternates between episodes of loose stools and constipation
○ Abdominal migraine – attacks involve pallor, nausea and sometimes vomiting in a child with a family (especially maternal) history of migraines
○ Functional abdominal pain syndrome – none of the above features but other causes excluded

General management has been outlined above; it is important to realise that functional abdominal pain is by definition a diagnosis of exclusion and that some laboratory investigations will often be necessary.

Family education and their acceptance of the diagnosis is very important and a positive prognostic factor. However, functional symptoms can occur in children with an underlying organic disease.

In children with functional abdominal pain practical management involves coping strategies and rehabilitation. It is important that the child returns to normal functioning, even if the pain cannot be completely eradicated. Input from a psychologist may be needed in difficult cases. Pharmacological treatment is generally not helpful unless there are specific problems such as constipation. Lifestyle strategies including healthy eating, plenty of fluids and regular exercise are generally helpful.

Regular follow-up to monitor progress, including school attendance, should be offered with the ability to deal with any arising complications and/or significant psychiatric co-morbidity.

2.5 CASE FIVE: CEREBRAL PALSY

Role

You are the Specialist Trainee

Setting

Outpatient department

You are talking to

Mrs and Mrs Melling and their 9-year-old son Ashley

Dear Dr...

Re: Ashley M

Thank you for seeing this 9-year-old boy who has spastic quadriplegic cerebral palsy. He has moved here from New Zealand recently and the family have come to see me to get him registered. His mother has a clinic letter from 6 months ago detailing his main problems. They are most concerned that his hips are getting more painful with significant spasm. His scoliosis is much more pronounced than it was a year ago. They could not attend his final appointment before they left for the UK. I thought it best that you meet up with the family soon. I would be grateful if you could also refer him to the correct agencies to continue/add to the multidisciplinary care provided in New Zealand.

Yours sincerely,

Dr S Smith

General Practitioner

Background information

Parents have forgotten the letter from New Zealand.

Additional information

Medications – sodium valproate 250 mg bd.

Preparation time (2 min): initial thoughts

You are not going to be able to take a complete, exhaustive history in the 13 min available. You are being asked to address the main problems (particularly contractures and scoliosis) in order to refer him to the most suitable agencies.

Consultation

Introduction, clarify role. Agree aims and objectives.

Remember to include patient in consultation – eye contact, etc.

History

- ○ When was the news first broken that Craig has cerebral palsy? How was it diagnosed and by whom? If there were obvious problems from birth, start with prenatal history
- ○ Results of previous investigations if relevant, eg neuroimaging. This is especially important to ask as there may be a known cause, such as polymicrogyria
- ○ Major medical problems – neurological, feeding and weight, musculoskeletal. Which problem is the biggest for parents and which for the child? This is a good question to ask when there is a multitude of problems and little time to discuss them all. Try to get an idea of the child's quality of life
- ○ Professionals involved so far (try to link with problems, eg feeding = dietician, speech therapist, paediatrician)
- ○ Previous management of contractures – professionals involved, especially physiotherapist (*in this case it is worth spending longer on this problem*)
- ○ Birth history (if not already taken) – with special attention to any problems antenatally
- ○ Developmental history

○ Medications
○ Social and family history

Warning bell rings; you have 4 min left with Ashley and his parents.
You have gathered the following information so far:

Ashley had an extremely difficult start to life. He was born by emergency caesarean section at 42 weeks for prolonged bradycardia. He needed intubating at birth and the parents recall him having cardiac massage. He was initially ventilated and needed three different drugs for neonatal seizures. He never managed to feed properly and had a nasogastric tube, which the parents learned to use at home when he was eventually discharged.

He had an MRI scan of his head as a baby, which showed some 'significant damage'.

His main problems are severe developmental delay, gastro-oesophageal reflux and poor weight gain (for which he had a gastrostomy and fundoplication) as well as progressive hip dislocation.

His parents feel that his hip pains are bothering him most. He was being seen regularly by a physiotherapist and orthopaedic surgeon for this problem, and he was being considered for hip surgery before the family moved. He is wheelchair-bound. Ashley can communicate using Makaton. His vision and hearing are normal.

Ashley has also been seen previously by a general paediatrician, community paediatrician, paediatric surgeon, dietician and occupational therapist.

In the remaining 4 min you try to focus on schooling and family life.

The family have already approached several schools and they will need written reports from the paediatric/community teams that will go towards a Statement of Special Educational Needs.

Their new home is a large ground-floor flat and they are already looking at ways to modify one of the rooms. Ashley is an only child. His parents run their own business from home and are experiencing problems finding clients in the UK. They are very concerned about this, as much of their income is spent on making Ashley as comfortable as possible.

The bell rings and you are left with the examiner.

Discussion with examiner (9 min)

Would you tell me what the main issues are for Ashley?

Ashley is a 9-year-old boy with quadriplegic cerebral palsy whose family have just moved to the country. His main problems at the moment are painful, dislocated hips and his progressive scoliosis. He should be referred to a paediatric orthopaedic surgeon and a spinal surgeon as well as a physiotherapist. His other problems are severe learning difficulties, nutritional and social issues.

What are the different ways in which you could help Ashley and his parents settle into their new country?

There are several options:

○ Medical – helping to co-ordinate all aspects of care; for example, occupational therapist to help place suitable equipment in the new flat, etc. This can be facilitated by conducting a **multidisciplinary meeting** so that parents can meet the professionals involved and agree upon an agenda including timelines for aspects of care

○ Financial – supporting application for Disability Living Allowance (DLA). Ashley would be entitled to both Care and Mobility components of the DLA

○ Helping with Statement of Special Educational Needs to ensure that he attends a suitable school – possibly residential, eg in the week

○ Giving his parents contact numbers for support groups in the area, and organisations such as Contact a Family

○ Arranging some respite care so that parents can have a break, especially as they are new to the country. Shared Care Network is a national organisation that provides family-based short breaks for disabled children

Why has Ashley got such severe feeding problems?

Pseudobulbar palsy is the most likely reason and this is present in many children with quadriplegic cerebral palsy. He could also have residual gastro-oesophageal reflux even after fundoplication.

Notes on management of cerebral palsy

Cerebral palsy is defined as a persistent, but not necessarily unchanging, disorder of movement and posture due to a *non-progressive* disorder of the immature brain.

This excludes diagnoses such as brain tumours and spinal cord disease. The term implies that motor function is not simply delayed, but also follows a course that is not seen in the normal child. Prevalence is 2 per 1000 live births.

Diagnosis

Cause unknown in many. Otherwise, categorised into prenatal (only 5% of causes), perinatal and postnatal. Unless cause is obvious (as in above example), try to ask about these following problems in the history:

Prenatal

- ○ Genetic forms – autosomal recessive and autosomal dominant
- ○ Cerebral malformation
- ○ Maternal alcohol consumption/substance abuse
- ○ Infection – *Toxoplasma*, rubella, cytomegalovirus
- ○ Intra-uterine growth retardation

Perinatal

- ○ Neonatal seizures? (neonatal encephalopathy)
- ○ Ventricular haemorrhage (ask about head scans)
- ○ Episodes of hypoglycaemia: severity and duration

Postnatal

- ○ Meningitis/encephalitis
- ○ Head injury

Different types of cerebral palsy and their specific problems

Hemiplegia

This leads to varying degrees of spasticity in the affected side of the body, requiring physiotherapy to prevent the worst deformities from developing. Weakness is usually more pronounced distally. The incidence of epilepsy and related disorders is related to cortical involvement – sensory defects, visual field defects and cranial nerve involvement should all be looked for.

Most children will walk by 18–24 months; if not, other pathologies should be considered or the cerebral palsy extent reviewed. Splints may be used at night to prevent contractures. Special shoes help to equal leg lengths, which may be discrepant due to limb shortening. Orthopaedic surgery has much to offer, with elongation of the Achilles tendon, although this is rarely required before 5 years of age. It is usually reserved for those with *diplegia*. In this situation the limbs on both sides of the body are affected, legs more than arms. More severely affected children never walk. It is more common in pre-term, low-birth-weight infants and in those who had an abnormal labour or delivery.

Quadriplegia

There is four-limb and often bulbar involvement, with the arms more severely affected than the legs. Initially young children are hypotonic with episodes of axial stiffening and extension. As they grow older the tone increases, producing rigidity with pyramidal signs. The windswept hip deformity is particularly characteristic, the adducting hip being at risk of dislocation. Scoliosis can be severe and should be treated aggressively.

Bulbar muscles, usually spared in hemiplegia and diplegia, are commonly affected. Severe mental retardation and fits are common. Many affected infants are microcephalic.

Children with spastic quadriplegia have many problems and require a considerable multidisciplinary input usually co-ordinated through the local child development unit.

Surgery to relieve contractures is often performed.

Ataxic

Here the motor disorder is cerebellar ataxia, but this is usually associated with diplegia. It is usually diagnosed relatively late – patients need to reach a certain stage of development before cerebellar deficit is noticeable. It is difficult to diagnose and you must look for other causes of cerebellar dysfunction, eg tumours and other progressive disorders (Friedreich's ataxia, ataxia telangiectasia, metachromatic leukodystrophy).

Athetoid

This involves involuntary movement of the limbs. Choreoathetosis is largely associated with hyperbilirubinaemia; the more severely disabled dystonic cases occur in severely asphyxiated term babies. The dystonic movements seen in the term asphyxiated infant involve slow movements with extension of the trunk and limbs. Other system involvement is common and should be looked for.

There are many children who fall into the category of mixed forms of cerebral palsy, eg ataxia and diplegia. The importance is not in categorising their cerebral palsy but in determining the overall ability and disability of the child and working with that. Remember that many children with cerebral palsy are able to understand you; do not make the assumption that no children with this problem have normal intelligence. Always acknowledge and talk to patients as well as parents in this station even if this is difficult and there is little reciprocation.

Investigation

You may be asked how to investigate a child with cerebral palsy. Clearly not all children with static cerebral palsy can be fully investigated, and this is usually reserved for those children with:

- The lack of an obvious cause
- Loss of skills
- Familial occurrence
- Encephalopathy
- Unusual features, eg nystagmus
- Lower motor neurone signs
- Symmetrical signs

Useful investigations include:

○ CT or MRI of head – MRI if neuronal migration defects are being considered
○ Chromosome analysis
○ Electroencephalogram
○ Congenital infection screen
○ Metabolic screen
○ Ophthalmological assessment
○ Hearing tests

Treatment

The treatment of cerebral palsy is something you may be expected to talk about at length and it is very important that you know all the aspects of management. This can arise in any part of the exam. Management involves a *multidisciplinary approach*, usually with the *involvement of a child development unit*. The team will comprise:

○ **Paediatrician**
  • usually in a co-ordinating role
○ **Physiotherapist**
  • provides the greatest day-to-day contribution
  • is involved with the child from an early stage
  • helps in preventing severe contractures and deformity as well as aiding as much normal motor development as possible
○ **Occupational therapist**
  • works closely with physiotherapist
  • is involved in adapting the environment to aid the child's functioning
  • is involved in adapting play within the home to aid development
○ **Communication therapist**
  • is involved early, providing help with feeding problems
  • is involved later with speech
  • encourages parents to stimulate their children, and to help them develop as much communication as possible, whether it be normal speech, sign language or a mixture of both
○ **Social worker**
  • works alongside all the therapists that have close links with the family
  • provides support for the family, helping with periods of stress

- • arranges holidays and social admissions/respite care should the need arise
○ **Others include**
  - • dietician; educational psychologist; psychologist; play therapist; teacher; ophthalmologist; orthoptist; audiologist; ear, nose and throat (ENT) surgeon; orthopaedic surgeon

2.6 CASE SIX: NEPHROTIC SYNDROME – RELAPSE

Role

You are the Specialist Trainee

Setting

Paediatric Assessment Unit

You are talking to

Mr Watts and his 8-year-old son, James

Dear Dr...

Re: James Watts

Thank you for seeing this 8-year-old boy who had nephrotic syndrome diagnosed 2 years ago. He was given a treatment course of prednisolone and required no other medications. He was not referred to a nephrologist. In the past 4 days he has had mildly puffy eyelids and 2+ of protein in his urine. He had just got over a cold. I am concerned that this is a relapse and would be grateful if you could review him.

Yours sincerely,

Dr. Black

General Practitioner

Background information

Weight going along 25th centile, systolic blood pressure 98th centile for height at GP surgery.

Preparation time (2 min): initial thoughts

You will need to focus on his previous illness and already start thinking about how he should be managed.

History

○ Introduction, clarify role. Agree aims and objectives
○ Ask about general health at the moment
○ When were parents first concerned this might be a relapse?
○ Any other symptoms apart from puffy eyelids?

Confirm and discuss previous diagnosis

○ How did he initially present?
○ Medications used to treat and days before achieved remission
○ Rule out previous complications such as difficulties in fluid management (hypovolaemia), infection, blood clots (thrombosis)
○ Ask if there are any other features that concerned doctors, such as high blood pressure, renal impairment, blood in urine (macroscopic haematuria). *Although he did not see a nephrologist, he may have been discussed with one*
○ Maximum weight if remembered
○ Ask if he is still under paediatric follow-up
○ Ask about other illnesses in the past (ask specifically if he has had chickenpox)
○ Medications
○ Immunisations (ask specifically if has had pneumococcal vaccine and influenza vaccine)
○ Family history of renal disease or any vasculitic illnesses such as systemic lupus erythematosus (SLE)

Bell rings for 4 min. You have obtained the following information:

James was diagnosed 2 years ago after having had puffy eyes for 5 days. This was thought to be due to hayfever and he was given an antihistamine. However, this swelling did not go down and his face then started to look swollen. He had put on half a kilogram in this time and so was referred to hospital. His urine dipstick test showed +++ of protein. Some other blood tests were taken and he was started on prednisolone daily. He was not given any other medications apart from penicillin. For a couple of days he produced less urine but his kidney function on the blood tests was normal and 'his protein levels were a bit low, but he didn't need any more'. After 16 days his urine dipstick was negative for protein.

He has been well since but developed a cold a week ago. The family had been told to dip his urine in the morning when unwell and this became positive for protein 3 days ago. His eyes look a bit puffy again.

You remember to obtain a family history, which is unremarkable for any renal problems. James lives with his parents and is an only child.

You ask the father if he has any other concerns; he is worried that this will happen again and again.

The bell rings and you are left with the examiner.

Discussion with examiner (9 min)

Tell me about this young man's problems

James was diagnosed with nephrotic syndrome 2 years ago and was treated with prednisolone. He went into remission after 16 days and had no complications. He now presents with a relapse of his nephrotic syndrome and has had a high blood pressure recorded at the GP's surgery.

What is your definition of a relapse of nephrotic syndrome and how common is this?

Relapse is defined as a protein of 2+ or more on dipstick for 3 days consecutively. Only one-third of patients will never have another relapse. Relapses often follow infections and parents should be told to dip their child's urine every morning if they are unwell.

Would you treat this child?

Yes, as he has had 4 days of proteinuria. Start prednisolone 60 mg/m^2 per day until remission, along with penicillin prophylaxis.

When would you discuss him with a paediatric nephrologist?

When there are any atypical features:

○ Age <1 year, >12 years
○ Renal impairment
○ Persistent hypertension
○ Gross haematuria
○ Systemic features of a vasculitis such as rash, arthropathy
○ Family history of systemic illness

And/or under the following circumstances:

○ There are any acute complications such as severe hypovolaemia, infection or thrombosis

○ Not in remission by day 28 of prednisolone
○ Two consecutive relapses on steroid treatment or relapse within 14 days of stopping steroids
○ Frequent relapses

At this moment in time I would not discuss him with a nephrologist but would reassess this on a regular basis.

What about his blood pressure? It was raised at the GP's surgery

Needs repeating on three occasions with the right-sized cuff. Look up blood pressure for height centile, age and sex on centile charts. If still over 95th centile, discuss with nephrologist.

Notes on nephrotic syndrome

This is a triad of:

○ Proteinuria (early morning protein:creatinine >200 mg/mmol)
○ Oedema
○ Hypoalbuminaemia (<25 g/l)

Presentation is usually between 18 months and 6 years of age and is sometimes confused for an allergic reaction when eyelids become puffy. Children can be brought up to the exam whether they are currently suffering from symptoms or not as there are many aspects to their management that discriminate good candidates from poor ones. Parents can quite easily pretend that their child has only just left hospital for the sake of the exam.

Investigations

These are undertaken to confirm the diagnosis and also to look for any atypical features and complications:

○ Urine dipstick, MC&S, early morning protein:creatinine ratio, urinary sodium
○ Blood for full blood count (FBC), urea and electrolytes (U&Es), albumin, cholesterol, C3 (reduced C3 is an atypical feature) and C4, varicella zoster titres, hepatitis B and C serology
○ If systemic or atypical features are present as outlined above, then further autoimmune profile including ANA, anti-double-stranded DNA
○ Anti-streptolysin O titre can be useful

General management

○ Dietician involvement – needs low-salt, normal-protein diet
○ Monitor and control fluid balance – need input/output charts, daily weights. Some patients need fluid restriction and diuretics. Need to watch for hypertension
○ Look for and manage complications (see below)

Steroid management

In Europe around 90% of children with nephrotic syndrome have steroid-sensitive nephrotic syndrome. These patients respond to initial high-dose prednisolone (60 mg/m^2) until remission followed by 40 mg/m^2 on alternate days then cessation. Relapses are treated in the same way.

If the patient is not in remission by day 28 they are said to have steroid-resistant nephrotic syndrome. Steroid-dependent nephrotic syndrome is defined as two consecutive relapses on steroid treatment or within 14 days of stopping steroids; renal biopsy will need to be considered. Both of these patient groups usually undergo a renal biopsy before alternative therapies are initiated.

Complications you may need to discuss

Poor knowledge of these is a good discriminator in exams, and effective treatment reduces mortality.

Hypovolaemia

Reduced capillary oncotic pressure (secondary to protein leak from kidneys) causes an efflux of plasma water from the circulation. Eventually, homeostatic mechanisms to conserve vascular volume cannot keep up and the patient becomes symptomatic. Clinical features are abdominal pain (splanchnic ischaemia), tachycardia, prolonged capillary refill time, wide core–peripheral temperature gap, decreased urine output with urinary sodium of <10 mmol/l, increased packed cell volume (PCV).

Treated by sensible amounts of isotonic saline, eg 10–20 ml/kg with assessment of clinical response. After discussion with the renal team, patient may need 20% albumin. Be aware that this can cause rapid refilling of vasculature and resultant left ventricular failure with severe pulmonary oedema so needs to be given slowly.

Infection

Patients are at increased risk of infection due to urinary loss of immunoglobulin. They are particularly prone to pneumococcal and *Haemophilus influenzae* infections, particularly peritonitis and septicaemia. Prophylactic penicillin should always be given while there is proteinuria. High-dose steroids may mask signs of infection and there can be diagnostic confusion with hypovolaemia, especially if patient is peritonitic, as both cause abdominal pain and circulatory compromise.

A suspicion of peritonitis warrants broad-spectrum antibiotics and a surgical opinion.

Nephrotic patients are also vulnerable to chickenpox (needs aggressive treatment with varicella zoster immunoglobulin (VZIG) and aciclovir if lesions) and measles. They are also defined as being immunocompromised from their steroids if they have had >1 weeks' worth of steroids in the past 3 months or any other form of immunosuppression in the last 3 months. Live vaccines should not be given to such patients. Pneumococcal and influenza vaccines are recommended. They should have been given a steroid card.

Thrombosis

Due to renal loss of antithrombin-3 and hyperviscous blood. Less of a risk if patients are adequately hydrated and mobilisation encouraged.

Parental education

This is an important part of management. Parents need to be given written information on the illness and should be aware of the complications. In particular they should be told to contact the ward urgently if their child develops abdominal discomfort. They should have a written regimen for tapering the steroids at home and be aware of side-effects (a common question in the communication station). Urine should be dipped daily until remission then twice weekly while still on a tapering dose of steroid or if their child is unwell at any time. Results can be recorded in a diary.

The above examples demonstrate the depth of knowledge required when preparing for examinations, and the different turns a consultation can take. We recommend you also look at referral letters for different problems, and see how the more senior members of staff managed that situation.

Try to make sure you have concise histories tailored to all of the major paediatric illnesses.

3

FURTHER SCENARIOS

3.1   Scenario one: Coeliac disease in a 4-year-old boy with loose stools and abdominal pain

3.2   Scenario two: Diabetic 12-year-old with morning hyperglycaemia

3.3   Scenario three: Multiple fits in a teenager – referred to you for an EEG

3.4   Scenario four: Failure to gain weight – 12-month-old whose weight has drifted from 50th to 9th centile in past 4 months

3.5   Scenario five: Down syndrome – yearly appointment, child now 11 years old and new to area

3.6   Scenario six: Severe constipation in a 6-year-old – first presentation to clinic

3.7   Scenario seven: Chronic diarrhoea in a 7-month-old – referred for investigations

3.8   Scenario eight: Inflammatory bowel disease – management of relapse in a 14-year-old boy with Crohn's disease referred to rapid access clinic

3.9   Scenario nine: Headaches – 9-year-old child referred for investigation

3.10 Scenario ten: Eczema – management of flare-up in a 6-year-old

3.11 Scenario eleven: Chronic fatigue syndrome (CFS) – 14-year-old girl referred to clinic

3.12 Scenario twelve: Review of patient with extrahepatic biliary atresia post liver transplant – main issues affecting patient (immunosuppression, etc)

This chapter contains some suggested topics for practice scenarios. Use the framework for approaching this station as provided and go through the examples with your colleagues. The 12 examples here (along with the 6 cases in chapter 2) do not constitute a syllabus for the examination but once you are comfortable talking through the main problems associated with this broad range of illnesses/scenarios you will feel better armed for the station. Many of the conditions mentioned here are covered in other sections of this book. The information that follows each scenario in this chapter is not exhaustive but has been adapted for this station and reflects the *questions you shouldn't miss asking* as well as *what you may be asked by the examiners*. Much of this knowledge base has been acquired from clinical experience, and also from any centralised guidelines such as those from the Royal College of Paediatrics and Child Health (RCPCH), National Institute for Health and Clinical Excellence (NICE) and the Scottish Intercollegiate Guideline Network (SIGN) that are available.

3.1 SCENARIO ONE: COELIAC DISEASE IN A 4-YEAR-OLD BOY WITH LOOSE STOOLS AND ABDOMINAL PAIN

Confirmed by positive histological examination of the duodenum, following suggestive tissue transglutaminase (TTG) test. First appointment since diagnosis and you have not previously met family.

History

○ Obtain history of symptoms, especially weight loss
○ Ask about other autoimmune disease symptoms – associations are type 1 diabetes (5%), hypothyroidism, hepatic, adrenal and mixed connective tissue disease
○ Ask about the impact this has already made on the family and if any other family members have the condition
○ Take a social history, bearing in mind that gluten-free products are expensive and many families need them on prescription
○ Ask about how much information the family has been given, or has sought for themselves

Management planning – issues that may be discussed

○ Gluten-free diet for life – resolves symptoms, reverses bone demineralisation that may have occurred, decreases chance of pubertal delay
○ Dietician input upon diagnosis is very important – parents need regular advice
○ Supermarkets are now more attuned to needs of sufferers; foods now more palatable
○ Contact groups – Coeliac UK (www.coeliac.co.uk)
○ Regular outpatient follow-up, looking at symptom resolution, growth and compliance to gluten-free diet. Be aware of potential complications. Joint clinic with dietician useful
○ The diagnosis is lifelong – this child has positive serology, a positive biopsy, and has responded to treatment. This child would not be re-challenged or have repeat biopsies as he is over 2 years old
○ Remember to tell parents about the increased incidence of small bowel malignancy, which decreases to that of the general population after 5 years on a strict gluten-free diet

3.2 SCENARIO TWO: DIABETIC 12-YEAR-OLD WITH MORNING HYPERGLYCAEMIA

There are many patients with diabetes who are well known to paediatric outpatient departments and who are invited to the examination, in particular to this station. It is well worth attending diabetic clinics to see the full range of problems with which diabetic patients and their families can present to the clinician. Also be aware that paediatricians are increasingly being contacted by phone about such problems where there is no diabetes nurse cover. Some hospitals have specific telephone advice proformas for such eventualities and there are now NICE guidelines on diabetes at www.nice.org.uk. Follow links to published clinical guideline CG15 on type 1 diabetes.

History

○ When was he/she diagnosed?
○ Current treatment – including any prior manipulation to try to resolve morning hyperglycaemia
○ Compliance with treatment and indicators of control – clinic attendances, last HbA1c, frequency of glycosuria. Diary of blood sugars?
○ Hospital admissions, previous hypoglycaemia (especially nocturnal) or diabetic ketoacidosis
○ Growth – is child thriving?
○ Impact on family and help they are receiving already
○ Comorbidity – renal disease, coeliac disease

Management planning – issues that may be discussed

○ Differential of this scenario – non-compliance, dawn phenomenon (hyperglycaemia coinciding with early morning growth hormone secretion), inadequate insulin administration are all possibilities
○ However, well-controlled children with early morning hyperglycaemia ± glycosuria and ketonuria may just be experiencing night-time hypoglycaemia. Rebound hyperglycaemia occurs by the morning due to compensatory hormonal mechanisms. Such children may have had their bedtime insulin increased to theoretically bring down their morning blood sugars, with the opposite

effect. You have established that there is good control from the replies to your history. This child needs regular nocturnal blood sugar measurements (BMs) to confirm your suspicions. This problem is more common when fast-acting insulins are used, and less with basal bolus regimens.

○ Discussion of different insulin regimens
○ Emergency management of hypoglycaemia

3.3 SCENARIO THREE: MULTIPLE FITS IN A TEENAGER – REFERRED TO YOU FOR AN EEG

Need to take a focused 'seizure' history. If there is a small number of events, try to describe each one from before event to recovery. If there are many and all sound the same, try to elicit the background to each event. Remember there are NICE guidelines on epilepsy at www.nice.org.uk, guideline reference CG20.

History

Before the event

○ Witnesses; where and at what time?
○ Behaviour at time – also ask child if they felt/saw/smelt anything unusual
○ Triggers – flashing lights, pain, noise

During event (some families are using mobile phones to record events)

○ Full description of movements and noises
○ Eyes open? Any sign of awareness?
○ Any unilateral features such as one-sided involvement/eye deviation?
○ Colour change, bladder and bowel incontinence
○ Total duration of event – often difficult for parents to recall
○ Did seizure terminate spontaneously or were anticonvulsants (± hospital admission) required?

After the event

○ Description of behaviour – levels of alertness. How long before child was back to normal?

General

○ When did problem start?
○ Are events getting more frequent? Associated morbidity, eg progressive headache
○ Need to take a good birth, drug, developmental and family history
○ Essential to elicit impact on schooling, family life, activities

Management planning – issues that may be discussed

○ Electroencephalogram and limitations of this. Consider MRI if concerns about space-occupying lesion. If diagnosis of epilepsy made:
   • Lifestyle issues such as supervision, driving (DVLA website), contraceptive advice, sleep hygiene
   • Discussion of risk/benefit ratio of medication, and side-effects of medications. See *British National Formulary for Children* (www.bnfc.org)

3.4 SCENARIO FOUR: FAILURE TO GAIN WEIGHT – 12-MONTH-OLD WHOSE WEIGHT HAS DRIFTED FROM 50TH TO 9TH CENTILE IN PAST 4 MONTHS

History

○ Ask about point at which weight became static; any preceding illness?
○ Food intake – has it changed, has child been weaned smoothly? How much of diet still consists of milk?
○ Stool frequency and consistency. Does stool ever contain blood?
○ Stool colour
○ Does infant vomit? If so, full description of character and frequency
○ Are there chest symptoms or any other symptoms of chronic illness such as pallor, lethargy?
○ Social history including support network for mother, how many other children to look after, possible maternal illness

Management planning – issues that may be discussed

○ Differential diagnosis – such failure to gain weight can logically be split into the following categories:
  • Reduced intake – infant not being given enough calories (occasionally due to neglect)/refusing food
  • Malabsorption – such as that caused by pancreatic insufficiency of cystic fibrosis, or acquired enteropathy including post infective/allergic or coeliac disease
  • Increased losses – diarrhoea and/or vomiting of acute or chronic illness, gastro-oesophageal reflux
  • Increasing energy expenditure – chronic illness, anaemia resulting from iron deficiency
○ Be prepared to discuss non-organic causes of failure to thrive, as these are far commoner than organic pathologies
○ Investigations depend on the history elicited; as a baseline it is reasonable to obtain a clean catch urine
○ Depending on symptoms and the most likely category based on the history and examination, first-line blood tests may include

full blood count and film, iron studies, U&Es and tissue transglut-aminase autoantibody screen for coeliac disease. Consideration should be given to sweat testing

○ Dieticians should be involved in all severe cases to assess the caloric intake and provide support for the family

○ GP, health visitor and community nurse should also be involved in such cases

○ Some patients and their families need an inpatient stay if this is in the child's best interests

3.5 SCENARIO FIVE: DOWN SYNDROME – YEARLY APPOINTMENT, CHILD NOW 11 YEARS OLD AND NEW TO AREA. NO CARDIAC DEFECT BUT HYPOTHYROID AND ON THYROXINE

History

○ Enquire as to child's general wellbeing; for example, many children have troublesome constipation
○ Ask specifically about symptoms of thyroxine over- or under-treatment
○ Ask about previous echocardiogram results; all children with Down syndrome should have been sent for an echocardiogram; In this case it is normal
○ Drug history, with attention to compliance and recent dose alterations. Was child under a paediatric endocrinologist in their previous area? How often were thyroid function tests (TFTs) being checked and when was last check?
○ Frequency of coeliac screening? Annual screen in most centres.
○ Results of last hearing test?
○ Ask about sleep; in particular, snoring, agitation and apnoeas. Around one-third of children with Down syndrome have obstructive sleep apnoea
○ Social history; in particular, ask about social and financial support. Any allowances?
○ Schooling – mainstream or special school? Statement of Special Educational Needs?

Management planning – issues that may be discussed

○ Plot child on adapted growth chart for patients with trisomy 21
○ Arrange hearing tests as necessary
○ Management of hypothyroidism – usually 6-monthly TFTs and initial communication with paediatric endocrinologist
○ Coeliac screen
○ Screening X-ray for atlanto-axial articular laxity if child wishes to be involved in contact sports in secondary school

○ Who decides upon the level of educational support this child may need in secondary school?
○ Talk about statementing

3.6   SCENARIO SIX: SEVERE CONSTIPATION IN A 6-YEAR-OLD – FIRST PRESENTATION TO CLINIC

The majority (90%) of cases are functional, but a good clinician will eliminate the possibility of Hirschsprung disease, hypothyroidism, spina bifida or meconium ileus equivalent. Much of this can be achieved with a focused history.

History

○ When did problem start and were there any notable circumstances, eg illness, holiday to hot climate, difficult potty training, etc?

○ Ask about stool frequency and consistency; what do parents/child mean by constipation?

○ Is defecation painful ± blood around stool (fissure)?

○ Diet (ask about fibre intake) and fluid intake

○ General health; enquire in particular about bladder problems, urinary tract infections, hypothyroid symptoms, behavioral problems. Is child thriving?

○ Any other health professionals, eg school nurse, involved thus far?

○ Medications; what has been tried?

○ Birth and past medical history – was stool passed in first 24 h and were there problems as a baby?

○ Social history, impact of problem on family, eg soiling

Management planning – issues that may be discussed

○ Remember that such children need a full lower limb neurological examination, with a lower back (ruling out obvious spinal abnormalities) and perianal inspection

○ Behavioural management – star charts, toileting

○ Community management – school nurse, community children's nurse

○ Consider referral to constipation clinics/nurse specialist if there is access to these services

○ Dietary advice and stress the importance of fluid intake

○ Medical therapy – initial therapy depends on extent of problem. If there is a mass below the umbilicus try a stool softener (eg **lactulose** or **docusate sodium**) followed by stimulant (eg **senna, sodium picosulphate** or **Movicol®**), with regular reviews as doses may need to be increased

○ Always consider if admission is warranted to clear out stool and ensure compliance. Try to avoid enema therapy as this can be distressing and can reinforce negative toileting experiences; sedation may be needed

○ Try to settle child onto regular maintenance therapy, usually consisting of a stool softener and a stimulant at a minimum dose that produces a regular, formed stool. It can take families a long time to get to this stage and they need to know that treatment can be required for many years

○ Multidisciplinary approach works best

3.7 SCENARIO SEVEN: CHRONIC DIARRHOEA IN 7-MONTH-OLD – REFERRED FOR INVESTIGATIONS

History

○ Ask about stool frequency and consistency; parents may have a different idea of what constitutes diarrhoea

○ When did problem start? A history of over 2 weeks' duration with no let-up in symptoms is indicative of chronic diarrhoea. Did an acute gastroenteritic illness precede this problem?

○ Enquire about blood or mucus in stool, and about systemic upset especially fever, rash, vomiting

○ Is child gaining weight?

○ Feeding history and recent dietary changes, eg introduction of cereal, bread

○ Birth, past medical/surgical and drug history

○ Travel history

○ Family history – enquire specifically about atopy/coeliac disease/cystic fibrosis/inflammatory bowel disease

Management planning – issues that may be discussed

○ The commoner differentials in this age group that may be discussed include:
  • Infection, eg *Giardia lamblia*, or post-infection with secondary lactose intolerance
  • Food intolerance, eg cows' milk protein or (very rarely) primary lactose intolerance
  • Coeliac disease
  • Cystic fibrosis

○ Investigations
  • Stool MC&S, virology, reducing substances
  • Blood count, electrolytes, albumin, liver function tests (LFTs), coeliac screen (TTG), inflammatory markers
  • Consider sweat test/faecal elastase
  • Consider duodenal biopsy

○ Management depends on most likely diagnosis; dietician may be involved and weight monitored

○ Pharmacological management not appropriate in this case, which turns out to be a post-infective (secondary) lactose intolerance

3.8 SCENARIO EIGHT: INFLAMMATORY BOWEL DISEASE – MANAGEMENT OF RELAPSE IN A 14-YEAR-OLD BOY WITH CROHN'S DISEASE REFERRED TO RAPID ACCESS CLINIC

History

○ Age at diagnosis and how diagnosed
○ How many relapses so far?
○ Current symptoms pertaining to this relapse; include stool frequency, consistency, presence of blood and mucus, abdominal pain
○ Systemic symptoms including extra-intestinal manifestations
○ Evidence of weight loss? Check growth status. Ask about pubertal status, as this is often delayed
○ Previous and current treatment (dietary, medical, surgical); ask about side-effects
○ Most recent levels of inflammatory markers, haemoglobin and albumin
○ Social history including effects of illness on family unit and schooling

Management planning – issues that may be discussed

○ Clinical assessment of unwell child with severe exacerbation, use of markers of increased disease activity – raised erythrocyte sedimentation rate (ESR), C-reactive protein (CRP), white cell count (WCC) with lowered albumin and haemoglobin
○ Home versus hospital management of relapses, and threshold for hospital admission
○ Discussion of different treatment approaches for relapses – elemental diets, steroids, azathioprine
○ You will need to know benefits versus risks of these treatments – remember that many patients become corticosteroid dependent or resistant
○ Management of gastrointestinal complications of Crohn's disease, eg toxic megacolon (colonic dilatation >6 cm), abscesses, fistulae

○ Indications for surgical treatment; remember that over 50% of patients will need an operation at some time in their life

○ Role of infliximab – a monoclonal antibody that inhibits the inflammatory cytokine tumour necrosis factor alpha. Risk of severe hypersensitivity reaction

Guidelines on British Society of Gastroenterology website (www.bsg.org.uk).

3.9 SCENARIO NINE: HEADACHES – 9-YEAR-OLD CHILD REFERRED FOR INVESTIGATION

History

○ How long have headaches been going on?
○ Patterns in relation to time of day/week
○ Description of onset, severity, duration and frequency
○ Characteristics of pain – especially location and severity, and whether or not the headache is exacerbated by coughing
○ Associated symptoms, eg vomiting, visual disturbance, vertigo or other neurological symptoms
○ Are headaches getting worse or more frequent?
○ Past medical history of note? Family history of headaches?
○ Dietary history
○ Social history, looking for any potential stressors
○ Effect on schooling, family life

Management planning – issues that may be discussed

○ Discussion of differential diagnosis based on history (many patients with *migraine* would be suitable to attend this station; remember that migraine can be on a spectrum with tension headache)
○ Tests in outpatient scenario – fundoscopy, visual fields, blood pressure, head circumference
○ Historical features of a headache that would warrant neuroimaging are: morning/recumbent headache, worse with coughing, increasing severity and frequency, change in behaviour or school performance
○ Sinister clinical features – meningeal signs, altered conscious level, papilloedema, hypertension, lateral rectus palsy

Management of migraine

○ Reassurance
○ Discuss any exacerbating factors, eg poor sleep, tensions at home, bullying (this patient was being bullied which contributed to his migraine and tension headaches)
○ Lifestyle and dietary advice

○ Headache and food diary to try to capture exacerbating factors
○ Pharmacological treatment – rescue, eg simple analgesia when headache first coming on; prophylaxis, eg **pizotifen, propranolol**

3.10 SCENARIO TEN: ECZEMA – MANAGEMENT OF FLARE-UP IN A 6-YEAR-OLD

Eczema is common, causes much morbidity and can have an impact on families as well as the child. A solid understanding of management and complications would be expected. The British Association of Dermatologists website contains up-to-date information on management (www.bad.org.uk)

History

○ When did child first develop eczema?
○ Precipitants
○ Enquire about food allergy; child may have been on an exclusion diet
○ Severity and frequency of exacerbations, hospital admissions
○ Current treatments – differentiate between creams and ointments, establish frequency of applications. Does child apply treatment at school?
○ Enquire about courses of oral antibiotics
○ Birth and past medical history; establish degree of atopy and any tendency for severe/recurrent infections
○ Family history of atopy very common (70%)
○ Ask about home environment (house dust mite exacerbates problem), impact on sleep, schooling, impact on parents

Management planning – issues that may be discussed

○ Avoidance of precipitants – commonly soaps/wool/rough clothing
○ Allergen avoidance
○ Nail care
○ Topical treatments:
  • Emollients for bath or shower; warn families that they can leave the bath very slippery
  • Soap substitutes, eg **Epaderm®** ointment mixed with water
  • Apply emollient directly onto skin, eg **Doublebase®** 3–4 times/day if possible

- Topical corticosteroids – remember that intermittent treatment with potent corticosteroids is as safe and effective as long-term hydrocortisone use. Topical antibiotic plus steroid combinations are no longer recommended
- Topical **tacrolimus** – especially useful on the face as there is no skin thinning. Remember side-effect of burning sensation. Need sun protection if on sites exposed to sun

Other issues

○ Bandaging – wet and dry wraps
○ Indications for oral antibiotics such as **flucloxacillin** (widespread) for moderate to severe infected eczema. Take skin swabs first and give a 10- to 14-day course
○ Indications for hospital admission. Remember that some families can cope with severe flare-ups better than others and that a written action plan/telephone advice can be useful

3.11 SCENARIO ELEVEN: CHRONIC FATIGUE SYNDROME (CFS) – 14-YEAR-OLD GIRL REFERRED TO CLINIC

Commonly seen in some outpatient departments. There are RCPCH guidelines on CFS management (Ref: EBG1) from which this advice is derived, which can be found at www.rcpch.ac.uk/Research/CE/Guidelines/RCPCH-guidelines. It will be sensible to have looked at them. Remember that CFS/myalgic encephalomyelitis (ME) is defined as generalised fatigue persisting after routine tests and investigations have failed to identify an obvious underlying cause. There are currently no specific diagnostic criteria.

History

○ Gradual/sudden onset of problems. Often a preceding illness (Epstein–Barr virus, influenza, pharyngitis)
○ Explore all symptoms – cardinal feature is *debilitating physical and mental fatigue, worsened by physical and mental activity*. Headaches, sleep disturbance, difficulty concentrating, myalgia and arthralgia can occur
○ Ask about depression/anxiety
○ General health and past medical history, psychiatric history, medications
○ Impact on child and family especially school days missed, family activities compromised

Management planning – issues that may be discussed

○ Importance of thorough physical examination should be mentioned
○ Differential diagnoses – anaemia, autoimmune disease, chronic infection, endocrine disorder (hypothyroidism and diabetes), depression, drugs, sleep disorder
○ Once positive diagnosis made, agree management plan with family and other health professionals
○ Stress that family need a co-ordinator of care
○ Inform Local Education Authority (with family's consent) especially if >15 days of school missed

○ Methods of establishing baseline activities, eg with diary. Patient should gradually increase with regular reviews. Warn patient that there will be 'payback' symptoms a day after excessive activity
○ Advice on diet/sleep, referral for co-morbidities such as psychiatric symptoms
○ Goal is gradual re-introduction to school and return to normal activities

3.12 SCENARIO TWELVE: REVIEW OF PATIENT WITH EXTRAHEPATIC BILIARY ATRESIA POST LIVER TRANSPLANT – MAIN ISSUES AFFECTING PATIENT (IMMUNOSUPPRESSION, ETC)

This is the kind of patient who would possibly be used in the clinical abdominal station on the same examination day and whose clinical features are covered in Chapter 9.

History

○ Age and mode of presentation – nearly all have prolonged jaundice, pale stools, dark urine
○ Associated malformations (splenic, cardiac, gut malrotation most commonly)
○ Investigations to confirm diagnosis: liver ultrasound ± hepatobiliary iminodiacetic acid (HIDA) scan (to evaluate whether there is obstruction to normal flow of bile), liver biopsy
○ Early complications, eg coagulopathy
○ Which specialist centre has managed/manages the patient?
○ Age at initial Kasai portoenterostomy? Better results before 8 weeks in several case series
○ Complications of surgery, eg ascending cholangitis
○ Reason for liver transplant
○ Discuss post-operative period and complications
○ Drug treatment post-transplant – especially immunosuppression and complications
○ Immunisations
○ Ask about intervals of follow-up, involvement of other health professionals, eg dietician, specialist nurse
○ Social history; acknowledge impact on family (such children spend long periods in hospitals that are often far from their home)

Management planning – issues that may be discussed

○ Outpatient management of prolonged jaundice – when to investigate, what to rule out

○ Discussion of Kasai procedure and indications for later liver transplant

○ Working a child up for a liver transplant – main considerations and awareness that donor supply is one of the main limiting factors

○ Immunosuppression, eg with **tacrolimus**, and general management including immunisations

○ Management of ascending cholangitis and liver failure

PART II

The communication skills station

INTRODUCTION AND SUGGESTED APPROACH

This section of the exam is intended to look at how you communicate in your everyday clinical practice and has been designed to mimic that closely. This is what is being examined. Remember it is not enough just to be a good listener – your job is to address patient's and their family's concerns appropriately and to provide them with reliable information about the child's condition and the management plan. This requires a broad knowledge of common paediatric conditions similar to that required in the written part of the MRCPCH exam and in preparing for this station you should concentrate as much on your background knowledge as you do on your communication style.

Read through the Royal College Anchor Statements as you prepare for this section of the exam.

You are being marked in three areas:

1. Conduct of interview
2. Appropriate explanation and negotiation
3. Accuracy of information given

The six main patterns of communication scenario described by the College are:

1. Information giving
2. Breaking bad news

3. Consent
4. Critical incident
5. Ethics
6. Education

Here are some suggestions for how to prepare for this section

1. Clear guidance about expectations and some comprehensive examples of cases are available from the Royal College and reviewing this information should be your first step.
2. The scenarios are realistic and commonly seen in everyday clinical practice. It is sensible to prepare for the exam by approaching your everyday communication with parents as though an examiner were watching you and expecting a perfect performance.
3. Make a shortlist of conditions that you plan to know in detail. This could be based on the most common conditions you see on the wards or in clinic. Ask your senior colleagues what most parents want to know about each condition; are there any common concerns that most parents have and what does your consultant tend to say in those situations? Plan to know about the usual treatments offered and practise how you would talk through the use of these treatments. No conditions should be considered too serious or too trivial to come up in the exam.
4. Ask someone to watch you practice. Give them a copy of the 'Anchor Statements' for the communication skills section. Ask for feedback and suggestions for improvement. Involve parents in the feedback process if you feel comfortable doing this.
5. Let your senior colleagues know that you are working on this and ask them to watch you explain management decisions to the parents during a ward round.
6. Role play with colleagues who are also preparing for the exam. Prepare scenarios for each other. Make sure you practise the scenarios you feel least comfortable with. Practise under 'formal' conditions and practise keeping to time.

SUGGESTED APPROACH

There now follow some broad categories of scenarios with a 'plan of attack' that could be applied to specific conditions. This is not intended to be a syllabus for studying for the communication skills section. However, if you have practised each of these scenarios as suggested and have a broad knowledge base about common conditions, you will be well prepared and will feel much more confident going into the exam.

Seeking consent

○ Check parents' understanding of their child's current health/ condition. Acknowledge any concerns/anxiety that they are experiencing
○ Explain the need for the procedure
○ Explain how it is done
○ Explain the anticipated outcome
○ Talk through any risks (be realistic about what parents should be told) and what will be done to minimise these risks
○ Talk through any alternatives
○ Give an opportunity for questions and address these immediately
○ Summarise what you've said and what has been decided, and check parents' understanding of this

Explaining a new treatment

○ Check patients' and parents' understanding of current status and need for change in management
○ Describe what the new treatment is
○ Explain how it works (use diagrams wherever possible)
○ Explain how it is administered
○ Explain how you can tell whether it is effective (desired/expected outcome)
○ Explain how long the patient will need to take it
○ Talk about side-effects, how likely they are, how to recognise them and what to do about them
○ Give an opportunity for questions and explore any concerns that the patient or their parents have about the new treatment
○ Summarise what you've said and check parents' understanding of this

Talking about chronic conditions

Frequently this takes the form of talking to a child or parent about a change in management because of a clinical deterioration. Parents and or children may disagree with the medical team's interpretation or plan. When parents or patients disagree with the team or need more convincing, a suggested approach is to:

○ Ask them what their concerns are
○ Acknowledge their concerns (write them down)
○ Discuss each concern: refer to any evidence you know that backs up a sensible medical plan (which could be published articles or national guidelines) or describe what is generally accepted practice
○ Talk through the benefits and drawbacks of any alternative management strategies
○ When there is potential for harm to the child if there is no agreement, then describe plainly what harm could arise, how likely this is to happen and the expected time frame
○ If they remain unconvinced, offer to take their concerns back to the team looking after them and arrange another time to discuss the issue further
○ Summarise what you have talked about, including concerns that have been raised and what was decided

Breaking bad news

○ Establish a common knowledge base
○ Talk about new information
○ Talk about the implications of the new information
○ Allow space for patient/parent to respond, expressing feelings, asking questions
○ Answer concerns honestly and sincerely
○ Talk about what is going to happen now
○ Summarise, giving the opportunity for more questions
○ Offer another meeting
○ Offer written literature, for example contact details for support group if appropriate

Telling parents about a medical error

○ Apologise in a sincere manner. Most angry parents will become angrier if they sense they are not going to get an apology or that the apology is insincere. Get a senior colleague to critique your 'apology' style.
○ Be prepared to discuss the following with the parent
 — what went wrong
 — what the likely risks are to the patient
 — what harm has already been done
 — what you are going to do about it to keep the patient safe now
 — what has been done so far about the mistake
 — what you will do to make sure this won't happen again

○ Be well aware of your hospital's complaints process and critical incident monitoring procedures

Having an ethical discussion about a case where the correct course of action is unclear

Prepare a general ethical framework that you can apply to many different situations. A suggested approach is discussed in detail in the Cases in Chapters 5 and 6.

SUGGESTIONS FOR HOW TO PREPARE YOURSELF DURING THE EXAM

○ Remember this is a 9-min station consisting of spoken inter-action. You will have up to 2 min before the start of the station to read about the task and prepare yourself

○ Use the full 2 min – make notes on key points that you need to get across if relevant

○ Also use the 2 min to put yourself in role: imagine yourself in this scenario in the right setting – your natural communication abilities are more likely to come across if you picture yourself in a real environment

○ Once you have introduced yourself, use the first minute of the consultation to establish an 'agreed agenda' with the parent. You need to spend some time listening to what the main concerns are; you also need to make the other person aware of what you need to cover. Then, when you know what needs to be covered, you can start the business of addressing each point individually. Some examples of how to do this are included in the individual Cases in Chapters 5 and 6

○ You will get a warning when there is 2 min to go. You need to think about how you are going to check the other person's understanding, summarise what has been talked about and bring the 9 min to a satisfactory conclusion. You could say, 'We are almost out of time. Can I quickly go over what we've talked about? Firstly ... Are there any other questions you had about what we've talked about so far?'

5

CASES

CONTENTS

5.1 Case one: Breaking bad news – new diagnosis of cystic fibrosis

5.2 Case two: Discussing an ethical dilemma – disclosure of HIV status

5.3 Case three: An education task – explaining the audit cycle

5.4 Case four: Obtaining consent for a blood transfusion

5.5 Case five: Apologising for a critical error – wrong breast milk

5.6 Case six: Talking about a chronic condition – poorly controlled diabetes

5.1 CASE ONE: BREAKING BAD NEWS – NEW DIAGNOSIS OF CYSTIC FIBROSIS

The following is a fully worked through example of a scenario that is typical of the sorts of cases you will be expected to deal with in the communication skills section. In keeping with the layout that you will encounter in the exam we have included boxed 'instructions to the candidate' as well as those given to the role player and examiner (who has a copy of all three 'instructions'). These are similar to the instructions seen within the specimen scenarios on the RCPCH website www.rcpch.ac.uk/Examinations/MRCPCH-Clinical. The intention is that this and the following scenarios can be used as templates so that you can develop a structured approach to this section of the exam, and become familiar with the level of background knowledge you will need in order to be fully prepared. This scenario could fit into the category of 'Breaking bad news' but will also test your ability to give information in layman's language and requires a working knowledge of cystic fibrosis.

Instructions to candidate

○ This station is a test of your ability to convey information based on the specific task given.

Timing –
Total time provided for this station is 9–min.

*There are **2 min** before you are called in to read this sheet and prepare yourself. A bell will signal the start of the station and you will be invited into the examination room – take your instruction sheet with you.*

*You will have **9 min** in total for the consultation; a warning will be issued when you have **2 min** left.*

You will not be assessed on the speed at which you communicate; you may find that you run out of time to finish the consultation.

You may take notes
You will not be asked to examine the patient

Role

A Specialist Trainee in paediatrics, working in a District General Hospital.

Setting

Interview room adjacent to a ward.

You are talking to

Mother of Jamie Saunderson, a 14-month-old boy admitted with his second episode of pneumonia requiring intravenous antibiotics. He has been on the ward for 3 days and is now well enough for discharge. Prior to becoming unwell he was waiting for an outpatient clinic appointment because his GP was concerned about his growth. You arranged a sweat test as well as immunoglobulins, coeliac screen and functional antibodies. Jamie's sweat test was positive and you have arranged to meet his mother to give her the result.

Other information

Jamie was born on the 50th centile for weight. He frequently has a cough and has had many courses of oral antibiotics from his GP to treat this. His health visitor has been monitoring his weight and this has gradually moved from the 50th to the 2nd centile. His parents do not smoke. He is an only child.

Task

To explain the implications of a positive sweat test.

You are not expected to gather any further medical history during this consultation.

Instructions to role player

(This is the information that is provided to whoever is playing the role of the parent.)

> *Total time provided for this station is 9 min.*
> *There will be a dialogue between you and the candidate only; you will not communicate with the examiner during the 9–min period.*

Role

Jenny Saunderson, a 28-year-old shop assistant and mother to Jamie, a 14-month-old boy.

Jamie has been in hospital for 3 days having intravenous antibiotics to treat pneumonia. He is much better and you anticipate he will be discharged home soon.

When he was 6 months old he was admitted to hospital with a chest infection and you were told that he had pneumonia. He was in hospital for a week on antibiotics. Jamie has had a cough since. You have seen your GP many times about this and Jamie has had many courses of antibiotics. These will take the cough away temporarily, but the cough will always return when the course has finished. In addition to this, your health visitor has told you that Jamie is not growing well. You were awaiting an appointment with a specialist to look into his growth when Jamie became unwell with high fevers and breathlessness. In hospital you were told that he had pneumonia again.

Your doctor has performed some tests because of the concerns about his growth and because it is his second admission to hospital with a serious infection. These tests included a sweat test looking for cystic fibrosis and some tests of his immunity. You have been told that your doctor would like to meet with you to discuss the test results.

Your general feelings

You have been concerned for several months that Jamie is not well and you feel that your GP has not taken you seriously. You are anxious that the test results will confirm that he has a serious condition.

What to expect from the candidate and what your feelings and *possible* further questions could be

○ The candidate should explain to you why Jamie has had a sweat test. They should also explain that the sweat test shows Jamie has cystic fibrosis

○ You should express that you do not know anything about cystic fibrosis other than seeing very sick children on a television appeal once

○ You should ask how he got this condition

After the candidate has explained what cystic fibrosis is and how it is treated your further questions might include

- ○ How will this affect his future (schooling, keeping up with other children)?
- ○ Will he ever get better from this?
- ○ Should you have noticed sooner that he had a serious condition?
- ○ You and your partner are hoping to have other children, will they be affected too?

Instructions to examiner

> *Total time provided for this station is 9 min.*
>
> *There will be a dialogue between the candidate and the role player only. Please warn the candidate when only 2 min of the consultation remain. Otherwise do not communicate with candidate or role player during the 9 min consultation.*

If the candidate finishes early, you should check that they have finished. If yes, they should remain in the room until the session has ended.

Guide notes towards expected standard

- ○ Explain why a sweat test was performed
- ○ Clear explanation about the effects of cystic fibrosis on the lungs and pancreas in particular
- ○ Appropriate summary of how cystic fibrosis is managed (physiotherapy, pancreatic supplements, antibiotics, multidisciplinary team involvement)

Suggested plan of attack

Preparation

In this scenario you are expected to give relevant information in an effective way, but you are also breaking bad news. A breaking bad news 'checklist' which could be adapted for this situation is given in the box. Remember that in real clinical practice when you are about to discuss something with a parent that you suspect will be distressing or sad for them you need to think about the following:

○ Environment: private and distraction free
○ Interruption free: hand over your bleep, tell your team where you are and what you're doing
○ Are the right people there? This includes relevant medical staff involved with the patient, also the parents'/patient's support network. Are you the right person to be talking about this now (should your senior colleagues be involved)?
○ Do you know all the facts: not only about the patient's background and medical history but about the condition you are talking about and how it is managed in your hospital

BREAKING BAD NEWS CHECKLIST

○ Establish common knowledge base
○ Talk about new information
○ Talk about the implications of the new information
○ Allow space for patient/parent to respond: expressing feelings, asking questions
○ Answer concerns honestly and sincerely
○ Talk about what is going to happen now
○ Summarise with opportunity for more questions
○ Offer another meeting
○ Offer written literature, contact details for support group if appropriate

Note how the 'task' instructions appear brief and relatively straightforward. Compare these to the expected standard and it becomes clear that there are several components to this task and all of them are being specifically watched for by the examiner. In the preparation time you should make a quick list of what you feel needs to be said to fully satisfy your task of 'explaining implications'. This could look like this:

1. Establish how much mother already knows (what is 'sweat test'/what is 'cystic fibrosis')
2. Sweat test results
3. Effects of cystic fibrosis
4. Cystic fibrosis team – 'multidisciplinary'

Introduction

You might like to start by saying to the examiner that you would have already handed over your bleep and arranged for a nurse to be present with you (before you say anything to the role player). This has the disadvantage of making it all seem less real, more like a practiced scenario and less like a consultation. The advantage is that you could refer to your imaginary nurse if you needed to later in the consultation (without having to invent them midway through).

When you introduce yourself, say where you fit into Jamie's care. Establish a common knowledge base.

> *'Good morning Mrs Saunderson, my name is Dr Goodwill. I'm the specialist trainee in the team looking after Jamie. I need to talk to you because we have some results available from the tests that were done on Jamie. First of all, can you tell me how much has already been explained to you about what tests we were doing and why?'*

Explanation

Don't spend a long time working up to telling the mother the diagnosis. After you have said it, allow some time for it to sink in. Don't be afraid of silence – what seems like a very long awkward pause to you may not seem like a long time to the parent. If you fill the silence with words because you feel awkward you will not make the patient feel any better and may say something you'll later regret. You will need to find a way of allowing the parent to set the pace of information following this silence, and you will also need to gently explain the key points on your list of information that needs to be conveyed.

> *'The sweat test results have shown that Jamie does have cystic fibrosis.'*

> *'Were you expecting us to find a reason like this for Jamie's health problems?'*

> *'Can I talk you through what this will mean for Jamie now?'*

Closing remarks

You need to check that she has understood one or two key points from the consultation and establish a plan for what will happen now.

> *'Mrs Saunderson, I realise that I've given you a lot of information and that it is a lot to take in all at once. The main things to remember are that Jamie has cystic fibrosis and will need to start treatment to help*

his lungs and digestive system. Is there anything you would like to ask me now before I go on?'

'What I am going to do now is talk to our hospital's CF team and arrange a time for them to come and meet with you later today. Can I suggest that you write down any questions that you would particularly like them to answer? Also you might like to arrange for someone to be there with you when you meet them – a family member perhaps. I'll also give you some patient information about CF including contact details for the CF Trust website (www.cftrust.org.uk) where you'll be able to find some useful information.'

Background notes

Diagnosing cystic fibrosis

Blood spot testing

- By 2007 most centres in the UK should offer cystic fibrosis (CF) screening with the Guthrie test
- Tests for immunoreactive trypsin (IRT) – very sensitive but not very specific
- Positive test does not mean the child has CF (needs further workup)
- If screen is positive a genotype is done – looks for the 29 most frequent mutations
- If one gene found – patient is referred for sweat test or second blood spot IRT
- Evidence that newborn screening influences long-term prognosis is inconclusive
- Benefits of screening include earlier diagnosis and treatment
- Drawbacks include increased parental anxiety and how to manage 'carrier' diagnoses
- IRT is inaccurate if there is meconium ileus present
- www.newbornscreening-bloodspot.org.uk is a good source of further information

Diagnosis of CF

- Affects 1 in 2500 (240 per year in the UK)
- 15% present with meconium ileus at birth

○ Can be diagnosed by antenatal screening (amniocentesis or chorionic villus sampling)

○ Gold standard is sweat test or testing homozygous for known CF mutations

○ Sweat testing can be performed on infants over 2 weeks of age

○ Need 100 mg of sweat

○ A sweat chloride of >60 mmol/l is considered positive (40–60 mmol/l is borderline)

○ Results are unreliable in dehydrated children or those with oedema, children on steroids or children with a rash affecting the area from which the sweat is being collected

○ www.cftrust.org.uk is a good source of further information

5.2 CASE TWO: DISCUSSING AN ETHICAL DILEMMA – DISCLOSURE OF HIV STATUS

Candidate information

Background

You are a Specialist Trainee in paediatrics. You have just finished seeing a patient on the ward round who was admitted several days ago with tuberculosis. She is 11 years old and has recently arrived from Africa with her parents. She speaks no English but her mother speaks English well. Her mother is HIV positive but has not told her family. The patient was tested and her test has also come back positive. When her mother was told, she said that she did not wish her daughter to know. A medical student who was observing the round now wants to talk to you about this patient.

Task

Discuss with the medical student the ethics behind the decision **not** to tell this patient that she has HIV.

Role player information

You are a final year medical student. You strongly believe that children should be fully involved in all aspects of their care and cannot understand why this information is being withheld.

Questions you should ask

○   Don't we legally have to tell her about it?
○   If she is not to be told now, when is she going to be told?

Questions you may ask

○   What about her father? Does he have a right to know? Could he decide to tell her?

Examiner information

Guide notes towards expected standard

○ Aware of reasons for and against informing the child of her HIV status
○ Able to explain these clearly and confidently
○ Shows respect for other's views

Suggested plan of attack

Preparation

This is a scenario where you are expected to explore the ethics behind a difficult situation. As with all these sorts of scenarios the examiner will be looking to see that you are able to understand both sides of an argument and that you can identify the issues involved, particularly those concerning conflicts in interests or rights. You will need to demonstrate your ability to do this and you have only got 9 min! It is unlikely that there will be any right or wrong answers although if there are any legal implications or college/General Medical Council guidance about an issue it is essential that this enters into your discussion. A list of key documents which have influenced this area is provided in a box at the end of the notes to this case.

> ## SUGGESTED STRUCTURE FOR AN ETHICAL DISCUSSION
>
> ○ Be clear about the question being asked
> ○ List 'arguments for' and 'arguments against'. As a way of categorising the various conflicting interests you could use the traditional medical ethical framework (autonomy, beneficence, non-maleficience, justice) but make sure you include some explanation of this as you will probably be talking to a medical student or junior colleague who may not have experience of discussing things in this way. The concepts behind the ethical framework are summarised in the box in the notes at the end of this case
> ○ Decide on a way forward – this could be a practical way of resolving some of the conflicts identified. Examples could

> include agreeing another opportunity to discuss things further, involvement of senior colleagues or the hospital ethics committee, seeking advice from specialist groups or looking for published evidence on the topic

Using the suggested structure given in the box, your list for the scenario could look something like this:

1. Main question, 'should an 11-year-old be told that they have HIV?'
2. Arguments for and against
   - ○ For
     - – 'Autonomy' – right to be actively involved in her own treatment
     - – 'Doing good' – able to offer more support if diagnosis known, can help to develop coping strategies
     - – 'Do no harm' – protecting her future sexual partners
   - ○ Against
     - – 'Do no harm' – less control over who knows, potentially exposing her and her family to stigma if she tells someone else, Mum's right to confidentiality
3. Way forward
   - ○ Explore reasons why Mum does not want her to know
   - ○ Negotiate phased disclosure
   - ○ Offer support

Introduction

You need to establish clearly what you are discussing and to seek out the medical student's views.

'That was a really difficult case. Deciding whether or not a child should know that they have HIV is a difficult decision to make. What do you think is the right thing for this mother to do?'

Explanation

You need to introduce a structured way of weighing up all the options (point 2 above, 'Arguments for and against').

'What do you think are the reasons in favour of her knowing that she HIV?'

'Can you think of any disadvantages for her or her mother if she is told that she has HIV?'

'One way that I have found helpful in weighing up difficult decisions is to think in terms of a doctor's obligations; for example, autonomy, doing good, doing no harm and treating people equally.'

Reasons for telling

Autonomy

○ The patient has the right to access support and information to help her understand her illness
○ She has the right to be actively involved in her care

Beneficence

○ Reduce anxiety
○ Compliance with medication will be important – she will want to know why she has to take medication/come to clinics and have blood tests
○ She may become sexually active in near future and will need to protect future partners

Reasons against telling

The mother knows her own child; the balance of benefits versus drawbacks cannot be made without reference to her views on what her child needs.

Non-maleficience

○ The mother has a right to confidentiality
○ Knowledge of her HIV status may alter her self-esteem
○ Knowing that she is HIV positive may not improve her sense of well-being
○ Protecting her from stigma at school

Closure

Try to find a practical way forward or 'next step' (point 3 above).

'It seems as though this mother will have major difficulties to face when she does decide to tell her daughter about HIV. It may help if when we next talk to her we outline the benefits to her daughter of knowing her diagnosis. We could also explore the reasons why she doesn't want her to know. There are lots of places where she could get

some more specific advice and support. This hospital has some HIV specialist nurses who are really experienced in talking through these issues with parents. There are also lots of support groups and websites where she can get some really practical help and advice for how to go about telling her daughter.'

Background notes

Ethical framework

This is an aid to decision making when faced with an issue where the 'right' course of action is unclear. Four different domains offer different ways of looking at a doctor's duties or obligations. When a difficult issue is defined in terms of these duties the fundamental conflicts that are present become more explicit. This helps a clinician who is weighing up different options to view the issue from various perspectives and to come to a clear decision that they can then justify.

The four domains are described in the box. Not all four domains will be relevant to each case. However, being able to define a thorny problem in terms of these obligations can help clarify the decision-making process.

THE FOUR DOMAINS OF THE TRADITIONAL MEDICAL ETHICAL FRAMEWORK

1. Autonomy – 'Deliberate self rule'

One of the things we like as individuals is to be able to think for ourselves and make our own choices. Ideally these choices should be based on logical and rational thought, having been presented with all the information required. Things that detract from autonomy include:

○ Paternalism
○ Lack of capacity (eg mental illness)
○ Pressure from society (eg peer pressure)
○ Lack of self-confidence

As a medical professional we can increase a patient's autonomy by:

○ Asking for and valuing their opinion
○ Seeking to remove external pressures
○ Giving timely and clearly understandable information
○ Enabling good communication with health professionals

An individual's right to decide for themselves is ultimately limited by:

○ The law
○ Others' rights and safety
○ Limited resources

2. Beneficence – 'Doing good'

This is the obligation to do whatever will deliver the greatest benefit to the patient in terms of their present and future well-being. It also necessitates balancing up the risks and benefits of the different options.

3. Non-maleficience – 'Do no harm'

A doctor has an obligation to avoid causing harm. Harm is something that undermines a patient's well-being or limits their potential. Harm from medical treatment may occur as a recognised risk of a particular course of action or may be accidental. Harm can be physical, mental, emotional or spiritual. There are some harms so unacceptable to an individual patient that they will take whatever course of action necessary to limit the risk of their occurring.

4. Justice – 'treating people equally'

This looks at the obligation to divide up resources fairly. How to judge what is fair is fraught with problems. There are advantages and disadvantages to distributing resources on the basis of societal values, evidence base, need or health economic measures such as QALYs (Quality Adjusted Life Years).

Telling a young person they have HIV

Once a child has been diagnosed with HIV most professionals would recommend informing them in a staged approach, starting with simple explanations and building up knowledge gradually. How and when they are told will depend on their age and development, their previous experience of HIV (for example in family members) and the need for treatment. In general the 'HIV' label is shared with children when they are about 12, but most will have prior knowledge of the basics of their condition, ie that it involves cells in their blood which are an important part of their immune system. It is essential they know their diagnosis and its implications prior to becoming sexually active. Learning about living with HIV is an ongoing process and information will need to be revisited and adapted as a child's needs and circumstances change.

There are many reasons why a parent might be apprehensive about their child knowing that they have HIV. A parent might have fears about who else their child will tell. They may worry how their child will cope with the information and whether it will affect their relationship. They may have feelings of guilt or fear or may be struggling to deal with their own diagnosis. There are many support groups and websites offering excellent resources for parents who want to talk to their children about HIV (eg Children With Aids Charity, www.cwac.org). If the parent feels they will become too upset talking about it, they could arrange to be present when a trusted health professional talks to their child. In general the benefits of a parent communicating openly with their child outweigh the upset or other difficulties that it may cause. The child may already be exposed to misinformation about HIV through the media and their peers. They may be on a lot of medication with significant risks associated with non-compliance. They will need time to develop coping strategies, and they may have a degree of anxiety and may feel more in control if they have more information. There are picture books available that parents and medical staff can go through with children to aid their understanding of this condition. They explain why the child has to go for blood tests and why they need to keep taking their medications.

HIV is not a notifiable disease and there is no legal need for the school to know. There is no evidence that there has ever been any HIV transmission in school. In general it is recommended that only their head teacher and one other teacher is informed, so that they can have some pastoral support if needed.

Confidentiality

Much of law about disclosure of health information concerns sharing information when a child is at risk of or has suffered abuse. In these cases the child's welfare is paramount and any threat to this needs to be taken seriously. Guidance is available from the General Medical Council and the Royal College of Paediatrics and Child Health.

○ Confidentiality must not stand in the way of protecting the child
○ Consent is normally required to disclose confidential information – this applies to information given by children in confidence
○ Information from a child can be disclosed without the child's consent if the clinician believes it is in the child's best interests (for example, to prevent them suffering further abuse), but the clinician will need to be able to justify this
○ It is good medical practice to inform the patient if you are going to pass on any information; tell them who you are passing it on to and why
○ If you decide disclosure is not in the best interests of the patient, you should talk to a senior colleague and be prepared to justify your position
○ Documentation is vitally important

KEY DOCUMENTS

The following is a list of key documents that influence the way we interpret ethical dilemmas in paediatrics. You need to be broadly familiar with these as they all influence the way paediatrics is practised in the UK.

○ Children Act 1989 – concerns welfare of children, parental responsibility and court orders required to protect children's welfare (www.dcsf.gov.uk/publications/childrenactreport)
○ Children Act 2004 – legal basis for 'Every Child Matters' (www.dcsf.gov.uk/publications/childrenactreport)
○ National Service Framework for Children, Young People and Maternity Services (http://www.standards.dcsf.gov.uk/eyfs/resources/downloads/04090552.pdf)
○ Every Child Matters: Change for Children – guidance for organisations working with children (eg concerning sharing information) aimed at ensuring that every child is able to 'be healthy, stay safe, enjoy and achieve, make a positive contribution and achieve economic well-being' (www.everychildmatters.gov.uk)

○ Good Medical Practice (www.gmc-uk.org)

○ *Seeking Patient's Consent: The Ethical Considerations* (GMC publication, www.gmc-uk.org)

○ RCPCH publications (eg *Child Protection Companion, Withholding or Withdrawing Life Sustaining Treatment in Children*) (www.rcpch.ac.uk)

○ *0–18 Years: Guidance for all Doctors* – published in 2007 by the General Medical Council, containing guidance on many aspects of working with children and young people, including consent and confidentiality

5.3 CASE THREE: AN EDUCATION TASK – EXPLAINING THE AUDIT CYCLE

Candidate information

Background

You are a Specialist Trainee in paediatrics working in a District General Hospital. An F2 comes to you asking for advice. He has been asked to perform an audit but not been given further guidance about how to go about this. He is a junior trainee and has not been involved in the audit process before.

Task

Explain the audit cycle to this F2.

Role player information

You are an F2. Your involvement in previous audits has been limited to looking at case notes and filling in some proformas. You now have to design an audit from scratch and do not know where to start.

Questions you should ask

○ Why do I need to do this?
○ What topic should I audit?

Questions you may ask

○ Who can help me with this?
○ Where can I find a gold standard?
○ Will doing the audit change anything?

Examiner information

Guide notes towards expected standard

○ Establishes level of prior knowledge
○ Clear and confident explanation
○ Ability to explain the audit cycle
○ Checks understanding

Suggested plan of attack

Preparation

This is an educational task and is checking not just your knowledge of the topic but your ability to teach it to another doctor. You should practise a clear structure for these sorts of tasks, which you can then apply to whatever subject is required.

A SUGGESTED APPROACH TO AN EDUCATIONAL TASK

In your preparation time, jot down these headings and which points you need to get across:

1. Establish common ground. Find out what they already know

2. Agree a learning agenda. You could use phrases like 'would it be helpful if I explain to you...?'

3. Outline the importance of what you are going to explain. Try to make it relevant to them

4. Explain it concisely and simply (you haven't got much time!). Use diagrams wherever possible

5. Summarise what you've said and check understanding. You could use phrases such as 'to summarise, tell me: what are the 5 main points to remember about...?'

Introduction

Aim to find out how much experience the trainee has had with audit, so that you can base your explanation on knowledge they already have. You need open-ended questions. Use the first few minutes to clearly establish what you are going to talk about and why it is important.

'I understand that you need to do an audit. What do you know about audits? Why do we do audits? Would it be helpful if we spent some time talking through the audit cycle? It's really important in this department because we use the results to improve patient care, and it will be an important aspect of your training for many years.'

Explanation

Try not to make this a lecture but a conversation. Keep checking that what you are saying makes sense to the listener. Try to give a structure by using a diagram, or a list of key points and make this structure explicit.

> 'A good way to work out how you are going to do your audit is to talk through the audit cycle. Have you heard of this before?'

Draw a diagram.

Closure

> 'Can I summarise what we've talked about. Firstly, tell me what are the steps of the audit cycle?'

> 'Remember that your ultimate aim is to improve patient care. In this hospital the audit department is a really good source of information and will be able to guide you through the process. You should talk to your educational supervisor as well and ask them to check through your aims and objectives once you've come up with them. Have you got any questions about what we've talked about this morning?'

Background notes

Audit cycle

The aim is to improve patient care by comparing what is being done with what should be done.

1. Identify a topic
   - Needs to be something that is important to you and a priority for your department. Ideally the department should decide together what the key priorities are for audit. These priorities could arise from:
     - New guidelines coming into operation (eg NICE guidance, new RCPCH guidelines, local derived guidelines)
     - New requirements (eg National Service Framework, Children Act, other government publications)
     - A local problem; for example, arising from critical incidents, or a resource issue

2. Decide what standards you will be measuring against
   ○ Need to agree (with colleagues) your audit criteria (must be definable, measurable and based on good evidence) and then decide what you think is an acceptable target (often expressed as a percentage)

3. Measure practices against standards

4. Identify key priorities for change
   ○ Occurs once information has been collected, collated and reflected on; usually involves presentation of data to colleagues for collective decision on key priorities and how to implement change

5. Implement change

6. Re-audit against standards to see what difference has been made and whether further changes are required

5.4 CASE FOUR: OBTAINING CONSENT FOR A BLOOD TRANSFUSION

Candidate information

Background

You are a neonatology Specialist Trainee. You are looking after a preterm baby called Toby Gibson. Toby was born at 26 weeks and is now 4 days old. The baby had initial problems with respiratory distress syndrome and hypotension requiring inotropes. You note that he is becoming anaemic and suspect this is because of frequent sampling from his umbilical arterial line for gases and bloods. You feel he would benefit from a transfusion. You have arranged to talk to his mother about this.

Task

Explain the reasons for the blood transfusion and obtain consent.

Role player information

- ○ This is your first child.
- ○ You have been very worried about Toby for the last few days.
- ○ You are anxious about the risks of blood transfusions.

Questions you should ask

- ○ Does he really need to have a transfusion; what would happen if he didn't?
- ○ Can you be sure that he won't get any infections from the blood?

Questions you could ask

- ○ Can I give him my blood for his transfusion?
- ○ Will the transfusion make him better?

Examiner information

Guide notes towards expected standard

- ○ Acknowledges parental concerns
- ○ Explains indication for transfusion

○ Explains expected benefit
○ Explains risks of transfusion (wrong blood/wrong patient/transmission of bacterial or viral infection)

Suggested plan of attack

Preparation

Make short notes about what points you need to cover. These could look like this:

1. Reason for anaemia (frequent sampling, immature bone marrow)
2. Reason for transfusion (oxygen requirement, hypotension, Hb unlikely to recover spontaneously in next few weeks)
3. Risks of transfusion and safety checks (mislabelling/wrong blood/infection checks on donated blood)

Introduction

Introduce yourself and explain where you fit into the team looking after Toby. Check parents' understanding of Toby's current situation.

'Hello Mrs Gibson, my name is Dr Goodwill. I am the specialist trainee looking after Toby. I need to talk to you about some of the plans we have for Toby's treatment.

Before we start, could I just check what has been explained to you about Toby's current situation?'

Talk about anaemia and its impact on Toby's ventilation and blood pressure management.

Explanation

○ How transfusion will help
○ Need for consent
○ Opportunity for questions
○ Talk through risks and explain what is done to minimise these

Closing remarks

Need to summarise what you've said and check the parent understands.

'Can I summarise what we've talked through. I've told you that Toby is stable but he is anaemic and unless he has a transfusion we expect this will affect his breathing and his blood pressure. We have talked

*about the risks of transfusion and how these are small and every effort
is made to minimise them with procedures for checking donors and
double checks to make sure the right blood is given to the right baby.
Have you got any further questions about anything I've said?'*

'Do we have your permission to give Toby a transfusion?'

Background notes

Notes on consent

○ Consent can be obtained from someone with parental responsibility
○ Only one person with parental responsibility is needed although ideally all parties with parental responsibility should consent
○ The child's birth mother always has parental responsibility unless the child has been adopted
○ The child's natural father has parental responsibility if they were married at the time of the child's birth, or if his name is on the birth certificate, or if he has acquired parental responsibility through the courts (residence order)
○ A step parent can consent if they have undergone a court process to assume parental responsibility
○ If a child is the subject of a care order then social services can consent on behalf of the local authority
○ Emergency Protection Order gives the local authority the ability to exercise parental responsibility if it is reasonably required to safeguard or promote the welfare of the child
○ A foster parent does not have parental responsibility
○ A child can consent for themselves if they are aged 16–18. This autonomy can be suspended by the courts in those under 18 years old where required
○ At any age a child can consent to treatment if they understand the issues involved; this is called 'capacity' (also 'Gillick competence'). The lower limit of Gillick competence age is related to the child's experience and the gravity of the treatment for which they are consenting. They can agree to treatment but cannot refuse treatment if they are under 16

What to do if parents disagree with you

Depends on degree of urgency. Can act to give treatment without parental consent if an immediate medical procedure is required to save life or prevent irreversible harm. In less urgent cases where there is a difference of opinion between medical staff and parents about what is in the child's best interests the following is a potential step-wise approach:

1. Consult local colleagues (eg senior colleagues/other consultants)
2. Consult more widely within the hospital (involve hospital ethics committee)
3. Consult another unit
4. Involve Royal College ethics committee
5. Involve the courts: a judge can issue a Specific Treatment Order. This gives permission to act without the parent's consent in one particular area but does not take away any other aspects of parental responsibility

In cases where parents are insisting on treatment that medical staff do not think is in the child's best interests a similar process can be followed. As a doctor you do not have to do anything that you think is wrong, even if the parents are insisting (it is the child who is your patient). You are required to supply a second opinion when requested to do so.

Risks of transfusion

Highest risks occur when blood is being given out of hours. The paediatric and neonatal population is over-represented in terms of transfusion risks (possibly because 1 unit of blood is a higher proportion of their circulating volume compared to adults, therefore reactions are more serious). Reactions are most likely to occur within the first 15 min of transfusion therefore start slowly for 15 min. Because there is a risk associated with transfusion, it is very important that the indications for transfusion are clearly documented, and that the discussion asking for consent is clearly recorded also. Most hospitals have a policy of giving written information about transfusions to patients or their parents.

The main risks are as follows:

1. Wrong blood/wrong patient
2. Haemolysis
3. Bacterial contamination

4. Anaphylaxis/allergy
5. Transfusion-associated acute lung injury
6. Risk of infection
   ○ Hepatitis B virus (HBV) – 1:900 000
   ○ Hepatitis C virus (HCV) – 1:30 million
   ○ HIV – <1:several million
   ○ Variant Creutzfeldt–Jakob disease (vCJD) – one possible case of transmission so far; potential for existence of transfusion-acquired vCJD still under debate. vCJD remains a rare condition in the UK (145 cases to date) but future prevalence is unknown so several precautions are in place (particularly for plasma-related products)

Jehovah's witnesses

○ Jehovah's witnesses do not accept transfusion of whole blood, red cells, platelets, white cells or plasma; other 'fractions' of blood (for example clotting factors) are left to the believer's own conscience
○ This is based primarily on the interpretation of Bible passages, backed up by knowledge of the risks and alternatives to transfusion
○ If an adult accepts a transfusion they risk excommunication. If their child is forced to have a transfusion by the courts this does not apply, yet the perceived spiritual consequences for their child will be distressing for their family irrespective of a court order

Some useful websites include:

○ www.blood.co.uk (National Blood Service website)
○ www.shotuk.org (Serious Hazards of Transfusion website)

5.5 CASE FIVE: APOLOGISING FOR A CRITICAL ERROR – WRONG BREAST MILK

Candidate information

Background

You are a neonatology Specialist Trainee. You need to talk to Mrs Tomes, the mother of a preterm infant called Kieran, born at 28 weeks and now 31 weeks' corrected gestation. He has had an uncomplicated neonatal course. He is currently on continuous positive airway pressure (CPAP) and having hourly nasogastric feeds of maternal, expressed breast milk. During the night his nurse realised that she had inadvertently given him another baby's expressed breast milk. The other baby has a similar name and the nurse misread this and didn't double check with a colleague or on the baby's label before giving the milk.

Task

Tell Mrs Tomes about the error and talk about the implications for her son.

Role player information

○ This is your first child
○ Neonatal Intensive Care Unit (NICU) admission has been traumatic and frightening for you
○ You do not feel involved in your baby's care
○ You have found it difficult and painful expressing milk for your baby
○ You are upset and angry about the error
○ You are worried that your baby may pick up an infection from the other mother's milk

Questions you should ask

○ How can I be sure this won't happen again?
○ Is there a risk that my baby could pick up an infection from the breast milk?

Possible further questions

○ How do I make a formal complaint?
○ Would it be safer if you gave my baby formula milk?

Examiner information

Guide notes towards expected standard

○ Appropriate conduct of interview
○ Explains how the error occurred
○ Apologises for the mistake
○ Describes critical incident documentation and action process
○ Explains infection risk from breast milk
○ Closure: reassures, final apology

Suggested plan of attack

Preparation

Make a short list of what you need to cover during the consultation. This could look like this:

1. Given wrong breast milk
2. Similar sounding name/inadequate checks
3. Critical incident form filled out/all staff reminded about checking process
4. Need to take blood from baby and donor mother

Introduction

Introduce yourself and explain where you fit into Kieran's care. Explain why you need to talk to them now.

> 'Good morning Mrs Tomes. My name is Dr Goodwill and I'm one of the specialist trainees who is looking after Kieran this week. I need to talk to you to explain about a mistake that was made overnight by the team who were looking after your son.'

Explanation

Come quickly to the point. Delaying the difficult parts will not make the information any more pleasant or less awkward to talk about. Allow space and silence for the parents to respond. Be humble and sincere. Make sure you invite questions and leave time for the parents to react.

'As you are aware we have been giving Kieran your breast milk because we feel it is the best thing for preterm babies who are establishing feeding. Unfortunately last night...'.

'All the staff on the unit are truly sorry that this happened.'

'Can I talk you through what action has been taken so far since the mistake happened?'

- ○ The critical incident form will be taken to the clinical governance meeting and discussed by senior staff
- ○ All staff on the unit are being further educated about the need for checking identification prior to giving feeds, and double checking with another staff member
- ○ The other baby's notes are being checked for anything that could make the breast milk less safe (maternal infection/medication) – no concerns found
- ○ The incident is clearly documented in the notes
- ○ 'Similar name' fluorescent stickers have been applied to the notes and incubators of both babies
- ○ As per protocol – planning to take blood from the mother whose breast milk was given to check for HIV/cytomegalovirus (CMV)/hepatitis serology
- ○ Will need to take blood from Kieran for viral serology with the next blood test

'Have you got any questions, either about the error or any other concerns you may have?'

Closing remarks

Offer a sincere apology again. Reassure the parents that Kieran has not suffered harm and that steps will be taken to make sure it doesn't happen again. Offer further meeting with senior nurse/consultant if there are ongoing issues to discuss.

Explain the complaints procedure if requested to do so.

Background notes

Some benefits of breast milk for preterm infants

- ○ Immunoglobulins found in breast milk
- ○ Reduced risk of necrotising enterocolitis

○ Enzymes in breast milk 'predigest' – easier on immature gut
○ Laxative effect

Infection risks from breast milk

HIV

○ Depends on viral load
○ 5%–20% of children born to HIV-positive mothers acquire infection through breast feeding
○ Overall risk of transmission is 10%–25% greater if the infant is being breastfed

CMV

○ Can be acquired from breast milk
○ If acquiring CMV from breast milk at term, there is a very low risk of permanent problems (eg hearing loss)
○ Preterm infants acquiring CMV infection have a much greater risk of permanent sequelae (this is why we give them CMV-negative blood)

Hepatitis C

○ No evidence of transmission via breastfeeding

Hepatitis B

○ Small amounts of surface antigen (HBsAg) are found in breast milk
○ There is no evidence of increased risk of transmission when a mother with hepatitis B breast feeds her own child; evidence for donor transmission unavailable
○ Donor milk banks screen mothers for hepatitis B

Bacteria

○ Preterm infants can be colonised with bacteria from breast milk; important bacteria to think about here are methicillin-resistant *Staphylococcus aureus* (MRSA) and group B streptococci

5.6 CASE SIX: TALKING ABOUT A CHRONIC CONDITION – POORLY CONTROLLED DIABETES

Candidate information

Background

You are a Specialist Trainee working in a paediatric diabetes clinic. Tina Collins is a 14-year-old diabetic. She had excellent control on her basal bolus regime but this has deteriorated over the last 2 years. Her most recent HbA1C was 11% and she has had a recent admission with diabetic ketoacidosis (DKA). She has not recorded any blood glucose readings. You are seeing her without her parents.

You do not need to take any more medical history.

Task

Talk to Tina about measuring her blood glucose levels more frequently.

Role player information

You have been diabetic since you were 6 years old. Since you started your new school you have found it difficult to make friends. You are having constant arguments with your parents because they say you are not taking enough care of your own diabetes. You give yourself your own injections but since you left hospital after being very unwell because of your diabetes your parents having been giving you your bedtime injection. You don't tend to check your blood sugars unless you are feeling unwell.

Your general feelings
- People who don't have diabetes don't understand what it is like
- Your parents should trust you more
- Being admitted to hospital was frightening
- You do not want to check your glucose levels at school because you are worried about what your friends will say

Examiner information

Guide notes towards expected standard

○ Appropriate conduct of interview
○ Invites Tina to share her own concerns
○ Explains need for more frequent blood glucose testing
○ Agrees a realistic plan of action with Tina

Suggested plan of attack

Preparation

This is a non-compliant teenager and an example of a scenario where you need to explore her attitude towards her condition. Similar issues arise in many adolescent patients with chronic conditions. Points to consider when you are faced with a non-compliant teenager are listed in the box.

With these points in mind, during your preparation you could list some key points to discuss. These could include:

1. Establish agreed agenda for consultation: invite her to express her concerns
2. Main difficulties for Tina
3. Outline problem (high HbA1c, need for more monitoring)
4. Outline health concerns if no change made (DKA/hypoglycaemia/long-term problems)
5. Action plan before next clinic
6. Extra support

POINTS TO THINK ABOUT WHEN YOU ARE FACED WITH A NON-COMPLIANT TEENAGER

1. Never assume they know everything they need to about their condition. Often the reasons behind the treatment are explained to the parents at diagnosis and then not revisited. The patient may have been too young to understand or may not remember being told some essential information. Make sure they are clear about the facts

2. Find something positive to say

3. Show respect and empathy – it's difficult for them to have this condition

4. Be honest about what you need from the consultation

5. Establish roles in the management of the condition. Define explicitly who has responsibility for which aspect of management

6. Ask the patient what their main concerns are and whether they can see any solutions for those. Ask them how they would like help

7. Try to agree on a way forward. Start from where they are at. Short-term goals are best. Aim for one small step at a time

8. Explore support network. Think of ways they could include their peers in their support network. Remember that specialised support groups exist and are sometimes extremely helpful

9. Think about how your multidisciplinary team could help

10. Consider psychological or psychiatric co-morbidities: suicidal ideation, risk-taking behaviour, bullying, family stressors, self-harm and depression

Introduction

Need to establish common ground and a common agenda.

'Good morning Tina, my name is Dr Goodwill. I am the specialist trainee at the diabetes clinic. It's great that you've come to clinic today. I need to talk to you about your diabetes. One of the main things I need to discuss with you is to do with checking your blood glucose. Before we do that, is there anything you need us to talk about as well?'

'What are your main concerns about your diabetes? At school? At home?'

'I'm concerned that you don't seem to have many blood sugar readings in your diary. Have there been any problems with checking your sugars recently?'

'Are there any difficulties you could see happening if you were to try to check your sugars more often?'

Explanation

'Your HbA$_{1c}$ was a little high and this could mean that the insulin you are on is not right for you. It's difficult for us to know if we need to change things if we can't see what is happening to your sugars. We'd like to avoid your having to come back in to hospital with DKA again if we can.'

'Any tests are better than no information. How many times a week do you think you would be able to manage a blood sugar test?'

'Is there anyone you would trust to help you remember to do this?'

Closure

Review what you've spoken about. Reiterate your agreed action plan and check that she has understood. Make space for any extra questions. Offer extra support; this could be a support group for children with chronic conditions, adolescent expert patients programme, or further support available through the diabetes multidisciplinary team (specialist nurse follow-up phone call, appointment with team psychologist).

'Tina, thanks for being so honest with me about how diabetes is affecting things for you. I feel the important things we've covered today are…

'By the next clinic appointment you are going to try to check your sugars at least twice a week, once before breakfast and once before tea. You're happy to ask your Dad if he will check that you've done this and tell him the results. Have you got any questions about that? Have you got any questions about anything else we've talked about?'

YOUR NOTES

FURTHER SCENARIOS

There now follow suggested scenarios to help direct your revision. These are all based on topics that have come up in the exam before. They are intended to be used as a starting point for you to practise adapting your structure and technique for this section of the exam to a range of different topics. Some background information is provided although this is not extensive and as with the scenarios previously gives guidance rather than precise answers. Practise in pairs with a facilitator where possible.

1. **A child has a congenital myopathy and is ventilator dependent on the neonatal unit. Her parents wish for a withdrawal of intensive care. Talk to a medical student about the ethics of withdrawing intensive care in this case**
   ○ *Withholding or Withdrawing Life Sustaining Treatment*; this document is accessible from the RCPCH website (www.rcpch. ac.uk) and lists five situations where it may be legal and ethical to consider withdrawal:
      – The 'brain dead' child
      – The 'permanent vegetative state'
      – The 'no chance' situation
      – The 'no purpose' situation
      – The 'unbearable' situation
   ○ Need to mention that this will be a team decision involving the full health care team and family
   ○ Need to mention palliative and terminal care

2. **Talk to a medical student about the ethics of offering neonatal intensive care to a child born at 23 weeks**
    ○ Make sure you are aware of the survival data and long-term morbidity of infants born at this gestation
    ○ Autonomy – consider the parents' right to decide, giving the child a chance of an autonomous life
    ○ Beneficence/non-maleficience – think about the impact on the family of the ups and downs of neonatal intensive care, and of looking after a potentially disabled child; for some people this would be a significant 'harm' and for others it would be a 'good'
    ○ Justice – NICU is expensive, beds in tertiary units may be scarce
    ○ Remember to seek the medical student's own personal views and experiences and discuss these too
    ○ In general a senior neonatologist will make this decision, taking the parents' view into account

3. **Talk to a Specialist Trainee who has been refusing to help clerk in general paediatric patients at busy times**
    ○ Talking to a colleague about a work-related problem is a common scenario in the exam
    ○ When you are jotting down key points in your preparation time, try using 'when you, I feel, because'; eg *'When you don't come and help out, I feel stressed and frustrated because it seems as though we are not working well as a team. Do you think that what I am saying is fair?'*

4. **Talk to a Specialist Trainee who is refusing to work the shift he has been allocated on New Year's Eve**
    ○ Be clear about the difficulty and what this means for others
        – *'When you say you won't work your allocated shift, I feel frustrated because it seems unfair for everyone else who has to cover for you'*
    ○ Try to understand why they are doing this and come up with a solution
        ○ *'I don't understand why you are doing this; could you explain it to me? Is there any way that we could help you to be able to work your share of the rota?'*

5. **Talk to an F2 who has not completed any discharge summaries for several months. Other juniors are complaining that he does not pull his weight**
   - ○ Aims should be to clearly explain why their behaviour is of concern and find out if there is an underlying reason for their behaviour (which might require your help or advice)
     - – *'How are you finding this job? Are there any areas you are finding particularly difficult?'*
     - – *'Something that I have noticed which is concerning me is.... Do you think that what I am saying is fair?'*
     - – *Do you think it would be helpful if I... so that you would be able to...?'*

6. **Talk to a medical student about why we use some medications that are unlicensed for children**
   - ○ Licensing refers to a drug being given marketing approval to be advertised for a specific clinical situation
   - ○ Pharmaceutical companies perform Phase 1, 2 and 3 trials before a licensing application
     - – **Phase 1 trial** = a few selected patients or healthy volunteers (looks at safety, pharmacokinetics, etc)
     - – **Phase 2 trial** = a few more patients (looks at best dose and whether the medication works)
     - – **Phase 3 trial** = comparison with best existing medication (randomised controlled trial with larger numbers)
     - – **Phase 4 trial** = after a drug has been made widely available (post-licensing)
   - ○ It is often felt to be unethical to perform randomised controlled trials on children, especially if a medicine clearly works in adults
   - ○ Newer medications take a very long time to become widely used in paediatrics because of this (and therefore have more years of 'adult' experience prior to their being used)
   - ○ There are some excellent sources of information about which unlicensed medications are acceptable and how these are generally used in paediatrics ('Medicines for children' available on the Medicines and Healthcare products Regulatory Agency website at www.mhra.gov.uk, and the *BNF for Children*, available online at http://bnfc.org)
   - ○ New European Union legislation is coming requiring pharmaceutical companies to make a plan for investigating whether their medicines can become available for children when they register them for adults

7. **Obtain consent for insertion of an umbilical arterial catheter**
   ○ Indications – blood pressure monitoring, blood sampling
   ○ Risks – failure to get the umbilical arterial catheter (UAC) in, blood loss, accidental displacement, line infection, necrotising enterocolitis, arterial thrombosis (particularly renal, distal ischaemia, eg in limbs)
   ○ Complications avoided by checking for correct placement, monitoring for complications and removing the UAC as soon as it is no longer needed

8. **Obtain consent for insertion of an intercostal drain in a neonate with spontaneous pneumothorax and respiratory distress**
   ○ Main risks: damage to intercostal vessels and nerves, damage to internal structures (heart, liver, spleen), scarring and damage to breast tissue

9. **Talk to a mother who is refusing to allow an F2 to insert a cannula into a well 2-year-old child with a petechial rash**
   ○ Explain why the procedure is being done, and what the likely benefit is (able to take blood for diagnosis, able to give antibiotics and fluids if required should child deteriorate suddenly)
   ○ Explain the risks of the procedure (failed attempts, pain and distress to child) and what will be done to minimise these (topical analgesia, distraction, experienced medical and nursing staff)
   ○ Explore alternative options available
   ○ Explore reasons why mother is resistant

10. **Apologise to the parents of a 3-year-old who was accidentally given a double dose of gentamicin**
    ○ Main risks: renal toxicity (often reversible), ototoxicity (tinnitus, ataxia), which can be permanent
    ○ What to do for the patient – check gentamicin levels, renal function, hearing if levels are high, monitor urine output and blood pressure
    ○ What to do to avoid another mistake – incident form, staff education, discussed at governance meeting

11. **Talk to the mother of a premature baby who has had a skin swab come back positive for MRSA. He has previously had negative swabs**
    ○ Apologise
    ○ Establish mother's current understanding of what MRSA is
    ○ Inform her that it lives on the skin without causing symptoms
    ○ Explain that if it causes an infection this can be more difficult to treat
    ○ No signs of infection needing treatment in your baby
    ○ Normally spread by touch
    ○ Need to prevent spread by using gloves/aprons/isolation, etc
    ○ No specific treatment is required as this doesn't normally cause harm – monitor with swabs and three negative swabs are needed before the patient can be considered clear

12. **You suspect a newborn baby has trisomy 21. Talk to her parents**
    ○ Start by describing abnormal examination findings – *'having examined your baby there are some features which are of concern. She seems generally very floppy, she also has what we call a 'sandal gap' which is…'.*
    ○ When we see all of these features together we worry that a baby may have Down syndrome
    ○ Pause
    ○ *'How much do you know about Down syndrome?'*
    ○ Finish with an action plan that includes how the diagnosis will be confirmed, when you are going to come back and talk to them some more, patient information, an opportunity for more questions, etc
       The Down syndrome association website (www.downs-syndrome.org.uk) contains information for new parents in the form of 'first questions' and reading through this would be good preparation for this sort of scenario

13. **Discuss the diagnosis of diabetes with the mother of a 5-year-old admitted with weight loss, polyuria, polydipsia and glycosuria**
    ○ *'How much do you know about diabetes…?'*
    ○ Draw diagrams wherever possible to explain
    ○ Stress that *'it is nobody's fault'*

○ Need for insulin injections, glucose monitoring
○ Will be lifelong
○ Referral to diabetes team/patient information booklet

14. **Talk to the parents of a child who was unexpectedly found to have ambiguous genitalia**
    ○ State that *'It is not possible to assign a gender'*
    ○ Do not register the birth yet
    ○ Referral to multidisciplinary team (endocrinologist, urologist, geneticist, psychologist)
    ○ Need for tests (karyotype, pelvic ultrasound scan, pituitary hormones, 17-hydroxyprogesterone)
    ○ Stay in hospital: monitor blood glucose/blood pressure/urea and electrolytes until congenital adrenal hyperplasia is excluded

15. **Discuss with the parents of a 26-week baby the implications of bilateral Grade 3 intraventricular haemorrhages (IVH), which have recently been diagnosed on cranial ultrasound**
    ○ Explain why preterm babies get IVH – fluctuations in blood pressure/carbon dioxide, etc
    ○ Complications – immediate (ventriculomegaly) and long term (developmental difficulties)
    ○ Explain that you are unable to predict the outcome with certainty based on ultrasound findings, but that there is an increased likelihood of problems with more significant and bilateral bleeding. Baby will be followed up through infancy and into childhood to detect and manage any developmental difficulties

16. **Talk about starting inhaled steroids with the mother of a wheezy 5-year-old who is concerned about effects on growth**
    ○ Establish common ground: what does she know about inhaled steroids, what are her main concerns?
    ○ Explain that poorly controlled asthma has significant effects on growth
    ○ Talk about bioavailability/drug delivery and how these lessen systemic effects

- ○ Reassure and emphasise the benefits of improved control
- ○ Make a plan for reassessing the need for steroids depending on response

17. **Talk to a 16-year-old diabetic who is anxious about being transferred to adult services**
- ○ Explore main causes for concern
- ○ Discuss transition clinics
- ○ Explain where they can go for further support (expert patients programme/Diabetes UK (www.diabetes.org.uk)/ adult diabetes specialist nurse)
- ○ Reassure and emphasise positive aspects

18. **Talk to a 14-year-old girl with cystic fibrosis about the need for (her first) admission to hospital for i.v. antibiotics**
- ○ Explain the need for treatment in hospital – frequent i.v. antibiotics/intensive physiotherapy input/aim to increase lung function
- ○ Explain what will be involved – staying in a cubicle/insertion of a short long line
- ○ Explore anxieties/main perceived difficulties
- ○ Emphasise benefits

19. **Your F2 finds a heart murmur in a baby on the postnatal wards. Talk to the parents**
- ○ Establish common ground – what do they know about heart murmurs?
- ○ Explain what a murmur is and potential causes for this (innocent/from closing duct/hole or narrowing in heart or blood vessels coming from heart)
- ○ Explain what will happen next – ECG/cardiology referral

20. **Talk about contraceptive choices with a sexually active 15-year-old girl who has epilepsy**
- ○ Check that no abusive situation is occurring
- ○ Check that she knows about safe sex and the risks and consequences of sexually transmitted diseases
- ○ Explain that anti-epileptics can interfere with the combined oral contraceptive pill, therefore she will need a higher than normal dose

- ○ Explain that the progesterone-only pill doesn't work in these circumstances
- ○ Explain that depot injections don't last as long (needed every 10 weeks)
- ○ Explain that a higher dose is needed for emergency contraception
- ○ Explain where to go for further help (family planning clinic/ general practitioner/specialist nurse/practice nurse/websites)
- ○ Explain that some anti-epileptic drugs can cause harm to an unborn baby, as can uncontrolled epilepsy in pregnancy
- ○ Explain that she will need to take higher than usual doses of folate when planning to become pregnant

21. **Explain the inheritance of Prader–Willi syndrome to a medical student**
- ○ Check prior knowledge – of imprinting
- ○ Describe Prader–Willi in terms of having 'no active paternal Prader–Willi gene'
- ○ Could be a new mutation in the child affecting the chromosome 15 that was inherited from the father
- ○ Could also occur from uniparental disomy – the child receives both chromosomes 15 from the mother (and so lacks a paternal copy of the gene)
- ○ Use diagrams

22. **Talk to the parents of a child with Down syndrome about the likelihood of future children having the condition**
- ○ Check prior knowledge about chromosome inheritance (meiosis) in general and trisomy 21 in particular
- ○ Best discussed using diagrams
- ○ 94% of babies with Down's occur because of meiotic non-disjunction
- ○ For most families where one child has had confirmed trisomy 21 there is a 1 in 100 chance of having a baby with another chromosomal abnormality
- ○ If the mother is over 35 years old, the risk of recurrence is double the baseline risk for age (increases with increasing age)

- 5% of babies have a translocation (onto another chromosome, 15, 22 or 21) – in a quarter of these one parent carries a balanced translocation
- The risk of recurrence is 10%–15% if the mother has a translocation and 2.5% if the father has a translocation (or 100% if the translocation is 21:21 – rare)
- 1% of babies with Down's show mosaicism – trisomy arises post-fertilisation during mitosis

23. **This 15-year-old boy has recently been diagnosed with epilepsy. Talk about how this will affect his lifestyle**
    - Advise him to tell anyone with whom he spends a fair amount of time what may happen and what to do if it does
    - Advise him to think about what would happen if he had a seizure in different situations
    - Tell him that showers are safer than baths, and to use a sign rather than locking the bathroom door
    - Tell him to take common sense precautions for sport activities
    - Advise him that this will affect driving if it is not controlled by then (stress the need for compliance with treatment) and that he can only apply for a license if he is seizure free for 12 months (or night-time only seizures for 3 years)
    - Advise him that anti-epileptic drugs can make him more sensitive to the effects of alcohol, and that alcohol can decrease the efficacy of his medication
    - Advise him to be aware of his own seizure triggers, eg lighting/late nights/missed meals
    - Tell him that having epilepsy may influence his career choice (eg the armed forces won't consider people with epilepsy)
    - www.epilepsyresearch.org.uk is a good source of patient orientated information about the effects of epilepsy on lifestyle

24. **An 8-year-old girl has had three afebrile seizures. You decide to start treatment. Talk to her parents about starting anti-epileptic medication**
    - Explain the reason for starting medication (preventing further seizures)
    - Explain how medication is administered (gradually increasing dose: start low/go slow)

○ List the main side-effects and what to do if the parents notice them – don't stop medication (needs to be tapered off), and contact the epilepsy team urgently

○ Explain when to review medication – no obvious benefit/unacceptable side-effects/at puberty/seizure free for 2 years

○ Main side-effects of:
  – Sodium valproate
    • Gastric upset
    • Hair loss (transient: regrowth after 6 months)
    • Sedation
    • Change in behaviour (hyperactive/aggressive)
    • Teratogenicity
    • Hepatotoxicity (some clinicians check liver function tests regularly)
  – Carbamazepine
    • Urticaria
    • Nausea/ataxia/visual changes (respond to more gradual dose increments)
    • Bone marrow suppression (need to tell parents what to look out for)
  – Lamotrigine
    • Rash
  – Topiramate
    • Headache/tiredness/weight loss
    • Memory/concentration difficulties
    • Nephrolithiasis

25. **Explain to this medical student the various different insulin regimes for children with diabetes**

○ Use diagrams to illustrate twice-a-day injections, basal bolus regime, insulin pump therapy

○ Talk about advantages and drawbacks with each type
  – Basal bolus
    • Appears more physiological
    • More flexibility, greater control over what and when to eat
    • More injections (at least four a day)
    • Able to 'carbohydrate count' – adjust insulin require-ments to meal characteristics
    • Need to inject at school (can be a problem for chil-dren and for schools)

   — Twice a day
- Fewer injections
- Need for regulated snacks to prevent hypos
- Timing of meals important

   — Insulin pump
- Precise control of insulin dose
- Need for frequent testing
- Expensive to set up and maintain a pump service
- Attached 24 h per day
- Risk of skin infections/marking

26. **This 1-year-old child has been diagnosed with an egg allergy. Talk to her mother**
   - ◯ The more processed the egg, the less allergenic it will be: talk about which forms to avoid
   - ◯ Explain that there is a strong likelihood that she will grow out of it
   - ◯ Consider an egg challenge after her second birthday depending on skin prick tests/specific IgE results. Some challenges are left until later if tests still very suggestive of ongoing allergy. Co-existent allergy/other medical problems may be relevant to the timing
   - ◯ Arrange dietician involvement, patient information
   - ◯ Make sure the family have a member of paediatric team whom they can contact with any concerns.

27. **You have prescribed an EpiPen® for this child with a peanut allergy. Talk to her parents**
   - ◯ Explain that anaphylaxis is life threatening
   - ◯ List the symptoms to watch out for (breathing problems, swelling in lips or mouth, pale, vomiting, drowsiness)
   - ◯ Explain how to inject
   - ◯ Pens for home and school
   - ◯ Second pen needs to be available as some children need extra pre-hospital dose of adrenaline
   - ◯ Arrange training for everyone who looks after child (including school) – allergy specialist nurse will help with this
   - ◯ Don't let pens go out of date
   - ◯ Consider recommending a training video (check one is available in your department)

28. **You suspect Kawasaki disease in this 3-year-old girl. Talk about the implications of this to her parents**
    ○ Explain how the diagnosis is made (5 days of fever, bilateral non-exudative conjunctivitis, erythema of the lips and oral mucosa, changes in the extremities, rash and cervical lymphadenopathy)
    ○ Talk about treatment
    ○ Explain about intravenous immunoglobulin
    ○ Aspirin at a high dose initially until the fever settles
    ○ Lower dose aspirin until 6 weeks after onset (if no aneurysms)
    ○ Heart investigations (explain about coronary aneurysms, which occur in 15%–25% of children with Kawasaki disease)
    ○ Arrange cardiology follow-up

29. **Talk to the mother who has a jaundiced neonate and who is unhappy that she is not able to take her baby home (because the baby needs phototherapy)**
    ○ Explain the cause of jaundice (breakdown of red cells, immature liver)
    ○ Explain the risks of jaundice – bilirubin crosses into the brain, causes drowsiness/poor feeding. Very high levels in children who are already sick can be more serious; permanent damage can be caused.
    ○ Treatment: exchange transfusion – avoid need for this by phototherapy/adequate hydration
    ○ Draw diagram of a bilirubin risk chart
    ○ Explain the need for blood tests and the likely length of stay in hospital

30. **Talk to this mother about the implications of premature delivery at 23 weeks**
    ○ Consider the following prior to talking to Mum
      - Mum's support network
      - How likely she will retain information (is she in active labour?)
      - Her previous experience of preterm deliveries
      - Any known antenatal problems so far
    ○ *'The most important thing to tell you is that this is a very high risk situation and by that I mean your baby may not survive'*
    ○ Many do not survive delivery (roughly half)
    ○ Of those admitted to the newborn unit many do not survive (roughly 25% survive)

○ Explain that the baby will be on the neonatal unit for 4–5 months, and may have problems with breathing, feeding, infection, bleeding into the brain and growth

○ Explain that many have long-term problems with development; particularly movement, vision and hearing problems (*'May not be able to walk and may not be able to talk'*)

○ Outline what will happen immediately after the baby is born (neonatal team present, intubation, transfer to NICU)

It is essential that you have a working knowledge of the EPICure study if you are embarking on discussing this topic. Though the cohort of babies studied were born in 1995 and much has changed since then, the study continues to influence how this area is discussed. EPICure 2 commenced in 2006. www.nottingham.ac.uk/human-development/Epicure is a good source of further information on both of these studies.

31. **This child has recently been admitted with a painful sickle crisis. Talk to her mother about pain relief**
   ○ Stepwise (paracetamol, ibuprofen, opioids)
   ○ Explain that they should come to hospital if the pain is severe (requiring opioids); also, explain the need to come to hospital for a high fever, pain in the chest, spine or abdomen, neurological signs
   ○ Don't forget other aspects of management of a crisis (think about rest, hydration, oxygen, antibiotics)

32. **Talk to the mother of this diabetic child about the management of hypoglycaemia**
   ○ When to treat low sugars (*'4 is the floor'*)
   ○ Symptoms – may be none, pallor/shaking/sweating followed by irritability/change in behaviour/drowsiness
   ○ How to treat mild symptoms (dextrose tablets or 50 ml Coke/Lucozade followed by long-acting carbohydrate, eg biscuits/bread/banana)
   ○ Hypostop® if drowsy, glucagon if unconscious
   ○ Explain that there is an increased risk associated with recurrent hypoglycaemia, alcohol, lots of exercise
   ○ Check understanding, offer written information and a diabetic nurse follow-up, who will go through this information again and have more information on how to treat

33. **The mother of a well-hydrated child with mild diarrhoea is insisting on i.v. fluids. Talk to her about the decision not to start i.v. fluids**
    - ○ Explain that the child will drink enough to keep well hydrated
    - ○ Explain that i.v. fluids can be harmful (distress and pain of cannula, iatrogenic electrolyte disturbance)
    - ○ Outline the conditions when a cannula would be required (vomiting all fluids, clinically dehydrated, drowsy)
    - ○ Negotiate plan for revisiting decision should things change

34. **Talk to the mother of this 6-year-old about his functional abdominal pain. She is insisting on further tests**
    - ○ Explain that it is a very common problem for children
    - ○ Focus on excluding serious pathology
    - ○ Focus on controlling symptoms
    - ○ Subjective experience of pain exacerbated by psychological factors (*'Some children find that if they are anxious or stressed it can make their pain more noticeable. Is there anything you can think of which might be making things worse like this?'*)

35. **Talk to this 15-year-old bradycardic anorexic girl about the decision to admit her into hospital**
    - ○ Establish common ground – what does she understand so far?
    - ○ Outline current concerns – life-threatening condition, slow pulse indicates that her body is not coping
    - ○ Plan for admission – bed rest, adequate fluids and nutrition, multidisciplinary team (dietician, psychiatrist, paediatrician), monitoring

36. **A 10–month-old boy has been diagnosed with developmental hip dysplasia. Talk to his angry parents**
    - ○ Spend time listening
    - ○ Explain that every effort is made to pick up abnormal hips clinically but the condition is not always able to be diagnosed at birth
    - ○ Explain that some cases are missed, and that of these many resolve spontaneously
    - ○ Explain that we cannot offer ultrasound screening to everybody

37. **Talk to the parents of an 18-month-old child who has been seen several times with uncomplicated viral infections. Her parents are demanding tests of her immune function**
    ○ Explain that immune function is investigated for recurrent severe, prolonged, or unusual infections
    ○ Explain that repeated viral infections are normal for this age group (at least eight per year is normal)
    ○ Explain that there is some evidence to suggest that viral infections in preschool children can have a beneficial effect on the immune system (reducing allergy)
    ○ Normal growth is reassuring
    ○ Offer follow-up

<u>YOUR NOTES</u>

PART III

Clinical stations

SHORT CASE PREPARATION AND TECHNIQUE

7.1 PREPARATION AND TECHNIQUE

Preparation and technique are intertwined. Many candidates fail the exam because of poor short case technique, and this is usually down to poor preparation of potential exam scenarios and a lack of awareness of what is expected of them in each station. The well-prepared candidate will give themselves many opportunities to pick up marks, just as the poorly prepared candidate will inevitably drop marks.

In particular if your examination technique is poor you will fail.

The RCPCH Anchor Statements for 'Expected Standard/Clear Pass' demonstrate that three key areas are assessed:

○ **Conduct of examination** – Introduces oneself, puts parent and child at ease. Displays an appropriate level of confidence. Appropriate pace without rushing. Acknowledges child fully and explains intended examination if deemed appropriate. Adjusts language and behaviour to suit age of child.
○ **Clinical examination** – systematic and uncluttered technique. Able to identify clinical signs and interpret their meaning.
○ **Discussion with examiners** – Sensible differential diagnosis. Able to suggest a sensible management plan, including investigations. Demonstrates an understanding of impact of findings on patient and family unit.

For example, if you are asked to examine the respiratory system, in order to pass the exam you will need to do more than just pick up and present findings. It may be you will need to present not only the most likely diagnosis, eg cystic fibrosis, but also suggest the different investigations that could have led to this diagnosis, such as the sweat test, genetic analysis or the Guthrie test looking at immunoreactive trypsin. This reiterates the philosophy that the exam reflects every-day clinical practice.

○ Examine the case
○ Pick up and present the abnormalities
○ Answer questions relevant to the case

It is essential to be completely clear about how to examine any system. Decide on your own method, learn it and practise it. Use this method throughout the preparation period when seeing short cases. Try not to change your approach in the run up to the exam. Remember there is no definitive way to examine any system; you need to find your own scheme. Whichever scheme you use, remember that the examiner is unlikely to tolerate imprecise or clumsy clinical examination and this should be avoidable with proper preparation. This book suggests an examination scheme for most potential scenarios. You are also referred to standard texts of paediatric examination, and to the RCPCH (2004) booklet, *Clinical Examination Technique in the Short Cases* (available online from www.rcpch.ac.uk).

Remember that confidence in the exam comes from knowing that your examination technique is not only correct but is also reproducible in a highly stressful environment. This comes from relentless practice of examination and presentation in the company of several different 'examiners'. It is important to be mock-examined by a range of colleagues, some whom you know and some of whom you don't. This reflects the six different examiners who will soon be assessing you in the clinical stations with no prior knowledge of your performance in a previous station, or indeed your performance in the workplace. At the very least you should go around in pairs and be very objective when assessing each other's performances. It will help to take a copy of the Anchor Statements with you to see how you measure up to the expected standard.

During the examination itself there are several common pitfalls:

○ Poor engagement with the child, including failure to look at a child to judge whether you may be eliciting pain. For example, repeated examination of an enlarged spleen may start to become uncomfortable for a patient if you are the fourth consecutive candidate to have seen them. It is important to be empathetic with the patient, just as you would be on the wards.

○ Failure to talk your way through an examination when it has been requested/is appropriate.

○ Lack of conviction in your findings, enabling an examiner to place doubt in your mind and throw you off balance. For example, a candidate was asked to examine an abdomen with bilateral masses and then asked to present her findings. She presented the patient as having an enlarged spleen and liver. The examiner was able to change the candidate's mind twice as to whether the masses were kidneys or liver and spleen in the subsequent discussion.

○ Stopping the examination when you have identified the organ in question. For example, there is a set routine for examining an enlarged liver and you must continue with your examination until you are stopped. Another candidate was asked to examine the abdomen. There was an enlarged liver and the child had a fever, having just returned from Africa. The candidate correctly identified malaria as the diagnosis but failed the short case. On counselling she was told that her examination of the liver was inadequate because she did not percuss its size.

○ Excluding a clear physical sign if you feel it does not fit in with other signs. Another candidate was asked to examine the cardio-

vascular system and to comment afterwards. She correctly identified the missing left brachial pulse and the left thoracotomy scar,
making the correct diagnosis of repaired aortic coarctation.
However, this candidate also heard a soft ejection systolic
murmur and could not fit it into the picture and did not mention
it. Of course, such a murmur is to be expected in coarctation.
Despite this the candidate passed.

○ Failing to come up with some common differential diagnoses in
the discussion. The differential diagnoses in this text are 'practical
differential diagnoses' focusing primarily on common scenarios
and ones that are likely to be seen in the exam. Many candidates
report that they are not given the chance to present a full differential diagnosis, but are asked for one or two possibilities relating
to the child they have seen. Where relevant, the most likely
differentials will be at the top of the list in this book.

BASIC FORMAT FOR CLINICAL EXAMINATION

○ Introduce yourself to the child and parent
○ Be prepared to talk about your findings as you proceed
○ Observe and be prepared to comment on:
   • General appearance and health – well or unwell? Ward
     patients are occasionally used
   • Dysmorphic features – syndromic or otherwise
   • Growth and nutrition – note obvious abnormalities. You
     may be asked to assess pubertal status
   • Development – neurodevelopmental abnormalities may
     be noted during examination of other systems. Many
     patients are eligible for two or more stations per exam
     session, for example Neurology and Child Development
   • Hands – colour, clubbing, nail abnormalities, poor perfu-
     sion
   • Face – cyanosis, anaemia, jaundice
   • General observations such as presence of a nasogastric
     tube
○ Palpate
○ Auscultate
○ Ask for permission to examine any other relevant part of the
   body

○ Describe your findings
○ Answer questions about your findings until the bell rings for the end of the station

7.2 PRESENTATION SKILLS

Presentation skills are important and particularly the first few sentences you say about a certain scenario need to be practised. Examples of how you should present cases are included in Chapters 8–13. When presenting, it is useful to have a few general words and phrases that can apply to most cases, eg 'Harry is a boy who looks well grown and I would like to plot his weight on a centile chart...'. This approach overcomes nerves and gives you time to compose yourself.

The information in this section of the book is presented partly in note form and partly as it would appear in the exam using case scenarios to illustrate the knowledge required on a particular topic. Additional information pertaining to many of the conditions seen in this section can be found in Parts I and II.

<u>YOUR NOTES</u>

CARDIOLOGY

CONTENTS

8.1   Introduction

8.2   Clinical examination
      Suggested approach to cardiovascular examination

8.3   Cases
      Case one: Complex cyanotic congenital heart disease
      Case two: Trisomy 21, with AVSD and Eisenmenger's
          syndrome
      Case three: Cavopulmonary shunt
      Case four: Innocent murmur
      Case five: Complex congenital cardiac disease
      Case six: Ventricular septal defect
      Case seven: Supravalvular aortic stenosis

8.4   Background notes
      Measuring JVP in children
      Innocent murmurs
      Dextrocardia
      Ventricular septal defect
      Atrial septal defect
      Pulmonary stenosis
      Aortic stenosis
      Coarctation of the aorta
      The cyanosed child
      Fallot's tetralogy
      Eisenmenger's syndrome

Cardiomyopathy
Infective endocarditis
Syndromes associated with cardiac lesions
Surgery for congenital heart disease

8.1 INTRODUCTION

Preparation

Cardiology short cases are a hard part of the exam. In this chapter we have tried to give useful information and to highlight some of the important areas and more common conditions seen. It is essential to have a good system of cardiovascular examination and some background knowledge (read through paediatric cardiology in one of the standard texts) to help with the interpretation of physical signs. The best places to see children with signs are on the cardiology ward (pre-elective operation) and in the cardiology clinic. These children will be most representative of the cases you are likely to see in your exam. You should ask a cardiology specialist trainee or consultant to critique your examination technique and point out to you how they would best elicit the relevant signs. There are many important physical signs that you may never have seen outside of a specialist clinic/ward. They are often surprisingly easy to elicit and once seen they are often not forgotten.

During the examination

It is important to adapt your examination, if appropriate, and to be responsive to whatever the examiner asks. Clearly, if the examiner asks you to do cardiovascular examination then the full examination should be done. If you are asked to examine the heart then it is less clear. There are different strategies to deal with this although no consensus view. It is, however, in our experience often best to do the full cardiovascular examination unless the examiner specifically tells you to take short cuts. If the examiner asks you just to listen to the heart then that may be all he/she expects in that instance. If you are unclear what is expected of you, then it is perfectly reasonable to check with the examiner directly.

It is not unreasonable in the case of a small child to move straight on to auscultation at the very beginning of the examination if the patient is quiet, in order to listen to heart sounds and murmurs before the child becomes upset. It is probably best to explain yourself to the examiner if you perform the examination this way. Remember to complete the examination.

Taking blood pressure and checking jugular venous pressure (JVP; see Section 8.4) are part of a complete examination and you should include them in all your practice cases so that you get used to doing them quickly under pressure for children at a variety of ages. Because they can often take up a disproportionate amount of time and are so often normal it may be acceptable to leave them to the end, but you should make every effort to let the examiner know that you haven't overlooked them and give the examiner the prerogative to stop you from attempting them if he or she does not think they are relevant. If in doubt – do it!

Particularly with the cardiovascular system, there are many signs that have the potential to give very accurate diagnostic information, but require years of experience to be fully appreciated, such as split second heart sounds and abnormal JVP waveforms. As a general rule, if a sign is not obvious it is probably not there or not worth mentioning. Don't spend so long on these aspects of the examination that you neglect the bigger picture.

In most short case scenarios it is sensible to talk your way through the examination of the case. In cardiovascular system examination however, particularly if the diagnosis is not obvious, then it is wise to keep your own counsel; although clearly if you see something obvious, eg Down syndrome, cyanosis or chest wall scarring, it is appropriate to mention it. Many of the signs you discover will be much easier to interpret once you have gathered all the information, particularly when it comes to interpreting murmurs. You would be wise to not volunteer any information about heart sounds and murmurs until you have listened as fully as you intend to, including checking for radiation and response to manoeuvres. This will give you the maximum time to assimilate all the information and put it together into a cohesive, reasonable sounding interpretation.

The keys to success in this station are to have a well-practised fluent technique, to be able to detect the relevant signs with confidence, to be able to formulate them into a sensible differential diagnosis and to have enough background knowledge of the more common conditions to be able to answer some questions about the significance of your findings and further management.

8.2 CLINICAL EXAMINATION

Suggested approach to cardiovascular examination

Examine this child's heart

This boy had a cardiac procedure as an infant, please examine his cardiovascular system

Examine this child's chest

Initial procedure

▨ Introduce yourself to the parents and the child

General observations

▨ Age
▨ Growth: more than just worth mentioning, growth is crucial to determining management in congenital heart disease
▨ Colour: pink, pale or blue (or jaundice as in Alagille's)
▨ Dysmorphic features (could give clue to underlying cardiac lesion)
▨ Monitoring (may have oxygen saturation probe)
▨ Supplemental oxygen
▨ Increased work of breathing (recession, tachypnoea)

Hands to arms

▨ Perfusion: cool or warm hands
▨ Clubbing: if you are unsure whether it is present, don't spend a long time looking for it, as it may not be significant enough to comment on. Best to look for 'loss of diamond' when comparing index fingers (first sign of clubbing). Clubbing is present after long-standing arterial desaturation (over 6 months). Could be present in pink, well-saturated children if they have recently had corrective cardiac surgery (or if it has a 'non-cardiac' cause)
▨ Evidence of endocarditis: see notes below
▨ Radial pulse (less relevant in babies) and brachial pulse: compare both sides
  • Make a show of counting pulse rate
  • Comment on rate (and whether this is normal for this age group; see Box), rhythm, character

NORMAL RANGES FOR HEART RATE (RESTING) IN BEATS PER MINUTE

Neonates	110–150
2 years	85–125
4 years	75–115
6 years and over	60–100

■ Brachial/carotid pulse characters
  • *Collapsing*: run off lesions, classically aortic regurgitation, could also be seen in patent ductus arteriosus, large arteriovenous fistula
  • *Thready*: congestive cardiac failure, circulatory shock
  • *Asymmetrical*: post-coarctation repair (using L subclavian flap)
  • *Slow rising* flattened pulse amplitude, implies impaired ejection from left ventricle (eg aortic stenosis)
  • *Pulsus paradoxus*: cardiac tamponade/pericarditis, severe asthma/high intrathoracic pressures

---

Tip

Don't suggest the pulse character is abnormal unless it is very obviously abnormal. If you are unsure, it is less likely to be significant and you should move on

---

Blood pressure

■ You should make a judgement about how quick and easy it would be to check the BP manually at this point. In older children this can be done rapidly and you should do it. In younger, less co-operative children it can take a while to do this but it is still an essential part of a complete, structured examination. If you plan to come back to BP at the end then make sure the examiners are aware of this or it may appear that you have simply forgotten. You will need to practise doing this on children of various ages so that you don't take too long over it in the exam. Your approach should be:

  • Explanation
  • Position child as you want them to be
  • Select correct cuff size

- Inflate the cuff whilst palpating the brachial/radial pulse until the pulse disappears
- Inflate the cuff a further 10 mmHg
- Place the stethoscope over the brachial artery
- Deflate the cuff slowly until regular sounds (the Korotkov's sounds) can just be heard through the stethoscope
- Note the systolic pressure as accurately as possible
- Continue to deflate the cuff slowly; the sounds get louder then suddenly become muffled and disappear
- Record the point at which the sounds become muffled as the diastolic pressure
- Interpret the results

▨ All children need an explanation of what is about to happen. This should start with *'have you had your blood pressure checked before?'* Young children need very careful reassurance and this should be well practised. It is likely that if the examiner has indicated that you should take the blood pressure of a young child then there will be a lot riding on your sensitive, paediatric approach

▨ Avoid cuffs that are too small as they may cause a falsely high BP. Cuff width should be approximately two-thirds of the length of the upper arm (or 50% of the circumference of the arm), and the bladder should encircle the limb almost completely

▨ Technically you should take at least two readings before you say what the blood pressure is. This is probably only necessary if you have been specifically asked to check the BP. You should let the examiner know what the result was from the first reading and then say *'I would normally confirm this with a second blood pressure reading'*

▨ *In reality BP is often measured by a Doppler machine or Dinamap®. If you are not familiar with how to use these you should ask one of the nursing staff to teach you. Don't be caught out by not being able to use a simple piece of equipment like a blood pressure monitoring machine!*

▨ Interpreting whether BP readings are normal is difficult. There are published normal ranges. As a rough guide a systolic BP should be no more than 90 plus double the child's age. If you find a BP that is outside this range you should comment on the fact that it is not a normal reading and that you would check the value against a table of normal ranges (Table 9.1). Remember particularly if the reading is abnormal to check a second one

Newborn	Mean BP should be equal to or above gestational age (eg mean of >40 mmHg for term infant)
Infancy	80–95 mmHg systolic
Preschool	80–100 mmHg systolic
School age	90–110 mmHg systolic
>12	100–120 mmHg systolic

Table 8.1: Approximate values for blood pressure in children

Face and neck

- Conjunctival pallor (approach with care)
- Central cyanosis – becomes clinically apparent when saturations are below 85%. This is not necessarily true if the patient is anaemic or dark skinned. You should say that the patient is not clinically cyanosed unless they are very obviously blue. In practice, for the purposes of the exam, if you are not sure and the patient is not clubbed, do not spend a long time looking
- Dental caries if present
- Carotid pulse character
- Jugular venous pressure – in older children (see notes below)

Chest

Inspection

- Expose fully wherever possible
- Shape (chest wall deformities)
- Comment on any visible impulses (could indicate hyperdynamic apex beat)
- Scars (see Box)

CAUSES OF CHEST WALL SCARS

Right lateral thoracotomy
- Modified BT shunt
- Lung causes (lobectomy)
- Tracheo-oesophageal fistula repair

Left lateral thoracotomy
- Modified BT shunt

- ○ Coarctation repair
- ○ Patent ductus arteriosus ligation
- ○ Pulmonary artery banding
- ○ Lung causes (lobectomy)

Median sternotomy

- ○ Any bypass surgery (most corrective surgery of intracardiac abnormalities requires bypass)

Chest drain scars

Mediastinal drain scars

Chest wall pacemakers (often in left pectoral region)

Palpation

- Apex beat (right or left): the first and most important thing is to look for dextrocardia at this point; if you miss it now it will be difficult not to look foolish when you eventually realise. Place a hand on each side of the chest and remove the hand that hasn't got the strongest impulse underneath it (if you detect dextrocardia you must remember to look for associated abnormalities/Kartagener's syndrome).
- You can then proceed to determine:
  - Site: normal (4th or 5th intercostal space, midclavicular line) or displaced
  - Character: hyperactive characterises lesions with volume overload (large left to right shunt/valvular regurgitation)
  - Right ventricular heave: a palpable right ventricular impulse indicative of high right-sided pressures (for example, right ventricular outflow tract obstruction)
- Thrills
  - Upper left sternal border – pulmonary stensosis (rarely patent ductus arteriosus)
  - Upper right sternal border – aortic stenosis
  - Lower left sternal border – ventricular septal defect
  - Suprasternal notch – aortic stenosis (occasionally pulmonary stenosis, patent ductus arteriosus, coarctation of the aorta)
  - Carotid arteries – aortic stenosis (occasionally coarctation of the aorta)

Auscultation

Listen in four areas:

1. Mitral (apex)
2. Tricuspid (lower left sternal edge)
3. Aortic (right second intercostal space)
4. Pulmonary (left second intercostal space)

Several candidates have been asked to point out the areas to the examiner.

Remember this is on the assumption that the heart is structurally normal and dextrocardia is not present.

Heart sounds

Take note of these before assessing the nature of any murmur

- Are they both present?
- First heart sound – loud when cardiac output high, eg when nervous or excited, anaemia and pyrexia. Soft when cardiac output is low or there is poor left ventricular function
- Is the second heart sound normal?
- If the second heart sound is louder than the first when listening over the apex, then this could indicate pulmonary hypertension

The following are classically heard by consultant cardiologists and medical students but very rarely by the rest of us. Once again, if it is not obvious don't spend a long time looking for it, as it is unlikely to be significant for the purposes of the exam. You should however know the significance and implications of the following and how to detect them if they are there:

1. Splitting of second heart sound
   - Pulmonary valve closes later than aortic valve in the normal cardiac cycle
   - Best listened for at the upper left sternal border
   - Increased separation between sounds in inspiration and decreased separation (becoming single second heart sound) in expiration are normal
   - Widely split: classically occurs in atrial septal defect where the right ventricle is overfilled and pulmonary valve closure is delayed, mild pulmonary stenosis and right bundle branch block
   - Fixed splitting of the second sound (atrial septal defect): when there is no variation with respiration, the two atria are functioning as one and respiration has the same effect on both the pulmonary and systemic circulations

- Single S2 occurs when there is pulmonary hypertension (pulmonary valve closes quickly), transposition of the great arteries or abnormal aortic or pulmonary valves (atresia or severe stenosis)
- Paradoxical splitting (aortic valve closes last) – left bundle branch block, severe aortic stenosis

2. Third heart sound ('Tennessee')
    - Often heard in normal children
    - Can indicate reduced ventricular compliance
    - Best heard with bell over apex/lower left sternal border

3. Fourth heart sound ('Kentucky')
    - This occurs shortly before the first heart sound
    - Almost always pathological but rare in children
    - Indicates reduced ventricular compliance

4. Gallop rhythm
    - Implies loud S3 or S4 and tachycardia
    - Always pathological

5. Ejection clicks
    - Classically occur in aortic valve and pulmonary valve stenosis, but may also be heard when there is a large dilated aorta in tetralogy of Fallot, coarctation of the aorta, patent ductus arteriosus or when there is a dilated pulmonary artery in pulmonary hypertension. The sound is made by the forceful opening of the valve
    - Aortic click – lower left sternal edge and apex
    - Pulmonary click – second left intercostal space

Murmurs

Make sure you have fully assessed a murmur before you comment on it. A full assessment consists of the following six components:

1. Timing in relation to cardiac cycle: patterns of murmur are given in Table 8.2

Systolic	**Diastolic**	**Continuous** ie overlaps both heart sounds, therefore is not confined to systole or diastole
Ejection systolic (crescendo/decrescendo) • Could be innocent • Aortic stenosis • Pulmonary stenosis Pansystolic • VSD • Mitral regurgitation • Tricuspid regurgitation Systolic click (occurs midsystole) with late systolic murmur • Mitral valve prolapse Ejection click (occurs early in systole) • Aortic valve disease	Early diastolic murmur • Aortic regurgitation (best heard at LLSB, with bell, in expiration, sitting forward) Mid diastolic • Mitral/tricuspid stenosis Opening snap/diastolic rumble • Mitral stenosis	• PDA • ASD • Blalock–Taussig shunt • AV malformation • Aneurysm • Collateral vessels • Venous hum • Peripheral pulmonary stenosis • Aortopulmonary window

Table 8.2: Patterns of murmur. ASD, atrial septal defect; AV, arteriovenous; LLSB, lower left sternal border; PDA, patent ductus arteriosus; VSD, ventricular septal defect

2. Site of maximal intensity (see Table 8.3)
   Remember this is on the assumption that the heart is structurally normal and dextrocardia is not present.

Upper left sternal edge = pulmonary area	**Upper right sternal edge** = aortic area	**Lower left sternal edge**	**Apex**
• Pulmonary stenosis • Pulmonary flow murmur • Pulmonary artery stenosis • PDA • RVOT obstruction (e.g. Fallot's)	• Aortic valve stenosis • Subaortic stenosis • Supravalvular aortic stenosis	• Aortic regurgitation (loudest over 3rd or 4th intercostal space) • VSD • AVSD • Vibratory innocent murmur (Still's) • HOCM • Tricuspid regurgitation	• MR • Mitral stenotic murmurs • Mitral valve prolapse

Table 8.3: Sites of maximal intensity. AVSD, atrioventricular septal defect; HOCM, hypertrophic obstructive cardiomyopathy; MR, mitral regurgitation; PDA, patent ductus arteriosus; RVOT, right ventricular outflow tract; VSD, ventricular septal defect

3. Character: high or low pitched/musical/vibratory/blowing
4. Murmur-enhancing moves:
   - Left lateral position – brings out S3 and mitral murmurs
   - Sitting forward – brings out aortic murmurs
   - Change with inspiration/expiration – expiration brings out left-sided murmurs
   - Valsalva – for hypertrophic obstructive cardiomyopathy
5. Radiation (neck, axilla and back)
   - To neck – aortic in origin
   - To back/sides of chest – pulmonary in origin (eg pulmonary stensosis, branch pulmonary artery stenosis, right ventricular outflow tract obstruction/infundibular stenosis as in Fallot's)
   - To axilla – pulmonary valve murmurs or mitral regurgitation
   - Look for murmur over the back at this stage (for coarctation – just below tip of left scapula)
6. Grade (I–VI)

GRADING OF MURMURS

I   Barely audible
II   Medium intensity
III   Loud but no thrill
IV   Loud with a thrill
V   Very loud but still requires stethoscope to be on the chest
VI   So loud, can be heard with stethoscope off the chest

Auscultate basal lung fields before moving on.

Abdomen

- Hepatomegaly
- Situs solitus (midline liver) or situs inversus: associated with atrial isomerism; association with malrotation so may have evidence of Ladd's procedure scar
- Abdominal pacemaker: epigastric scar; may not be able to feel pacemaker box
- Scars from postoperative peritoneal dialysis (sometimes necessary for fluid/ascites management post bypass surgery)
- Ascites

▨ Evidence of protein-losing enteropathy (can occur after bidirectional Glenn procedure)

▨ Splenomegaly (occurs in infective endocarditis)

Groin

Announce that you are about to do this and remember to preserve modesty in older children

▨ Scars from cardiac catheterisation/central lines

▨ Femoral pulses: compare character with upper limb pulses and look for radio-femoral delay (a sign that collateral circulation has developed to bypass an aortic coarctation)

Don't forget to mention

▨ Blood pressure if not already done

▨ Jugular venous pressure if not already done

▨ Femoral pulses if not already done

▨ Check growth chart

▨ Peripheral or sacral oedema

▨ Fundoscopy/dipping urine for evidence of infective endocarditis

---

8.3 CASES

The following are representative of some of the cases that you may see in the exam

Case one: Complex cyanotic congenital heart disease

> *Patient: 8-month-old girl. She appears small for her age although I would like to plot her on a centile chart. She is tachypnoeic at rest. She is centrally cyanosed. She has no dysmorphic features. She is clubbed and has peripheral cyanosis. She has an absent right brachial and radial pulse, there is no radio-femoral delay. She has a right-sided thoracotomy scar. On auscultation she has a normal first heart sound and a single second heart sound. She has a continuous murmur over the right side of her chest. (At the end of this examination you should suggest palpating the abdomen for a liver and taking the blood pressure.)*

This set of clinical signs would fit with a child who has a complex cyanotic congenital heart lesion and has had a shunt procedure.

Notes

Possible diagnoses include:

❍ Pulmonary atresia without a ventricular septal defect
❍ Double outlet right ventricle
❍ Univentricular heart with pulmonary atresia

You would not be expected to come up with that diagnosis, but carefully eliciting the clinical signs will allow a best guess. In this case, with the shunt and the single second heart sound, a diagnosis of pulmonary atresia would be the first best guess. Fallot's is less likely because there is no systolic murmur of pulmonary stenosis and in pulmonary stenosis there should be two components of the second sound.

Case two: Trisomy 21, with AVSD and Eisenmenger's syndrome

> *Patient: 13-year-old girl. She has facial features of Down syndrome. She is deeply cyanosed at rest. She is clubbed and peripherally cyanosed. Her pulses are normal in character and the rate is 95 beats per minute. There is no radio-femoral delay. There are no scars visible on the thorax. Her apex beat is not displaced. She has a right ventricular heave. On auscultation she has a normal first heart sound, a loud second heart sound and a pansystolic murmur, maximal at the left sternal edge but heard all over the chest. I would like to go on to palpate her abdomen for a liver.*

This young girl with Down syndrome is most likely to have atrioventricular septal defect with shunt reversal resulting in Eisenmenger's syndrome.

Notes

Down syndrome children who have no scars and are cyanosed at the age of 13 are likely to have a defect causing Eisenmenger's – be prepared to talk about Eisenmenger's syndrome and its prognosis. This case could just as well be seen in the History Taking/Management Planning Station or the Communication Station.

Case three: Cavopulmonary shunt

> *Patient: 20-month-old girl. She appears to be thriving although I would like to plot her on a centile chart. She has no dysmorphic features and appears to be comfortable at rest. She is mildly cyanosed centrally. Her pulses are normal throughout. She has no radio-femoral delay. She has a median sternotomy scar but no thoracotomy scars. Her apex beat is localised to the 5th intercostal space on the right; there are no heaves or thrills. She has normal heart sounds on the right side and appears to have dextrocardia. There is a continuous murmur.*

This set of clinical signs would fit with a child who has a complex congenital cardiac defect and who is likely to have had a central shunt procedure, eg cavopulmonary anastomosis.

Notes

If the heart sounds are difficult to hear, as a matter of routine listen to the right side of the chest to exclude dextrocardia. Mild cyanosis in a child with a median sternotomy scar suggests a palliative shunt procedure for those children for whom definitive surgery is not possible. The case described had a complex cardiac defect involving right atrial isomerism, dextrocardia, a complete AV canal defect and a single ventricle with pulmonary atresia. A precise diagnosis would not be expected.

Case four: Innocent murmur

Patient: Jack, aged 4. He looks well and is thriving. There is no clubbing. His pulse and blood pressure are normal. There are no scars. His apex beat is normal and in the 5th left intercostal space. There are no heaves or thrills. There is a 2/6 ejection systolic murmur, maximal in the pulmonary area, which does not radiate. The murmur is loudest when the child sits forward. The heart sounds are normal. Chest X-ray and ECG are normal.

This is likely to be a pulmonary flow murmur.

Case five: Complex congenital cardiac disease

Patient: 3-year-old boy. He looks well and is not tachypnoeic at rest. His right radial pulse is absent. He has a scar from cardiac catheterisation. He has a right thoracotomy scar and midline sternotomy scar. I presume he has complex congenital heart disease, now repaired, and I would like to proceed to listen to the heart ...

It is not possible to achieve a specific diagnosis in this case.

Case six: Ventricular septal defect

Patient: 12-year-old boy who appears to be well and thriving. On examination he has a grade 3/6 pansystolic murmur, heard maximally at the lower left sternal edge. There is no radiation and no variation with posture or expiration. There are no other detectable heart murmurs. His heart sounds are normal; his apex beat is normal in character and site. There are no other abnormalities in the remainder of his cardiovascular examination.

My impression is that these signs would be consistent with a diagnosis of a small ventricular septal defect. I would now like to check his blood pressure to complete my examination.

Case seven: Supravalvular aortic stenosis

Patient: 3-year-old boy who appears to be short for his age. He has some facial characteristics of Williams syndrome. He appears well and is pink. There is no clubbing or evidence of infective endocarditis in his hands. His radial and brachial pulses are normal and symmetrical in character. He has no chest wall deformities or scars. His apex beat is not displaced and is normal in character. He has a suprasternal and carotid thrill as well as a thrill over his aortic area. He has a loud, grade 4/6 ejection systolic murmur in the aortic area, which radiates to the carotids and is increased in expiration. He also has an ejection systolic murmur, grade 2/6, heard over the pulmonary area and widely radiating to the back and sides of the chest. This is not associated with a thrill. There is no ejection click or diastolic murmur. His heart sounds are normal. His femoral pulses are normal with no radio-femoral delay. There were no other abnormalities on cardiovascular examination.

My impression is that this boy has aortic stenosis, which, given the absence of an ejection systolic click and the features suggestive of Williams, I would expect to be a supravalvular aortic stenosis. He also has some evidence of branch pulmonary stenosis. I would now like to examine his blood pressure, look in his eyes for evidence of a stellate iris and examine his development.

8.4 BACKGROUND NOTES ON THE CARDIOVASCULAR STATION

Measuring jugular venous pressure (JVP) in children

This can be time consuming and relies on co-operation and the presence of a neck; therefore, it is only normally attempted in older children. It can give useful information about fluid status in general and also about the condition of the right heart. Because it is time consuming it would pay to mention as part of your structured examination that you would normally measure the JVP and that you will come back to it at the end. That way if the examiner would like to see how you do it they can prompt you at this point. If they don't then you will need to remember to come back to it, as it may give you very useful information that you can use to inform your diagnosis. Don't forget that children who have had a bidirectional Glenn procedure will not have a JVP, so attempt with caution in cyanosed children.

Spend time getting the patient positioned exactly how you would like, doing this means that you are much more likely to be successful. Use pillows behind their head if necessary to get the sternocleidomastoid muscle completely relaxed. If you are not used to measuring JVP in children find a consultant (preferably a cardiologist or a nephrologist) to show you how they do it.

1. Position patient
   - Head resting on bed – adjust to an angle of approx 45°
   - Turn them slightly to the side to relax the sternocleidomastoid muscle
   - Ideally have the patient lit from the side
2. Locate pulsation: you can confirm that it is an internal jugular pulsation by:
   - Wave form (multiphasic wave form is normal for JVP; not seen in carotid pulsation)
   - Rises with pressure over the liver (ask if they have pain first); hepatojugular reflex
   - Non-palpable
   - Stops with pressure applied to the base of the neck
   - Position changes with raising/lowering the head
   - Varies with respiration
3. Measure height above sternal angle
   - 4 cm above the sternal angle is quoted as within the normal range for adults

Characteristics of the JVP

The JVP pulsation consists of three wave forms:
- ○ a wave – corresponds to right atrial contraction
- ○ c wave – corresponds to ventricular contraction – causing pressure on the tricuspid valve as the atria are filling
- ○ v-wave – corresponds to blood filling the right atrium prior to the tricuspid valve re-opening again

Associations between conditions and abnormal JVP findings

- ○ Increased a wave is seen in pulmonary hypertension
- ○ Tricuspid regurgitation increases the v wave
- ○ Cannon a waves are seen when the atria are contracting against a closed tricuspid valve (complete heart block)
- ○ Raised JVP seen in constrictive pericarditis/cardiac tamponade (unlikely exam case), right sided heart failure

Innocent murmurs

Features

1. Asymptomatic
2. Normal heart sounds
3. Systolic or continuous (never solely diastolic)
4. Vary with position and respiration
5. Soft (grades 1–3)
6. Normal ECG and chest X-ray

Some examples of innocent murmurs

1. Pulmonary flow murmur
   - ○ Very common
   - ○ Characteristically it is brief and in mid-systole
   - ○ Loudest with the patient supine and during expiration
   - ○ Occurs in children and adolescents of all ages
   - ○ Commonly heard during hyperdynamic states such as fever
2. Still's murmur
   - ○ Peak age 2–6 years, resolves towards adolescence
   - ○ Grades 1–3 present in early systole, heart sounds normal
   - ○ Maximum intensity at lower left sternal edge
   - ○ Vibratory
   - ○ Best heard with the patient supine, reducing in intensity or disappearing when the patient sits up

3.   Venous hum
   ○   Continuous murmur most commonly heard in children aged 2–6 years
   ○   Diastolic component is usually loudest
   ○   Best heard over the supraclavicular fossa on the right with the head turned to the other side
   ○   May radiate and is often heard on both sides
   ○   Sometimes an associated thrill
   ○   Disappears on lying flat or if the neck veins are compressed

Dextrocardia

○   It is essential not to miss dextrocardia in the exam. Cases are quite common and readily available to the examining centre to put into the exam to catch people out. If you have any difficulty locating the apex either on palpation or auscultation it is worth checking the right side of the chest. It is probably sensible to include it in your examination as a matter of routine in order to show to the examiner that you remember to look.

○   Dextrocardia is when the heart apex points to the right. The term dextrocardia in association with situs inversus indicates that the left atrium is on the right, the right atrium is on the left, the three-lobed right lung is on the left, the two-lobed left lung is on the right, the stomach and spleen are on the right and the liver is on the left. This, in association with normally related great arteries, is most often a functionally normal heart. Dextrocardia without situs inversus (and levocardia with situs inversus) is most often complicated by severe cardiac malformations that include various combinations of single ventricle, arterial transposition, pulmonary stenosis, atrial septal defects, ventricular septal defects, atrioventricular septal defects, total anomalous pulmonary venous drainage, tricuspid atresia and pulmonary artery hypoplasia/atresia

○   Abnormalities of the position of the heart are also associated with asplenia and polysplenia syndromes

○   Dextrocardia is also associated with immotile cilia syndrome (dextrocardia, bronchiectasis, situs inversus, infertility, sinusitis, dysplasia of the frontal sinuses and otitis media)

○   If you find dextrocardia on examination, it is important that you go on to palpate the abdomen to find the position of the liver and to listen to the lung fields for bronchiectasis.

Ventricular septal defect

Pathophysiology

Ventricular septal defects (VSDs) are the commonest congenital heart defects (30%). Defects usually occur in the membranous part of the septum with extension into the muscular septum, the so-called perimembranous VSD, although they may occur anywhere. The main haemodynamic effect is left ventricular volume overload and increased pulmonary blood flow. There is often a misconception that the right ventricle is overloaded due to the left-to-right shunt of blood. When the blood is being shunted in systole, the right ventricle is ejecting blood into the pulmonary artery, thus the blood is shunted directly into the pulmonary artery and hence into the lungs. This then returns to load the left ventricle during diastole.

Investigations

ECG, chest X-ray, echocardiogram (two-dimensional with colour flow Doppler). The latter is useful to help estimate the size of the shunt by examining the degree of volume overload of the left atrium and left ventricle. Cardiac catheterisation is not usually required.

Presentation

In a small defect where the shunt is insignificant, there is usually no haemodynamic derangement, and the patient is asymptomatic. An ECG will be normal. A chest X-ray will also be normal. A large defect producing a shunt with haemodynamic significance may cause signs of heart failure, with cardiomegaly, a diastolic murmur at the apex due to increased blood flow into the left ventricle from pulmonary veins in diastole, and a loud second heart sound due to an increase in pulmonary blood flow. The ECG may show a left ventricular volume overload or biventricular hypertrophy with left ventricular hypertrophy predominant if the defect is large enough. Chest X-ray may show cardiomegaly, enlarged pulmonary arteries and increased vascular markings from pulmonary oedema, again if the defect is large.

Diagnosis

If the defect is asymptomatic and the murmur is very suggestive of a VSD, the patient is monitored clinically. As 80% of the defects close spontaneously, a reassuring line can be taken. Prophylactic antibiotics are indicated for surgical and dental procedures.

If the defect is haemodynamically significant, or if there is doubt about the diagnosis, echocardiography should be performed. If the lesion is large enough to be symptomatic, echocardiography is essential to confirm the diagnosis and assess the shunt size.

Treatment

○ In haemodynamically significant defects, treatment is indicated. Medical management aims to control congestive cardiac failure and to prevent the development of pulmonary vascular disease, with the maintenance of normal growth using calorie supplementation if appropriate. This involves the use of diuretics and angiotensin converting enzyme inhibitors such as **captopril**.

○ Surgical management is reserved for those with a significant shunt who are not responding to medical management. The size of the intracardiac shunt is usually expressed as the ratio of pulmonary to systemic blood flow. If the cardiac shunt is small, ie a pulmonary to systemic flow ratio of less than 2:1, the cardiac chambers are unlikely to be enlarged and the pulmonary bed is likely to be normal. If the shunt is large with a pulmonary to systemic flow ratio greater than 2:1, left atrial and ventricular volume overload occurs and there is significantly raised pulmonary arterial pressure leading to pulmonary hypertension. This will ultimately lead to irreversible damage and the development of Eisenmenger's syndrome (see later). Cardiac surgery is usually considered if the pulmonary to systemic flow ratio is greater than 2:1. In complicated cases of patients with pulmonary hypertension who are not suitable for early surgery, pulmonary artery banding is sometimes carried out, eg multiple VSDs – 'Swiss cheese' defect. Infants who require medical management will normally be repaired before 6 months. For a moderate defect, if growth is normal and no medical management is required, they may have surgical repair aged 2–5 years. For very small defects, watch and wait (may close spontaneously).

Examination finding in asymptomatic VSD

This is one of the commonest short cases.

Inspection
○ Normal, patient appears well
○ No tachypnoea or tachycardia
○ Hands – no clubbing/cyanosis
○ Pulses normal
○ Blood pressure normal

○ Normal face
○ No scars

Palpation

○ Position and character of apex beat are important in determining the haemodynamic significance of VSD
○ Active praecordium – an indication of volume loading secondary to left-to-right shunt – unlikely to find this in an older child (as most haemodynamically significant VSDs present with symptoms and are corrected in infancy)
○ Thrill, normally at the left sternal edge

Auscultation

○ Pansystolic murmur, maximal at the left sternal edge
○ No radiation, but heard all over the chest wall
○ Specifically mention second heart sound
○ A loud second heart sound suggests elevated pulmonary arterial pressure, ie a haemodynamically significant VSD causing pulmonary hypertension, therefore you must mention the second heart sound
○ A diastolic rumble at the apex or any clinical features of heart failure imply a large defect with a significant shunt
○ When presented with what you feel is a simple VSD in the exam you must include a statement about whether or not it is likely to be haemodynamically significant in your summation

---

Features to look for in a haemodynamically significant VSD

- Murmur may be softer (implying larger lesion)
- Hyperactive praecordium
- Loud second heart sound (has already developed complications)
- Displaced apex beat
- Diastolic murmur
- Effects on growth
- Tachypnoea/symptoms

Supplementary questions frequently asked

○ How would you confirm this is a VSD?
○ How would you follow this child up?
○ What advice would you give the parents?
○ Give the options for management

○ What are the indications for surgery?
○ How would you differentiate between VSD and innocent murmur?

Atrial septal defect

Pathophysiology

The most common site of the defect is in the fossa ovalis (ostium secundum). Other sites include the septum primum (ostium primum defect, more recently called partial atrioventricular septal defect or partial AVSD) and the atrioventricular septum (atrioventricular septal defect, atrioventricular canal defect, more recently called complete AVSD). The main haemodynamic abnormality is right ventricular volume overload during diastole with an increased pulmonary blood flow secondary to the shunt. Most children are asymptomatic and the lesion is discovered on routine examination. Symptoms of an ASD rarely develop before the third decade. Patients may then go on to develop atrial arrhythmias, pulmonary hypertension and heart failure.

Investigations

○ ECG
  • Ostium secundum: right axis deviation, partial right bundle branch block
  • Ostium primum (also called partial endocardial cushion defect, part of a spectrum that can include AVSD with involvement of atrioventricular valves). Occurs in the lower part of the septum: left axis deviation, partial right bundle branch block
○ Echocardiogram

Treatment

Treatment is usually surgical closure in the fourth or fifth year of life, or earlier if symptomatic. If left untreated, the defect will cause symptoms in adult years. Currently a child of 5 or over may be suitable for repair using a transcatheter closure device. The procedure is considered to be low risk. Antibiotic prophylaxis required for surgical and dental procedures for 6 months following repair. Bypass surgery may be required for larger defects or defects which are unusually shaped (and therefore not suitable for device closure).

Examination findings in ASD

General
○ Normally ASD is asymptomatic: should be well grown, not clubbed, etc

Palpation
○ Apex beat normal, may have parasternal heave, no thrills

Auscultation
○ Heart sounds both heard
○ Second heart sound is widely split, with fixed splitting
○ Ejection systolic murmur upper left sternal edge (alternatively there may be no murmur). The ejection systolic murmur is due to increased flow across the right ventricular outflow tract. It is normally grade 2–3/6
○ May be diastolic murmur due to high flow across the tricuspid valve (lower left sternal border), which is an excellent diagnostic sign. Occurs when there is a large left-to-right shunt

Supplementary questions frequently asked
○ How would you confirm the diagnosis?
○ How would you manage the patient?
○ What are the indications for surgery?

Pulmonary stenosis

Pathophysiology
○ Present in 5%–8% of children with congenital cardiac disease
○ Can be subvalvular (same as infundibular; uncommon if not part of Fallot's tetralogy), valvular or supravalvular
○ Haemodynamically, pulmonary stenosis causes pressure overload of the right ventricle and a relatively fixed cardiac output

Presentation
○ Patients are usually asymptomatic if the stenosis is mild or moderate
○ Neonates can get critical pulmonary stenosis with cyanosis due to shunting across the foramen ovale. This is a separate entity and requires urgent surgery

Investigations

○ ECG: usually normal, with severe stenosis there may be evidence of right ventricular overload with right ventricular hypertrophy and tall spiked P waves

○ Chest X-ray: usually normal, although you may see a prominent pulmonary artery due to post-stenotic dilatation. May see prominent right atrium and right ventricle

○ Echocardiography: diagnostic

Treatment

○ Surgery is usually not indicated unless there is fixed subvalvular stenosis or grossly thickened pulmonary valves, commonly seen in Noonan's syndrome. Prognosis is excellent. Timing of surgery is governed by the pressure gradient across the stenotic area

○ Remember, in the exam children are often seen post repair

○ Post repair the child is likely to have a residual systolic and diastolic murmur (secondary to pulmonary incompetence). There may be a midline sternotomy following complete repair. Younger children are likely to have had a balloon angioplasty at cardiac catheterisation which does not require open heart surgery, ie there will be no scars

Examination findings in pulmonary stenosis

Inspection

○ Most likely to be asymptomatic

Palpation

○ May have thrill over pulmonary area

○ May have right ventricular heave (uncommon)

Auscultation

○ Ejection systolic murmur maximal at the upper left sternal edge, radiation through to the back

○ If it is a critical stenosis there may be no murmur; it will present in the neonatal age group but outside of this age group louder and longer murmurs mean more severe stenosis

○ Heart sounds both heard: widely split second heart sound, with a softer pulmonary component, can even be absent if the stenosis is severe

○ Ejection click

Further examination

○ Usually normal but look for the stigmata of Noonan's syndrome or Williams syndrome

○ Look for evidence of right ventricular failure. This is unlikely as the lesion is likely to have been repaired before this stage, but you will need to show the examiners that you are aware that this is a complication of pulmonary stenosis.

Aortic stenosis

Pathophysiology

○ 5% of congenital heart disease: valvular, subvalvular, supravalvular

- **Valvular** (most common): usually this means that the valves are abnormal with one or two cusps (bicuspid) rather than the usual three (tricuspid)
- **Supravalular**: this is a diffuse/localised narrowing immediately above the aortic sinuses and the coronary arteries. Most commonly occurs as part of Williams syndrome. Many patients have peripheral pulmonary artery stenosis in addition
- **Subvalvular**: long narrowing of the left ventricular outflow tract
- **Subaortic stenosis**: this is a fibrous diaphragm just below the aortic valve, often associated with an abnormal subaortic region. It is often seen with coarctation. Clinical presentation is similar to that of aortic stenosis although it is often not severe. There is no ejection click. Treatment consists of excision of the fibrous diaphragm in all but the mildest of cases as it can be easily performed without interfering with other structures. Subaortic stenosis patients are particularly prone to bacterial endocarditis

○ The main haemodynamic effect is systolic overload (pressure overload) of the left ventricle and a fixed cardiac output. This constant pressure load stimulates left ventricular hypertrophy

○ Symptoms include chest pain on exertion and syncope, although most patients are asymptomatic

○ Syncope is important as it indicates severe disease

Investigations

○ ECG is normal in mild obstruction. In severe lesions there may be left ventricular hypertrophy on the ECG, but it is often surprisingly normal:
  - ECG signs of left ventricular hypertrophy
    – Tall R waves V5–V6
    – Inverted T waves in 1, aVL, V5–V6
  - ECG signs of ischaemia (in very severe lesions)
    – ST depression
    – T wave inversion
○ Chest X-ray may show a prominent left ventricle
○ Echocardiography is always indicated. It is diagnostic and will assess the gradient across the stenosis

Treatment

Treatment is conservative in most cases, avoiding valve replacement in the young patient. If the gradient across the valve is greater than 60 mmHg, intervention is indicated. This is usually in the form of a balloon valvuloplasty by cardiac catheter, or surgical valvuloplasty. Aortic regurgitation can develop after balloon procedures, which often needs surgical correction.

As with pulmonary stenosis, the patient may present post repair, with the murmur of aortic stenosis still present and the murmur of aortic regurgitation due to the residual incompetence of the valve postoperatively. If the patient is older, they may have had the stenosis repaired via an open valvuloplasty and could have a median sternotomy scar. Younger children may have had a catheter repair and will not therefore have a sternotomy scar.

Associations with aortic stenosis

○ Turner syndrome
○ Williams syndrome – supravalvular aortic stenosis
○ Coarctation of the aorta
○ Other cardiac abnormalities, eg hypoplastic left ventricle, mitral valve abnormalities

Examination findings in aortic stenosis

Take care to note associated aortic regurgitation findings if the child has had a procedure to relieve gradient across aortic stenosis.

Inspection
○ Normally asymptomatic
○ Look for dysmorphic features (Turner/Williams in particular)

Pulse
○ May be collapsing (if associated with aortic valve incompetence post procedure to open stenotic area), although usually normal
○ If the defect is severe, pulse pressure may be low causing weak peripheral pulses

Blood pressure
○ Normal or slightly raised, narrow pulse pressure
○ In supravalvular aortic stenosis it is possible to get a higher blood pressure reading in the right compared to the left arm

Palpation
○ Supra-sternal and carotid thrill
○ May also have thrill over aortic area (upper right sternal edge)
○ Apex beat may be displaced and forceful

Auscultation
○ Heart sounds normal
○ In severe stenosis the second heart sound may be reduced in intensity or absent
○ Ejection click heard best at the lower left sternal edge and apex
○ Ejection systolic murmur at the lower left sternal edge, in the aortic area and radiating into the neck – 'harsh' sounding
○ Early diastolic murmur (decrescendo) is associated with aortic regurgitation

Further examination
○ Ask to feel femoral pulses and feel for radio-femoral delay as sometimes aortic stenosis is associated with coarctation
○ Listen at the back to confirm (aortic stenosis does not radiate to the back – coarctation does)

Coarctation of the aorta

Pathophysiology
This is present in 8%–10% of patients with congenital heart disease.

In 98% of cases it originates just below the origin of the left subclavian artery, at the origin of the ductus arteriosus – the juxtaductal coarctation. The remaining ones are pre-ductal and often associated with arch hypoplasia. The male:female ratio is 2:1. Pre-ductal is more serious and often presents in the neonatal period due to its severity. The juxtaductal type may be mild and often does not present until late childhood. Even then it is often asymptomatic and comes to light during the investigation of hypertension.

The classical signs are of a disparity in pulses and blood pressure between the arms and the legs, hence the pulses in the arms and legs should always be palpated together at some point in a cardiovascular examination. The delay occurs due to the fact that the blood flow to the descending aorta is dependent on collaterals, hence the femoral pulse is felt after the radial. The blood pressure difference should be measured in all four limbs. Normally, the systolic pressure in the legs is 10–20 mmHg higher than in the arms, in coarctation it is lower. If the BP is higher in the right arm than in the left, it suggests involvement of the left subclavian artery in the coarctation.

Investigation

○ Chest X-ray: usually normal in the juxtaductal coarctation unless it does not present until after the first decade when there may be mild to moderate cardiac enlargement due to left ventricular prominence. Rib notching occurs in children with long-standing coarctation (>7 years).
○ ECG: usually normal unless late presentation as above, when there may be signs of left ventricular hypertrophy.
○ Echocardiography: demonstrates the presence and position of the coarctation. Will also determine the pressure gradient across the coarctation and exclude an intracardiac abnormality.

Surgical treatment

A subclavian flap, Gore-tex® graft or end-to-end anastomosis can be used to repair the abnormal segment. Repair is through a left-sided thoracotomy (if aortic arch is on the normal side!). Complications include residual hypertension and re-coarctation. The latter can be treated with balloon dilatation, although occasionally further surgery is required. Subclavian flap repair causes the loss of the pulse in the left arm. This could be confused with a modified Blalock–Taussig shunt, which is also performed through a thoracotomy and sometimes causes loss of the pulse. If these two signs are present, you must listen for a shunt murmur, and if it is absent and the child is not cyanosed, think of a coarctation repair with a subclavian flap. Older children (>10) can be treated by insertion of a stent during cardiac catheterisation.

Endocarditis prophylaxis

Endocarditis prophylaxis is recommended because of frequency of associated abnormalities and recoarctation.

Examination findings in coarctation of the aorta

Inspection
○ Look for dysmorphic features (Turner syndrome)
○ Check blood pressure

Pulses
○ Right radial pulse normal
○ Compare radial pulses; left radial may be absent
○ Femoral pulses may be weak
○ May be radio-femoral delay

Scars
○ None unless there has been a repair. It is likely that if you see a case in the exam it will be post repair (left thoracotomy scar)
○ If the scar is associated with a reduced left radial pulse volume, think subclavian flap repair

Palpation
○ Apex beat is usually normally placed, no heaves or thrills

Auscultation
○ Systolic murmur is loudest at the back (left interscapular area). Alternatively the murmur may be non-specific or absent
○ Ejection click at the upper left sternal edge if there is a bicuspid aortic valve
○ There may be a diastolic murmur from collaterals in the older patient

Further examination
○ Could be directed at looking for evidence of Turner syndrome
○ Offer to do four-limb blood pressure measurement

Associations

○ Turner syndrome
○ Bicuspid aortic valve in 70%
○ Over half of the patients with coarctation have other lesions, eg ventricular septal defect, mitral valve abnormalities and aortic stenosis. Associated abnormalities are more likely if coarctation is symptomatic in infancy

The cyanosed child

Cases in the exam are often quite difficult. Many will have had surgery and the cardiac lesions are likely to be complex. It is important to describe what you see and to make sensible statements about potential causes. It is therefore essential to have a good overview of cyanotic congenital heart disease. Some useful information is summarised below. While thinking about this it is important to remember that children seen in the exam who have had definitive surgery for cyanotic congenital heart disease will be pink (eg transposition of the great arteries or tetralogy of Fallot) and will present as a pink child with a central sternotomy scar with, in some cases, an additional shunt scar. Children seen in the exam who have cyanosis due to cardiac causes are likely to have complex cyanotic congenital heart disease.

Cardiac causes of cyanosis

○ Decreased pulmonary blood flow, eg tetralogy of Fallot, pulmonary atresia, Ebstein's anomaly, tricuspid atresia
○ Poor mixing, eg transposition of great arteries
○ Common mixing, eg truncus arteriosus, double outlet right ventricle, total anomalous pulmonary venous drainage, univentricular heart. Cyanosis in these conditions may be mild enough to be difficult to detect clinically

Management

Fallot's tetralogy

See below for details on how to manage this condition.

Pulmonary atresia

Pulmonary atresia with or without an intact intraventricular septum is a difficult problem, and usually requires several shunt procedures; definitive repair is often not possible. Often there is a poor prognosis.

Blood supply to the lungs may be provided by major aorto-pulmonary collateral arteries (MAPCAs), which may cause pulmonary oligaemia or pulmonary oedema depending on their size and distribution. Treated by unifocalisation, which involves fashioning a main pulmonary artery-like structure out of whichever vessels best suit. This can then be incorporated into a Glenn or Fontan circulation if the right ventricle is small. If the right ventricle is normal or near normal in size and function then repair would involve attaching a graft which links the right ventricle to the newly fashioned pulmonary arteries, bypassing the atretic pulmonary valve (Contegra graft).

Transposition of the great arteries

Transposition of the great arteries is the second commonest cyanotic lesion, comprising 4% of all congenital disease. Infants at presentation need a prostaglandin infusion, followed by urgent transfer to a cardiology unit. Treatment has recently changed. Until approximately 2003, a balloon atrial septostomy was performed, the infant returned home to thrive and then a permanent procedure was carried out at 6–9 months (Mustard or Senning operations). Now, in some centres, the arterial duct is maintained by a prostaglandin infusion and a definitive repair is carried out within the first few days (arterial switch). If there is likely to be a delay in definitive surgery, or if there is inadequate mixing through the ductus, an atrial septostomy may be performed.

Truncus arteriosus

Truncus arteriosus is rare, comprising 0.5% of all lesions. Often associated with chromosomal abnormality (22q deletion syndrome).

Double outlet right ventricle

Double outlet right ventricle is rare. A very heterogeneous group of conditions. Early pulmonary banding (if pulmonary blood flow is high) or shunt procedure (if pulmonary blood flow is inadequate) followed by definitive repair at a later date.

Total anomalous pulmonary venous drainage

Total anomalous pulmonary venous drainage is rare, comprising 1% of all cardiac cases (40% have other associated cardiac lesions). Definitive repair early for obstructive lesions.

Univentricular heart

Univentricular heart is as common as transposition: 4% in certain published series. Many different types. No correction, only palliation. Often die early. If cyanosis is severe, may need shunt procedure early.

Pulmonary artery banding if the pulmonary artery flow is high. If the pulmonary outflow tract and pulmonary arterial tree is underdeveloped the patient may need a palliative shunt procedure, which will encourage the vessels to grow. New shunts may be needed as the patient grows, or a Glenn procedure (superior vena cava to pulmonary artery). If they reach 3–5 years, surgery to palliate the defect is indicated, involving the Fontan/modified Fontan procedure (total cavo-pulmonary anastomoses), bypassing the ventricle.

Fallot's tetralogy

Pathophysiology

Fallot's tetralogy forms 10% of congenital heart disease and is the most common cyanotic lesion beyond infancy.

The constituents of Fallot's tetralogy are:

1. Obstruction to the right ventricular outflow tract (could be infundibular stenosis, pulmonary valve stenosis or both)
2. Ventricular septal defect
3. Overriding aorta
4. Right ventricular hypertrophy

Rarer variations exist:

○ 25% of cases have a right-sided aortic arch
○ Tetralogy of Fallot with absent pulmonary valve: a rudimentary pulmonary valve results in post-stenotic dilation of the pulmonary artery, which can cause compression and poor development of lung architecture

Investigations

○ Hb/packed cell volume if cyanosed
○ Chest X-ray: prominent right ventricle, small pulmonary arteries, pulmonary oligaemia
○ ECG: right axis deviation, right ventricular hypertrophy. P wave is tall and peaked
○ Echocardiogram: demonstrates the lesion and the size of the pulmonary arteries as well as the side of the aorta, obviating the need for cardiac catheterisation

Treatment

Depends on the severity of the right ventricular outflow tract obstruction. If it is severe then a palliative shunt (modified BT shunt) procedure may be performed as above. This decreases the amount of hypoxia and allows increases in linear growth as well as growth of the main pulmonary arteries. Corrective surgery can then take place. The optimum time for corrective surgery varies from child to child and depends on the clinical severity of the lesion, the type of anatomy demonstrated at investigation and the size of the child. There is a wide spectrum of severity and it depends on individual cardiology review. The current recommendation is that surgery is carried out between 4 and 12 months of age.

Complications

○ Exertional dyspnoea – squat for relief
○ Cerebral thrombosis/brain abscess
○ Infective endocarditis
○ Arrhythmias (in years following repair)
○ Paroxysmal hypercyanotic spells
  • The infant becomes restless and cyanotic; with increasing cyanosis, gasping respiration may occur followed by syncope. Murmur becomes less audible during the attack. The attacks are most common after exertion and during the first 2 years of life.
○ Treatment of paroxysmal hypercyanotic spells
  • Bring baby's knees to their chest (reduces venous return and increases systemic resistance, reversing the shunt)
  • Morphine
  • Sodium bicarbonate if acidotic
  • Vasoconstrictors
  • Beta blockers

Examination findings in Tetralogy of Fallot

This is a classic short case and frequently seen. It will usually have been operated on by the time the child is seen.

Inspection

○ Untreated, most patients are symptomatic – cyanosed/clubbed
○ May have no cyanosis in milder forms
○ Failure to thrive
○ Hands: early clubbing
○ Pulse
  • Normal
  • May be absent left-sided pulse in association with left thoracotomy scar (or a similar situation on the right)

○ Face: central cyanosis (if uncorrected)
○ Scars
   • If untreated, none
   • May be left/right thoracotomy scar in association with an absent pulse on the corresponding side (classical **Blalock–Taussig shunt** – usually right side performed first; modified Blalock–Taussig shunt: Gore-Tex® conduit side to side from the subclavian artery to the homolateral branch of the pulmonary artery)
   • There may be bilateral thoracotomy scars suggesting the failure of one shunt and the need for a second shunt procedure (not uncommon)
   • Central sternotomy scar indicates that definitive repair has been carried out. If the definitive repair has been carried out the child will not be cyanosed, but may still have signs of right ventricular outflow tract stenosis

Palpation
○ Apex beat normally located
○ Right ventricular impulse may be palpable
○ 50% have a systolic thrill palpable at the upper left sternal edge

Auscultation
○ Loud (grade 3–5/6) ejection systolic murmur maximal at upper left sternal edge, transmitted widely especially to the lungs
○ Shunt murmur in younger children (you wouldn't expect to hear this if there is a median sternotomy scar, and it indicates definitive repair) on the side of the thoracotomy
○ Heart sounds: second heart sound is either single or the pulmonary component is soft
○ May have an aortic ejection click

Eisenmenger's syndrome

Pathophysiology

This is a condition in which there is pulmonary hypertension due to high pulmonary vascular resistance, with a reversed or bidirectional shunt at the aortopulmonary, ventricular or atrial level. It may occur in patent ductus arteriosus, aortopulmonary window, ventricular septal defect or atrial septal defect. It has also been applied to more complex defects when a very high pulmonary vascular resistance causes a dominant right-to-left shunt, such as persistent truncus, single ventricle, single atrium, atrioventricular defect and total anomalous pulmonary venous drainage. When Eisenmenger's occurs the defect must be large, although children with Down syndrome and ventricular septal defect or atrioventricular septal defect are particularly liable to develop pulmonary hypertension and reversal of shunt at an early age.

Presentation and investigations

Patients are generally cyanosed with clubbing, and signs are those of pulmonary hypertension. The pulse is of normal volume. There is a right ventricular heave. There is a short ejection systolic murmur (ejection of blood into the dilated pulmonary artery) often preceded by an ejection click and a very loud second heart sound. The chest X-ray shows right ventricular prominence with small peripheral pulmonary vessels (giving a 'peripheral pruning' appearance). The ECG shows peaked 'P' waves due to right atrial hypertrophy, right axis deviation and moderate or marked right ventricular hypertrophy with tall R waves in V4R and VI.

Treatment

Treatment is difficult; surgical closure is not possible. Heart–lung transplant is the only life-saving procedure. Medical treatment involves use of pulmonary vasodilators (eg sildenafil).

Cardiomyopathy

Hypertrophic cardiomyopathy

○ Ventricular filling is impaired because of relaxation difficulty
○ Usually familial (autosomal dominant in 30%–60%)
○ May be associated with septal hypertrophy or abnormal mitral valve movement – both causing variable obstruction to left ventricular outflow (also called hypertrophic obstructive cardiomyopathy or HOCM)
○ Can cause angina, syncope, arrhythmias or sudden death
○ May also present with easy fatigability or pulmonary oedema symptoms (secondary to abnormal left ventricle filling)
○ Clinically may have symptoms of left ventricle failure in end-stage disease
○ Murmur may be ejection systolic murmur from left ventricular septal hypertrophy or murmur from mitral regurgitation secondary to abnormal movement of the anterior leaflet

○ Treated medically with beta blockers, and endocarditis prophylaxis
○ If surgery is required a myectomy is performed. Occasionally patients also need surgery to mitral valve

Dilated cardiomyopathy

○ Most common cardiomyopathy
○ Normally idiopathic
○ May be caused by toxic myocardial insult (from infections/ chemotherapy or other drugs/metabolic disease)
○ Causes dilation of all four chambers
○ Presents with symptoms of weakness and pulmonary oedema
○ Poor prognosis
○ Managed medically (diuretics/**digoxin**/**captopril**/bed rest) – may require cardiac transplantation
○ Clinical findings may include:
   • Displaced apex beat
   • Mitral regurgitation or tricuspid regurgitation murmur
   • Third heart sound
   • Signs of left heart failure
     – Increased work of breathing
     – Bi-basal crackles
   • Signs of right heart failure
     – Raised JVP
     – Oedema
     – Hepatomegaly

Infective endocarditis

Normally requires predisposition of structural heart abnormality resulting in turbulence/pressure gradients, leading to platelet aggregation/ potential for thrombus. Following bacteraemia this abnormal area can become infected resulting in vegetation formation. Bacteraemia is often associated with diseased teeth and/or dental procedures.

Signs of endocarditis

○ Fever
○ Osler's nodes: painful, red/raised lesions on fingertips (from immune complex deposition)
○ Janeway lesions: non-tender, erythematous/haemorrhagic macules or nodules on palms or soles
○ Splinter haemorrhages: dark red linear streaks in nail bed

○ Conjunctival/buccal petechiae
○ Clubbing
○ Hepatosplenomegaly (in 20%)
○ Congestive cardiac failure (depending on severity of valvular disease)
○ Murmur (20%–80% of patients)
○ Roth's spots: retinal haemorrhages with pale centre, seen on fundoscopy
○ Microscopic haematuria
○ Neurological abnormalities
○ Look at dentition/gingival disease

Endocarditis prophylaxis

Antibiotic prophylaxis is only recommended for certain conditions and procedures. This is given orally 1 hour before the procedure, or parenterally 30 min beforehand. The choice of antibiotic depends on the site of surgery: dental or respiratory tract/ear, nose and throat procedures require cover for *Streptococcus viridans*, while genitourinary or gastrointestinal procedures direct cover against enterococci. As a general rule most cardiac lesions are classed as moderate to high risk and therefore require prophylaxis. Low-risk lesions are as follows

○ Secundum atrial septal defect
○ Innocent murmurs
○ Kawasaki disease lesions
○ Surgically repaired atrial septal defect/ventricular septal defect/patent ductus arteriosus – for 6 months after surgery

Patients should be counselled by their cardiologist as to whether they require prophylaxis and carry information with them about what regime is appropriate.

Syndromes associated with cardiac lesions

Table 8.4 is a list that may help when faced with a dysmorphic child in the cardiac station. It is not an exhaustive list and there are many more syndromes that can be associated with cardiac lesions. As a general rule in this situation you should concentrate on diagnosing the cardiac condition (if you recognise the syndrome and know which lesion it is likely to be associated with, this will help you to elicit the signs confidently). The relevance of the syndrome comes when you comment on the dysmorphic features as part of your general observation, and when you seek clarification of the syndromic diagnosis by looking for associated abnormalities in your 'further examination'. For example:

> *'She is a 6-year-old girl who appears well. On general inspection she has some features which would be consistent with Turner syndrome. These include...* She has features of aortic stenosis which consist of ejection systolic murmur at the upper right sternal edge... Given her other examination findings I would expect this to be caused by a bicuspid aortic valve. There is no evidence of associated coarctation; specifically she does not have.... I would now like to check her blood pressure and plot her growth on a Turner's specific chart.'

Syndrome	Cardiac lesions	Other findings
Down syndrome	• Up to 50% are quoted to have some congenital heart defect • Ventricular septal defects are the commonest lesions followed by atrioventricular septal defects • Patent ductus arteriosus and tetralogy of Fallot are less common • All children with Down syndrome should be routinely sent for an echocardiogram • Children with Down syndrome develop pulmonary vascular disease earlier than other children, and hence those with large cardiac defects will develop the Eisenmenger's complex at an earlier stage	• Down facies • Single palmar crease • Sandal gap • Middle ear disease • Hypotonia • Effects on development and growth • Many others

Table 8.4: Associations between syndromes and cardiac lesions

Syndrome	Cardiac lesions	Other findings

Turner syndrome (XO)	• Bicuspid aortic valve, usually non-stenotic, in one-third of patients
	• Coarctation of aorta, less common but more serious
		• Hypoplastic and hyperconvex nails
		• Short 4th/5th metacarpals
		• Widened carrying angle (cubitus valgus)
		• Low posterior hairline
		• Prominent ears (look in ears ?glue ear)
		• Neck webbing
		• High arched palate
		• Shield chest
		• Widely spaced nipples
		• Excessive naevi
		• 'Also need to examine'
		  – Plot growth – on special Turner syndrome growth chart
		  – Thyroid status (autoimmune hypothyroidism?)
		  – Abdomen (?horseshoe kidney)
		  – Formal audiology
		  – Pubertal staging/breast development

Noonan's syndrome (phenotypically like Turner, but autosomal dominant)	• Pulmonary stenosis in a usually dysplastic valve, and hence not amenable to treatment by valvuloplasty • Atrial septal defect • Cardiomyopathy	• Short stature • Typical facies – hypertelorism, anti-mongoloid slant, epicanthic folds, ptosis, micrognathia, low set ears • Wide spaced nipples, cubitus valgus, short stature and pubertal delay • Cryptorchidism, hernias
Williams syndrome	• Supravalvular aortic stenosis • Branch pulmonary artery stenosis	• Round facies with full cheeks and lips • Stellate pattern in the iris • Strabismus • Supravalvular aortic stenosis • Branch pulmonary artery stenosis • Hypercalcaemia • Mental retardation, friendly personality

Table 8.4: continued

Syndrome	Cardiac lesions	Other findings
di George 22q deletion also called • CATCH 22 • Velocardio – facial syndrome • Shprintzen syndrome All on a spectrum with subtle differences between each description	• Aortic arch abnormalities • Truncus arteriosus • Pulmonary atresia and ventricular septal defect	May have various combinations of: • Structural (cleft)/functional palatal abnormalities • Nasal speech • Hypotonia • Developmental delay • Hypocalcaemia • Immunodeficiency • Long face • Narrow palpebral fissures • Thin alae nasi • Squared nasal root – bulbous tip • Hypospadias/cryptorchidism • Long/tapering fingers
CHARGE association	• Fallot's tetralogy • Ventricular septal defect • Atrial ventricular septal defect • Double outlet right ventricle	• Coloboma • Heart disease • Atresia choanae • Retarded growth and development and/or CNS abnormalities • Genital anomalies and/or hypogonadism • Ear anomalies and/or deafness
VACTERL association	• Fallot's tetralogy • Ventricular septal defect	• Vertebral defects • Anal atresia • Cardiac defects • Tracheo-oesophageal fistula • Renal defects • Limb abnormalities. This is an updated version of the VATER association
Infant of diabetic mother	• Hypertrophic cardiomyopathy • Ventricular septal defect	• Macrosomia • Sacral agenesis

Table 8.4: continued

Syndrome	Cardiac lesions	Other findings
Trisomy 18 – Edwards' syndrome	• Ventricular septal defect • Atrial septal defect • Patent ductus arteriosus • Coarctation of aorta • Bicuspid aortic valve	• Abnormal tone • Microcephaly • Wide fontanelle • Severe growth retardation • Rocker bottom feet • Overlapping fingers • Many other dysmorphic features
Trisomy 13 – Patau syndrome	• Ventricular septal defect • Atrial septal defect • Patent ductus arteriosus • Coarctation • Bicuspid aortic valve	• Scalp defects (aplasia cutis) • Cleft lip and palate • Rocker bottom feet • Polydactyly • Omphalocele • Many other features
Marfan syndrome	• Aortic aneurysm • Aortic regurgitation • Mitral regurgitation	• Tall stature • Hypermobility • Arm span greater than height • High arched palate • Lens abnormalities • Scoliosis
Ehlers–Danlos syndrome	• Aortic root dilatation	• 'Cigarette paper' scars/ tissue fragility • Easy bruising • Joint hypermobility • Flattened arch of foot
Fetal alcohol syndrome	• Ventricular septal defect • Patent ductus arteriosus • Atrial septal defect • Tetralogy of Fallot	• Absent/ flattened philtrum • Developmental delay • Coarse features
LEOPARD syndrome (genetically similar to Noonan's syndrome: same site but different mutation)	• Pulmonary stenosis • Long PR interval • cardiomyopathy	• Lentigines • Electrocardiographic conduction abnormalities • Ocular hypertelorism Pulmonary stenosis • Abnormalities of genitalia • Retardation of growth • Deafness Also have characteristic facial features and café-au-lait spots

Table 8.4: continued

Surgery for congenital heart disease

Many of the cardiac cases seen in the exam will have had surgery, often definitive. In some cases it is clear what surgery has been carried out and the underlying diagnosis is clear. For example, a child who is pink with an absent left brachial pulse and a left lateral thoracotomy scar has probably had a coarctation repair. In other cases it is less clear, such as the child with a central sternotomy scar who may have had straight-forward surgery, eg ventricular septal defect or the repair of complicated congenital heart disease. It may not be possible to give an underlying diagnosis but a broad knowledge of the principles behind the timing of cardiac surgery, as well as an understanding of what signs to expect at which age for each of the major congenital cardiac lesions should prevent you from saying things that are clearly impossible.

Procedures can be for repair or palliation.

Repair procedures aim to create a heart that is functionally and anatomically normal. Examples of these include:

○ Ventricular septal defect repair
○ Atrial septal defect repair
○ Tetralogy of Fallot repair (traditionally a full tetralogy of Fallot correction occurs at approx 1 year for size/weight reasons although definitive repair procedures are now being performed earlier than this because of evidence suggesting improved outcomes)
○ Arterial switch procedure for transposition of the great arteries (TGA)

Palliative procedures can be temporary or permanent. Temporary procedures are necessary to prevent or minimise physiological instability pending more definitive surgery. Examples of these could include:

○ BT shunt (to allow for pulmonary blood flow, which encourages development of the pulmonary vascular tree, until the child has grown enough to safely have more definitive surgery)
○ Pulmonary banding (eg to prevent overloading the pulmonary circulation pending repair of a large ventricular septal defect)
○ Atrial septostomy (for example, if there is transposition with inadequate mixing despite a patent duct)

Examples of procedures which are considered permanent palliative procedures include creation of a Fontan circulation.

Timing of surgical intervention

The principles governing the age of surgical correction for individual cardiac defects have already been described in this chapter. The timing and choice of corrective and palliative procedures can vary from unit to unit depending on local expertise. Advances in this field mean that current practice is constantly evolving. Because of this we have tried to avoid being too specific about surgical management. What follows is a description of the general principles behind timing and choice of surgery, so that you can have a system with which to make rational conclusions about the causes of a scar, or the causes of a murmur with no scar, should you encounter this in the exam.

POINTS TO CONSIDER IN THE TIMING OF SURGICAL INTERVENTION

Symptoms; for example, poor growth or difficulty feeding due to cardiac failure

Duct-dependent lesions – these may require definitive repair early (in the first week), such as TGA/coarctation, or they may require a palliative procedure with further procedures later

Prevention of long-term problems, eg pulmonary hypertension from left to right shunts with increased flow, or ventricular dysfunction in tetralogy of Fallot

The lesion might close spontaneously

Intervention is less risky in larger children

○ Within first week
- Duct-dependent lesions require surgery in the first week of life (either repair or palliative depending on condition)
- Severe obstructive lesions
○ Within first few weeks of life
- Some lesions require a fall in pulmonary pressures, either for diagnosis or for physiology which is favourable for surgical repair. Surgery is carried out within the first weeks of life. An example of this could be PA banding, or the creation of a BT shunt
- Obstructive lesions (eg total anomalous pulmonary venous drainage) could present after the first week of life and be repaired soon after diagnosis

○ Infants
  • Conditions with a significant left-to-right shunt will require surgery to prevent pulmonary hypertension; this will be done earlier if there is concern about faltering growth and cardiac failure, or later if the child is growing well. Occasionally they will have had a PA band to allow for growth prior to a full repair
  • In general most symptomatic left-to-right shunts will be repaired within the first 6 months of life
  • Lesions with right ventricular outflow tract obstruction (such as Fallot's) may be repaired at this time – avoiding the development of severe right ventricular hypertrophy or cyanotic spells
  • Glenn procedures (cavo-pulmonary shunt) are often performed within the first year of life. The timing could depend on the size of the child, how well they are growing and what their oxygenation is like (falling saturations could indicate they are outgrowing their BT shunt and are ready for the next palliative procedure).
○ Older children
  • Staged repairs – in children who have already had some palliation, for example the conversion of a cavo-pulmonary shunt (superior vena cava to pulmonary artery) to a Fontan circulation (total cavo-pulmonary anastomosis)
  • Surgery to close asymptomatic lesions, to prevent further complications. An example of this could include an atrial septal defect repair, using either a cardiac catheter device or bypass surgery (for larger or unusually shaped lesions)
○ Adolescence
  • Surgery for acquired disease (for example valve replacement following endocarditis)
  • Stent procedures (for example for non-duct-dependent coarctation of the aorta)
  • Repeat procedures, for concerns which have developed following previous cardiac surgery (eg redo pulmonary homograft)

Note that in aortic stenosis and pulmonary stenosis – timing of operation is more dependent on symptoms and the pressure gradient across the lesion than on age. Ballooning is the favoured treatment. Subaortic stenosis is more likely to cause symptoms because the obstruction is dynamic (worse with exercise).

Long-term post-operative complications following cardiac surgery

○ Diaphragmatic palsy
○ Arrhythmias (treated with pacemakers/internal defibrillators/ Maze procedure)
○ Vocal cord palsy
○ Protein-losing enteropathy (following Fontan procedure)
○ Developmental problems

YOUR NOTES

9

GASTROENTEROLOGY AND HEPATOLOGY

CONTENTS

9.1 Introduction

9.2 Clinical examination
Suggested approach for the examination of the gastrointestinal system

9.3 Nutrition
Assessment of nutritional status
Nutritional supplementation/concentrating feeds
Malnutrition – cases
Gastrostomy tube feeding
Obesity

9.4 Cases and conditions
Cystic fibrosis
Crohn's disease
Coeliac disease
Constipation
Umbilical hernia
Ascites
Hepatomegaly and splenomegaly
Glycogen storage disease
Splenomegaly
Cirrhosis and liver transplantation
Extra-hepatic biliary atresia – post Kasai procedure

9.1 INTRODUCTION

This chapter contains information on examination of the gastrointestinal system. Abdominal examination includes looking for splenomegaly. Some of the causes of splenomegaly are discussed in the section on haematology in Chapter 12, others in this chapter. We have tried to avoid duplication where possible. We have also included a detailed review of nutritional assessment and supplementation. This can be applied to any pathology, whether gastrointestinal or related to disease in another system. Such knowledge would also stand you in good stead for the History Taking/Management Planning Station.

The conditions listed in this chapter are those likely to be seen in the Abdomen/'Other' Stations.

9.2 CLINICAL EXAMINATION

Suggested approach for the examination of the gastrointestinal system

Find your own system with which you are comfortable. Always remember to position the child correctly, make them comfortable and maintain good eye contact. The following is a suggested scheme.

Initial procedure

- Introduce yourself

Inspection – ensure adequate exposure

- Does the child look well?
- Normal or dysmorphic?
- Nasogastric tube, intravenous cannula?
- Well nourished? – comment on nutritional status
- Mention the need to plot on a growth chart
- Look for xanthoma – they suggest a raised cholesterol as in cholestasis. They are usually on the extensor surfaces, and occasionally around the eyes

Hands

- Clubbing – such a patient in this station may have inflammatory bowel disease, cirrhosis, chronic malabsorption, cystic fibrosis
- Koilonychia – iron deficiency anaemia

■ Palmar erythema
■ Pallor

Eyes

■ Jaundice
■ Anaemia
■ Blue sclera – iron deficiency anaemia
■ Xanthoma

Mouth

■ Pigmentation – Peutz-Jeghers
■ Mouth ulceration
■ Tongue – stomatitis, large tongue (Down syndrome, Beckwith–Wiedemann syndrome)
■ Teeth – should be looked at carefully as they are a good indicator of general nutrition. Dental caries predominant at the back in gastro-oesophageal reflux and at the front with poor diet, eg prolonged bottle feeding with sugary drinks

Chest

■ Spider naevi
■ Gynaecomastia

Abdomen

■ Scars (laparoscope, groin, loin); see notes below
■ Umbilical hernia
■ Abnormal vessels – caput medusae (drain from the umbilicus)
■ Distension
■ Superficial palpation – all over once
■ Deep palpation – all over once
■ Liver
■ Spleen
■ Kidneys

Further examination

This should be done as appropriate and depends on the previous findings. For example, it is not necessary to look for shifting dullness if the abdomen is not distended.
■ Percussion
■ Bowel sounds

- Abdominal distension – stand child up and look at buttocks, as they may also be wasted suggesting malabsorption
- Ascites – fluid thrill, shifting dullness (only if distended); see notes below
- Can I see the back?
- Can I see the genitalia?
- Hernia orifices

Notes on abdominal scars

An abdominal scar would not be an uncommon way to begin a short case. The more common childhood surgical conditions and the position of the scars associated with the surgery are listed. It is important during your revision to look at scars, to understand the possible procedures that may have resulted in that scar and to be able to talk about them.

Laparotomy scar

The finding of a laparotomy scar could incorporate a whole host of intra-abdominal pathology, but look for **surrounding clues** that might lead you to the diagnosis. Context is all-important.

- ○ **Down syndrome baby** with a laparotomy incision: look for the site of a colostomy on the abdomen, and think of **Hirschsprung's disease**; alternatively, if there is a laparotomy scar and no colostomy scar there may have been an **atresia**
- ○ Are there any signs of **cystic fibrosis**, and could this be a **meconium ileus repair**?
- ○ Could this be an **ex-premature infant** who had **necrotising enterocolitis** during the neonatal period?
- ○ Is there an **associated thoracolumbar incision** suggesting a **renal transplant**? (Feel for mass in right iliac fossa as this is the site of implantation of the donor kidney)
- ○ **Other possibilities**:
  - Kasai procedure for biliary atresia
  - Malrotation
  - Intussusception
  - Tumour removal

Other scars – by site

○ **Below right subcostal margin – Kocher's incision.** Allows access to the liver and the biliary tree and is seen after cholecystectomy and gallstone removal. Patients with sickle cell disease or hereditary spherocytosis may have had such surgery

○ **Transverse upper abdominal incision** – repair of congenital diaphragmatic hernia. These are more common on the left than the right

○ **Upper abdominal midline incision** – Nissen's fundoplication; is this child handicapped, is there an associated gastrostomy scar?

○ **Small right upper transverse ('rectus cutting') incision** is the site of Ramstedt's pyloromyotomy, more common in boys

○ **Right iliac fossa scar** – appendectomy

○ **Lateral thoracolumbar incision** – nephrectomy. Commonly performed in children with cystic dysplastic kidneys to prevent infection in a redundant kidney and the development of hypertension in adult life

○ **Sub-umbilical/umbilical scar** – suggests gastroschisis or exomphalos, again think of associated conditions. Alternatively could be an umbilical hernia repair

○ **Groin scars** suggest inguinal hernia repair, more common in ex-premature male infants

○ **Laparoscopy scars** are frequently seen as laparoscopic surgery is becoming more common. Scar sites are usually small and multiple

Examination of the liver, spleen and kidneys

▦ Important to do correctly
▦ Liver/spleen – start in right iliac fossa
▦ If organomegaly found confirm with percussion – **measure** if appropriate

Liver

▦ Edge – regular or irregular
▦ Surface – smooth or nodular
▦ Texture – firm or hard
▦ Tenderness
▦ Is there a rub?
▦ Is there a bruit?

Spleen

- As above
- ? Hepatomegaly and ascites
- Associations, eg jaundice – hereditary spherocytosis

COMMON EXAM QUESTIONS

○ How do you differentiate between a liver, spleen and kidney?

○ Why is it a liver?

○ Why is it a spleen?

These are straightforward but commonly asked questions that are often answered badly. If you find organomegaly it is important that you assess its character carefully and make it clear to the examiner using the criteria below that you are demonstrating a liver, spleen or kidney.

Liver

- Right hypochondrium
- Cannot get above it
- Moves with respiration
- Dull to percussion

Spleen

- Left hypochondrium
- Cannot get above it
- Moves with respiration
- Dull to percussion
- Has a notch

Kidney

- Can get above it
- Doesn't move with respiration
- Resonant
- Ballotable

Tip

Whenever you are practising, get into the habit of justifying your findings in such a manner

9.3 NUTRITION

Assessment of nutritional status

The assessment of nutritional status is very important and knowledge can be tested in different sections of the exam. The information in this section could help you in more than one station! Firstly the general case and appropriate comments are considered then specific scenarios with notes on how to deal with them are provided.

Instructions to candidate

Look at this 10-year-old boy and comment on his nutritional status

Case

John is comfortable at rest. He looks thin. I would like to plot him on a growth chart. His muscle bulk is poor with a reduced mid-arm circumference and his subcutaneous fat mass is poor with a reduced skinfold thickness. I note he has a gastrostomy tube in situ. I would like to proceed with a full examination. He looks pale...

Notes on nutritional assessment

This is an essential part of the general examination of a patient and applicable to children with pathology from the gastrointestinal or other systems. Commenting on nutritional status is all part of making a general comment about a patient. If in any doubt about nutritional status it is sensible to suggest to the examiner that you would plot the child onto a height and weight chart. Even if your performance of a measurement, eg skinfold thickness, may not be tested, you will still be expected to **ask** to measure/plot it. If the nutrition looks poor then the following scheme may be helpful.

Scheme

- ○ Look for and comment on obvious pathology, eg cystic fibrosis
- ○ Presence of nasogastric tube, gastrostomy
- ○ Nails (koilonychia)

○ Pallor – hands, mucous membranes, skin
○ Hair – thinning
○ Pubertal status, if older
○ Carefully plot height, weight and head circumference
○ Triceps and subscapular skinfold thickness – gives an impression of the subcutaneous fat mass
○ Mid-arm circumference – gives an impression about muscle bulk

Notes on malnutrition

It is useful to give some thought to potential mechanisms as poor nutrition is frequently multifactorial. Cystic fibrosis provides the best example and is commonly seen in the exam. Others include congenital heart disease, bronchopulmonary dysplasia, severe neurological handicap and chronic inflammatory bowel disease.

The aetiology of malnutrition is often complex and various factors play a role. For example, in cystic fibrosis:

○ Malabsorption causing increased losses
○ Increased energy needs
  • Chronic cough
  • Dyspnoea
  • Recurrent infection
  • Inflammation
○ Reduced intake
  • Anorexia
  • Vomiting
  • Psychological problems

All these together result in an **energy deficit**. All factors need to be taken into account when nutritional supplementation is considered.

Nutritional supplementation/concentrating feeds

Nutritional supplementation should be done with the help of a paediatric-trained dietician. Try to attend a dietetic clinic to observe the dietetic management at first hand.

Basic information – normal weight gain

○ Normal birth weight for term infants in the UK is 3.3–3.5 kg for both sexes

○ Loss of weight occurs in the first 5–7 days, then birth weight regained within the next 14 days
○ Thereafter, average weight gain is
  • 200 g/week for first 3 months
  • 150 g/week for second 3 months
  • 100 g/week for third 3 months
  • 50–75 g/week for fourth 3 months

Supplementation

Nutritional supplements (see Box) are generally required for those infants who are **failing to thrive on normal feeds** or who are **fluid restricted**. Care needs to be taken not to present too high an osmotic load as diarrhoea may result.

Carbohydrate supplements
○ Glucose polymers are used: examples include Caloreen®, Maxijul®, Polycal® (all hydrated cornstarch)

Fat supplements
○ Usually fat emulsions, examples include Calogen®, Liquigen®
○ Calogen® – arachis oil (not if peanut allergic as it is a crude oil and so may have traces of protein)
○ Liquigen® – medium-chain triglycerides (MCT) oil

Combined carbohydrate and fat supplements
○ Duocal®, which includes cornstarch, maize oil and coconut oil

Protein supplements
○ Whole protein, peptides or amino acids
○ Rarely required without an accompanying increase in other energy sources
○ Examples include Maxipro HBV®, which is whey protein

Concentrating infant feeds

Concentrating infant feeds increases the density of energy and protein, and has the advantage of providing this without the need to add a series of supplements. If feeds are concentrated then this also concentrates up electrolyte, vitamin and mineral replacement, which may be a problem.

○ Most normal baby milks are made up to **13%**, providing **65 kcal per 100 ml** and a **protein content of 1.5 g/100 ml**. Making a feed up to **15%** provides **75 kcal/100 ml** and **1.7 g/100 ml** of protein
○ Carbohydrate and fat can still be added if required

There are multiple commercially available high-calorie-density milks that have the appropriate electrolyte, mineral and vitamin contents, eg Infantrini® (Nutricia) 100 kcal/100 ml.

Malnutrition – cases

Specific scenarios arise within the different systems and need to be considered. Note that such questions could easily be asked at the end of the History Taking/Management Planning Station when you are left with the examiner.

Case one

This 6-month-old infant has congenital heart disease with faltering growth – comment on his nutritional status. What nutritional supplementation would you recommend?

> *In this infant the poor nutritional state will be as a consequence of increased metabolic demands (respiratory drive) and poor intake secondary to breathlessness. Supplementation would be by increasing the calorie density of feeds and consideration of other methods of administration such as a nasogastric tube.*

Case two

This 6-month-old infant has chronic lung disease and severe faltering growth. Comment on possible causes.

> *In this infant the poor nutritional state will be as a consequence of increased metabolic demands (for example work of breathing causing increased energy requirements) and poor intake secondary to breathlessness. In addition other factors may be relevant such as gastro-oesophageal reflux. Supplementation would be by increasing calorie density and considering using a nasogastric tube. In addition investigating for gastro-oesophageal reflux may be considered, as treatment in tandem with dietary manipulation may result in better weight gain.*

Case three

This 13-year-old boy has cerebral palsy. Comment on his nutritional status. What strategies could be used to improve it?

> *This child's principal problem will be with intake, either because of reflux or secondary to the bulbar problems or both. In addition to nutritional supplements this child may benefit from help with feeding practices including the involvement of a communication therapist and occupational therapist. Other medical problems may be relevant. Consideration needs to be given to nasogastric tube or gastrostomy tube feeding if appropriate. In some instances a fundoplication will also be required.*

Case four

This boy has cystic fibrosis and is malnourished. Comment on the cause. What can be done to help?

> *The additional factor in this child is malabsorption for which pancreatic supplementation is required. Children with cystic fibrosis often dislike food and need either a nasogastric tube or gastrostomy to help with administration. The energy requirements are high and calorie supplementation with energy-dense supplements is required.*

Gastrostomy tube feeding

It is essential to have seen and to recognise a gastrostomy tube. They are generally inserted endoscopically (percutaneous endoscopic gastrostomy). Complications are rare.

Indications

- ○ In chronic disease with nutritional impairment, eg cystic fibrosis, bronchopulmonary dysplasia
- ○ For nutritional therapy, eg Crohn's disease
- ○ Because of difficulties with feeding, eg cerebral palsy, particularly with an associated bulbar palsy
- ○ In severe gastro-oesophageal reflux with a fundoplication
- ○ Children dependent upon nasogastric feeding for any other reason

> **Tip**
>
> Gastrostomy tube plus transverse abdominal incision = gastrostomy plus Nissen's fundoplication

Obesity

This is defined as a body mass index (BMI) above the 98th centile for age and sex. There is an increase in childhood obesity in many parts of the world, with the UK being no exception. The causes are nearly always due to excess energy intake with reduced expenditure. In the UK the increasing consumption of carbonated drinks and high-fat foods along with an increasingly sedentary population have meant that in some population studies the prevalence is up to 15% of 15-year-olds. Childhood obesity is a strong predictor for obesity in adulthood. National Institute for Health and Clinical Excellence (NICE) guidelines recommend consideration of tailored clinical interventions for children with a BMI at or above the 91st centile. Children with a BMI at or above the 98th centile should undergo a comorbidity assessment.

It is currently unlikely that you will be asked to examine a child in the clinical section who is obese due to excess food intake but remember that there are other causes of obesity (see Box). It may also be that weight is relevant in one of the other cases you see.

Remember that children with an endocrine or genetic condition may be **short as well as overweight** and may have dysmorphic features. Children with physiological obesity are usually tall.

OTHER CAUSES OF OBESITY (ONLY 5% OF CASES)

○ Chromosomal/genetic
- Down syndrome
- Kleinfelter syndrome
- Prader–Willi syndrome
- Lawrence–Moon–Biedl syndrome

○ Endocrine
- Hypothyroidism
- Cushing's syndromes

- Polycystic ovarian syndrome
- ○ Oncological
  - Pituitary tumour

Physiological obesity/metabolic syndrome

Problems that older obese children face include hypertension, non-alcoholic steatohepatitis, hypercholesterolaemia, insulin resistance (associated with acanthosis nigricans), type 2 diabetes and obstructive sleep apnoea. Many such children are bullied at school and depression is becoming increasingly recognised. Girls who are adolescent and obese may have polycystic ovarian syndrome

Management of functional obesity

- ○ Prevention – public health campaigns, eg healthier school dinners, free fruit, banning drinks machines in schools, reduction in TV advertising of "junk foods"
- ○ Weight reduction programmes – works better when the whole family are on board. Involves healthy eating, portion control, 'prescribed' exercise, reduction of sedentary behaviour eg limitation of TV/computer time to less than 2 h a day

9.4 CASES AND CONDITIONS

Cystic fibrosis

Case one: 12-year-old boy

Peter is a thin-looking boy and I would like to plot him on a growth chart. He has reduced subcutaneous fat and muscle bulk. There is a gastrostomy tube in situ. He is clubbed, tachypnoeic and there is a Harrison's sulcus. Examination of his abdomen reveals hepatomegaly which is firm in consistency. There is splenomegaly and caput medusae...

I suspect he has cystic fibrosis complicated by liver disease – presumably cirrhosis associated with portal hypertension...

Case two: 10-year-old girl

> Sarah is a well-looking Caucasian girl. I would like to plot her growth parameters. She is clubbed. She has a hyperexpanded chest. On examination of the abdomen there is a transverse incision. She also has a palpable mass in the right iliac fossa.
>
> I wonder if she has cystic fibrosis and distal intestinal obstruction syndrome...

Gastrointestinal manifestations of cystic fibrosis

More detailed notes can be found in Chapter 10.

Pancreatic

- Insufficiency occurs in around 85%
- Pancreatitis
- Abnormal glucose tolerance in up to 10% by the second decade
- Insulin-dependent diabetes mellitus in 7% of patients; remember that diabetic ketoacidosis is rare in this group

Intestinal

- Meconium ileus
- Atresias
- Rectal prolapse
- Distal intestinal obstruction syndrome (DIOS)
- Strictures secondary to high-dose pancreatic supplementation

Hepatobiliary

- Cholestasis in infancy – leads to obstructive jaundice
- Fatty liver
- Focal biliary fibrosis
- Multilobular cirrhosis
- Abnormalities of the gall bladder
- Cholelithiasis
- Obstruction of the common bile duct

Crohn's disease

This may be seen in more than one section of the exam and therefore a good knowledge base of the various aspects is required. The clinical signs are not particularly specific but an illustrative case is included.

Case

> *This 14-year-old boy looks pale and thin. I suspect he is short and I would like to plot him on a growth chart. His muscle bulk and subcutaneous fat mass are poor. I would like to look in his mouth for gum hyperplasia and aphthous ulceration. There is mild right iliac fossa tenderness but no other abnormalities on abdominal examination.*
>
> *I would like to check his pubertal status and examine his peri-anal region for skin tags, fissures and fistulae...*

There may also be:

○ Nasogastric tube or gastrostomy
○ Signs of steroid toxicity
○ Scars from previous surgery

Notes on Crohn's disease

Crohn's disease is an idiopathic chronic inflammatory disorder of bowel involving any region from mouth to anus, with many cases involving the terminal ileum. The inflammation is transmural (thus effectively narrowing the lumen) with skip lesions. Affected mucosa is interspersed with deep ulcers, giving a cobblestone appearance.

There has been an increase in incidence since the late 1990s.

Symptoms and signs

○ The commonest presenting symptoms are abdominal pain, diarrhoea and weight loss
○ Systemic upset, lethargy and fever can occur
○ Extra-intestinal manifestations can occur and are worth looking for in a known case:
  • Eyes – uveitis or episcleritis
  • Joints – peripheral arthritis
  • Skin – erythema nodosum

○ Growth failure with delayed bone maturation and delayed sexual development is common. The aetiology of this is complex and includes poor nutritional state, disease activity, endocrine disturbance and the side-effect of corticosteroids when used

Diagnosis

Made on the basis of clinical symptoms, raised inflammatory indices and diagnostic test including barium radiology (upper GI series) and ileo-colonoscopy with biopsy.

Treatment

The disease often runs a chronic relapsing course. The aim of treatment is to induce a disease remission and facilitate normal growth and development whilst minimising treatment toxicity.

○ Exclusive enteral nutrition is the most widely used treatment in children, with an elemental or polymeric diet lasting for up to 8 weeks followed by a period of controlled food reintroduction. This induces remission in up to 80% of patients. Repeat courses may be needed for relapses.

○ Anti-inflammatories – maintenance is with oral 5-aminosalicylic acid (5-ASA) derivatives. Rectal disease can be treated with 5-ASA enemas.

○ Corticosteroids for severe flare-ups and relapses, particularly if systemic upset is present. Once remission is achieved these can be tapered down. Dependence or resistance can occur and additional immunosuppression with drugs such as azathioprine may be necessary. Anti-tumour necrosis factor (TNF) monoclonal antibody therapy such as infliximab is increasingly used in frequently relapsing cases.

○ Antibiotics for abscesses and fistulae – ciprofloxacin and metronidazole are often used.

○ Surgery – indicated if there are persistent symptoms despite optimal medical therapy, intolerable side-effects of medical therapy, abscesses that are unresponsive to conservative treatment, or life-threatening toxic megacolon. The need for surgery increases with age. Relapse following surgical resection is common.

Coeliac disease

This may be seen in the Abdomen Station or the History Taking/Management Planning Station and so can be found in these parts of the book (see for example Chapter 3).

Case

Examine this child and suggest a diagnosis

Clinical features:

- Often short
- Pale
- Thin with reduced subcutaneous fat, poor muscle bulk and buttock wasting
- Abdominal distension

> *I saw a 2-year-old girl. She looks pale and is thin. I would like to plot her on a growth chart. Her muscle bulk and subcutaneous fat mass are reduced. Abdominal examination is unremarkable apart from marked distension. On standing, her distension increases and I can see buttock wasting. I suspect she has a malabsorption syndrome.*
>
> *Coeliac disease would be the most likely diagnosis.*

Supplementary questions (could also apply to History Taking/Management Planning Station)

- What are the investigations?
- What is the management?
- What are the indications for a gluten challenge?

Notes on coeliac disease

Coeliac disease is a gluten-sensitive enteropathy with an increasing prevalence in symptomatic and screened populations. There is genetic susceptibility with an increased incidence in first-degree relatives.

The intolerance is to gluten, which is present in wheat, rye and barley. Oats are usually cross-contaminated during production.

Symptoms and signs

○ Coeliac disease usually presents after 6 months of age (ie after gluten has been introduced into the diet) with **chronic diarrhoea** and **poor weight gain**
○ Older children may present with non-specific gastrointestinal symptoms, iron deficiency or short stature
○ Dermatitis herpetiformis is occasionally seen and is an intensely itchy, blistering skin rash

Other features include:

○ Anorexia
○ Lethargy
○ Irritability – patients are characteristically very miserable
○ Abdominal distension
○ Pallor

Diagnosis and treatment

The standards for the diagnosis of coeliac disease are set out by the European Society of Paediatric Gastroenterology, Hepatology and Nutrition. Diagnosis is confirmed if characteristic features are found on endoscopic biopsy of the duodenum or jejunum. These features are sub-total villous atrophy, crypt hypertrophy, intra-epithelial lymphocytes and a lamina propria plasma cell infiltrate. **It is of crucial importance that the child's gluten intake is adequate at the time of the biopsy.**

Treatment is with a gluten-free diet for life, which should result in remission of symptoms. **If it does not the diagnosis should be reviewed.** There is a long-term risk of small bowel lymphoma if the patient does not adhere to the diet. The gluten-free diet itself has no long-term complications.

There are indications for a subsequent gluten challenge and these include initial diagnostic uncertainty and when the diagnosis is made under the age of 2 years. The latter is because at that age there are other causes of a flat jejunal biopsy such as cows' milk protein sensitive enteropathy. A gluten challenge involves an initial control biopsy on a gluten-free diet followed by a period on gluten with a repeat biopsy after 3–6 months and then again after 2 years, sooner if symptoms develop. There are reports of late relapse following gluten challenge.

Antibody testing in the screening of children with faltering growth and in the ongoing management of children with coeliac disease is helpful. The most widely used antibody tests are the IgA anti-endomysial and the IgA tissue transglutaminase (tTG) antibodies. False negatives are seen in children who are IgA deficient, and 10% of children with coeliac disease have a selective IgA deficiency. IgG antibodies can be used in this group. All children with positive antibody screening go on to have a biopsy (while still on a normal diet) in order to make the diagnosis.

The other associations of coeliac disease are an increased incidence of autoimmune thyroid disease, mixed connective tissue disease, pernicious anaemia and diabetes mellitus (HLA B8 associations) and dermatitis herpetiformis.

Differential diagnosis of the 'malabsorptive' picture (= malabsorption syndrome)

- ○ Coeliac disease
- ○ Cows' milk protein intolerance
- ○ Cystic fibrosis
- ○ Immunodeficiency
- ○ Others = many, eg infection, giardiasis, soya intolerance, autoimmune disease, etc

Constipation

This is the commonest cause of an abdominal mass and children may be recruited from the ward on exam day if there is a shortfall in cases for the Abdomen station.

It has been reported by candidates to be a common short case.

Case

> *This 9-year-old girl looks well. I would like to plot her on a growth chart ... proceed through examination... She has a full abdomen with a palpable mass arising from the pelvis. This is hard and indents. I suspect it is faeces and that she has chronic constipation with a megarectum. I would like to examine her peri-anal region as she may have overflow soiling and it is essential to exclude local pathology such as a fissure.*

Notes on constipation

Most children with constipation do not have an underlying cause and their constipation is functional. If associated with a megarectum then soiling is common. This should be distinguished from encopresis, a primarily psychological problem in which stool is passed in to the pants at inappropriate times and in inappropriate places with no underlying constipation.

Underlying causes that need to be considered for the purpose of the exam include:

○ Hirschsprung's disease – this is very rare in children who have at some stage of their life had a normal bowel habit and usually presents in the neonatal period
○ Thyroid disease
○ Meconium ileus equivalent
○ Spina bifida

The management of chronic functional constipation is multidisciplinary and is further outlined in History Taking/Management Planning (Section 3.6). Many factors are often involved including local pathology such as anal fissure, poor diet, poor fluid intake, previous difficult toileting experiences and psychosocial problems. Drugs used include stimulant and bulk laxatives. Remember that enema therapy can reinforce difficult toileting experiences and should be reserved for the more difficult cases.

Umbilical hernia

A common condition, which presents in infancy. Unlike inguinal hernias of infancy it almost never obstructs. Usually resolves by age 2 years. If it has not resolved by then it is unlikely to and therefore surgery should be considered, preferably before school age.

Remember the associated conditions:
○ Hypothyroidism
○ Storage disorders, eg mucopolysaccharidoses
○ Beckwith–Wiedemann syndrome
○ Trisomy 18
○ Trisomy 13

Ascites

What is ascites?

How do you examine for it and what are the potential causes?

Clinical features

- Not obvious clinically in 50%
- Bulging of flanks
- Protrusion of umbilicus
- Scrotal swelling
- Fluid thrill
- Shifting dullness

Differential diagnosis

Wide – four main groups of pathologies:
- Cirrhosis
- Congestive cardiac failure
- Nephrotic syndrome
- Protein-losing enteropathy

Hepatomegaly and splenomegaly

Hepatomegaly, splenomegaly and hepatosplenomegaly may well be encountered in the abdominal station. It is important to have wide differential diagnosis but try to focus on the most likely causes in the patient you have seen. Cases more likely to be seen in the exam are listed below.

Hepatomegaly

- Glycogen and other storage disorders
- Right-sided heart failure

Splenomegaly

- Portal hypertension
- Idiopathic thrombocytopenic purpura
- Myeloproliferative disease
- Hereditary spherocytosis
- Sickle cell disease
- Infection – glandular fever

Hepatosplenomegaly

○ Congenital hepatic fibrosis
○ Cystic fibrosis
○ Thalassaemia
○ Mucopolysaccharidoses

Case

Examine this child's gastrointestinal system. Talk me through your examination.

This is a 10-year-old girl. She looks well. She appears small. I would like to plot her on a height and weight chart.

(Proceed to examine – lift hand)

There is no evidence of clubbing or palmar erythema.

(Her facies are a little immature – may or may not notice; assess conjunctiva)

There is no pallor or jaundice. Her mouth looks clear with no aphthous ulceration or stomatitis. There are no spider naevi on the chest. Her abdomen is full. There are no scars or abnormal vessels.

(Palpate – superficial then deep palpation – should at this stage be able to feel the large liver, then assess formally)

She has a large liver palpable in the right hypochondrium. The liver is hard, non-tender and measures 6 cm below the costal margin.

(Percuss to confirm upper border; feel for spleen)

There is no associated splenomegaly. Kidneys are impalpable.

(Occasionally may be impalpable). (If clear about findings can stop there)

In summary this is a well 10-year-old girl. She has massive hepatomegaly but no other signs of liver disease. I suspect she may have glycogen storage disease type one.

Notes on hepatomegaly

You may be asked for a full differential diagnosis of hepatomegaly in which case you will need to have one available. We have included one below based on different categories – infection, infiltration, idiopathic, storage disorder, obstruction, miscellaneous. Avoid mentioning rarities and give just one or two examples in each category.

You don't want to be mentioning some rare differential you don't know much about and then be asked about it by the examiner – black hole! **The most likely scenario is that you will be asked for a diagnosis that would be appropriate in the child you have seen.** For example, you would not expect to be taken to see a child who was jaundiced with a large tender liver and infective hepatitis. Equally, one would not expect to be asked to palpate the liver of a child with extensive metastases. You are more likely to see a stable and well child with a glycogen storage disease or other storage disorder, or a child with portal hypertension or a stable child post-Kasai procedure for biliary atresia. Such patients will usually be able to tolerate repeated, similar examinations a few times in a row if required. This means you need to ensure you give an appropriate and relevant answer to the questions asked and remember that many causes of organomegaly in the abdomen are not likely to be used as short cases for the exam.

There may be no physical signs in a child with liver disease such as chronic hepatitis B infection.

Differential diagnosis of hepatomegaly

○ **Infection**
  • Hepatitis A
  • Hepatitis B
  • Epstein–Barr virus (EBV) infection
○ **Infiltration**
  • Primary liver tumours
  • Secondary tumour, eg lymphoma, leukaemia, neuroblastoma
○ **Idiopathic**
○ **Storage disorders**
  • *Fat*
    – Cystic fibrosis
    – Obesity
    – Malnutrition
    – Total parenteral nutrition (TPN)
  • *Lipid*
    – Gaucher's disease
  • *Sphingomyelin – cholesterol*
    – Niemann–Pick disease

- *Glycogen*
  - Glycogen storage disease – see notes below
○ **Obstructive**
  - Hepatic vein thrombosis
  - Congestive cardiac failure
○ **Miscellaneous**
  - Wilson's disease
  - Alpha 1 antitrypsin deficiency
  - Congenital hepatic fibrosis

VERY LARGE LIVER

You may examine a patient with a huge liver – remember to start palpating low down in the right iliac fossa!

○ Storage disorder
○ Reticuloendothelial disease, eg leukaemia
○ Gross fatty change
○ Malignancy
○ Congestive cardiac failure

Glycogen storage disease

Notes on glycogen storage disease type I – von Gierke's disease

An example of a very rare disorder with disproportionately high representation in the exam. You may not have encountered such a case so far in your career, so you will need to fall back on your notes!

This is an autosomal-recessive disorder and is the most common glycogen storage disease seen. It is due to reduced glucose-6-phosphatase activity and usually presents within the first 6 months with **hypoglycaemia** or **asymptomatic hepatomegaly**. Diagnosis used to be from liver biopsy with estimation of hepatic glucose-6-phosphatase activity, but genotyping can now be used.

Clinical findings
○ Often short
○ Doll-like facies

○ Large liver – due to the accumulation of glycogen and fat
○ Large kidney – occasionally

Main problems

○ Can present as fasting hypoglycaemia with no response to glucagon
○ Hypoglycaemia is accompanied by lactic acidosis – patients need overnight glucose infusions and frequent feeds when unwell
○ For older children use corn starch, which is a slow-release carbohydrate
○ Long-term risk of renal calculi and hepatoma
○ Platelet dysfunction
○ Reduced intellectual development often seen

Notes on other storage diseases

Glycogen storage disease type III

This is a debranching enzyme deficiency of liver and muscle. Important clinical features are:

○ Massive hepatomegaly
○ Myopathy
○ Developmental delay

Patients often develop cardiomyopathy in their late teens or adulthood. Liver cirrhosis is also a risk.

Glycogen storage disease type IV

A rapidly progressive hepatic disease with hepatomegaly, ascites and portal hypertension leading to cirrhosis.

Glycogen storage disease type V

○ Muscle only
○ Poor prognosis

Gaucher's disease

○ Autosomal recessive with different forms – infant, juvenile and adult
○ Deficiency in glucosylceramide beta-glucosidase (glucocerebrosidase) resulting in lipid accumulation in reticuloendothelial cells
○ Can progress to portal hypertension and cirrhosis

Splenomegaly

Case

Examine this child and suggest a likely diagnosis.

> *Callum is a 10-year-old boy who appears well grown. He is pale. Caput medusae are visible. His abdomen is full but not distended and he has a large spleen extending to 6 cm below the costal margin. Ascites is also present. No other signs...*
>
> *The likely diagnosis is* **portal hypertension** *secondary to pre-hepatic portal vein obstruction.*

What are the complications of portal hypertension?

Notes on splenomegaly

The **aetiology** of splenomegaly can be split into the following categories:

○ Hyperplasia of the reticuloendothelial system
○ Excessive antigenic stimulation – infection
○ Disorders of immunoregulation – autoimmune disease
○ Excessive destruction of blood cells – haemolytic anaemia
○ Neoplasia
○ Disorders of splenic flow – portal hypertension
○ Infiltration – metabolic lesions
○ Extramedullary haemopoiesis

Differential diagnosis of splenomegaly

Infection

○ Bacterial, viral or protozoal
○ Septicaemia
○ Infectious mononucleosis
○ Malaria

Autoimmune disease

○ Juvenile idiopathic arthritis
○ Systemic lupus erythematosus (SLE)

Haemolytic disorders
○ Hereditary spherocytosis
○ Sickle cell anaemia (early)

Neoplastic
○ Acute leukaemia
○ Hodgkin's disease

Disordered splenic flow
○ Portal hypertension
○ Cirrhosis
○ Cardiac failure

Infiltration
○ Gaucher's disease

Extramedullary haemopoiesis
○ Thalassaemia

Notes on portal hypertension

The cardinal feature of portal hypertension is splenomegaly. **Portal hypertension does not necessarily imply liver disease.**

○ If there are no clinical or biochemical features of liver disease and the liver is not enlarged, portal vein obstruction is the most likely diagnosis
○ If the liver is large and there are no stigmata of cirrhosis then congenital hepatic fibrosis should be considered

Clinical features of portal hypertension
○ Failure to thrive, reduced muscle bulk on overall inspection
○ Splenomegaly
○ Liver small, normal size or enlarged
○ Cutaneous portosystemic shunts (caput medusae – flow from the umbilicus, venous hum above the umbilicus, haemorrhoids)
○ Ascites

Main problems

○ As a consequence of the portosystemic shunts there may be gastrointestinal haemorrhage (oesophageal varices, internal haemorrhoids) and encephalopathy

○ As a consequence of the large spleen (hypersplenism) patients are often thrombocytopenic, anaemic and leukopenic

Commonest causes of portal hypertension

○ Cirrhosis
○ Portal vein obstruction
○ Congenital hepatic fibrosis
○ Hepatic vein outflow obstruction

Portal vein obstruction

In 50% there is no obvious aetiology, and it is probably a developmental defect. Other causes include congenital abnormalities of the portal vein and intra-abdominal sepsis. Presentation is usually either with asymptomatic splenomegaly or life-threatening bleeding. Occasionally the presentation can be with failure to thrive.

Congenital hepatic fibrosis

Autosomal recessive. Child looks well. Large hard liver with well preserved liver function. Large spleen secondary to portal hypertension. Large polycystic kidneys (75%).

Differential diagnosis of portal hypertension

Having given the most likely diagnosis for your particular case, you still may be asked for some more causes of portal hypertension, so a full list is included:

Pre-hepatic

○ Portal vein thrombosis

Intra-hepatic

○ Pre-sinusoidal
   • Neoplasia, schistosomiasis, hepatic cyst

○ Sinusoidal
  • Congenital hepatic fibrosis, cirrhosis, biliary atresia, neonatal hepatitis, alpha 1 antitrypsin deficiency
○ Post-sinusoidal
  • Veno-occlusive disease

Post-hepatic
○ Budd–Chiari syndrome
○ Right ventricular failure
○ Constrictive pericarditis

In general a child with portal hypertension in whom the underlying diagnosis is unclear would be referred to a liver centre for assessment. The main priority is treatment of the underlying cause.

Cirrhosis and liver transplantation

There are numerous disorders that can lead to cirrhosis. The most likely scenario seen will be a child with biliary atresia who has had a Kasai procedure and has progressive liver disease. Other cases can be seen but rarely. The differential diagnoses should be known and will need to be presented if a child with the stigmata of chronic liver disease/cirrhosis is seen.

Tip

Remember that a cirrhotic liver is usually small (except in cystic fibrosis)

Notes on cirrhosis

Differential diagnosis of cirrhosis

Biliary tract disorders
○ Biliary atresia
○ Choledochal cyst
○ Congenital hepatic fibrosis
○ Cystic fibrosis
○ Sclerosing cholangitis

Genetic and metabolic causes

- ○ Alpha 1 antitrypsin deficiency
- ○ Wilson's disease
- ○ Glycogen storage disease

Infection

- ○ Hepatitis B and C
- ○ Cytomegalovirus

Autoimmune

Drugs and toxins

- ○ Alcohol

Nutrition

- ○ TPN

NB. **Chronic active hepatitis** refers to inflammation, necrosis and fibrosis that can lead to cirrhosis. The commonest causes are hepatitis B and C and autoimmune liver disease.

Clinical features of cirrhosis

- ○ Faltering growth – always ask to plot patient
- ○ Hands – clubbing, palmar erythema
- ○ Eyes – pale conjunctivae of anaemia, jaundice evident in sclerae (variable), xanthelasma
- ○ Spider naevi
- ○ Large hard or small impalpable liver

Complications of cirrhosis

You may be asked about the main problems that a patient with cirrhosis will encounter (and the management of such problems) in this station or the History Taking/Management Planning Station.

- ○ Portal hypertension
- ○ Bleeding diatheses
- ○ Increased susceptibility to infections
- ○ Ascites with danger of secondary bacterial peritonitis
- ○ Pulmonary hypertension
- ○ Hepatoma
- ○ Malnutrition

○ Gallstone formation
○ Renal failure
○ Hepatic encephalopathy
○ Endocrine changes
○ Impaired hepatic metabolism of drugs and hormones
○ Impaired neurodevelopment

Management of cirrhosis

This is multidisciplinary and the team will be headed by a paediatric hepatologist:

○ Determine the cause if possible and treat the underlying condition – it is hoped that this will minimise further liver damage
○ Diet containing adequate protein and essential fatty acids, trace elements and vitamins for growth and normal activities; plus adequate calorie intake. Specialist dietician to implement and review this regimen
○ Ascites best dealt with by restricting salt intake and/or diuretics

Emergencies

○ Alimentary bleeding – admit, even if small, for assessment as patients may have a slow initial bleed followed by a massive bleed. Should have a reliable i.v. line, and cross-match. Further prevention and management of varices includes sclerotherapy, variceal ligation, surgical portosystemic shunts.
○ Bacterial peritonitis – should be managed by adequate parental education leading to early detection and then treatment with appropriate antibiotics.
○ Hepatic encephalopathy – prevent the accumulation of ammonia, remove/correct identifiable precipitating factors, improve liver function by reducing protein intake, use antibiotics (neomycin). Lactulose to encourage excretion of waste products via the stool.
○ Hepatorenal failure is usually a terminal event requiring liver transplant

LIVER TRANSPLANTATION

You may see a child who has had a liver transplant in this section of the exam or the History Taking/Management Planning Station

○ **Indications**
- End-stage chronic disease – likelihood of death within 12 months or evidence of deterioration that will worsen the prognosis for liver transplantation
- Unacceptable quality of life
- Fulminant or subacute liver failure – age <2 years or INR >4
- Metabolic disorders, eg Wilson's, alpha 1 antitrypsin, galactosaemia
- Liver tumours
- Bleeding varices
- Grossly encephalopathic
- Persistent severe ascites

○ **Donor**
- A supply of suitable donors is a major limiting factor. Can split organ between recipients or use one part of the liver from a related donor

○ **Complications**
- The acute rejection rate can approach 50%–60%
- Sepsis is the primary cause of deaths post-transplant
- Biliary leaks in up to 20%

○ **Prognosis**
- There is around a 90% 2-year survival, 64%–75% 5-year survival. Patients need lifelong immunosuppression. The chronic rejection rate is around 5–10 %

Extra-hepatic biliary atresia – post-Kasai procedure

This is a very common clinical case in the examination and patients may also be used for the History Taking/Management Planning Station. Pointers relevant to this station are given in the History Taking/Management Planning section of this book (Section 3.12).

Case

What do you think of this girl's scar?

Examine the abdomen, what do you find, can you give a sequence of events to explain this?

Clinical findings

- ○ Characteristic scar
- ○ Liver may be palpable
- ○ Signs of portal hypertension may be present
- ○ Signs of chronic liver disease may be present

Notes on extra-hepatic biliary atresia

Currently biliary atresia is the commonest indication for liver transplantation in childhood. Most of this is extra-hepatic biliary atresia. The incidence is 1 in 8000 to 1 in 20 000 live births. The disorder is thought to be acquired and presents as neonatal cholestasis.

Investigation is complex and any infant with prolonged jaundice that is predominantly conjugated needs to be referred to a liver centre for further assessment.

Treatment is with a porto-enterostomy (Kasai procedure). The outcome is much better if surgery is carried out before 3 months of age, which is why delays between finding unexplained conjugated jaundice and referring it to a liver centre can be detrimental to the patient. Post-operatively there is a high risk of cholecystitis and children need intravenous antibiotic therapy if unwell. A proportion go on to get chronic liver disease and a number require transplantation.

Notes on other causes of cirrhosis

Intra-hepatic biliary atresia

This is less common and can be either syndromic or non-syndromic. Alagille's syndrome is an example worth remembering.

Alagille's syndrome

- ○ Paucity of intra-hepatic bile ducts
- ○ Characteristic facies with growth retardation, mental retardation

○ Vertebral arch defects/hemivertebrae
○ Hypoglycaemia
○ Heart disease – usually peripheral pulmonary stenosis

Alpha 1 antitrypsin deficiency

Autosomal-recessive phenotype determined by Pi (protease inhibitor) typing. The condition presents with cholestasis in infancy, cirrhosis in childhood and chronic obstructive pulmonary disease in early adult life.

Wilson's disease

Incidence is 1 in 500 000. Autosomal-recessive inheritance. The pathology is as a consequence of decreased biliary excretion of copper and impaired caeruloplasmin production. Caeruloplasmin is the plasma protein that transports copper.

Presentation

Note that the condition does not present under the age of 5 years.
○ Younger children tend to present with liver disease – asymptomatic hepatomegaly, acute hepatitis, chronic active hepatitis, portal hypertension (ascites, oedema, variceal haemorrhage) or fulminant hepatic failure.
○ Adults usually present with neurological symptoms – the lenticular degeneration usually presents with a tremor.

Diagnosis and features of illness

Diagnosis is suggested by a low plasma caeruloplasmin level and high urinary copper excretion. The latter can occur in other forms of hepatitis and a liver biopsy is often required. In equivocal cases the increased copper excretion after chelation with D-penicillamine is of diagnostic importance.

Kayser-Fleischer rings are seen and are said to be **pathognomonic**. Other abnormalities include sunflower cataract, renal tubular disorders and haemolysis.

Treatment

Untreated the condition is fatal but treated the prognosis is good. Treatment is with oral penicillamine as a copper-binding agent in conjunction with a low-copper diet. Patients on penicillamine require vitamin B6 supplements as it is an antimetabolite.

10

RESPIRATORY MEDICINE

CONTENTS

10.1 Introduction

10.2 Clinical examination
Suggested approach for examination of the respiratory system

10.3 Cases and conditions
Asthma
Bronchiolitis
Cystic fibrosis
Bronchiectasis
Primary ciliary dyskinesia
Chronic lung disease of infancy
Kyphoscoliosis
Stridor
Miscellaneous notes
– Pierre-Robin sequence
– Enlarged tongue
– Tracheostomy

10.1 INTRODUCTION

The respiratory examination is straightforward and should be revised thoroughly and practised frequently. The conditions seen are common – cystic fibrosis, other chronic suppurative lung disease, asthma and bronchopulmonary dysplasia. Patients with these chronic conditions are among the first to be contacted when an examination centre is recruiting families to help on exam day. Studying these conditions (approach to examination, clinical signs and knowledge of the underlying condition) well will present a good opportunity for you to pick up marks and boost confidence during the exam.

Some of the conditions discussed in this chapter may also come up in the History Taking/Management Planning or the Communication Skills Station. The notes about these conditions will therefore be useful for other sections of the exam as well as the short cases section.

10.2 CLINICAL EXAMINATION

Suggested approach for examination of the respiratory system

Find your own system, with which you are comfortable. It is important to start with a general assessment looking for dysmorphology, nutritional status and any other specific features. The following is a suggested scheme.

Baby/infant/toddler

It is reasonable to be opportunistic in this situation and change the order of examination to gain the maximum amount of information before the baby starts to cry.

Include the following:

- Observation – dysmorphology, supplementary oxygen, nutritional status, cyanosis, recession, respiratory rate, chest expansion, scars
- Auscultation (remember apices and right middle lobe)
- Apex beat and heart sounds
- Percussion (may not be helpful in infants and toddlers)
- Clubbing
- Anaemia

- Tracheal position
- Hepatomegaly/liver edge pushed down by hyperexpanded lungs
- Ear, nose and throat (ENT)

The last three are more likely to elicit some protest so may be best left to the end

Older child

- Look at the child from the end of the bed and make some general observations. Are they wasted? Children with cystic fibrosis (CF) may have a gastrostomy. Check for a BCG scar
- Look around the room for inhalers/nebulisers, pancreatic enzymes, peak flow meter, sputum pot
- Examine hands for clubbing, peripheral cyanosis (can be seen in nails) and anaemia
- Count pulse and respiratory rate – and be seen to be doing this
- Assess chest shape – look for pectus excavatum/carinatum and Harrison's sulci. Might the child have kyphoscoliosis?
- While you are looking at the child's hands, arms and chest wall you may notice eczema; be prepared to comment on this as it may be relevant to your diagnosis
- Assess respiratory effort while you are still inspecting the child. Look for nasal flaring, recession, tracheal tug, abdominal respirations. Look and listen for features of upper airway obstruction (stridor, nasal congestion)
- Look in the mouth for central cyanosis
- Feel suprasternal notch for tracheal deviation
- Lift each arm in turn and look for scars (eg lateral thoracotomy) and palpate for axillary then cervical lymphadenopathy
- Assess chest expansion. Is it equal on both sides? Don't forget to look from the side for increased anteroposterior (AP) diameter as seen in obstructive airways diseases such as asthma
- Palpate apex beat (an indicator of mediastinal shift, or Kartagener's syndrome if on right)
- Percuss (anteriorly, posteriorly and laterally). Practise distinguishing between resonance and hyper-resonance, dullness and stony dullness. Practise your technique for percussion
- Auscultate (anteriorly, posteriorly and laterally). Comment on whether breath sounds are vesicular or bronchial. Be prepared to describe added sounds such as crackles (coarse or fine?) and wheezes (monophonic or polyphonic?) along with their timing
- Assess for tactile vocal fremitus, vocal resonance if appropriate (eg suspected consolidation)

At the end of your examination

■ Palpate the abdomen for a liver edge (pushed down by hyperexpanded lung or genuine hepatomegaly)
■ Ask to examine the ears, nose (look specifically for polyps) and throat
■ You may be shown a sputum pot (whether or not you remember to ask for one!) and be asked to describe its contents
■ Ask to measure peak flow rate (if appropriate)
■ Ask to see a growth chart; one may be produced for comment

Different instructions may be given and you need to adapt your examination accordingly. Remember that there are 9 min per station so it is likely you will be asked to perform a complete systems exam. If in doubt about whether you should, talk your way through the examination.

■ Examine this child's chest
■ Examine this child's respiratory system
■ Look at this child's chest and tell me what you see – hyperexpansion, thoracotomy scars, Harrison's sulci, wasting
■ Just listen to this child's chest
■ The GP says this child does not have asthma – do you agree? Perform a full respiratory examination. The examiner is expecting you to comment on distinguishing features such as Harrison's sulci and hyperexpansion, and to ask the child to perform a peak flow measurement

Notes on examination of the respiratory system

Signs of respiratory distress

Severe signs in bold are very unlikely to be **seen** in the exam situation but you may be **asked** about them:

○ Audible wheeze
○ Tachypnoea
○ Tachycardia
○ Nasal flaring
○ Intercostal/subcostal/sternal recession
○ Tracheal tug
○ **Abdominal respirations/see-sawing of abdomen**
○ **Drowsiness and confusion**
○ **Cyanosis**

Clubbing

How to assess

This can be difficult if early but is often asked. We know of one candidate who was asked to stage clubbing once he recognised it. Clubbing is graded according to stages of its development:

○ Stage 1: Fluctuant bogginess of the nail bed
○ Stage 2: Loss of nail fold angle then occurs (Schamroth's sign); this is most easily seen by asking the child to hold their thumbs together nail to nail and looking through the gap which will have lost its normal 'diamond' shape
○ Stage 3: Increased curvature of the nail bed
○ Stage 4 :Enlargement of the distal phalanx (later sign)

CAUSES OF CLUBBING

Respiratory
○ Bronchiectasis/cystic fibrosis
○ Primary ciliary dyskinesia
○ Empyema/lung abscess
○ Pulmonary tuberculosis
○ Fibrosing alveolitis

Cardiac
○ Cyanotic congenital heart disease
○ Bacterial endocarditis

Gastrointestinal
○ Biliary cirrhosis
○ Chronic active hepatitis
○ Inflammatory bowel disease

Other
○ Malignancy
○ Idiopathic/familial

Hyperexpansion

This implies **obstructive airway disease** and is an extremely important physical sign. Practise the assessment of hyperexpansion. Look from the front first and then assess by looking at the child from the side and examining AP diameter and chest excursion during the respiratory phases. Comment on asymmetry if seen.

Causes of hyperexpansion – common conditions seen in the exam

○ Asthma
○ Cystic fibrosis
○ Bronchiectasis
○ Bronchopulmonary dysplasia – look for neonatal sequelae, eg head shape, chest drain/i.v. scars, nasal cannulae for low-flow oxygen
○ Recurrent aspiration – commoner in children with cerebral palsy
○ Repaired tracheo-oesophageal fistula

Tip

Hyperexpanded chest plus clubbing implies cystic fibrosis or other chronic suppurative lung disease

Hyperexpanded chest without clubbing implies asthma or bronchopulmonary dysplasia

---

Harrison's sulcus

Harrison's sulcus is visible as a bilateral fixed indrawing of the anterior portion of the lower ribs. It is caused by chronic airway obstruction encouraging excessive diaphragmatic use. This eventually causes a deformity where the diaphragm inserts into the ribcage.

Spirometry

The routine use of lung function testing has become more widespread and most children over the age of 5 years will be able to have their lung function tested. You may be asked to interpret a test result.

Values obtained by spirometry are:

○ PEFR: Peak expiratory flow rate. Effort dependent and used more for home monitoring
○ FVC: Forced vital capacity. Total amount of air forcibly exhaled
○ FEV_1: Forced expiratory volume in the first second (if diminished indicates large- and medium-sized airway obstruction)

○ FEV_1/FVC: Preserved in restrictive disease, lowered in obstructive diseases such as CF and asthma

○ FEF_{25-75}: Average expiratory flow between points where 25% and 75% of FVC has been expired. Represents small airways function and, as resistance increases, the flow–volume loop becomes more concave or scalloped

It will be sensible in the run up to the exam to attend the local respiratory clinic and discuss the results on individual patients.

10.3 CASES

Asthma

Children with asthma may be brought down from the ward to the Respiratory Station on exam day. This is also one of the chronic illnesses that may appear in other sections of the exam.

Instructions to candidate

Examine this child's chest
Comment on the appearance of this child's chest

Case

> Simon is a well-looking 9-year-old boy who looks well grown for his age. I would like to plot his height and weight on a growth chart.
>
> There is no clubbing or cyanosis. On inspection of his chest he has bilateral Harrison's sulci. His respiratory rate is 48 breaths per minute. Auscultation of his chest reveals bilateral expiratory wheeze with a prolonged expiratory component. The most likely diagnosis is **asthma**. I would also like to ask Simon to perform a peak flow measurement...

Clinical examination

- ○ Hyperexpansion, chest wall deformity (Harrison's sulci, pectus carinatum)
- ○ Signs of respiratory distress
- ○ Wheeze and prolonged expiration
- ○ Peak flow

Also look for: clubbing, wasting, coarse crepitations, focal signs, central lines, neonatal scars.

If these are present then an alternative diagnosis is more likely.

> ### Tip
>
> Clubbing is not seen in children whose only diagnosis is asthma

DIFFERENTIAL DIAGNOSES OF ASTHMA – YOU MAY BE ASKED THIS

○ Bronchiectasis
○ Bronchiolitis (infants)
○ Bronchopulmonary dysplasia (ex-prematures)
○ Foreign body
○ Congestive cardiac failure (myocarditis/congenital heart disease (CHD))
○ Gastro-oesophageal reflux (severe resulting in aspiration)
○ Tracheo-oesophageal fistula – post repair
○ H-type tracheo-oesophageal fistula (very rare)
○ Vascular ring
○ Lymphadenopathy causing extrinsic small airway compression (TB/Hodgkin's/sarcoidosis)

Notes on asthma

Epidemiology

Prevalence: 10% of pre-school rising to 30% of school-age children in some areas. Threefold increase in past 40 years.

Each year 70 % of asthmatic children are admitted to hospital. There are around 50 deaths per year under the age of 16 in the UK, which is a relatively static figure.

Management – summary

See Section 2.2 in History Taking and Management Planning for detailed management notes.

General measures

○ Allergen avoidance: damp dusting, changing carpeted bedroom floors to laminate flooring, washing/freezing toys, avoiding animal dander, bed covers
○ Avoiding cigarette smoking /passive exposure
○ Weight reduction in obese patients
○ Regular exercise

Drug therapy

Keep up to date with joint British Thoracic Society (BTS) and Scottish Intercollegiate Guidelines Network (SIGN) guidelines at www.britthoracic.org.uk. or www.sign.ac.uk

Acute attacks

Oxygen, inhaled or nebulised beta-2 agonists and oral steroids. The small proportion of patients who don't respond require intravenous (i.v.) salbutamol, i.v. aminophylline, i.v. hydrocortisone, and occasionally magnesium sulphate.

A very small proportion of children need ventilating on the Paediatric Intensive Care Unit (PICU).

Long-term treatment

See Box.

SUMMARY OF BRITISH THORACIC SOCIETY (BTS) GUIDELINES FOR STEPWISE THERAPY

Step 1: Inhaled short-acting beta-agonist as required

Step 2: As Step 1 + regular inhaled prophylactic steroids

Step 3: Inhaled steroids plus add-on therapy such as long-acting beta-2 agonists (LABA) or leukotriene receptor antagonists

Step 4: As Step 3 + increase inhaled steroid in over-5s, refer to respiratory paediatrician if under 5

Step 5: As Step 4 + regular prednisolone + refer to respiratory paediatrician

---

Delivery devices

Remember that one of the key aspect of asthma management is educating patients and families on how to use the medication prescribed. You may be tested on this in the Respiratory Station by being asked to explain delivery devices to a patient, parent or examiner.

Many candidates who attend Part Two clinical courses are unable to use many of the devices correctly. This does not give the examiner a good impression. Most hospitals have a Paediatric Asthma Nurse who demonstrates these devices every day and it would be wise to utilise their help before the exam! There are NICE guidelines for inhaler devices for children with chronic asthma (www.nice.org.uk). The central principle of these guidelines is that the child's needs and likelihood of compliance come before cost.

Babies and toddlers – up to the age of 5 years

○ **Metered dose inhaler** coupled to a **spacer device**, eg **Volumatic®/Nebuhaler®**. The spacer slows down the particles and requires no co-ordination to use. For under-2s who are unable to breathe directly into the mouthpiece a soft rubber **mask** is supplied.

○ Spacers must be replaced when they become scratched. When they are cleaned they must be left to drip-dry, not wiped with a cloth, as the static charge produced reduces effective particle delivery to the lungs. While most toddlers cope well with this device, babies tolerate it less well.

○ There are devices with a smaller volume and a more pliant valve to match the tidal volume of the baby, eg **Babyhaler®**. If this does not work then it may be necessary to deliver the medication via a **home nebuliser**. This is mentioned in the NICE guidelines; there are few other indications for home nebulisers.

Age 5–15 years

○ Pressurised metered dose inhaler **and** spacer device for corticosteroid therapy.

○ **Dry powder inhalers** such as the **Accuhaler®** and **Turbohaler®** are simple to use and are popular with school children. **Diskhalers®** can be very useful and are easy to carry to school. You will need to learn the technique of loading and using this inhaler as it is different from all the others.

○ **Self-activating devices with propellant** such as **Easibreathe®** and **Autohaler®** devices. The child still needs to be able to take a deep breath and hold it when using them. Inhalers should now be chlorofluorocarbon free.

Bronchiolitis

Case

> Jade is 6 months old. She appears to be well grown. I would like to plot her on a growth chart. She is in headbox oxygen and is in respiratory distress with tachypnoea of 60 breaths per minute, nasal flaring and intercostal recession. There is no cyanosis. Auscultation of her chest reveals bilateral inspiratory and expiratory wheeze and bilateral fine crepitations. The most likely diagnosis is **bronchiolitis**...

Clinical examination

- Hyperexpanded, barrel-shaped chest, nasogastric (NG) tube, headbox/low-flow oxygen
- Signs of respiratory distress – mainly tachypnoea, recession
- Bilateral wheeze and crackles. Air entry may be unequal due to consolidation caused by atelectasis (around 30% of patients)

Differential diagnoses include

- Heart disease: ventricular septal defect/atrioventricular septal defect, myocarditis, total anomalous pulmonary venous drainage
- Bronchopneumonia: bacterial (staphylococcal or pneumococcal), aspiration, pertussis. Patients with a high fever (axillary temperature of >39°C) should be assessed for features of bacterial infection
- Post viral wheeze
- Foreign body

Notes on bronchiolitis

Bronchiolitis is an acute viral respiratory illness affecting infants up to 1 year of age with a peak incidence at 6 months. It occurs in winter epidemics in both hemispheres. The underlying pathophysiology is inflammation of the small airways (bronchioles). The main causative agent is respiratory syncytial virus (RSV) in 50%–90% of cases (sero types A and B). The remainder of cases are due to parainfluenza, mycoplasma and adenovirus. Infants are at increased risk of developing bronchiolitis if their parents smoke and if they live in crowded conditions. Breast feeding is partially protective, presumably through passive transfer of anti-RSV immunoglobulin.

The illness starts with a few days of coryza followed by a moist cough and sometimes wheeze. The child may have a fever. Very young or ex-premature infants can present with or develop apnoeas. Diagnosis is clinical, with certain groups of patients requiring confirmation by immunofluorescence of a nasopharyngeal aspirate (NPA). This viro-logical diagnosis can aid decisions about cohorting.

Management

For more information there are SIGN guidelines for bronchiolitis available from www.sign.ac.uk, guideline no. 91.

Mainstay is **supportive care** with **frequent monitoring**

○ Supplementary humidified oxygen by headbox or nasal cannulae; mandatory if saturations in air are less than 93%. Additional respiratory support may be required either by continuous positive airway pressure or transfer to a PICU if ventilation is required. Bronchiolitic patients can be very difficult to ventilate.
○ Hydration and providing help with feeding. Nasogastric feeds (small, frequent amounts) are more physiological but may not be tolerated very well. Intravenous fluids may be required, bearing in mind that many patients develop the syndrome of inappropriate antidiuretic hormone (SIADH).
○ Suction and saline nose drops can be useful as secretions are usually profuse and contribute to the airway obstruction and poor feeding.

Pharmacotherapy

○ You may be asked about the role of pharmacotherapy. **The vast majority of patients do not benefit from any drugs and this should be stated to the examiners if you are asked.**
○ It is useful to be aware of the various therapies that are being considered and trialled as you may need to know this informa-tion in the History Taking and Management Planning or Communication Skills Stations.
○ **Ipratropium bromide** via nebuliser reverses some of the short-term effects of bronchiolitis but has not been shown to alter mortality or length of hospitalisation.

○ More recently there has been considerable interest in the use of **nebulised adrenaline** but it is currently not recommended.
○ **Nebulised** ribavirin reduces viral shedding and shortens the duration of illness but systematic reviews have shown no reduction in mortality. It is also difficult to administer.
○ **Palivizumab**, an anti-RSV monoclonal antibody, is available for treatment and prophylaxis in high-risk patients (see below – contraindicated in cyanotic congenital heart disease). However it is very expensive so cost-effectiveness is an issue.
○ **Steroids** are of no benefit during the acute phase. They are of some use in obliterative bronchiolitis, a destructive form of bronchiolitis, usually associated with adenovirus and resulting in bronchiectasis.
○ **Antibiotics** are of no benefit in straightforward bronchiolitis but are occasionally required if there is clinical suspicion of superadded bacterial infection – around 5% of patients in some centres.

High-risk groups

○ Congenital heart disease
○ Cystic fibrosis
○ Chronic lung disease (ex-premature babies at higher risk even if they do not have CLD)
○ Immunodeficiency

Prognosis is slightly worse in the high-risk group (mortality 3.5% versus 1%).

Discharge

Consider when baby has had sats of >94% in room air for over 8–12 h, including during sleep, and is taking over 75% of feeds. The social set-up is also relevant. On discharge parents should be warned that around 50% of babies take 2–4 weeks to recover as they are left with hyper-reactive airways. Such babies can re-present multiple times to their GP or Paediatric Unit with episodes of wheeze. These patients very rarely benefit from steroid prophylaxis.

Cystic fibrosis

Cystic fibrosis patients are seen very commonly in the Respiratory Station. A thorough knowledge of all aspects of this condition is required for this *and* for other parts of the exam. Remember, cystic fibrosis is a multisystem disorder.

Instructions to candidate

Examine this child's chest – crackles/wheeze/central line

Examine this child's hands – clubbing

Look at this child – wasting/nasogastric tube

Examine this child's chest – what else would you like to examine? (Abdomen, nutritional status, ENT, cardiac)

General examination

○ Visible central line or gastrostomy
○ Cyanosis, supplemental oxygen
○ Wasting – reduced muscle bulk (mid-arm circumference), reduced subcutaneous fat (skinfold thickness)
○ Obvious hyperexpansion and respiratory distress
○ Scars – thoracotomy, abdominal
○ Around the bed – pancreatic enzymes, peak flow and nebulisers in evidence
○ Remember to measure/ask about height and weight, and offer to plot on centile chart

Case

> John is a 15-year-old boy who is lying in bed, comfortable at rest. There is a central line and gastrostomy tube in situ. He looks thin with a poor muscle bulk and reduced subcutaneous fat. I would like to plot him on a height and weight chart. Looking at his hands he appears clubbed.
>
> He is obviously hyperexpanded and using his accessory muscles of respiration. His respiratory rate is 24 breaths per minute...

On examination

Hands/face

○ Clubbing – in older child, CF unlikely in the absence of clubbing
○ Peripheral and central cyanosis
○ Pulse
○ Pallor
○ Jaundice
○ Nasal polyps

Chest

○ Tachypnoea
○ Hyperexpansion
○ Crackles, wheeze
○ Peak flow
○ Sputum sample (ask at end)

Abdomen

○ Scars – meconium ileus
○ Gastrostomy
○ Caput medusae
○ Ascites
○ Hepatosplenomegaly
○ Rectal prolapse
○ Palpable faecal mass – distal intestinal obstruction syndrome (DIOS) or meconium ileus equivalent

Cardiovascular system

○ Signs of right-sided heart failure secondary to pulmonary hypertension (raised JVP, dependent oedema, hepatomegaly)

Endocrine system

○ Poorly grown, delayed puberty
○ Insulin injection sites

Joints

○ Arthritis – occurs in 1% of patients and is fleeting. Knees and ankles most commonly affected. Thought to be due to circulating immune complexes. Improves with lung function

> **Tip**
>
> Patients with multisystem involvement may be asked to cover other stations – see Section 9.4 in Chapter 9.

Background notes on cystic fibrosis

Inheritance is autosomal recessive. Prevalence 1:2500, carrier frequency 1:25. Cystic fibrosis transmembrane conductance regulator (CFTR) is a cAMP-mediated chloride channel. In the lungs, normal CFTR causes efflux of chloride ions across apical membranes of the submucosal glands. Sodium and water follow. Abnormal CFTR (reduced production, defective processing or ATP-binding site defects) causes an inability to secrete chloride, sodium and then water, resulting in viscid secretions, the hallmark of CF. A similar problem occurs in the pancreatic and biliary ducts, and also in the reproductive tract. The inspissated mucus in the bronchi causes failure to clear pathogenic organisms. These then colonise the airways and the resulting inflammatory reaction predisposes to repeated infections and chronic suppurative lung disease. However, in the skin the function of the sweat glands is to absorb chloride from the isotonic sweat. CFTR defects therefore cause a high sweat chloride, the basis of the sweat test.

Genetics

There are now more than 1500 alterations at the gene locus on chromosome 7. Delta F508 is the commonest mutation and is present in 75% of patients (two-thirds homozygous, one-third heterozygous for Delta F508 and one other mutation). Different phenotypes exist, and the genotype/phenotype correlation is strongest for pancreatic insufficiency and sweat chloride, eg all Delta F508 patients have pancreatic insufficiency whereas those with the R117H mutation have some preservation of pancreatic function.

Diagnosis

You may need to explain the following to a proxy parent; see Chapter 5.

○ Antenatal chorionic villous sampling (at 8/40 to 10/40), amniocentesis (at 16/40 to 18/40) for gene analysis if mutation within the family has been previously identified.

○ Guthrie test looking at immunoreactive trypsin (IRT). Single raised IRT has low specificity and so genetic testing is then performed. If one gene is found the child is referred for a sweat test or a second blood spot IRT. Screening and thus early diagnosis has been shown to help optimise nutritional status – an important aspect of management. All babies are screened in Wales, Scotland, Ireland and screening is now being rolled out across England. Rest of world – varies as the incidence obviously varies dramatically.

○ Genetic analysis – in all children who have been diagnosed, as this provides more information on genotype/phenotype correlations. Also used when sweat test is equivocal.

○ Sweat test – sweat chloride of >60 mmol/l diagnostic; need over 100 mg of sweat but there are newer methods being developed that need less.

Clinical problems in cystic fibrosis – summary

More detailed notes on the following problems can be found in Section 2.1 in Chapter 2.

Respiratory

○ Bacterial colonisation and infection – typically *Staphylococcus*, *Haemophilus*, *Pseudomonas*
○ Cor pulmonale
○ Allergic bronchopulmonary aspergillosis (ABPA)

Gastrointestinal/hepatic

○ Pancreatic insufficiency with resultant malabsorption (85%)
○ Meconium ileus
○ Distal intestinal obstruction syndrome (DIOS) or meconium ileus equivalent
○ Rectal prolapse (toddler presentation)
○ Chronic liver disease – mainly in teenage children (around 20%)

Endocrine

○ Insulin-dependent diabetes in 7% of patients – usually over-10s

Metabolic

○ Salt deficiency state: hyponatraemic, hypochloraemic metabolic alkalosis

Genitourinary

○ Azoospermia: male infertility

Management of cystic fibrosis

Multidisciplinary and often outpatient-based. Annual review or 'MOT' advised.

○ **Physiotherapy**: Percussion and vibration techniques, positive expiratory pressure (PEP) mask followed by coughing. Regular exercise.
○ **Optimise nutrition**: Required because patients with cystic fibrosis have increased metabolic demands, malabsorption and poor appetites. Involve paediatric dietician – high-calorie, high-protein diet with regular plotting of height and weight.
○ **Pancreatic enzyme supplements** (pancreatin) in pH-sensitive polymer capsules.
○ **Vitamin A, D and E supplementation** is necessary, as these are fat soluble. Plasma concentrations should be measured at annual review.
○ **Antibiotics**: Used to **reduce colonisation** and **treat acute chest infections.**
  • Flucloxacillin is used either prophylactically from diagnosis or long-term after colonisation with *Staphylococcus*
  • **Nebulised tobramycin/colomycin** in *Pseudomonas* colonisation
  • Acute infections are treated as they arise – often using results from the last cough swab/sputum samples
  • Oral **(ciprofloxacin)** or intravenous **(ceftazidime/ piperacillin** plus an aminoglycoside such as **gentamicin)** therapy can be started as appropriate
  • Be vigilant for *Burkholderia cepacia*.
○ **DNase**: To digest viscous DNA fragments derived from inflammatory cells.

○ **Treatment of co-existent conditions/complications**
- Asthma: bronchodilators
- ABPA: corticosteroids
- Constipation: laxatives
- DIOS: laxatives and hydration, through to Gastrografin® or even surgical treatment
- Liver disease: ursodeoxycholic acid.
- Cor pulmonale: heart–lung transplant.

○ **Separation of patients in clinic settings**: to reduce spread of harmful organisms such as *Burkholderia cepacia*.

○ Gene therapy: be aware of this although still in early stages.

Bronchiectasis

The chest presentation is as for cystic fibrosis, and cystic fibrosis is part of the differential diagnosis.

Aetiology

Some cases are idiopathic or due to the chronic presence of a foreign body. The rest are listed below:

○ Primary ciliary dyskinesia
○ Bronchiolitis obliterans (adenovirus, RSV, pertussis)
○ Alpha 1 antitrypsin deficiency
○ Asthma
○ Recurrent aspiration (H-type tracheo-oesophageal fistula or TOF)
○ Lobar sequestration
  • A non-functioning mass of embryonic tissue within the chest that receives its entire arterial supply from the aorta
  • Haemoptysis is common
  • There is a continuous murmur over the lesion
  • Needs aortography before removal because feeding vessel usually arises from abdomen
○ Immunodeficiency
  • Hypogammaglobulinaemia
  • IgA deficiency
  • Complement deficiency
  • Hyper IgE (Job's) syndrome
  • AIDS

Management

○ Education; aids compliance with treatment
○ Regular physiotherapy for life; encourage exercise where appropriate
○ Prophylactic antibiotics
○ Bronchodilators as bronchospasm is usually a prominent feature
○ Mucolytics when appropriate
○ Prompt immunisation – including influenza

Monitoring – regular clinic appointments to look at following:

○ Spirometry
○ Sputum cultures to detect colonising organism and its sensitivities
○ Monitor for cor pulmonale

○ Growth and nutrition are very important (can suffer due to a combination of increased metabolic rate and reduced intake). Offer nutritional supplements if necessary or feed in alternative ways, eg overnight nasogastric or gastrostomy feeds

Surgical treatment

○ Lobectomy may be necessary – involve Paediatric Surgeons early as need a window to operate when the child is clinically well enough for the procedure

Primary ciliary dyskinesia (PCD)

This is an autosomal-recessive group of disorders, the most common being Kartagener's syndrome.

Case

> Peter is a well-looking 7-year-old boy who appears small for his age and I would like to plot him on the appropriate height and weight centile charts. On examination he has clubbing, and is not cyanosed. Palpation of his apex beat reveals dextrocardia and auscultation of his chest reveals coarse crepitations at both bases. The most likely diagnosis is **Kartagener's syndrome**. I would like to examine the abdomen and enquire about a history of sinusitis...

Features of primary ciliary dyskinesia

- Bronchiectasis
- Nasal polyposis
- Chronic sinusitis
- Chronic suppurative otitis media
- Male infertility (common)

Half of all patients with PCD have Kartagener's syndrome with all of the above features plus:

- Dextrocardia (palpating for the apex beat, which will not be on the left *but on the right*, should alert you to this diagnosis!)
- Visceral situs inversus

Notes on ciliary dyskinesia

There is a defect in cilial ultrastructure, mobility or both. The most obvious effect is on the mucociliary escalator, which depends on cilia wafting mucus from the lower airways in a cephalic direction from where it is usually swallowed. The cilia look grossly normal but have ultrastructural defects of the dynein side arms. Primary ciliary dyskinesia occurs in 1:15 000 of the population, accounting for as much as 5% of children with recurrent respiratory disease. It usually presents with bronchiectasis after a troublesome period of chronic wet cough, sinusitis, nasal polyps and chronic suppurative otitis media. This condition should be considered in neonates with unexplained persistent tachypnoea, pneumonia with no risk factors and of course dextrocardia with situs inversus.

Diagnosis is made and management implemented with the help of the PCD Diagnostic Service, based in a small number of UK centres.

A useful initial test is to place a drop of saccharin on the nasal mucosa and measure the time until a sweet taste is sensed in the mouth (normally 11 min). Patients need to sit still for 1 h and not sniff, cough, eat or drink, which precludes testing many younger children! Patients as young as about 4 years can be screened using nasally exhaled nitric oxide measurements.

Nasociliary brushings are performed and motility assessed in vitro by photometry, giving a beat frequency and a comment on whether movement is dyskinetic. Electron microscopy will reveal ultrastructural abnormalities.

Prognosis: some patients have a normal lifespan, especially if they are diagnosed relatively early so that lung disease progression is modified (by educating patient about avoiding smoking/allergens and teaching them physiotherapy) and recurrent infections treated.

Chronic lung disease of infancy

This is a very common short case and a typical 'cross-over' case with the History Taking and Management Planning Station (see Section 2.3).

Case

> Jordan is 6 months old but looks small for his age. I would like to plot his weight, length and head circumference on a centile chart. He has nasal cannulae in situ which are connected to an oxygen cylinder. He also has a long, narrow head shape.
>
> There is no clubbing. He has a hyperexpanded chest. There is mild intercostal recession. He has two chest drain scars on the right and the dorsum of both hands have venepuncture scars. Auscultation of the chest reveals bilateral wheeze. The most likely diagnosis is **chronic lung disease.**
>
> I would like to perform a developmental examination...

Notes on chronic lung disease

The definition of chronic lung disease states that the child must have been ventilated after birth and be oxygen dependent at 28 days with evidence of respiratory distress and an abnormal chest X-ray. The incidence is rising as survival of extremely premature babies improves. Prevalence is 20% of all ventilated babies.

Associations: high levels of inspired oxygen, barotrauma and volutrauma, patent ductus arteriosus (PDA), air leak.

Clinical features

○ General appearance will be of an infant who is obviously small for chronological age

○ Head may have a characteristic scaphocephalic appearance and the face may look cushingoid (dexamethasone). Scaphocephaly refers to a long and narrow head shape (literally means 'boat shaped') and can occur from postnatal moulding in preterm infants or more rarely from premature closure of the sagittal suture

○ Chest drain or venesection scars should be looked for, and a thoracotomy scar suggests previous PDA ligation
○ Chest is usually hyperexpanded
○ Comment on the presence of cyanosis (unlikely in the exam), or respiratory distress
○ Stridor (secondary to prolonged intubation) or wheeze (reduced small airway diameter) may be present
○ Ask to examine the heart, in particular, for a PDA or a loud second heart sound of pulmonary hypertension
○ There may be an abdominal scar for a Nissen's fundoplication or gastrostomy
○ Last of all, mention that you would go on to perform a developmental examination

Differential diagnoses of this picture

○ Other causes of hyperexpanded chest/bronchiectasis
○ Immunodeficiency, eg severe combined immunodeficiency/chronic granulomatous disease
○ Chronic aspiration due to gastro-oesophageal reflux/repaired tracheo-oesophageal fistula
○ Congenital heart disease (eg atrioventricular septal defect), cardiac failure

Treatment

Current best evidence suggests the following:

○ Supplemental oxygen to maintain good saturations above 94%; if ventilated try and avoid volutrauma and barotrauma (permissive hypercapnoea)
○ Nutrition – additional calories are essential to combat increased energy expenditure
○ **Dexamethasone** if necessary – proven benefit in weaning off ventilator or decreasing oxygen requirement.
However, while glucocorticoids can improve lung function there are significant potential complications including hyperglycaemia, hypertension and intestinal perforation. They have not been shown to improve mortality. Some long-term follow-up studies have raised concern about an increased rate of cerebral palsy in patients given glucocorticoids although confounding factors make this difficult to interpret. Current practice is to

reserve glucocorticoid treatment for those who are on maximum ventilatory support with a high oxygen requirement and not showing signs of improvement. Because of the uncertainty about effects on neurodevelopmental outcome this decision is normally discussed with the parents

○ **Diuretics** are also shown to have short-term benefits in improving lung function but there is no evidence that they affect long-term outcome. Increase risks of nephrocalcinosis and electrolyte imbalance

○ Physiotherapy as appropriate

○ Gastro-oesophageal reflux is frequently present and a trial of therapy is worthwhile in difficult cases

○ Assess and treat complications, eg PDA, right-sided heart failure

Prognosis

○ Most weaned off oxygen prior to discharge

○ Long-term respiratory function tends to recover

○ High risk of hospital admission with intercurrent infections

○ Remember vaccinations including influenza and palivizumab (passive immunity vs RSV)

Kyphoscoliosis

○ Positional if disappears on bending down, otherwise it is structural and pathological

Aetiology

Commonly
○ Idiopathic (usually in pre-pubertal girls)
○ Cerebral palsy

Others
○ Duchenne muscular dystrophy
○ Spinal muscular atrophy (type II/III)
○ Friedreich's ataxia
○ Poliomyelitis
○ Neurofibromatosis type 1
○ Homocystinuria
○ Osteogenesis imperfecta
○ Marfan syndrome
○ Klippel–Feil sequence (fused cervical vertebrae, webbed neck, facial asymmetry, deafness, ventricular septal defect, renal anomalies, Sprengel shoulder)
○ Alagille's syndrome (broad forehead, prominent chin, posterior embryotoxon (opaque border to cornea), peripheral pulmonary artery stenosis, butterfly vertebrae, cholestasis)
○ Mucopolysaccharidoses (short, large head, macroglossia, hepatosplenomegaly, cloudy cornea in Hurler's)

Notes on kyphoscoliosis

Scoliosis is lateral curvature of the spine accompanied by rotation of the vertebral bodies and viscera. It causes a reduction in chest wall compliance and its major importance is reduction of lung volumes causing a restrictive defect. The earliest manifestation of this is a fall in P_aO_2 due to ventilation–perfusion mismatch at the bases. Later, hypoventilation results in hypercapnia. Finally, cor pulmonale develops in response to pulmonary hypertension. Investigation includes plain X-rays to demonstrate the angle of the scoliosis (correlates well with severity of reduction in lung volumes) and lung function testing to assess the restrictive defect. Overnight O_2 saturation monitoring assesses the degree of hypoxia, and is often combined with CO_2 studies.

Treatment involves monitoring for complications and treating as appropriate with the eventual need for corrective orthopaedic surgery in some.

Prognosis depends on the cause. Idiopathic scoliosis usually has a good outcome; outcome of scoliosis due to other causes depends on the prognosis of the underlying condition.

Stridor

It is just possible that you might see a (stable) child with stridor, which is a 'crowing' inspiratory noise due to upper airway obstruction.

Instructions to candidate

Look at this child's chest and tell me what you see and hear; what is the most likely reason for this?

What investigations are appropriate?

Case

> John is a well looking 2-month-old infant who looks well grown for his age, although I would like to plot him on a growth chart. There is audible stridor with slight sternal recession. There is no tachypnoea. There are no scars and I cannot see any haemangiomas on inspection of his skin. Chest expansion looks normal and there is no abnormality on auscultation. (Ask mother about feeding.) He is currently feeding without any problems. The most likely diagnosis is **laryngomalacia**, but I would also consider the following in my differential diagnosis...

Notes on stridor

The commonest cause of stridor is **laryngomalacia** or 'floppy larynx'. This condition presents soon after birth. If present at birth an alternative diagnosis should be sought. It is characteristically better when the child is laid prone. It normally has a benign course and resolves by 18 months. Some neonates and infants run into problems with feeding and a combination of poor intake and increased energy expenditure (accessory muscle use) may necessitate nasogastric tube feeding for a while. Patients sometimes need hospital admission during intercurrent respiratory infections.

Other causes to exclude:

○ **In a sick pyrexial child: acute epiglottitis, bacterial tracheitis, severe croup**
○ Inhaled foreign body
○ Prolonged neonatal intubation – subglottic stenosis

- Tracheo/bronchomalacia
- Pierre–Robin sequence
- Intraluminal web or haemangioma
- Extrinsic compression from vascular ring (double aortic arch, pulmonary sling or aberrant subclavian artery), lymphoma, branchial/thyroglossal cyst, cystic hygroma

Investigations

In children with laryngomalacia in whom a confident diagnosis can be made and there are no complications (eg failure to thrive, apnoea, respiratory distress, hoarseness), no investigations are required. In children in whom there is doubt about the diagnosis or an underlying cause is suspected, then fibre-optic laryngoscopy and bronchoscopy should be performed. A barium swallow and transoesophageal ECHO may be required to exclude a vascular ring.

Miscellaneous conditions

Pierre-Robin sequence

This sequence is caused by posterior attachment of the tongue (genioglossus) together with a small mandible. This results in glossoptosis and pseudomacroglossia. The tongue commonly falls back and obstructs the airway. There is sometimes a cleft palate. The mandible usually grows sufficiently within 6 months, but some children with severe recurrent obstruction will need either a nasopharyngeal airway or tracheostomy whilst this occurs.

Enlarged tongue

May also be seen in the "'Other' Station". Causes:
○ Hypothyroidism
○ Mucopolysaccharidoses/GMI gangliosidosis
○ Congenital hypothyroidism
○ Trisomy 21
○ Pseudomacroglossia
○ Beckwith–Wiedemann syndrome

Tracheostomy

Patients with a tracheostomy are usually well known to the examination centre and those who are well enough to be at home are often used for a few sessions on exam day. Their background condition may mean they can crop up in other stations. Management of blocked tracheostomy may be asked – please refer to *Advanced Paediatric Life Support – The Practical Approach* (An ALSG manual published by the BMJ group, currently in its 4th edition).

Indications
○ Subglottic stenosis (high tracheostomy)
○ Prolonged intubation
○ Severe gastro-oesophageal reflux
○ Irradiation
○ Neuromuscular weakness
○ Severe sleep apnoea

Complications

○ Hypoxia – due to partial (secretions) or complete obstruction
○ Decannulation
○ Ulceration
○ Infection
○ Bleeding
○ Arrhythmias (during suctioning)

YOUR NOTES

NEUROLOGY
(INCLUDING EYE EXAMINATION)

CONTENTS

11.1 Introduction

11.2 Cranial nerves and eyes
Suggested scheme for examination of the cranial nerves – older child
Suggested scheme for cranial nerve examination of the infant
Facial nerve palsy
Bell's palsy
Muscular disorders causing facial weakness
Suggested scheme for examination of the eyes

11.3 Cases and conditions: Cranial nerves and eyes
Ptosis
Squint
Nystagmus
Fundoscopic findings – notes on various signs
Systemic conditions with eye signs
Miscellaneous eye problems
Coloboma
Duane syndrome
Moebius syndrome
Uveitis

11.4 Central and peripheral nervous system
Suggested scheme for examination of the central and peripheral motor system

Suggested scheme for examination of gait
Suggested scheme for sensory examination
Suggested scheme for cerebellar examination
Abnormalities of posture and movement
11.5   Cases and conditions: central and peripheral nervous system
Cerebral palsy
Neuromuscular disease
Ataxia
Spina bifida
Neurocutaneous syndromes

11.1 INTRODUCTION

Neurology is a difficult subject about which to provide information on how to assess cases in the exam. There is a very large amount of potential information including considerable background information on specific subjects. We have confined ourselves principally to discussion of the potential scenarios you are likely to meet in the exam, along with thumbnail sketches of commoner conditions seen in the exam. We would recommend further reading of neurological examination as the information presented is intended to be a summary, and the neurological signs change in relation to age of the child.

11.2 CRANIAL NERVES AND EYES

The cranial nerves and the eyes have been included together because of the considerable overlap between the two subjects; they are best revised with this in mind.

Tip

Patients with eye signs may also be in the "Other" clinical station

---

Cranial nerve examination needs to be confident and it is essential to develop an examination scheme and practise it with colleagues. It is essential also to practise and be familiar with examination of the eyes. It is particularly important to remember that early on in the eye examination some assessment of visual acuity needs to be made. Do not be caught out by a blind child. The best way to practise eye examination and to learn about the common eye conditions is to sit in on clinics with the orthoptists and ophthalmologists. In particular this will ensure that you are clear about the formal assessment of visual acuity and can quickly and competently assess a squint.

Suggested scheme for examination of the cranial nerves – older child

This is a very commonly examined topic in short cases and your technique must become second nature. It is essential to practise cranial nerve examination on patients and, if necessary, on colleagues. In the past you were unlikely to be asked to examine all the cranial nerves in one case but now there are 9 min to fill. Be prepared for many different scenarios!

Tip

Always inform the child what you are about to do and if possible why

---

- Enquire about sense of smell (**olfactory nerve**), and be prepared to examine formally if requested
- Test visual acuity (**optic nerve**). Establish if the child can see (both eyes). If the child wears glasses offer to test the visual acuity with them on. This can be done grossly at the bedside by asking the child to read from an age-appropriate book, or to read a poster on the wall
- Comment on any obvious abnormality such as squint and go on to examine formally if present
- Examine visual fields – sit with your face opposite the child's, one metre apart. Cover your left eye and ask child or parent to cover child's right eye. Ask the child to say 'yes' when they can see your finger 'wiggling'. Move your finger in from the periphery at 2, 5, 8, 11 o'clock and 'wiggle' it. Test both eyes.
- **Examine eye movements (cranial nerves III, IV, VI)** – this is really very simple as long as you remember the patient's perspective. Ask the child to follow your finger/toy with their eyes. Keep the object being followed approximately 0.5 m from their face. The plane of movement should be parallel to the child's face. Keep your other hand on the child's forehead to steady it. Ask the child to tell you if they can see two of the object. Test lateral gaze and then vertical gaze

---

Tip

A common pitfall is to test to the extremes of vision, where most of us will have diplopia

---

▓ Check for nystagmus – present at extremes of gaze

▓ Test the **sensory divisions of the trigeminal nerve.** Ask the child to shut their eyes and to say 'yes' when they feel your touch. Gently touch the face at irregular intervals with a wisp of cotton wool, on each side, in each division of the nerve – ophthalmic, maxillary and mandibular. Ask the child if it feels the same on both sides

▓ Test the **motor component of the trigeminal nerve (V)** by asking the child to close their jaw tightly and palpate temporalis and masseters

▓ Mention corneal reflexes at the end

▓ Test the **motor division of the facial nerve (VII)**. Ask the patient to raise their eyebrows, puff out their cheeks and smile. Look for asymmetry. Remember the sensory division, which supplies the anterior two-thirds of the tongue with taste – not usually necessary to test

▓ Test the **auricular nerve (VIII)** grossly by asking the child if they can hear a very quiet noise that you make in each ear, eg whisper a number the child can repeat and occlude the other ear. Offer and know how to test formally (see Chapter 13). Ask parent about hearing

▓ The **glossopharyngeal nerve (IX)** can be tested by the gag reflex. This should not be attempted in the exam but do mention it. Remember that the gag reflex tests the glossopharyngeal (sensory) and vagal (motor) nerves. The glossopharyngeal nerve also supplies the posterior one-third of the tongue with sensation.

▓ Test the **vagal (X) nerve** by asking the child to say a short sentence. The voice will be hoarse if there is a vocal cord paralysis. The vagus can also be assessed at this point by asking the child to say 'ah' and looking at the soft palate

▓ Test **accessory nerve (XI)** by forced rotation of the head against resistance to check for sternomastoid weakness

▓ The **hypoglossal nerve (XII)** is tested by asking the patient to stick out their tongue and move it from side to side. Look for wasting and weakness

At the end of the examination (if you have not already done so) you should ask to:

▓ Examine patient's glasses

▓ Look at fundi

▓ Assess pupillary responses to light and accommodation, offer to check corneal (V) reflexes

Suggested scheme for cranial nerve examination of the infant

Don't panic! Observation is the key. Squint and facial nerve palsies would be the most likely scenarios in the Neurology Station. Babies are used far less frequently as the candidates do not get a uniform experience. You may be allowed to substitute questions for parts of the examination; making a baby cry to see if they have a facial palsy would not go down well! A modified Cranial nerve examination is summarised in Table 11.1.

Notes on cranial nerve lesions

Origins

○ III–IV: mid brain
○ V–VIII: pons
○ IX–XII: medulla or bulb

Olfactory nerve (I)

Traverses cribriform plate to frontal lobes, so lesions are most commonly detected in upper respiratory tract infections (URTIs), basal skull fractures, purulent meningitis, hydrocephalus. Remember anosmia also occurs in Kallman syndrome (associated hypogo-nadotrophic hypogonadism) caused by embryological neuronal migration defect.

Optic nerve (II)

Nerve fibres pass through the optic disc to the optic nerve. Nasal fibres decussate at the chiasm and optic tracts carry impulses to the lateral geniculate bodies. The optic radiation carries the impulses to the visual cortex.

Patterns of visual defect

Patterns of visual field defect occur thus:

○ **Blindness in one eye** – retinal, lens, optic nerve (chronic uveitis, optic nerve glioma, optic atrophy, septo-optic dysplasia)
○ **Bitemporal hemianopia** – craniopharyngiomas, pituitary tumours
○ **Homonymous hemianopia** – lesions posterior to chiasm, eg cortical lesions such as cerebral palsy
○ **Scotoma** – irregularly shaped visual field deficit arising from anywhere along the visual pathway; could be bilateral or monocular

Cranial nerve(s)	Activity	Comment
I	Smell	At least mention
II	Visual acuity	Response to examination?
III	Eye movement	Up, down, in
IV	Eye movement	Down and out
V	Chewing	Ask parent if baby can chew
VI	Eye movement	Lateral
VII	Crying? Smiling?	Ask re facial symmetry when crying
VIII	Hearing	Is there a startle reflex
IX	Gag	Do not test gag in exam!
X	Phonation	Palatal movement
XI	Head turning	Equal both sides
XII	Tongue protrusion	Central?
V, VII, IX	Sucking	If absent, is there hypotonia?
IX, X, XI	Swallowing	Ask if intact

Table 11.1: Summary table of cranial nerve examination – infant

Oculomotor nerve (III)

Palsy is apparent as a dilated pupil that faces 'down and out'. Usually congenital, associated with chromosomal abnormalities or cerebral palsy. Acquired palsy may indicate tumours, infection or head injury.

Trochlear nerve (IV)

This nerve controls the superior oblique muscle. Usually presents subtly as head tilt towards the unaffected eye. On examination there is upward deviation of the eye and diplopia on downward vertical gaze. Causes include raised intracranial pressure as the nerve has a long intracranial course. Will need surgical correction if head tilt is significant.

Trigeminal nerve (V)

Has three sensory divisions (ophthalmic, maxillary, mandibular), which pass into the trigeminal ganglion at the apex of the petrous temporal bone. The motor fibres originate in the pons and supply the muscle of mastication.

Lesions are caused by:

○ Brainstem gliomas
○ Infarction/AV malformation

O   Acoustic neuromas
O   Chronic suppurative otitis media
O   Cavernous sinus thrombosis

Abducens nerve (VI)

The abducens nerve controls the lateral rectus muscle. Lesions of this nerve cause a marked convergent paralytic squint. The affected eye is turned nasally and is unable to abduct fully. Causes include raised intracranial pressure, tumours, arteriovenous (AV) malformations, meningitis.

Facial nerve (VII)

The facial nerve has a long intracranial course: initially it is closely related to the sixth nerve (lesions in the pons therefore tend to affect both nerves) and then it emerges from the cerebellopontine angle (lesions here also affect nerves V, VI and VIII) and runs in the petrous bone in close relation to the middle ear.

An upper motor neurone lesion causes weakness of the lower part of the face on the side opposite the lesion; the forehead is spared as it is bilaterally innervated. Lower motor neurone lesions cause weakness of the whole side of the face on the same side as the lesion.

Auditory nerve (VIII)

Passes through cerebellopontine angle.

Glossopharyngeal (IX), vagus (X) and hypoglossal (XII) nerves

All leave through the jugular foramen and are affected by lesions at the base of the skull such as achondroplasia and Arnold–Chiari malformation

Cases related to nerve lesions

Facial nerve palsy

This is a very common short case.

Examination

O   Smile

○ Frown
○ Raise the eyebrows
○ Puff out the cheeks
○ Whistle
○ Close the eyes and keep them closed against a resistance
○ **Finally**, offer to check blood pressure, look in the ears for signs on infection or rash, inspect the skin for a rash (?erythema migrans), assess hearing (?acoustic neuroma) and look for signs of exposure keratitis in the eyes (from incomplete lid closure)

Tip

Lower motor neurone lesion affects the upper and lower face
Upper motor neurone lesion spares upper face

Aetiology of facial nerve palsy

Lower motor neurone lesions

○ Bell's palsy (by far the commonest)
○ Ramsay–Hunt syndrome – an eruption of herpes zoster vesicles on the posterior wall of the ear canal accompanied by a lower motor neurone facial nerve palsy. Spontaneous recovery is the rule
○ Chronic serous otitis media
○ Intracranial tumours
○ Mumps
○ Lyme disease
○ Guillain–Barré (usually bilateral)
○ Congenital – associated with obstetric forceps
○ Skull fractures

Upper motor neurone lesions

○ Cerebral palsy
○ Tumours
○ Moebius syndrome – loss of function of motor cranial nerves; child will have a strabismus and an immobile face because cranial nerves VI and VII most commonly affected. Extremely rare

Bell's palsy

Usually unilateral; most are idiopathic

Management

○ Exclude hypertension
○ Exclude other causes
 - Lyme disease, particularly if bilateral. Many centres advocate serological testing for any patient with Bell's palsy who has visited a tick-infested area in the preceding few months.
 - Varicella (varicella titres)
 - Leukaemia (thorough examination and screen with FBC and film)
○ Treat with steroids, oral **aciclovir** (some evidence of benefit) and eye drops (artificial tears)

Prognosis

○ The prognosis is generally good and is better in children than in adults
○ All patients show signs of recovery by 4 weeks if they are going to recover

Muscle disorders causing facial weakness

○ Myotonic dystrophy
○ Facioscapulohumeral muscular dystrophy
○ Congenital myopathies
○ Mitochondrial myopathies
○ Myasthenic syndromes

Bulbar and pseudo-bulbar palsy

A **bulbar palsy** describes a **lower motor neurone** lesion resulting in weakness of the muscles supplied by those cranial nerves whose nuclei lie in the medulla (or bulb), ie IX–XII. It is very unusual in children.

A **pseudo-bulbar palsy** results from bilateral supranuclear **upper motor neurone** lesions of the lower cranial nerves, resulting in poor tongue and pharynx movement. This is far more common than bulbar palsy, particularly in association with spastic quadriplegia.

Signs of a pseudo-bulbar palsy

○ Stiff spastic tongue that is not wasted
○ 'Dry' voice and dysarthria
○ Preserved gag and palatal reflexes
○ Exaggerated jaw jerk

Suggested scheme for examination of the eyes

- Look at the child for any obvious clues, eg squint, ptosis, dysmorphology
- Does the child wear glasses?
- Look at the eyes – conjunctiva, pupils, lids
- Can the child see? Test both eyes separately; visual acuity
- Visual fields
- Eye movements
- Check for nystagmus
- Accommodation
- Pupil responses – direct and consensual light reflexes
- Cover test
- Fundoscopy

Notes on eye examination

Observation

- This is very important, much pathology being visible on observation.
- Look first at the child
  - Do they look normal, are there any obvious dysmorphic features?
  - Is the child thriving?
  - Is the child displaying behaviour suggestive of visual impairment, such as light gazing (cortical disease) or eccentric fixation with nystagmus?
- Look closely at the eye for the following
  - Squint
  - Coloboma
  - Corneal clouding
  - Lesions of the iris
  - Ptosis
  - Anophthalmia (glass eye)
  - Microphthalmia

THE EFFECT OF GLASSES

This is clearly of importance and it is sensible to look at a few children with their glasses on before the exam to assess their vision and the effect of glasses.

Convex glasses correct long sightedness (difficulty with near vision)

Concave glasses correct short sightedness (difficulty with distant vision)

Visual acuity

For a **small child** the information you will gain will be limited and should be augmented by comments about their behaviour. Check that they can fix and follow in the horizontal and vertical planes. Use an interesting but silent toy or your face.

Tip

Take care to keep quiet because if you give auditory clues you will render the examination invalid

For **older children** use a suitable picture or story book (age dependent – don't ask a 4-year-old to read!) for near vision and use a Snellen chart for far vision. Test both eyes separately with and without glasses (if worn).

Tip

Check vision in both eyes separately and don't get caught out by unilateral visual loss. If you suspect early on that a child is blind in one eye continue to examine both eyes as instructed

Visual fields/eye movements/nystagmus

See 'Suggested scheme for examination of the cranial nerves – older child' (Section 11.2) and see Section 11.3 for nystagmus.

Accommodation

Ask the child to fix their gaze on your finger held in front of your face. Move your finger towards the child until it is touching their nose. Note their eye movements and pupillary responses.

Squint testing

See below.

Pupil responses

Test direct and consensual light reflexes.

Fundoscopy

Many candidates are asked to do this and you must appear proficient. Remember to examine for the red reflex first (from a distance of around 20 cm), then examine the anterior chamber and then the fundus.

11.3 CASES AND CONDITIONS: CRANIAL NERVES AND EYES

Ptosis

This is a very common short case and you will be invited either to comment on or examine the patient's eyes.

Instructions to candidate

Examine this 12-year-old boy with ptosis

Case

> *This young man has a left ptosis. He is a well-looking boy and there are no dysmorphic features. I would like to examine his eyes. His eyes look normal. The pupils are symmetrical. There is no obvious squint. I would like to test his vision – candidate gets him to read – vision appears normal in both eyes (tested separately). His visual fields and eye movements are normal. His direct and consensual reflexes and his ability to accommodate are normal.*
>
> *I suspect therefore that his ptosis is congenital.*

Notes on ptosis

The examiner will expect you to examine the eyes carefully and in doing so come up with a likely cause of the ptosis. The ptosis will become apparent on inspection. At this stage, on noting the ptosis you need to have a clear differential diagnosis in your mind.

Ptosis may be broadly classified as syndromic or neurological in origin and so it is a condition where you can earn 'points' by suggesting other systems/organs to examine.

Most likely in exam:

○ Horner's syndrome
○ Third nerve palsy
○ Myasthenia gravis
○ Congenital

Full differential diagnosis of ptosis

Syndromic

- Noonan's syndrome
- Rubinstein–Taybi (microcephaly, broad thumbs and toes, mental retardation)
- Smith–Lemli–Opitz syndrome
- Marcus Gunn (aberrant innervation causes the affected lid to raise and wink when the child chews or cries)

Neurological

- Third nerve palsy
- Horner's syndrome (see below)
- Myasthenia gravis
- Dystrophia myotonica
- Craniosynostosis
- Neuroblastoma

Others

- Congenital (evaluate early to prevent amblyopia)
- Ocular tumours (rhabdomyosarcoma)

Notes on Horner's syndrome

Lesion of the sympathetic nervous system in association with the brainstem, cervical cord or a lesion of the sympathetic plexus in association with the carotid artery.

Features are:

- Partial ptosis
- Pupil constriction
- Enophthalmos
- Ipsilateral anhidrosis
- Heterochromia iridis (complete when one iris is a different colour from the other; partial when part of one iris is a different colour from the rest) – indicates congenital Horner's syndrome
- Normal direct and consensual reflex

Squint

Examination of a squint (see Box) is commonly asked in the exam and needs to be practised carefully. It is best to get an orthoptist to help you to perfect your technique.

EXAMINATION OF SQUINT

○ Check the child can see first – with both eyes!
○ Corneal reflections
○ Eye movements
○ Cover test

Notes on squint examination

Go straight to this after testing visual acuity. If you pick up a squint offer to test the child first without and then with their glasses, if prescribed. The child needs to be co-operative for this to work.

Corneal reflections

Observe both eyes whilst shining a point source of light at both corneas (corneal reflections). The light source should be held about 30 cm from the eyes and in different planes. If the eyes are straight the reflection from both corneas will be symmetrical. If a squint is present the reflection will be asymmetrical. Beware of epicanthic folds or hypertelorism giving a false impression of squint.

Eye movements

Eye movements should be examined in all directions using an interesting object. If the eyes deviate, ie there is asymmetry, then a squint is present. If the deviation is worse in one direction then it is paralytic. If it is equal in all directions, it is non-paralytic.

If it is paralytic you should be able to say which cranial nerve is involved (III, IV, VI) (see Box).

FEATURES OF A THIRD (OCULOMOTOR) NERVE LESION

○ Complete ptosis
○ Diplopia
○ Downward and lateral gaze (unopposed lateral rectus and superior oblique muscles)
○ Pupil dilatation
○ Failure of the pupil to react to light or to accommodate

FEATURES OF A FOURTH (TROCHLEAR) NERVE LESION

○ Diplopia
○ Failure of inferior-lateral gaze (failure of the superior oblique muscle) – difficult to read

FEATURES OF A SIXTH (ABDUCENS) NERVE LESION

○ Diplopia
○ Medial gaze (failure of the lateral rectus muscle)

The following tests should be done at near and far vision, first with glasses and then without. This avoids missing a squint caused by excessive adduction secondary to hypermetropia. Inward deviation is denoted by eso-; outward deviation, exo-.

Cover/uncover test

This examines for a **manifest (-tropia) squint**. Ask the child to fix on an interesting object at 1 m and then 6 m. Cover the eye that appears to be fixing. If the other eye takes up fixation then there is a manifest squint present.

Alternate cover test

Again, ask the child to fixate on an interesting object at 1 m and then 6 m. Alternately, cover each eye back and forth. Look at each eye as it is just uncovered: if it moves to take up fixation then a **latent (-phoria) squint** is present.

Non-paralytic squint

Most squints will be **non-paralytic**. You may be asked about treatment of non-paralytic squint. There are two main aims. The first is to achieve the best possible vision in each eye. Any underlying defects such as cataracts or refractive errors are corrected, and amblyopia is prevented with occlusion therapy. Secondly, achieve the best possible ocular alignment.

Surgery is commonly required.

Nystagmus

Instructions to candidate
Look at this boy's eyes

Case

> Jack is a well-looking 10-year-old boy who has pale skin, blue eyes and fair hair. Examination of his eyes reveals that he usually wears sunglasses, there is nystagmus and reduced visual acuity. Red reflexes are easily visible. I suspect he has oculocutaneous albinism.

What are the long-term consequences?

○ Blindness and skin cancer

What is the inheritance?

○ Autosomal recessive (ocular albinism alone is X-linked recessive)

Notes on nystagmus

○ **Cerebellar nystagmus** is the most important type to recognise. It is usually horizontal and worsens on looking to the side of the lesion, with the fast component directed towards the side of the lesion

○ **Vestibular nystagmus** differs in that the slow phase is directed towards the side of the lesion

○ **Vertical nystagmus** is usually due to a lesion of the brainstem at the pontomedullary junction (roughly at the foramen magnum), eg achondroplasia, or Arnold–Chiari malformations

○ **Ocular nystagmus** with slow searching movements occurs in blindness

○ **Congenital nystagmus** appears after a few months, is usually bilateral and often improves with age

Fundoscopic findings – notes on various signs

Papilloedema

The stages of papilloedema are:

1. The optic nerve becomes hyperaemic
2. Small capillaries on the optic disc disappear as they become compressed
3. Venous pulsations are no longer seen
4. The border of the optic disc becomes indistinct
5. Flame-shaped haemorrhage appears around optic disc

Causes

○ Raised intracranial pressure – late sign
○ Brain tumours – craniopharyngioma, brainstem glioma, astrocytoma, medulloblastoma
○ Leukaemia
○ Benign intracranial hypertension
○ Hydrocephalus
○ Hypertension
○ Pseudotumour cerebri
○ Infection
○ Encephalopathy
○ Intracranial haemorrhage
○ Craniosynostosis

Cherry red spot – causes

○ Tay-Sachs disease
○ Niemann–Pick disease
○ GM1 gangliosidosis
○ Sandhoff disease
○ Mucolipidosis

Lens dislocation – causes

○ **Marfan syndrome** – lens dislocation is present in 80% of adults and 50% of 5-year-olds with Marfan syndrome. It usually dislocates superiorly and temporally. Symptoms include blurred vision, due to refractive changes, and diplopia. If the pupil is dilated the edge of the lens may be seen as a black crescent on ophthalmoscopic examination. A clearer view is obtained with slit lamp examination; mention this in the exam
○ Homocystinuria
○ Ehlers–Danlos syndrome

Cataracts – causes

○ Metabolic disease, eg galactosaemia
○ Wilson's disease
○ Hypoparathyroidism
○ Diabetes
○ Dystrophica myotonica
○ Intrauterine infections
○ Traumatic insult to the eye

Corneal clouding – causes

○ GM1 gangliosidosis
○ Fucosidosis
○ Mucopolysaccharidosis
○ Mucolipidosis

Systemic conditions with eye signs

Condition	Sign
Neurofibromatosis	Lisch nodule, ptosis
Wilson's disease	Kayser–Fleischer ring
Ataxia telangiectasia	Conjunctival telangiectasia
Down syndrome	Brushfield spots – not pathognomonic
Hyperthyroidism	Exophthalmos, lid lag
Juvenile chronic arthritis	Iridocyclitis

Table 11.2: Systemic conditions with eye signs

Miscellaneous eye problems

Coloboma

Sometimes seen in the examination. Either inherited (autosomal dominant) or as part of the conditions listed below:

- Aniridia – Wilms' association
- CHARGE association
- Goldenhar syndrome

Duane syndrome

A congenital abnormality of innervation causing simultaneous contraction of medial and lateral recti on attempted adduction of the affected eye. On examination they may have exotropia or esotropia, and on testing eye movements they may have failure to abduct or adduct the affected eye.

Moebius syndrome

This is manifest as a (usually) bilateral but asymmetrical lower motor neurone facial nerve palsy, associated particularly with sixth nerve palsies. These cause failure of abduction and paralytic convergent squints of the affected eyes. The cause is unknown, but as both cranial nerves are closely related it may be due to underdevelopment of the cranial nerve nuclei.

Uveitis

This is inflammation of the uveal tract consisting of the inner vascular coat of the eye, the iris, the ciliary body and choroid. Iritis may occur alone or in conjunction with the ciliary body as iridocyclitis. This commonly occurs insidiously without symptoms and for this reason children with seropositive (ANA) arthritis need to have regular eye review.

Case

Jane is a well-looking 8-year-old girl. She appears cushingoid. Examination of her eyes reveals conjunctival injection. The visual acuity of her left eye is markedly reduced. It was not possible to examine the visual fields. The pupil responses are present but slow on the left. Ophthalmoscopy reveals clouding of the cornea on the left. There is normal visual acuity in her right eye with normal pupil responses and no clouding of the cornea.

*This would fit with **chronic uveitis**. I would like to proceed to a full systemic examination, paying particular attention to the joints and looking for the side-effects of steroids.*

11.4 CENTRAL AND PERIPHERAL NERVOUS SYSTEM

Suggested scheme for examination of the central and peripheral motor system

This needs to be done carefully and correctly. It is essential to practise and make your technique second nature. Remember to look for obvious clues first (eg obvious neurological deficit such as cerebral palsy, orthoses, wheelchairs). The examiner may limit you to the arms or the legs. You should have a different approach to infants compared with older children.

Infants

Most information is gained by **observation** and so spend some time watching and playing with the infant. Have a look at the child from head to toe when you walk into the room:

- Look for any obvious dysmorphology
- Try to get eye contact – see if the child will fix and follow in the horizontal and vertical planes
- Is the child moving any limbs? Remember that a baby lifting their right arm has at least grade 3 power in that limb. Ask the mother about hand preference, which is abnormal under 1 year
- Look specifically for leg scissoring (spastic diplegia), paucity of movement on one side (hemiplegia), overall paucity of movement (spinal muscular atrophy)

Perform a brief **neurodevelopmental assessment**. It is essential to know the normal milestones (see Section 13.2, Chapter 13). During this assessment you will be able to assess **tone** and **power**.

- Pull the child to sit – use one hand to pull up both hands and the other to support the head. This is the best way to assess head control because if the child is held prone and the head is extended, this may reflect extensor spasm
- Hold the child by the trunk in the sitting position
- Assess standing posture if possible
- Hold the child up prone looking at tone and head control
- Place the child on the bed prone to see if the child supports its head, supports itself on its forearms (3 months) or on outstretched hands (6 months)

▓   Proceed with further examination dependent upon the initial findings, eg tone and power in all four limbs

Proceed to examine the **tendon reflexes** as you would in an older child. Remember to examine for **ankle clonus** (one or two beats are normal under 1 year) and **plantar reflexes** (up-going until 1 year).

Finally, examine for the presence of the **primitive reflexes,** eg Moro, asymmetric tonic neck reflex, grasp, etc. These are described in Chapter 13. Give some warning before attempting a Moro reflex; it is sometimes unpleasant for the infant and it may be enough just to ask if you can perform it.

Older children

This should be done more conventionally as most older children can co-operate. Observe the child as you walk in and introduce yourself. Ask the child to walk first unless there is an obvious reason why they cannot (eg in a wheelchair). Look for clues as above. Their gait may tell you where to focus the rest of the examination.

▓   Look at their muscle bulk, symmetry and for scars, eg tendo-achilles shortening
▓   Examine tone – include testing for clonus
▓   Examine power
▓   Examine reflexes
▓   Examine co-ordination
▓   Further examination as appropriate eg sensory, cerebellar

You may well be asked to focus on just a part of the neurological examination such as a cerebellar assessment.

Upper motor neurone or lower motor neurone lesion?

This relatively straightforward piece of information (Table 12.3) is often asked for and is a reproducible discriminator between a good and bad candidate. It is very important to be ready for this question with the correct answer as a number of candidates when asked this do not appreciate what information the examiner is requesting.

Observe for clues then examine tone, power and reflexes.

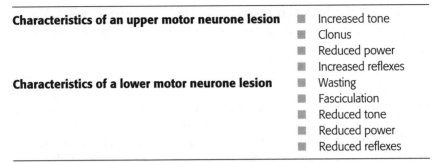

Characteristics of an upper motor neurone lesion	Increased tone
	Clonus
	Reduced power
	Increased reflexes
Characteristics of a lower motor neurone lesion	Wasting
	Fasciculation
	Reduced tone
	Reduced power
	Reduced reflexes

Table 11.3: Characteristics of upper and lower motor neurone lesions

Tell the examiner which type of lesion this is and clearly explain how you came to this conclusion.

Suggested scheme for examination of gait

The examination of gait is very important and often asked. The question can either be a direct one or be phrased indirectly such as '**examine this child's legs**' when, providing the child can walk, gait examination is the appropriate first step.

Gait problems can be due to the following:

- Hemiplegia
- Diplegia
- Ataxia
- Neuromuscular disease
- Orthopaedic problems (can develop from spasticity)
- Rheumatological disorders (more likely to be in 'Other' Station)
- Secondary to a limp

Children with abnormal gaits need to be viewed (try child development unit or general outpatients) so that you have seen common abnormalities and are able to spot them in the exam. It is sensible to use a scheme for examination and one is suggested below. Before you launch into an examination, first check with the child or parents that they can walk.

- Look at the child – do they look dysmorphic, is there an obvious cerebral palsy, is there a built up shoe?
- Look at their surroundings for equipment – are there sticks or a wheelchair nearby?
- Ask them to walk and decide whether their gait is spastic, ataxic or due to a neuromuscular problem. These categories are your best bet as you are in a Neurology station!

░   Don't forget to **look at the spine** at some point in the examination. It is an essential part of examining the lower limbs and candidates have failed for missing it out

Spastic gait

Ask the child to walk unaided – look at arm and leg movement for signs of a hemiplegia. The arm will be flexed on the affected side. If you suspect hemiplegia ask the child to walk fast or walk on tip toe, which will make the neurology more pronounced. Continue looking – are the legs stiff and adducted, if so a diplegia is likely. A diplegia will also become more pronounced if you ask the child to walk fast or on tip toe.

░   If the child has either a hemiplegia or a diplegia you can then take the child to the examination couch and confirm the neurology with a careful peripheral neurological examination
░   You may then be asked if you want to examine anywhere else – upper limbs, cranial nerves, skin (neurocutaneous syndrome)

Ataxic gait

If the gait is not spastic and seems unsteady and/or broad based the next thing to consider is whether it is ataxic. Ataxia is the incoordination that results from either **sensory loss** or **cerebellar dysfunction**. In children the latter cause is by far the most common.

░   Ask the child to walk heel-to-toe; you will need to demonstrate this. If the child is ataxic this will be difficult
░   Then ask the child to stand still – they should fall over towards the side of a cerebellar lesion
░   Ask the child to close their eyes. If the lesion is cerebellar there should be no deterioration. If the ataxia is as a consequence of a dorsal column problem the child will fall (Romberg's sign). The latter is rare in childhood
░   If you feel the gait is ataxic and due to a cerebellar lesion confirm this with a **cerebellar examination**. This is detailed later below in 'Suggested scheme for cerebellar examination'

Neuromuscular problem

If neither of the above seem applicable the next possibility is that you are dealing with either a neuromuscular or a lower motor neurone problem:

░   Look for a **waddling gait** and **foot drop**
░   Examine for **Gower's sign**. Ask the child to sit on the floor and then stand up without using their hands for assistance. A positive Gower's is when the

child rises from the floor by pushing off and crawling up their legs with their hands, to overcome proximal pelvic weakness

▓ If the Gower's sign is positive a peripheral neurological examination should be carried out and the back checked for a scoliosis or spina bifida

Others

Finally, consider either an orthopaedic or a rheumatological problem.

Notes on examination of gait

Limp

The aetiology of limp is divided into two groups: non-painful and painful.

Non-painful limp is also known as a **Trendelenburg gait**. Here the child shifts their centre of gravity over the affected side for balance and this is an indicator of proximal muscle weakness or hip instability. Trendelenburg positive implies the affected hip is lower than the unaffected hip. Causes are:

○ Congenital hip dislocation
○ Neurological (muscular dystrophy)
○ Slipped capital femoral epiphysis

Painful limp gives the child an **antalgic gait**. Here the child spends the least amount of time possible on the affected limb. This is Trendelenburg negative, which implies that the affected hip is higher than the unaffected hip as the centre of gravity is shifted away from it.

Causes are:

○ Infection
○ Trauma
○ Perthes' disease
○ Rheumatological (juvenile idiopathic arthritis)

Suggested scheme for sensory examination

This would be very difficult in the context of the exam. The appropriate equipment should be provided. Your approach to the child will be important and you need to encourage co-operation to gain maximum information. For older children you should have a polished technique so that you not only put the child at ease, but are able to concentrate on the signs elicited. How you phrase your questions and the precise instructions you give are the key to giving a convincing, confidence-inspiring performance. When preparing for this station, get a colleague or senior to watch you doing this and give feedback.

○ Pain, light touch and temperature – spinothalamic tracts
○ Joint position sense, vibration and proprioception – posterior columns

You may then be asked to give a sensory level if appropriate. This will require a thorough knowledge of dermatomes.

Suggested scheme for cerebellar examination

There is no definite order in which to do this. Fortunately it is rarely called upon. However, if asked to examine cerebellar function you need to have your own scheme. Make sure you do not move the child around more than is necessary.

Below is a suggested scheme.

○ Introduce yourself and ask the child a question – listen for dysarthria
○ Think of the causes of ataxia whilst observing the child and look for associated signs, eg telangiectasia or pes cavus
○ Ask the child to walk. Observe the gait, which will be ataxic and broad based, leaning towards the side of the lesion if unilateral
○ Ask the child to sit to check for truncal ataxia
○ Examine the arms and legs for hypotonia and hyporeflexia
○ Test eye movements and look for nystagmus – horizontal and maximal looking to the side of the lesion
○ Test co-ordination. Ask the child to touch their finger and then your nose with their index finger. Look for past pointing or intention tremor. Assess rapidly alternating movements (dysdiadochokinesis)
○ Stand the child up and examine for **Romberg's sign** to differentiate sensory posterior column disease from cerebellar disease. The child is asked to stand with their feet just sufficiently apart to become steady. The child then closes their eyes. If the child has a cerebellar problem there is no deterioration in balance. If the child has a sensory ataxia then he or she will fall

Abnormalities of posture and movement

During your neurological examination you may notice sustained abnormalities in the child's movement or posture. These abnormalities can usually be categorised as **tremor, myotonia, dystonia, chorea, athetosis or tics.**

Remember that dystonia and choreoathetosis are abnormalities of posture and movement secondary to extrapyramidal dysfunction.

Tremor

○ Physiological
○ Drug induced – salbutamol, thyroxine
○ Benign essential tremor – positive family history, intentional
○ Cerebellar – not present at rest (intentional)
○ Parkinson's (rare) – present at rest (not intentional)

Myotonia

○ The failure of muscle to relax after contraction

Dystonia

○ Abnormal posturing of the limbs, trunk and face
○ Can occur in association with choreoathetosis
○ For example, cerebral palsy, drug induced, Wilson's disease

Chorea

○ Rapid irregular repetitive jerking, either generalised or affecting one part of the body

Athetosis

○ Slow writhing movement of the limbs

Tic

○ A sudden brief and purposeless stereotyped movement which can, at least to some extent, be suppressed by voluntary effort

When you have picked up signs of disordered movement or posture present your findings succinctly to the examiner as in the case below.

Case

John is a 12-year-old boy in a wheelchair. He is mentally alert but has dystonic posturing with choreoathetoid movements. The diagnosis is cerebral palsy and likely causes of the cerebral palsy include perinatal asphyxia or kernicterus.

Useful lists

These lists are essential knowledge and will enhance the way you present an abnormality. For example, an examiner may disagree with your grading of power and ask you how you derived it.

Reflexes – spinal segments and nerve roots involved

Reflex	Spinal segment	Nerve
Biceps	C5,6	Musculocutaneous
Supinator or brachioradialis jerk	C5,6	Radial
Triceps	C6,7	Radial
Superficial abdominal	T7–12	
Knee	L2–4	Femoral
Ankle	S1	Tibial
Plantars	S1	

Table 11.4: Reflexes – the spinal segments and nerve roots involved

Spinal levels of some cutaneous reflexes

- Superficial abdominal: T7–12
- Cremasteric: L1
- Plantar: S1
- Anal: S4–5

Power – MRC grading

0	No contraction
1	Flicker or trace of contraction
2	Active movement with gravity eliminated
3	Active movement against gravity
4	Active movement against gravity and resistance
5	Normal power

Myotomes

Movement tested	Nerve root
Shoulder abduction	C5/6
Elbow flexion	C5/6
Elbow extension	C7/8
Finger flexion	C8
Finger abduction	C8/T1
Hip flexion	L1
Hip adduction	L2
Knee extension	L3
Foot dorsiflexion	L4
Foot plantar flexion	S1
Knee flexion	S2
Hip flexion	S3

Table 11.5: Myotomes

11.5 CASES AND CONDITIONS: CENTRAL AND PERIPHERAL NERVOUS SYSTEM

Cerebral palsy

Children with varying types and severities of cerebral palsy may be seen in the examination. The cases used as examples are meant to get you thinking about how to deal with and talk about children with cerebral palsy who you see in the exam. You need to make contact with whoever runs the child development unit in your area and arrange to see and discuss some cases.

Remember the definition – cerebral palsy is a **persistent, but not necessarily unchanging, disorder of movement and posture due to a non-progressive disorder of the immature brain.** As this excludes diagnoses such as brain tumours and spinal cord disease, try not to mention them as causes!

Children with cerebral palsy and their families are often asked to help out in the History Taking and Management Planning Station. Such a case is discussed in the relevant section, along with extensive notes on this variable condition.

NB When interacting with a child who has cerebral palsy do not make the assumption that no children with this problem have normal intelligence. Many children have a cognitive ability that exceeds their ability to communicate. Always talk to patients as well as parents even if this is difficult and there is little reciprocation – after all this should be normal practice on the wards and in outpatient clinics.

Cases

For the Clinical Station, most patients with cerebral palsy can be categorised into those with hemiplegia/monoplegia, quadriplegia, ataxia or dyskinetic (eg athetoid) cerebral palsy.

NB Some children have a mixed form of cerebral palsy.

Case one

> *Peter is a thin 5-year-old boy who walks with a Trendelenburg-positive gait, there is muscle wasting and decreased tone in the left leg. He has brisk reflexes with up-going plantars and short tendo-achilles in the left side. No involvement of the left arm or any other limb.*

Diagnosis – monoplegia involving the left leg.

Discussion points

○ You may be asked to go through causes. Remember to categorise them as prenatal, perinatal or postnatal and to appreciate that the cause may well be unknown

○ Why has he got a tight tendo-achilles on the affected side (contractures)?

○ How would you treat his shortened Achilles tendon (physiotherapy and surgery if necessary)?

Case two

Jade is a thin-looking 10-year-old girl with gross muscle wasting of all four limbs. She is lying in a windswept position (alternatively, she could be in a wheelchair with support). She is drooling. There is generalised hypertonia with contractures and increased reflexes. Both plantars are up-going...

The **diagnosis** is **spastic quadriplegia**. I would like to examine the cranial nerves as she may have a pseudo-bulbar palsy.

Discussion points

○ Why might there be problems feeding her orally (pseudo-bulbar palsy)?

○ What alternative methods of feeding could be used (gastrostomy)?

Case three

Ellie is a thin 9-year-old girl who is sitting supported in a wheelchair. She is drooling. There is truncal hypotonia with four-limb hypertonia and hyper-reflexia with striking choreoathetoid movements...

The **diagnosis** is **athetoid cerebral palsy**.

Discussion points

○ This type of cerebral palsy falls under the group of **dyskinetic** forms, which result from a lesion in the extrapyramidal system or basal ganglia. In dyskinesia there is increased muscle tone and abnormal posturing, as well as involuntary movements. These are more obvious when the child is attempting an activity voluntarily

○ What uncommon neonatal problem might be the cause (perinatal asphyxia, hyperbilirubinaemia leading to kernicterus)?

Case four

> Robert is a well-nourished 14-year-old boy with a broad-based ataxic gait. He has increased tone and brisk reflexes in his legs, with normal tone and reflexes in his arms. He has nystagmus and an intention tremor with past-pointing. He is Romberg's negative.

Diagnosis – cerebellar ataxia with a diplegia, which therefore suggests ataxic cerebral palsy.

Discussion points

○ This would be a difficult case and a good differential of the causes of cerebellar ataxia would be called for. The important thing is to demonstrate good examination technique and have confidence in your findings, even if you have difficulty pulling them together to make a diagnosis

Neuromuscular disease

This is another group of disorders seen with disproportionately high frequency in the exam and hence you need to know about them in considerable detail. These include diseases affecting the lower motor neurone at one of the following sites: **anterior horn cell, nerve fibre, neuromuscular junction or muscle.**

There are certain cases that are frequently seen in the exam.

There are two main scenarios, which we will deal with separately: the older child with neuromuscular disease and the floppy infant.

The older child

Commonly seen cases in the exam

- Duchenne muscular dystrophy
- Kugelberg–Welander disease
- Dermatomyositis
- Peroneal muscular atrophy

Differential diagnosis of neuromuscular disease in the older child

This may well be asked for once you have presented your findings (see Table 11.6). The easiest way to remember this for most people is to think of the reflex arc and start 'proximally' at the anterior horn cell and move distally from the nerve fibre to the neuromuscular junction and then muscle. More likely diagnoses in the exam are listed first in each section.

Anterior horn cell	Spinal muscular atrophy	
	Poliomyelitis	
Nerve fibre	Peroneal muscular atrophy	
	Infectious polyneuritis – Guillain–Barré syndrome	
	Leukodystrophies	
	Poisons	
Neuromuscular junction	Myasthenia gravis	
Muscle	Muscular dystrophy	Duchenne
		Becker's
		Facioscapulohumeral dystrophy
		Limb girdle dystrophy
	Dystrophia myotonica	
	Inflammatory, eg polymyositis, dermatomyositis	
	Metabolic disease, eg glycogen storage disease	
	Thyroid disease	
	Steroids	

Table 11.6: Differential diagnosis of neuromuscular disease in the older child

Neuromuscular disease in the older child: cases

Case one

> Andrew is a thin-looking 14-year-old boy who walks with a waddling gait. He has a positive Gower's sign. Examination of his peripheral nervous system shows reduced muscle bulk, hypotonia and absent tendon reflexes. There is a proximal muscle weakness. When his arms are outstretched, he has winging of the scapula and a fine tremor.
>
> The diagnosis is **spinal muscular atrophy type III** (Kugelberg–Welander disease) which affects the anterior horn cells.

Notes on spinal muscular atrophy type III

- Autosomal recessive and gene deletion known – diagnosis possible from the DNA
- Presents at age 5–15 years with waddling gait and proximal muscle weakness, which often manifests itself when the patient is trying to climb the stairs.
- Gower's positive
- Hypotonia
- Reduced power – mostly proximal
- Reduced reflexes
- Tongue fasciculation

Differential diagnosis

Limb girdle muscular dystrophy – see 'Notes on other muscular dystrophies' below. The two conditions have similar clinical features and it is difficult to distinguish between them. This needs DNA analysis, electromyography and nerve conduction studies.

Case two

Instructions to candidate

Examine this girl's legs.

Jennifer is a well-looking 10-year-old girl who is lying flat in bed. She has reduced tone in her lower limbs and symmetrical weakness, which is more pronounced distally than proximally. She has depressed tendon reflexes.

The diagnosis is **Guillain–Barré syndrome**; I would also like to examine her cranial nerves and perform spirometry.

Notes on Guillain–Barré syndrome

- You may see a case if there is a patient on the ward in the recovery phase and there is a shortfall in cases for the Neurology Station
- It starts 10–14 days after a viral prodromal illness and involves the nerve fibres
- It is characterised by a **symmetrical ascending flaccid paralysis – although a degree of minor asymmetry is not uncommon as the condition evolves (if there is marked asymmetry an alternative diagnosis should be sought)**
- **Distal sensory loss** or **paraesthesia** occur but are less marked than the motor symptoms and signs. Neuropathic pain is not uncommon
- Examine for reduced tone and absent or reduced tendon reflexes
- There will be a flexor plantar response
- Examine the cranial nerves as they are prone to **ptosis** and **seventh nerve palsies**
- The illness must be monitored with daily spirometry as the onset of respiratory failure is insidious and life threatening. Some patients need ventilating and those with severe disease can have autonomic involvement with blood pressure instability and arrhythmias contributing to morbidity and sometimes mortality.
- Some patients are given i.v. immunoglobulin or even plasmapheresis.
- The main prognostic indicator is time to initial improvement after maximal weakness, with those only starting to recover beyond 16 days having a worse prognosis

NB **Polio** starts with an influenza-type illness followed by muscle pain and then progressive ascending **asymmetrical** paralysis, worse in the legs. Less likely to see this in an examination in the past, but its prevalence has increased because of emigration of families from countries where this illness is relatively more common.

Case three

Instructions to candidate

Look at this child's legs and in particular his feet.

> Jordan is a 12-year-old boy who has pes caves. There is associated weakness and wasting of the distal muscles of the leg, in particular he has weakness of foot dorsiflexion. His plantar response is down-going. I would like to test the sensation in his feet.
>
> The diagnosis is **peroneal muscular atrophy.**

Notes on peroneal muscular atrophy

○ A disorder of the nerve fibres – also known as **hereditary motor and sensory neuropathy type I**, it usually begins in late childhood. The peroneal and tibial nerves are damaged, causing foot drop and the characteristic distal wasting

○ Sensory nerves conveying proprioception and vibration also become involved

○ The main differential diagnosis is **Friedreich's ataxia**, which is characterised by ataxia, Romberg's positivity, absent tendon reflexes and up-going plantars

○ Treatment is by stabilisation of the ankle joint with ankle–foot orthoses

Case four

> Samuel is an 8-year-old boy who is able to walk with the aid of a walking frame and foot orthoses. He has a wide-based gait and an exaggerated lumbar lordosis. His calves are hypertrophied. On examination of the peripheral nervous system it is apparent he has a positive Gower's sign and reduced muscle bulk of his thighs; there is weakness of his hip flexors. There are absent knee jerks but brisk ankle jerks. I would like to examine his back for a scoliosis.
>
> The above findings suggest a muscular disorder. The diagnosis is **Duchenne muscular dystrophy.**

Questions

How do you confirm the diagnosis?

What is the differential diagnosis?

What is the prognosis?

Notes on Duchenne muscular dystrophy

○ Commonest disabling neuromuscular disorder of childhood. X-linked recessive inheritance with an incidence 1 in 3500 live born males. Gene locus known and is at Xp21; a third of cases represent a new mutation. Females may be symptomatic as a consequence of the random inactivation of one of the X chromosomes

○ Usually presents between the ages of 3 and 5 with delayed walking, waddling gait and difficulty with stairs. Calf muscle hypertrophy is often present. Most reflexes disappear early in the disease, apart from the ankle jerk which disappears late. Variable degree of cognitive impairment is often present and speech delay is often seen in tandem with or before the delayed walking

○ Creatinine phosphokinase is usually abnormally high at birth and at diagnosis. Diagnosis is by DNA studies looking at the dystrophin gene. Electromyography (EMG) and muscle biopsy for histochemical studies can also be done, particularly if DNA studies are inconclusive. Both show typical features

○ Complications arise from cardiac, respiratory and skeletal muscle involvement. Cardiomyopathy can be a significant problem as the child enters adulthood, with left ventricular failure and arrhythmias often needing medical intervention

○ Scoliosis is common and is seen in around 80% of patients; it exacerbates their pre-existing restrictive lung disease. Spinal fusion surgery is often needed. Physiotherapy input is important

○ These children lose their ability to walk unaided between 7 and 12 years of age. A walking frame is used first, followed by a wheelchair as the child enters their second decade

○ Although non-invasive ventilation can increase life expectancy by a few years, this condition is usually fatal during the second or third decade, with respiratory failure being the commonest cause of death

Notes on other muscular dystrophies

Becker's muscular dystrophy

○ Incidence is 1 in 30 000. Presents later than Duchenne muscular dystrophy. The gene defect is at the same locus as Duchenne muscular dystrophy. Cardiac and respiratory muscle involvement is rare. The creatinine phosphokinase is high at diagnosis. EMG and muscle biopsy are helpful in establishing a diagnosis; dystrophin is abnormal

Facioscapulohumeral muscular dystrophy

○ Facial and shoulder girdle muscles are affected. The face is typically expressionless and there is also winging of the scapula, with shoulder muscle weakness

Limb girdle muscular dystrophy

○ Hips and shoulder muscles are affected and the condition progresses distally. Affected children can get calf muscle hypertrophy and ankle contractures, which causes confusion with Becker's muscular dystrophy. Onset is in late childhood and most are wheelchair bound by age 30

Tip

Another condition that can present with muscle weakness is dermatomyositis, which is covered in Chapter 12 (Section 12.2). Asymmetry helps to distinguish it from other muscle disease, eg limb girdle dystrophy

---

The floppy infant

Commonly seen cases in the exam

1. Werdnig–Hoffman disease
2. Myotonic dystrophy
3. Down syndrome
4. Failure to thrive

Differential diagnosis

You may see a hypotonic infant and be asked for a full differential diagnosis. It is important when reviewing the list to remember that there are many causes of the 'floppy infant' that can be seen in the exam and that both neurological and systemic conditions need to be considered.

A full systematically organised differential diagnosis is listed (Table 11.7). Try to organise your differential diagnosis in a similar way to the approach of neuromuscular disease seen previously.

Central	Encephalopathy
	Intracranial haemorrhage
	Degenerative disease, eg infantile Gaucher's disease
	Neurometabolic disease, eg Zellweger's
Spinal cord	Spina bifida
	Transection of the cord, eg following complicated breech delivery
	Haematoma
	Tumour
Anterior horn cell	Spinal muscular atrophy (Werdnig–Hoffman disease)
	Poliomyelitis
Nerve fibre	Demyelinating disease, eg Guillain–Barré syndrome
Neuromuscular junction	Transient neonatal myasthenia gravis
	Botulism
Muscle	Congenital myopathies
	Congenital myotonic dystrophy
	Congenital muscular dystrophies
	Pompes disease
Other causes of hypotonia	Trisomy 21
	Prader–Willi syndrome
	Acute and chronic childhood illnesses: Hypercalcaemia Renal tubular acidosis Rickets Hypothyroidism Coeliac disease Cystic fibrosis Failure to thrive

Table 11.7: Differential diagnosis for floppy infant

Neuromuscular disease in the floppy infant: cases

Anterior horn cell

Case

> Samantha is a happy-looking 6-month-old child who is visually alert. She is lying flat on her back with obvious paucity of movement and only minimal antigravity movement. She has a bell-shaped chest and para-doxical 'see-saw' respiration. When pulled to sit and on ventral suspension there is head lag and poor tone. She has no sitting posture. Tendon reflexes are absent.

Diagnosis infantile spinal muscular atrophy type I (Werdnig–Hoffman disease)

Different mutations in the gene for spinal muscular atrophy produce different illnesses in terms of age of onset and rate of progression. Type I is the most severe.

Discussion points

○ Investigation and differential diagnosis
○ Genetic counselling – gene probe available
○ Care of the infant with a life-threatening condition

Notes on spinal muscular atrophy type 1

○ Autosomal recessive chromosome 5q12
○ Presents in the first year
○ On inspection, infant is watchful and alert, but immobile with a frog-like posture, bell-shaped chest with see-saw respirations
○ On examination will have muscle weakness, hypotonia, reduced or absent reflexes and fasciculation. Legs more severely affected than arms
○ Patients are never able to sit and their life span is 12–18 months
○ Diagnosis is essentially a clinical one. Gene probe available

Patients with spinal muscular atrophy type II have a later onset of symptoms but most are affected by 12 months of age. They will never be able to stand but life expectancy is longer – early teens through to middle age depending on respiratory complications.

Notes on muscle

Myotonic dystrophy (dystrophica myotonica)

Myotonia is the failure of muscle to relax after contraction. Myotonic dystrophy is an autosomal-dominant condition that shows genetic anticipation. The gene has been isolated to chromosome 19 and the involvement of geneticists is essential as the extended family needs advising. The condition is characterised by progressive myotonic weakness particularly affecting the face, jaws, neck and distal muscles.

The early presentation is as the hypotonic floppy infant (= congenital myotonic dystrophy). The clue is the mother, who is likely to have a relatively expressionless, immobile face and myotonia (failure to relax) when you shake her hand. Older child will present with a myotonic, expressionless, immobile face, hypotonia, poor muscle bulk, weakness and reduced or normal reflexes. The extent of the motor defect is quite variable.

One important management point is that administration of a general anaesthetic to a patient with myotonic dystrophy (which may be mild and not noted preoperatively) is potentially very dangerous. Gene carriers should have a Medicalert bracelet for this reason.

Congenital myotonic dystrophy

There is often a history of reduced fetal movements. The infant is floppy **from birth** – the myotonia presenting later. There is a facial diplegia with a triangular facies. There are often respiratory problems after birth. Associations in infancy include talipes and hip problems. The most severe form presenting in the neonatal period has a mortality of 75% in the first year.

In the majority of cases it is the mother who is affected but it can be the father. The investigation of choice is an EMG.

Ataxia

Remember that ataxia can be due to a **cerebellar** or a **dorsal column** problem. In a ward or outpatient setting the most common cause is infectious/post-infectious.

Although rare in absolute terms, the commonest cases seen in the examination have been:

1. Friedreich's ataxia
2. Ataxia telangiectasia
3. Ataxic cerebral palsy

Differential diagnosis of ataxia

Best split into acute, intermittent and chronic.

Acute

○ Infectious and post-infectious, eg chicken pox, *Mycoplasma*, measles
○ Structural lesions, eg tumours, hydrocephalus
○ Drugs, eg phenytoin toxicity
○ Metabolic disorders
○ Vascular, eg basilar artery thrombosis

Intermittent

○ Migraine
○ Epilepsy
○ Inherited recurrent ataxia (eg Hartnup disease)

Chronic

○ Perinatally acquired, eg hypoxic ischaemic encephalopathy
○ Cerebellar malformation, eg Dandy–Walker syndrome
○ Spinocerebellar degeneration, eg Friedreich's ataxia
○ DNA repair abnormalities, eg ataxia telangiectasia, xeroderma pigmentosa
○ Metabolic, eg Wilson's disease, leukodystrophies, abetalipoproteinaemia, Batten disease
○ Refsum disease – phytanic acid storage disorder with peripheral neuropathy, deafness and retinitis pigmentosa
○ Vitamin E deficiency – abetalipoproteinaemia
○ Dysgenesis of the cerebellar vermis, eg Joubert syndrome

Case

> Peter is a well-looking 12-year-old boy who on walking has an ataxic gait. He is Romberg's positive. He has pes cavus of his feet, up-going plantar responses and absent ankle jerks.
>
> The diagnosis is **Friedreich's ataxia.**
>
> I would also like to examine his cardiovascular system.

Notes on Friedreich's ataxia

This is a progressive ataxia with pyramidal tract dysfunction. Inheritance is usually autosomal recessive. The gene locus is on chromosome 9. It usually presents before the 15th birthday with loss of position and vibration sense. Other features include:

○ Absent tendon reflexes
○ Extensor plantars
○ Sensory ataxia (positive Romberg's)
○ Nystagmus
○ Pes cavus
○ Kyphoscoliosis
○ Cardiac abnormalities (hypertrophic cardiomyopathy)
○ Increased risk of diabetes mellitus

Treatment is largely supportive. Death is usually secondary to cardiac complications.

Tip

Older child with ataxia plus positive Romberg's – think Friedreich's ataxia

Ataxia telangiectasia

This condition has autosomal-recessive inheritance; the gene locus is on chromosome 11.

The ataxia is cerebellar and usually presents in early childhood. The telangiectasia is characteristic and usually starts at age 5–6 years. The main areas initially are the bulbar conjunctiva and ears.

A third of these children develop malignancy (50–100 fold greater chance of developing lymphoreticular malignancy as well as brain tumours) and there is also an increased risk of recurrent infection as there are low levels of IgA and IgG. The alpha-fetoprotein is usually raised.

Spina bifida

Case one

> John is a well-looking, 8-year-old boy who is unable to walk alone and uses a wheelchair. He is wearing a nappy. Examination of his lower limbs reveals reduced muscle bulk proximally and distally. There is reduced power and tone in his legs and tendon reflexes are absent. I would like to examine his back ... which reveals a healed surgical scar in the lumbosacral area and a scoliosis.
>
> The diagnosis is **spina bifida**.

Case two

> Jessica is a well-looking 3-year-old girl who is able to walk with the aid of calipers and a walking frame. She has a waddling gait and neurological signs consistent with a lower motor neurone lesion. Examination of her back reveals a surgical scar over the lumbar region.
>
> The diagnosis is **spina bifida**.
> I would like to examine her for scoliosis and measure her head circumference...

Discussion points

○ What associated problems might you expect?
○ How do we attempt to prevent spina bifida?

Notes on spina bifida

○ Folic acid supplementation before conception and during the first trimester has been shown to reduce the risk of spina bifida
○ In all but the mildest sacral lesions there is some degree of hydrocephalus caused by a hind-brain malformation. This is displacement of the fourth ventricle below the foramen magnum causing obstruction of the cerebrospinal fluid (CSF) as it tries to drain to the basal cisterns. Patients need regular head circumference measurement

Associated problems

○ Joint contractures
○ Scoliosis
○ Ulcers on feet (sensory neuropathy)
○ Incontinence of urine and faeces with patulous anus and palpable bladder
○ Learning difficulties

Neurocutaneous syndromes

These are uncommon in clinical practice but are commonly used as short cases in the exam. You need to know in detail the clinical signs and be able to discuss issues around each case.

1. Neurofibromatosis
2. Tuberous sclerosis
3. Sturge Weber syndrome
4. Incontentia pigmenti

Case one – 8-year-old boy

Instructions to candidate

> *Examine this child's skin. What else would you like to examine?*
>
> *Simon has multiple brown macules, which are irregularly shaped. These are café-au-lait spots. He also has axillary freckling. I suspect the under-lying diagnosis is **neurofibromatosis type I**.*
>
> *I would like to examine his gait and his eyes...*
>
> *I would like to examine his mother for café-au-lait spots...*

Discussion points

What other systems might be involved; is there anything else you would like to examine?

Rest of examination

○ Visual fields – examine for evidence of optic nerve gliomata which also cause proptosis and ptosis. Offer to examine the eye with a slit lamp for Lisch nodules
○ Blood pressure – measure the blood pressure and listen for renal bruits
○ Head circumference – measure the head circumference (macro-cephaly is common, hydrocephalus due to aqueduct stenosis is not)
○ Examine the back for kyphoscoliosis

Notes on neurofibromatosis

Neurofibromatosis is an autosomal-dominant disorder that affects the bone, soft tissues and skin as well as the peripheral and central nervous systems. Occurs in 1:2500 to 1:3300 births worldwide. There are two clearly defined genetic disorders: NF-I and NF-II.

Type I (90%)

Autosomal-dominant inheritance, 50% new mutations, gene locus on chromosome 17. Encodes a protein called neurofibromin, which normally acts as a tumour suppressor.

Diagnosed if **two** of the following features are present:

- A first-degree relative with neurofibromatosis
- Axillary or inguinal/perineal freckling (often develop in early puberty)
- Optic gliomas (15%)
- Distinctive osseous lesion, eg kyphoscoliosis, tibial bowing
- Two or more neurofibromas or one plexiform neurofibroma. Can be found at any point along a nerve. Can be cutaneous, subcutaneous or plexiform (specific for NF-I). 'Buttonhole' invagination when pressed with a finger is pathognomic
- Two or more Lisch (iris) nodules – hamartomas of iris seen on slit lamp examination
- **Five or more café-au-lait spots greater than 5 mm diameter – Pre-pubertal child,**
- **Six or more café-au-lait spots greater than 15 mm diameter – Post-pubertal child**

Tip

Café-au-lait spots are best defined as brown macules that are irregularly shaped and evenly pigmented. A small proportion of healthy children (less than 1 in 100) have three or more, and one or two may be seen in normal individuals.

Type II (10%)

Autosomal-dominant inheritance, mostly new mutations, gene locus on chromosome 22.

Diagnosis

○ Bilateral acoustic neuromas (also called vestibular schwannoma)

or

○ Unilateral acoustic neuroma and first-degree relative with neurofibromatosis type II

or

○ Two of the following:
  * Schwannoma (most common tumour in NF-II)
  * Neurofibroma
  * Meningioma
  * Glioma
  * Juvenile posterior subscapular lenticular opacities

Clinical course of neurofibromatosis

The clinical course of neurofibromatosis is variable and different systems can be involved as time goes on. Patients with NF-I have an additional 3%–15% increase in their lifetime risk of malignant disease. Astrocytomas, meningioma and ependyoma are associated with neurofibromatosis. At least one-third of patients with NF-I will have significant learning disabilities.

Endocrine problems are more common than in the general population, specifically short stature and growth hormone deficiency. Phaeochromocytomas can occur.

Management

Management is multidisciplinary and you may be asked at the end of the station to reel off a list of health professionals potentially involved in such a case:

○ Paediatrician – overall management, assessment at least yearly including checking neurofibromas for signs of malignant change, monitoring growth, looking for scoliosis and measuring blood pressure

○ Paediatric surgeon – excision of neurofibromas that are painful or increasing in size

○ Orthopaedic surgeon – management of kyphoscoliosis
○ ENT surgeon – excision of acoustic neuromas
○ Plastic surgeon – correction of facial deformities
○ Child psychiatrist/educational psychologist
○ Geneticist for counselling as condition has autosomal-dominant inheritance
○ Audiologist
○ Ophthalmologist
○ Endocrinologist
○ Speech and language therapist
○ Radiologist to help guide neuroimaging

Case two – 15-year-old boy

Instructions to candidate

Please examine this boy's skin then tell me what else you would like to examine.

> *Christopher has wart-like lesions along his naso-labial folds which I think are adenoma sebaceum. He has several café-au-lait spots on his trunk and a shagreen patch on his lower back.*
>
> *The diagnosis is **tuberous sclerosis**.*
>
> *I would also like to use a Wood's lamp to look for depigmented macules, and check his head circumference and blood pressure...*

Notes on tuberous sclerosis

Autosomal-dominant inheritance with a 50% recurrence risk in offspring. Caused by mutations of the TSC1 and TSC2 tumour suppressing genes on chromosomes 9 and 11; 70% are new mutations.

Diagnosis is based on major and minor features. Prevalence in children is 1:10 000 to 1:15 000.

Seizures are common (70%) often presenting as infantile spasms. All seizure types except petit mal have been described in tuberous sclerosis. The age of seizure onset and the severity of mental handicap are directly related, with most children in whom seizures develop under the age of 2 years suffering mental handicap. The prevalence of mental handicap is 30%–60% and autism is present in around 25% of patients.

Clinical features

Skin

- Hypopigmented macules – leaf-shaped, best seen with Wood's lamp
- Adenoma sebaceum present in 85% over the age of 5 years. Rash more fully developed when sebaceous glands hypertrophy at puberty. Seen as a warty lesion along the naso-labial folds (look at parent's hand as they are more commonly seen in adults)
- Periungual fibromas
- Shagreen patches
- Café-au-lait spots

Teeth

- Enamel hypoplasia

Eyes

- Choroidal hamartoma
- Retinal phakomas

Central nervous system (CNS)

- Cerebral astrocytoma
- Malignant glioma
- Hydrocephalus

Kidney

- Renal angiomas
- Polycystic kidneys

Cardiac

- Rhabdomyomas

Gastrointestinal

- Rectal polyp

Investigation

- Renal ultrasound as renal tumours are common

○ Echocardiography to detect cardiac rhabdomyomas – mostly seen in neonates
○ ECG if suspicion of arrhythmias; Wolff–Parkinson–White commoner in this group of patients than in the general population
○ Skull X-ray
○ ECG useful when there is epilepsy
○ CT or MRI is performed in all patients

Management

Patients should be seen in specialist multidisciplinary clinics as well as at a local level wherever possible. Seizures respond well to anticonvulsants but rarely with complete seizure control. Vigabatrin is indicated, particularly in seizures associated with hypsarrhythmia on the EEG. Neurodevelopmental follow-up is essential.

Outlook is variable; early death may occur due to seizures or tumours affecting the CNS, heart or kidney. Genetic counselling should be offered.

Sturge Weber syndrome

In this station you may see a child with a facial naevus. If you do, it is important to be able to look for the associated CNS complications seen in some but not all children with a facial naevus. As this is a 9-min station it is likely that the child will have an associated neurological finding as part of Sturge Weber syndrome. In this disorder there are angiomas (residual embryonal blood vessels) involving the skin of the face and also the leptomeninges.

Notes on Sturge Weber syndrome

Facial naevus (port wine stain)

○ Present at birth = capillary haemangioma
○ Sporadic
○ Unilateral usually, but can be bilateral
○ Upper face and eyelid but can be more extensive
○ Glaucoma is an occasional complication

CNS associations – not present in all

○ Involvement of ipsilateral meninges (leptomeningeal angiomas) and cortex
○ Intracranial calcification
○ Seizures – 75%–90% of patients. Result from cortical irritability caused by cerebral angiomata
○ Hemiparesis in around one-third of patients
○ Developmental disorders and mental retardation – 50%–60% and more likely if bilateral involvement

Investigation

○ Skull X-ray: intracranial calcification – 'rail track' calcification seen by 2 years
○ EEG
○ CT with contrast/MRI

Management

○ Anti-epileptics
○ Hemispherectomy/lobectomy occasionally considered as the epilepsy is very difficult to control
○ Management of glaucoma if present
○ Cosmetic – pulsed laser is used for the port wine stain

Incontinentia pigmenti/Hypomelanosis of Ito

You will be presented with a girl with a very obvious rash, which will be in the pigmented stage. You should offer to measure the head circumference and perform a full neurodevelopmental assessment as well as eye examination and ask the parent about seizure activity.

You may be asked about the inheritance as it is unusual:

○ X-linked dominant
○ Usually lethal in males

Notes on incontinentia pigmenti/hypomelanosis of Ito

Clinical features of incontinentia pigmenti

- Rash (present in neonatal period as an erythematous bullous rash that fades to pigmented lesions which are splashed across the skin as if by a paint brush)
- Seizures
- Mental retardation
- Spasticity
- Ocular abnormalities (benign mass in posterior chamber)

Hypomelanosis of Ito

This is a distinct syndrome with whorled, marbled areas of hypopigmentation. Half the children have neurological signs and symptoms. Most cases are sporadic.

<u>YOUR NOTES</u>

YOUR NOTES

12

'OTHER' STATION

CONTENTS

12.1 HAEMATOLOGY

12.1.1   Introduction

12.1.2   Terminology

12.1.3   Clinical examination
         Suggested approach to haematological examination

12.1.4   Cases and conditions: Haematology
         Lymphadenopathy
         Purpura
         Anaemia
         Hereditary spherocytosis
         Thalassaemia
         Sickle cell disease

12.1.5   Disorders of haemostasis – haemophilia and
         von Willebrand's disease
         Haemophilia
         Notes on haemophilia A
         Notes on von Willebrand's disease

12.2 RHEUMATOLOGY

12.2.1 Introduction

12.2.2 Clinical examination
Suggested approach to joint examination
Specific joints
Suggested approach to hand examination

12.2.3 Cases
Case one – juvenile idiopathic arthritis
Case two – psoriatic arthritis; 'hand' examination
Case three – haemophilia
Case four – osteogenesis imperfecta
Case five – median nerve injury

12.2.4 Neonatal hip examination

12.2.5 Hypermobility

12.2.6 Juvenile idiopathic arthritis (JIA)
Systemic-onset juvenile idiopathic arthritis (formerly Still's disease)
Oligoarticular juvenile idiopathic arthritis
Enthesitis-related arthritis
Polyarticular rheumatoid factor negative juvenile idiopathic arthritis
Polyarticular rheumatoid factor positive juvenile idiopathic arthritis
Juvenile idiopathic arthritis – management

12.2.7 Other conditions
Psoriatic arthritis
Juvenile dermatomyositis
Osteogenesis imperfecta
Hemihypertrophy
Miscellaneous conditions

12.3 DERMATOLOGY

12.3.1 Introduction
12.3.2 Clinical examination
12.3.3 Skin conditions commonly seen in the exam

Eczema
Psoriasis
Mongolian blue spot
Strawberry naevus
Sebaceous naevus
Lipodystrophy
Vitiligo
Molluscum contagiosum
Ichthyosis
Ectodermal dysplasia
Epidermolysis bullosa
Erythema multiforme

12.4 ENDOCRINOLOGY AND GROWTH

12.4.1 Introduction
12.4.2 Assessment of growth
12.4.3 Tall stature
        Suggested approach to tall stature examination
12.4.4 Conditions and cases associated with tall stature
        Marfan syndrome
        Homocystinuria
        Klinefelter syndrome (47XXY)
        XYY syndrome
        Sotos syndrome (cerebral gigantism)
12.4.5 Short stature
        Suggested approach to short stature examination
        Notes on short stature
12.4.6 Conditions and cases related to short stature
        Turner syndrome
        Noonan syndrome
        Russell–Silver dwarfism
        Mucopolysaccharidoses
        Skeletal dysplasia
        Achondroplasia
12.4.7 Cushing syndrome
12.4.8 Thyroid gland
        Suggested structure for examination of the thyroid gland
        Suggested structure for examination of thyroid status

12.4.9   Neck lumps
          Suggested structure for examination of the anterior neck
12.4.10   Puberty

12.5 NEPHROLOGY

12.5.1 Introduction
12.5.2 Renal masses
12.5.3 Nephrotic syndrome
12.5.4 Steroid toxicity
12.5.5 Beckwith–Wiedemann syndrome

12.1 HAEMATOLOGY

12.1.1 Introduction

Many haematological conditions are encountered during the examination of other systems, for example:

○ Skin: purpura – Henoch–Schönlein purpura
○ Joints: swollen joint – haemophilia
○ Abdomen: splenomegaly – hereditary spherocytosis
○ General appearance: short stature, malar hypertrophy – thalassaemia

It may be that you will be asked to examine the haematological system, and if you are then remember that the examiner is looking for a clinical assessment of the following:

○ Immunodeficiency
○ Red cell disease: signs of anaemia, extramedullary haematopoiesis (bones, liver, spleen, rarely skin) and complications of the underlying cause
○ Platelet or clotting factor deficiencies and their complications
○ Complications from underlying disease or treatment
○ Dysmorphic features which point to a diagnosis with haematological implications

You will not just be looking for a diagnosis but also seeking some evidence of severity and whether or not any complications have already occurred (eg cholecystectomy for spherocytosis, neurological complications in sickle cell disease). Alternatively, the examiner may be much more specific and ask for an examination of the reticuloendothelial system or for the assessment of a child with purpura. Schemes for these scenarios are given later in this chapter. Individual conditions with a haematological emphasis are discussed, pointing out the key clinical features to look out for. Splenomegaly is also covered in Chapter 9.

12.1.2 Terminology

The **reticuloendothelial** system is the mononuclear phagocyte system and consists of cells in the bone marrow, peripheral blood and tissues highly specialised for the function of endocytosis and intracellular digestion. It plays a role in inflammation but also acts as the main line of defence against bacteria in the bloodstream and controls the haematogenous dissemination of organisms.

Hypersplenism is a clinical syndrome in which normal splenic function becomes excessive as the spleen and its mononuclear phagocyte tissue enlarge. The most common cause is venous obstruction such as that seen in extra-hepatic venous obstruction. Pancytopenia usually occurs.

Hyposplenism refers to diminished splenic function associated either with the absence of the spleen (congenital or following splenectomy) or functional impairment, eg sickle cell disease. The main consequence of hyposplenism is the risk of overwhelming bacterial septicaemia. Prophylactic penicillin and appropriate immunisations are required.

12.1.3 Clinical examination

Suggested approach to haematological examination

Initial procedure

Introduce yourself.

General

■ Comment on growth and whether the child looks ill or well
■ Comment on ethnicity (particularly if thinking of thalassaemia, hereditary spherocytosis or sickle cell disease) as this is highly relevant; comment on the parents' ethnicity as well if you think it is appropriate
■ Comment on obvious pallor or jaundice; remember haemochromatosis 'bronzing'
■ Note dysmorphic features, (eg TAR syndrome, ie thrombocytopenia, absent radius; Fanconi syndrome is also associated with upper limb abnormalities)
■ There may be obvious bruising, pallor or jaundice

Hands and arms

■ Clubbing
■ Koilonychia
■ Scars from cannulae
■ Pallor
■ **Assess pulse**: if there are any concerns then check blood pressure (BP), otherwise you could mention checking BP later (think symptomatic anaemia; although this would be uncommon in the exam scenario you may be asked to talk about it)

Head and neck

■ Frontal bossing, malar prominence
■ Eyes, pallor or jaundice, conjunctival haemorrhage
■ Lymphadenopathy
■ Lips (angular cheilitis)
■ Look at gums (hypertrophy in neutropenia) and dentition
■ Tongue
■ Tonsils

Chest

- Heart murmur (flow murmur from anaemia)
- Hickman line or Port-A-Cath®
- Comment on the presence or absence of increased work of breathing (think sickle chest syndrome which is unlikely to present to clinical exams but is an important part of the examination)

Abdomen

- Scars – think splenectomy, cholecystectomy
- Liver and spleen
- Bruises from injection sites
- Inguinal lymph nodes

Legs

- Signs of infection
- Scarring or bruising
- Joint disease (think haemophilia)

Finally

- Axillary lymph nodes – very difficult if children are even slightly ticklish so leave until the end, but don't forget about it
- In a male you would normally palpate the testes; indicate to the examiner that you would complete the examination by doing this (looking for testicular lymphoma or testicular relapse of haematological malignancy)
- Neurology – especially for sickle cell disease
- Check temperature (crucial for neutropenic or immunodeficient patients)
- Do parents have evidence of disease?

12.1.4 Cases and conditions: haematology

Lymphadenopathy

It is important to have a differential diagnosis if you find lymphadenopathy. This will depend upon whether the lymphadenopathy is localised or generalised. Cervical nodes are, for example, very common in children with either current or recurrent upper respiratory tract pathology.

Tip

Normal nodes do not exceed 2.5 cm in diameter.

Simple differential diagnosis of generalised lymphadenopathy

○ Infection – infectious mononucleosis, cytomegalovirus, HIV
○ Autoimmune disorders
○ Leukaemia/lymphoma
○ Storage diseases (rare)

Investigation of lymphadenopathy

There are NICE guidelines for when it is appropriate for GPs to refer children with lymphadenopathy for paediatric opinion (when there is no evidence of local disease) at www.nice.org.uk. Look up Clinical Guideline CG27 (*Referral Guidelines for Suspected Cancer*, date of issue June 2005, Section 1.14.11), which gives the following indications for further investigation:

○ Non-tender, firm or hard lymph nodes
○ Lymph nodes >2 cm
○ Lymph nodes progressively enlarging
○ Other features of general ill health, fever or weight loss
○ Axillary node involvement (without local disease)
○ Supraclavicular node involvement

Investigation of lymphadenopathy largely depends on the history and physical characteristics of the enlarged node. History taking and physical examination should also focus on excluding serious causes of lymphadenopathy.

Options for investigation include

○ Watch and wait
○ Full blood count (FBC) and film
○ Lactate dehydrogenase (LDH), erythrocyte sedimentation rate (ESR)
○ Serology, monospot – looking for infectious causes of chronic lymphadenopathy
○ Imaging – looking either at the node itself or for evidence of lymphoma elsewhere (chest X-ray, abdominal CT/ultrasound)
○ Biopsy

Purpura

Purpura reflects a bleeding tendency and if purpura are seen in the exam it is important to remember the differential diagnosis:

○ Infection – meningococcal disease
○ Thrombocytopenia – neonatal thrombocytopenia, idiopathic thrombocytopenic purpura (ITP), leukaemia
○ Coagulation disturbance – disseminated intravascular coagulation, haemophilia, von Willebrand's disease
○ Vasculitis – Henoch–Schönlein purpura (HSP)

Children with purpura are unlikely to be acutely unwell with meningococcal disease but may be shown in the recovering phase. All children with purpura need a full systemic examination with particular focus on the reticuloendothelial system in order to elicit a cause. In addition it is sensible to mention basic investigation, which includes a FBC, blood film and clotting screen.

Henoch–Schönlein purpura

Instructions to candidate

Look at this child's legs, what do you see?

Case

> Jenny looks well. On inspection of her legs I can see a purpuric rash, limited to the extensor surfaces and buttocks. There is also urticaria in places. On palpation it does not blanch with pressure. She also appears to have a swollen left ankle, not hot to touch, not red, not tender but with limitation of movement in all directions. The right foot does not appear abnormal and...

What is your diagnosis?

Henoch–Schönlein purpura.

What is the differential diagnosis?

○ Other vasculitis, eg systemic lupus erythematosus
○ Thrombocytopenia although this wouldn't explain the swollen joint
○ Sepsis but the child does not look unwell
○ Could be leukaemia

List clinical features/problems

- ○ Urticarial/purpuric rash, mostly on extensor surfaces and buttocks
- ○ Joints: arthritis in 60%–80%
- ○ Gastrointestinal involvement: including colicky abdominal pain, vomiting, GI bleeding, intussusception, pancreatitis; occurs in 50%–70%
- ○ Renal involvement in 20%–90%: including microscopic haematuria, frank haematuria and proteinuria, nephrotic/nephritic picture, renal failure and hypertension
- ○ Neurological involvement is recognised, but usually mild
- ○ Lung involvement is rare
- ○ Testicular involvement may manifest as uni/bilateral orchitis

Notes on Henoch–Schönlein purpura (HSP)

Commonest vasculitis of childhood with incidence of 14:100 000 to 18:100 000 children per year. Half of cases occur in children under 5 years, 75% in those under 10 years. Commoner in males and in winter months. Aetiology unclear, often there is a history of preceding viral upper respiratory tract illness. There are no specific laboratory diagnostic tests. Treatment remains controversial. Use of steroids for abdominal pain is generally well accepted although there are concerns that steroids may mask a worsening gastrointestinal picture or a lymphoproliferative disorder. Joint symptoms should be treated as required with analgesia and rest. The treatment of renal complications requires the help of a paediatric nephrologist. All patients with significant renal involvement require long-term follow-up. The morbidity is principally due to renal involvement, and hence the prognosis depends on the degree of renal involvement.

Idiopathic thrombocytopenic purpura (ITP)

This is an immunologically mediated condition that is often triggered by a viral infection. It presents with multiple petechiae and purpurae. Course is usually self-limiting and benign. If it lasts over 6 months (10%–15%) it is termed chronic. Most cases can be diagnosed by excluding other causes of thrombocytopenia (clinical history, examination, FBC and film). Platelet count is typically very low. If the patient has any other cell lines affected or their diagnosis is unclear a bone marrow biopsy is indicated after liasing with a paediatric haematologist.

Management involves education (advised to avoid contact sports) and treatment of complications such as severe haemorrhage. There is no benefit in platelet transfusing an asymptomatic patient. Oral steroids are occasionally used in severe disease. The biggest fear of patients and parents is intracranial haemorrhage, which is very rare, occurring in fewer than 0.3% of patients in most case series. Intravenous immunoglobulin is the treatment of choice for all severe bleeds. Some patients with chronic ITP go on to have a splenectomy. Therapy with **anti-D, vincristine, cyclophosphamide** and **cyclosporin** has also been used with some success.

Other causes of thrombocytopenia that may be seen in exam are shown in the box.

WISKOTT–ALDRICH SYNDROME

○ X-linked condition
○ Severe eczema, thrombocytopenia, immunodeficiency

THROMBOCYTOPENIA, ABSENT RADIUS (TAR) SYNDROME

○ Autosomal recessive
○ Absent radii is the most common finding
○ Cardiac, renal or other skeletal malformations may occur
○ High mortality from bleeding in the first year of life

Anaemia

You may be shown a child who is obviously pale and be asked to show the examiner features of anaemia (see Box) and to come up with a differential diagnosis. The cause may range from iron deficiency (common) to red cell aplasia (very rare) but marks will be gained for conducting a focused examination and giving a sensible differential.

CLINICAL FEATURES OF ANAEMIA

○ Patient may look pale and tired – comment on this
○ Is patient jaundiced? Will narrow down differential diagnosis
○ Hands – koilonychia (spoon-shaped nails)
○ Mucous membranes (look at conjunctiva) and nail beds for pallor
○ Flow murmur

Tailor the rest of your examination to initial findings, eg if jaundiced look for other signs of haemolysis and examine for spleen, etc.

Notes on anaemia

Anaemia is a reduced (2 SD below mean) haemoglobin level for the age and sex of that individual. It will be broadly due to defective production, loss or excessive destruction of red cells (see Box for summary).

CAUSES OF ANAEMIA

Defective production/maturation of red cells
○ Iron deficiency
○ Chronic disease with decreased erythropoietin production, prematurity
○ Vitamin B_{12} and folate deficiency

○ Marrow failure – aplastic anaemia, infiltration, pure red cell aplasia (Diamond–Blackfan), drugs

Loss of red cells

○ Haemorrhage – through, for example, menstruation, non-steroidal anti-inflammatory drugs (NSAIDs) or inflammatory bowel disease. Worldwide, blood loss from hookworm is a very common cause of anaemia
○ Excessive destruction
○ Haemolytic anaemias

Initial investigations to aid in narrowing down the differential diagnosis are blood film (for red cell morphology), reticulocyte count (increased if loss or destruction, decreased if defective production) and iron indices.

Iron deficiency

Commonest cause of anaemia in children – present in 10%–30% of inner city UK preschool children. You may get a case in the exam if it is severe enough to show signs. Occurs when there is insufficient iron for erythropoiesis, especially in the context of increased demand during the rapid growth phase from 6 months to 3 years combined with a suboptimal diet. For this reason there is also a peak in incidence during the adolescent growth spurt.

Clinical problems arising from iron deficiency anaemia are many and include:

○ Faltering growth
○ Decreased exercise tolerance – 'tired all the time'
○ Decreased attention span and thus learning ability
○ Pica

You may be asked how to address iron deficiency in infants. Current advice is to breastfeed (or use an iron-fortified formula) then wean onto iron-containing foods by 6 months of age. Cows' milk should be avoided at this time. Sources of iron are well known but often sparse in many children's diets, so supplementation (with advice and monitoring from a paediatric dietician if available) may be required. Appetite improves as the condition is treated.

Fanconi anaemia

Very rare in actuality but if there is a patient in the region they may well be invited to the examination. This is an autosomal-recessive aplastic anaemia with a pre-malignant potential. There are characteristic physical findings in 50%–75%. Pancytopenia develops towards the end of the first decade.

Characteristics

- Short stature
- Hyperpigmentation
- Microcephaly
- Microphthalmia
- Hypoplasia/aplasia of the thumb
- Renal anomalies
- Skeletal anomalies
- Mental retardation

Hereditary spherocytosis

This is a very common clinical case in the examination.

> **Tip**
>
> Northern European child plus pallor, jaundice and splenomegaly = hereditary spherocytosis until proved otherwise

Instructions to candidate

Examine this child's abdomen; why is he jaundiced?

This boy presents with abdominal pain, pallor and a palpable spleen. What are your thoughts? What would you do?

Clinical findings

- ○ Northern European child
- ○ Looks well
- ○ Jaundice (mild)
- ○ Pallor
- ○ Cholecystectomy scar (occasionally)
- ○ Splenomegaly or a splenectomy scar (scars may be laparoscopic)

Case one

> *This is a well-looking boy. I would like to examine him. His conjunctiva are pale and he is mildly jaundiced. He has a palpable spleen. There are no other abnormalities. I suspect that he has **hereditary spherocytosis**...*

Case two

> *This is well-looking boy. There is no pallor or lymphadenopathy. He has a cholecystectomy and splenectomy scar. The underlying diagnosis is most likely to be hereditary **spherocytosis**...*

Notes on hereditary spherocytosis

Autosomal-dominant condition. Incidence is 1 in 5000 in Northern Europeans. Usually presents in childhood with the classical triad of anaemia, jaundice and splenomegaly. The jaundice is unconjugated and worsens during infections. Pigmented gallstones are present in 85% by the second decade. Aplastic crises can occur.

The diagnosis is made on clinical grounds, by observing the sphero-cytes on a blood film and by the increased osmotic fragility of red cells when tested. Treatment is with folic acid supplements and later by splenectomy, particularly if the haemoglobin is consistently less than 10 g/dl. Cholecystectomy is occasionally required. The spleen is the site of red cell destruction. Removal of the spleen will reduce haemolysis and reduce the incidence of gallstones. There is however an increased risk of pneumococcal and other infections and splenec-tomy is reserved for the most severe cases only. Once a child is asplenic, pneumococcal, meningococcal and haemophilus influenza type B immunisation and lifelong prophylactic penicillin need to be given.

Differential diagnosis

Other causes of haemolytic anaemia include:
○   Hereditary elliptocytosis
○   Pyruvate kinase deficiency
○   Autoimmune haemolytic anaemia

Thalassaemia

Thalassaemia and the different variants are often seen in the exam. If you work in a hospital where such cases are rare then it is essential to read about and try to get to see some cases.

Case

> This is a well-looking boy of Asian origin who looks well grown. On inspection of his hands he has three scars from i.v. cannulae. His sclerae show a tinge of jaundice and on examination of his abdomen he has a palpable spleen... I also noticed that he had some patches of depigmentation on his abdominal wall.
>
> I think this child has **thalassaemia major**....

Clinical findings
- Mediterranean/African/Indian/SE Asian child
- Multiple i.v. cannula sites in the hands, may be a Port-A-Cath®
- Jaundice (mild), pallor
- Multiple depigmented patches on abdominal wall from subcutaneous desferrioxamine administration
- Palpable spleen

The above refers to a well-controlled thalassaemic on a regular transfusion regime. A poorly controlled thalassaemic or someone who is well controlled now but was previously poorly controlled may have signs of **extra-medullary haemopoiesis** (see notes below):

- Frontal bossing
- Malar hyperplasia
- Hepatomegaly
- Splenomegaly
- Previous long bone fracture sites

Notes on thalassaemia

- The thalassaemias are a heterogeneous group of recessively inherited disorders characterised by deficient synthesis of either alpha or beta chains of haemoglobin. There are various different types and there are approximately 100 different mutations known to cause thalassaemia, many of which are unique to localised geographical areas. These notes are about **thalassaemia major** – the transfusion-dependent form of β-thalassaemia. This occurs in the populations mentioned above and produces a severe progressive haemolytic anaemia during the second 6 months of life. This presents as pallor, failure to thrive and feeding difficulties in a child who is found to have hepatosplenomegaly.

○ The anaemia is **microcytic and hypochromic**, with poikilocytes and target cells on the peripheral blood film. There are large numbers of nucleated red cells and a marked increase in HbF.

○ In untreated or inadequately transfused patients there is proliferation of medullary and extramedullary haemopoiesis with massive expansion of the skull and face causing characteristic facies. The spleen and liver are enlarged, the bones become weak and have pathological fractures, growth is impaired and puberty delayed. Diabetes mellitus occurs due to pancreatic siderosis and cardiac failure due to cardiac siderosis. Iron deposition can cause a range of endocrinopathies. With the modern technique of management many of these complications can be avoided and others ameliorated and their onset delayed.

Treatment

Aims to control the ineffective erythropoiesis and thus reduce the likelihood of hypersplenism and its complications.

○ **Hyper transfusion regime**: blood transfusions on a regular basis to maintain haemoglobin above 10 g/dl. Haemosiderosis is however a complication of hyper transfusion and should be prevented with chelation.

○ **Chelation therapy** with **desferrioxamine** should commence when the ferritin has reached 800–1000 mg/l, usually around the 12th–14th transfusion. It is given as a subcutaneous infusion over an 8- to 12-h period 5–6 nights per week. The injection sites give rise to the depigmented patches on dark skin that are seen in most patients. Ask about compliance in adolescents.

○ **Folic acid supplementation**: increased erythropoiesis uses up folic acid.

○ **Splenectomy** may be necessary. This will often reduce the transfusion requirement but there is a high risk of bacterial sepsis.

○ **Bone marrow transplantation** is considered to be curative, and is being used with increasing success. However, it carries a considerable morbidity and mortality, and currently is only used if there is a non-affected HLA-compatible sibling donor.

Sickle cell disease

Like thalassaemia, sickle cell disease is commonly seen in the exam. Due to the multiple ways in which the condition can present (including as a 'paediatric emergency') children and families are also asked to attend the History Taking/Management Planning Station. If you work in an area where sickle cell disease is rarely seen then you need to read about and be very familiar with the condition.

> ### Tip
>
> Afro-Caribbean child with pallor, jaundice and no palpable spleen = sickle cell disease until proven otherwise

Instructions to candidate

Examine this 11-year-old child, what do you find?

Case

> Jimmy is an Afro-Caribbean child who looks well. He does look short for his age and I would like to plot him on a centile chart. On close inspection of his sclerae he looks jaundiced. His conjunctivae look pale. He has what I think is a cholecystectomy scar but the rest of his abdominal examination is normal. In particular I cannot feel his spleen...

Why can you not feel his spleen?

This child presents with a pyrexia, unwell, how would you manage him?

This child presents in acute respiratory distress, what are the possibilities and how would you manage him?

Clinical findings
- Afro-Caribbean child, usually appears well. May have short stature
- Jaundiced (mild), pallor (seen as pale conjunctivae)
- May be cholecystectomy scar
- Splenomegaly in an infant, spleen not usually palpable in an older child
- Otherwise examination unremarkable

If acutely unwell look for
- Signs of infection
- Signs of dehydration
- Chest – sequestration
- Abdominal – acute splenic enlargement
- Joints – dactylitis

Notes on sickle cell disease

Sickle cell disease is caused by a point mutation in the beta-globin gene causing deoxygenated HbS to polymerise and distort the shape of the red blood cell, decreasing red cell lifespan. The red cell membrane damage that occurs leads to a haemolytic tendency. Sickled cells tend to sludge in the microcirculation leading to vaso-occlusive syndromes.

It is most common in Africa, the Mediterranean, the Middle East and India.

Diagnosis is based on haemoglobin estimation, blood film (contains target cells, poikilocytes and irreversibly sickled cells) and haemoglobin electrophoresis, which shows >80% HbS. The Hb electrophoresis result is confirmed with a further test, eg electrophoresis at acidic pH. Antenatal diagnosis can be made via chorionic villus biopsy but cannot distinguish carriers from diseased fetuses.

Main clinical problems and their management

Usually asymptomatic until 5–6 months, when production of haemoglobin switches from HbF to HbA. Acute dactylitis is often the first manifestation. The problems that follow are due either to **haemolysis** or more frequently **vaso-occlusion** – this inevitably involves the spleen which renders the patient functionally asplenic.

Haemolysis
- Chronic anaemia – in general transfusions are limited to those patients with disabling chronic pain
- Jaundice – raised unconjugated bilirubin due to increased red cell breakdown
- Aplastic crises. In common with other patients with chronic haemolysis, patients with sickle cell disease are at risk of developing aplastic crises secondary to parvovirus infection. Transfusion is warranted in some instances

○ Cholelithiasis: cholecystectomy can be required
○ Delayed growth and sexual maturation

Vaso-occlusion (acutely termed as 'sickle crisis')

○ **Recurrent acute pain:** can be severe, sometimes requiring hospitalisation. The quoted mean incidence is one episode per patient-year. This obviously varies, with some patients having more episodes and some never experiencing pain. Abdominal pain is common, as is bone pain. Dactylitis (hand/foot syndrome) can be another presentation.
Triggers include infection, dehydration and exposure to cold. Treatment: warmth, hydration, oxygen, powerful analgesia, antibiotics

○ **Splenic sequestration:** young children may have rapid splenic enlargement associated with haemolysis and progress to hypersplenism. This causes circulatory collapse, which may require life-saving blood transfusions

○ Whether patients have splenic enlargement or autosplenectomy (from multiple infarcts), they all have **functional asplenia** by around 1 year of age and are therefore at risk of overwhelming infections from encapsulated organisms such as *Pneumococcus*. Patients must maintain full immunisation status and be on prophylactic penicillin from at least 3 months. They need prompt help if they become febrile with parenteral antibiotics. Salmonella osteomyelitis is another danger

○ **Acute chest syndrome:** lung infarction ± infection leading to symptoms not dissimilar to those of a severe pneumonia but with circulatory compromise and chest pain. Treat with oxygen, pain relief, warmth, hydration, i.v. antibiotics, transfusion if required. Can be life-threatening and is responsible for a quarter of all deaths in children with sickle cell disease

○ **Stroke:** occurs in 5%–10%. Can present with hemiplegia and cranial nerve involvement. An urgent exchange transfusion is needed along with other management strategies for vaso-occlusive crises

○ **Other problems:** papillary necrosis, avascular necrosis of femoral head, proliferative retinopathy (can lead to blindness), leg ulcers, priapism

GENERAL MANAGEMENT POINTS

○ Use hydroxyurea to increase HbF fraction, leading to reduction of hospital admissions as complications are rare if HbS is less than 30%

○ Open access set up for patients along with an individualised letter for Accident and Emergency staff concerning the risks of sepsis/sickle crisis for any given sufferer of the disease Particularly relevant in regions where the condition is rarely seen

○ Manage acute vaso-occlusive crises: admit, warmth, oxygen, hydration, i.v. analgesia, i.v. antibiotics

○ Recognise and manage functional asplenia: immunise, i.v. antibiotics if evidence of infection and unwell

○ Top-up/exchange transfusions mainly reserved for emergencies such as acute chest syndrome or stroke

○ Genetic counselling

Variants

Hb SC disease is a milder variant with moderately severe anaemia and splenomegaly. Vaso-occlusive episodes are less frequent and usually milder. Aseptic necrosis of the femoral head is common.

12.1.5 Disorders of haemostasis – haemophilia and von Willebrand's disease

> ## Tip
>
> In a child with traumatic mucosal (toothbrushing) or dental/surgical bleeding think about platelet deficiency or von Willebrand's factor deficiency
>
> If there is prolonged bleeding or spontaneous bleeding think about haemophilia

Haemophilia

The haemophilias are the commonest and the most serious of the congenital coagulation disorders. About 80% of cases are X-linked haemophilia A, causing a majority to have reduced factor VIII activity and factor VIII antigen.

Haemophilia B exhibits varied genetics and is associated with low factor IX levels. Because factor IX levels are normally low in neonates it can be difficult to diagnose in patients under 6 months. Treatment is with recombinant factor. There is a 3% chance of improvement at puberty.

Notes on haemophilia A

Incidence is around 1 in 12 000 males.

Numerous mutations in gene structure have been described. In 70% of cases the family history is positive. The degree of severity is similar among family members. The severity of disease depends on the level of factor VIII activity in the plasma:

○ Severe cases have <1% of normal activity
○ Moderate cases have 1%–5%
○ Mild cases have 6%–30%

Prenatal diagnosis is now possible. The gene is known and there is a gene probe that can detect carrier status.

Clinical presentation

The commonest time of presentation is when ambulation begins. The hallmark is haemarthroses; knees, ankles and elbows are the most commonly affected joints. The bleeding itself occurs from the vascular synovium. Repeated haemorrhages may cause degenerative changes with osteoporosis, muscle atrophy and eventually a fixed immobile joint.

The factor VIII deficiency causes a greatly prolonged activated partial thromboplastin time (APTT), with a normal platelet count, bleeding time and prothrombin time.

Management

Management of haemophilia and other bleeding disorders requires multidisciplinary expertise, mostly in haemophilia centres. The mainstay of medical treatment, for those with severe haemophilia, is the administration of **factor VIII concentrates**. These can be given in two ways: either as prophylaxis against haemorrhage (aiming to get over 2% activity) or as required for acute bleeding; up to 100% activity is needed when treating an intracranial haemorrhage. The problems with factor VIII replacement therapy fall into two main groups:

○ Blood-borne diseases, particularly HIV, hepatitis D and hepatitis C: this has been helped by the development of recombinant factor VIII concentrate, which is in use but expensive
○ The development of factor VIII inhibitors, which render factor VIII replacement therapy ineffective through antibody neutralisation and require progressively higher doses to be given. This affects 30% of patients with severe disease

Mild to moderate haemophiliacs often only require the administration of vasopressin (DDAVP), which releases endogenous factor VIII from its stores. **Tranexamic acid tablets can be used for minor mouth bleeds.**

Physiotherapy is important in patients who are recovering from joint bleeds as muscles will otherwise atrophy through lack of use.

Notes on von Willebrand's disease

Von Willebrand factor (vWF) is needed to protect circulating factor VIII from enzymes and to mediate platelet adhesion. Von Willebrand disease occurs when vWF synthesis is reduced or when abnormal vWF is produced. Platelet function is thus impaired.

Unless severe the majority of patients are asymptomatic, unless they are having surgery. There are three types:

○ Type 1: mild decrease in vWF levels and activity. Treat bleeding with DDAVP (watch sodium and fluid balance)
○ Type 2: normal or slightly low amounts of vWF but abnormal vWF function
○ Type 3: severe disease, complete absence of vWF. Presents in neonatal period

MANAGEMENT POINTS TO CONSIDER FOR PATIENTS WITH A SEVERE BLEEDING DISORDER

○ If antenatal diagnosis: plan delivery (no forceps/ventouse)
○ Avoid intramuscular injections, aspirin, NSAIDs
○ Subcutaneous hepatitis A and B vaccines (because of risks associated with frequent blood products)
○ Inform GP and dentist
○ Multidisciplinary team management
○ Educate parents
○ Think about preparing action plan for management of complications (who to ring, what blood products to give)
○ Physiotherapy, eg for joint bleeds
○ Genetic counselling
○ Involve haematologist for treatment of acute events

YOUR NOTES

12.2 RHEUMATOLOGY

12.2.1 Introduction

The examination of joints can come up as part of the examination of another system or as a station in its own right. It is an opportunity to score well if you have good knowledge of joint examination and abnormal pathology. It is essential to practise joint examination carefully and frequently and to recognise and understand the range of normality.

12.2.2 Clinical examination

Suggested approach to joint examination

There are some golden rules, which will help you structure your examination and appear confident and professional:

■ Always take a general look at the child first
■ When examining limbs, remember to compare both sides, simultaneously wherever practical
■ Always ask about pain (in general first and then specifically before you touch or move the patient)
■ Bear in mind the symptoms of joint disease

SYMPTOMS OF JOINT DISEASE

○ Pain
○ Stiffness
○ Swelling
○ Instability
○ Locking
○ Clicking
○ Loss of function

Examination involves the following components:
1. Look
2. Feel
3. Move
4. Assess function

General

The following is a guide only. Not all aspects of joint examination necessarily need to be carried out in every short case. If there is an obvious abnormality, eg swollen left knee or swollen interphalangeal joints, then you need to focus on it.

Look

- General appearance of the child. Any obvious clues, eg orthoses, shoes, splints. Remember growth
- Look for any deformity, erythema, swelling around the joint, scars from previous infection or surgery and muscle bulk
- Compare with normal joint
- Comment on posture/movements where relevant

Feel

- Watch patient's face while palpating the joint
- Feel for skin temperature, tenderness, and joint effusion

Move

- Ask the child to move the joint before you move it to ensure that movement is not painful and to get some idea of the range of movement possible. It is important to do this as you don't want to cause pain as soon as you touch the patient!
- Compare with normal joint

Function

- Ask the patient to stand up and walk a short distance (gait) with exposure
- For upper limbs, get the patient to do things that he/she finds difficult, eg drinking from cup, grasping large objects such as a bottle/box and small objects, eg paper clips, etc. Make him/her write, draw, comb hair, take off shirt, etc.

TRENDELENBURG GAIT

- ○ Non-painful limp
  Trendelenburg positive implies the affected hip is lower than the unaffected hip, eg hip dislocation, instability or muscle weakness
- ○ Painful limp
  Trendelenburg negative implies the affected hip is higher than the unaffected hip, eg Perthes' disease

If the affected joint is not obvious, the order for examination may be from hand to head, and head to toe, ie hands, wrists, elbows, shoulders, temporomandibular joints, spine, hips, knees, ankles, feet.

Finally

Many rheumatological conditions are associated with physical signs elsewhere (eg eyes, skin, cardiac). It may be relevant to extend your examination to look for extra-articular manifestations of joint disease. This is covered in more detail under the notes on specific conditions. The following is a rough guide for where else to look after you have discovered the primary rheumatological abnormality.

Further examination after finding of inflammatory arthritis

- Eyes: blue sclerae, evidence of visual impairment (from uveitis), conjunctival pallor (can be iron deficient from chronic disease or from NSAID use or both)
- Skin: psoriatic lesions, dermatomyositis rash, striae from steroid use, neurocutaneous stigmata, systemic lupus erythematosus (SLE) rash, salmon pink rash
- Nails: psoriatic changes, iron deficiency changes
- Dactylitis: if present can help with differential diagnosis
- Abdomen: hepatosplenomegaly
- Look for evidence of overgrowth or undergrowth of affected limb (eg measure for leg length discrepancy)
- Look for evidence of infection if joint pain is known to be of recent onset (reactive arthritis)
- Check temperature (particularly relevant for systemic-onset juvenile idiopathic arthritis or JIA)
- Think about growth and nutrition

Further examination after finding of scoliosis

- Skin: look for neurocutaneous stigmata, scars from previous surgery
- Neurological examination
- Mention pubertal staging: may be relevant (as scoliosis tends to worsen during puberty)
- Respiratory examination if scoliosis is severe (?evidence of respiratory failure)
- Look for evidence of Marfan syndrome if tall

Specific joints

Hands

- Described under examination of hand (see 'Suggested approach to hand examination' below)

Wrists

- Wrist is held in flexion with pronation of forearm in cerebral palsy
- Diffuse swelling of wrist may be seen in arthritis
- Palpate to localise tenderness
- Range of movements: flexion 80°, extension 70°, radial deviation 20° and ulnar deviation 30°

Elbows

- Range of movement: flexion 135°, extension 0°, supination 90° and pronation 90°
- Supination and pronation are tested with elbows flexed

Shoulders

Range of movement can be tested easily (this method also covers function):

- *'Put your hands above your head'*; tests flexion (90°) and abduction (180°)
- *'Give yourself a hug'*; tests adduction (45°)
- *'Scratch your back'*; tests external rotation (45°)
- *'Hide your hands behind your back'*; tests internal rotation (55°) and extension (45°)

Jaw and cervical spine

- Movement at temporomandibular joint should be examined with the child opening and closing mouth
- Feel for crepitus over temporomandibular joint
- Look for acquired micrognathia and dental malocclusion
- Range of movement at cervical spine is as follows: flexion (45°), extension (50°), rotation (80°) and lateral flexion (40°)

Thoracolumbar spine

- Examine child for kyphoscoliosis when they are standing and bending forward
- Feel for tenderness and check range of movement: flexion (should be able to touch toes), extension (30° at lumbar area), lateral bending (50° to each side), lateral rotation (30° to each side)

▓ Functional evaluation: ask the child to pick an object up from the floor or put their socks and shoes on

Lower limbs

▓ Examine the gait whatever the joint in question
▓ Make the child squat (for proximal muscle weakness)
▓ Make child stand on each leg (for Trendelenburg sign).

Hips

▓ Look for muscle wasting
▓ Note the resting position
▓ Feel for tenderness
▓ Measure true leg length between anterior superior iliac spine and medial malleolus
▓ Range of movement: flexion (120°), extension (30°), internal rotation (35°), external rotation (45°), abduction (50°) and adduction (30°). Stabilise the pelvis before checking the range of movement. Internal and external rotation are measured with hip flexed and these are the movements most likely to cause pain if there is any hip pathology – be careful!

Knees

▓ Look for quadriceps wasting
▓ Feel for tenderness, raised local temperature and effusion
▓ Check range of movement: flexion (135°), extension (up to 10°). Check for abnormal movement
▓ There are manoeuvres to check the stability of the ligaments in the knee You should know what these manoeuvres are, but they are more relevant to traumatic knee injuries and you would be very unlucky to need to demonstrate these in this station

Ankles and feet

▓ Range of movement at ankle: plantar flexion (50°), dorsiflexion (20°). Inversion (5°) and eversion (5°) occur at the sub-talar joint. Abduction (10°) and adduction (20°) occur at mid-tarsal joints. First metatarsophalangeal joint permits plantar flexion (45°) and extension (70°)
▓ Some joint deformities are more obvious when the patient is weight bearing. As part of assessing function ask the patient to stand and observe what happens to their feet and ankles. Looking at footwear may also give some information about function.

Suggested approach to hand examination

This is very important and is the starting point of the clinical examination of most systems. Alternatively, you may be asked just to look at the hands. In most cases the features are obvious and lead you on to further examination. In other circumstances a more detailed review of potential pathology in the hand is required and the following is a suggested scheme.

Instructions to candidate

Examine this child's hands
Look at this child's hands and describe what you see

Introduce yourself and ask the child, *'please would you roll up your sleeves?'*

Inspection

Look first for any obvious abnormality which, if found, will determine the rest of your examination. Remember to examine both hands at once. If there is no obvious lead then work through the sequence below.

1. Inspect dorsum of hands first, looking specifically at:
   - Deformity
     - Trauma
     - Arachnodactyly – Marfan syndrome
     - Pseudohypoparathyroidism – short 4th, 5th metacarpal
     - Broad hands, stubby fingers, curved little finger, simian crease – Down syndrome
     - Large – acromegaly (rare)
   - Asymmetry
   - Muscles and soft tissues
     - Muscle wasting could point to arthritis, myopathy or neurological disease (for example, combination of claw hand and interosseous wasting points to an ulnar lesion proximal to the wrist). Remember to look for wasting at the thenar eminence and interosseous muscles in particular
     - Subcutaneous fat and palmer fascia – Dupuytren's contracture (rare in childhood) – indicative of chronic liver disease
     - Blood vessels – Raynaud's phenomenon in primary Raynaud's disease
     - Tendon sheaths – in rheumatoid arthritis thickening of the synovial sheath leads to swelling on the dorsum of the wrist and the front of the fingers and wrist
     - Joints – arthritis can cause anything from mild spindling of proximal interphalangeal joints to gross disorganisation of the hand with

subluxation of joints and wasting of small muscles. Psoriatic arthritis involves the distal interphalangeal joints and nails

■ Nails: abnormalities include:
  - Clubbing
  - Psoriasis – pitting of nails, onycholysis and arthropathy of distal inter-phalangeal joint
  - Koilonychia – iron deficiency anaemia
  - Splinter haemorrhage
  - White bands (horizontal) – abnormal zones of nail growth in serious illness, malnutrition and chemotherapy
  - Nail bed telangiectasia in dermatomyositis
  - Haemorrhage in nail fold in vasculitis, eg dermatomyositis, rheumatoid arthritis and scleroderma

■ Skin
  - Eczema
  - Contact dermatitis
  - Scleroderma

■ Posture
  - 'Claw hand' – hyperextension of the metacarpophalangeal joint and lack of extension of the interphalangeal joint due to weakness of the interossei (damage to the medial cord of the brachial plexus at birth)
  - Hemiplegia – flexed hand and arm
  - Wrist drop – radial palsy
  - Ulnar deviation – rheumatoid arthritis

■ Stigmata
  - Neurocutaneous syndromes
  - Evidence of bacterial endocarditis

■ Scars – especially preterm venepuncture marks

2. Inspect the nails from the side to look for
  ■ Clubbing
  ■ Hyperconvex nails (Turner syndrome)

3. Inspect the palms following same regime as above (minus the 'Nails')
  ■ Deformity
  ■ Asymmetry
  ■ Muscles and soft tissues
  ■ Skin
  ■ Posture
  ■ Stigmata
  ■ Scars

Palpation

- Colour, temperature, sweating
- Palpate any swellings to see if they are bony or soft tissues
- You could assess sensation at this point – remember dermatomes and radial/ulnar/median sensory distribution

Move

1. Comment on tremors/spontaneous movements

2. Range of movement
   - Metacarpophalangeal joint – flexion 90°, extension 30°
   - Proximal interphalangeal joint – flexion 100°
   - Distal interphalangeal joint – flexion 90°, extension 10°

Tip

Remember to compare both sides

---

3. A quick way of assessing hand movements is
   - *'make a fist'* : finger flexion at each joint is assessed by looking at symmetry – assesses median and ulnar nerve supply
   - *'make a star'* (fingers spread out and extended): radial nerve extends and adducts the thumb; the ulnar nerve supplies the intrinsic hand muscles (responsible for abduction) – can test symmetry of finger abduction power
   - *'make a circle'* (with thumb and index finger): median nerve opposes and flexes thumb – can test symmetry and power of this

If there are any abnormalities in the above movements, you can then go on to assess nerves individually in more detail.

Function

The function of the hand is best assessed by simple tests such as

- Grip strength
- Use of spoon, knife and fork
- Holding cup
- Drawing with pencil
- Writing
- Doing and undoing buttons

Nerve injuries with physical signs in the hand

Nerve injuries make good spot cases and should be revised carefully (see Box).

ULNAR NERVE PALSY

- Sensory loss medial 1½ fingers
- Motor – claw hand, weakness and wasting of small muscles with sparing of the thenar eminence

MEDIAN NERVE PALSY

- Sensory loss of the thumb and lateral fingers (up to and including the lateral half of the middle finger) with wasting of the thenar eminence.
- Motor – weakness of the thenar eminence, opponens pollicis, lateral two lumbricals, adductor pollicis brevis

RADIAL NERVE PALSY

- Sensory loss in anatomical snuffbox
- Motor loss at the wrist, finger and thumb extension, weakness of extensors of the wrist, thumb, metacarpophalangeal joints of the fingers, 'wrist drop'

Erb's palsy

C5,6; right > left. Can be bilateral. Occurs secondary to difficult deliveries, particularly shoulder dystocia. Usually reflects compression with haemorrhage and oedema and there is a good recovery. Occasionally the nerve is torn.

Features
- Asymmetrical Moro
- Adduction and internal rotation at the shoulder
- Extension at the elbow
- Pronation of the forearm
- Flexion of the wrist (waiter's tip)
- Limb is hypotonic with a reduce biceps jerk

Associations

- Fractured clavicle
- Horner's syndrome

Management

- Physiotherapy
- Surgery (rarely)

Klumpke's

Much less common = claw hand (C8, T1)

12.2.3 Cases

Case one – juvenile idiopathic arthritis

Instructions to candidate

Please examine Bethany's hands. She is 10 years old.

> *(Introduce yourself) I would like to plot her height and weight on the centile chart. Bethany has got bilateral swollen wrists. There is painful restriction of range of movement at both wrists to around 120°. I can also see marked swelling of proximal interphalangeal joints of index and middle fingers bilaterally. I would like to do a detailed examination of all joints... (proceed).*

This scenario gives you a good opportunity to say what else you would examine.

For example:

- I would like to examine for signs of eye disease
- I would like to review the growth
- I would look for signs of steroid toxicity
- I would like to check the skin

Case two – psoriatic arthritis; 'hand' examination

Instructions to candidate

Examine John's hands. He is 12 years old.

> *John is 12 years old. I would like to plot his weight and height on a centile chart. Examination of his hands shows diffusely swollen right index finger at the distal interphalangeal joint. On closer examination, I can clearly see multiple pits on the nail of this finger. I would like to carry out further joint examination and look for the rash of psoriasis.*

Supplementary questions

What else would you like to examine?

- Joint examination: asymmetric oligoarthritis of large and small joints
- Rash: typical of psoriasis. Erythematous papules that coalesce to form plaques with silvery or yellow-white scales. Preferred sites are scalp, knees, elbows, umbilicus and genitalia

○ Nails may show multiple pits, vertical or horizontal ridging; onycholysis is uncommon

○ Eye examination may show chronic uveitis similar to juvenile chronic arthritis

Case three – haemophilia

Instructions to candidate

Examine this young man's elbow.

> *(Introduce yourself) On inspection, there is no obvious swelling or redness. On feeling the joint, there is no tenderness. On both passive and active movement there is a fixed flexion deformity of the elbow, although the joint is not painful. I note there is also some bruising to the upper arm.*
>
> *This would be compatible with **haemophilia**.*

Supplementary questions

○ How does arthropathy reflect the seriousness of the haemophilia?

○ How do you treat bleeding into the joint?

Case four – osteogenesis imperfecta

Instructions to candidate

Examine Clara's eyes please.

> *(Introduce yourself) The most obvious feature is the blue sclera.*

Supplementary questions

With that in mind, what would you like to examine?

> *I would like to go on and look for bony deformities in the arms and legs, with the diagnosis of osteogenesis imperfecta in mind.*

Mum may be in a wheelchair in which case that is an obvious clue.

This is a very common short case. The main clues being the blue sclera and the presence of the mother in a wheelchair reflecting the autosomal-dominant inheritance of the condition.

○ What different types of osteogenesis imperfecta are there?
○ What is the inheritance?
○ What is the differential (non-accidental injury?)?
○ What do you see in the skull of the newborn? (Wormian bones)

Case five – median nerve injury

Instructions to candidate

Examine Steven's hands. He is 10 years old.

> Steven looks well. Looking at his hands, there is atrophy of thenar muscles and loss of the thenar eminence in the right hand. Hypothenar muscles are well preserved. I would like to do a full motor examination of both upper limbs ...

Examine also for:

○ Muscle wasting of arms, forearms
○ Classic signs of brachial plexus lesions: 'claw hand' in Klumpke's palsy; 'waiter's tip' hand in Erb's palsy
○ Classic signs of peripheral nerve lesion: wrist drop in radial nerve palsy; 'monkey hand' in median nerve palsy; and 'claw hand' in ulnar nerve palsy
○ Fasciculation indicative of anterior horn cell disease
○ Contractures
○ Scars in the hand, neck and the back
○ Scoliosis

12.2.4 Neonatal hip examination

There is a 'hip' doll available and it is often used in the exam. Therefore, you need to know precisely the correct methods of hip examination (see Box), the potential abnormalities and how they are dealt with. You may also be asked about the role of ultrasound in the detection of hip problems in the neonatal period.

> **BARLOW TEST**
>
> This is the test for the 'dislocatable' hip (ie femoral head in joint but shallow acetabulum). Stabilise the pelvis with one hand by lying the child on its back with its hips flexed and knees bent. Place the middle finger of your hand over the greater trochanter and the thumb on the inside of the thigh opposite the lesser trochanter. Push down on the hip, creating a posterior force, and you should feel the hip dislocate if abnormal.
>
> **ORTOLANI TEST**
>
> This is the test to relocate the recently dislocated hip. The hips are flexed and abducted and the femoral head should move back into the acetabulum.

In practice, the Barlow and Ortolani tests are performed together in one movement.

Other quoted physical signs for hip dysplasia are:

- Leg length discrepancy
- Unequal abduction (most valuable)
- Asymmetrical buttock (not thigh) creases (least valuable)

Notes on abnormalities detected on neonatal hip examination

The abnormalities detected fall into different groups:

- Dislocated
- Dislocatable
- Unstable/click

The first two groups require urgent orthopaedic input and splinting – double nappies, Aberdeen splint or a Pavlik harness. The last group requires further assessment and follow-up and many in this group improve with time. It would be sensible to discuss with your local orthopaedic surgeons their strategy for the management of hip problems in the neonatal period. In some units ultrasound is offered either to all babies or to families with risk factors. Other hospitals do not offer this and there is no consensus as yet. The ossific nucleus in the femur appears at 4–8 months; after 8 months hip dysplasia should be obvious on X-ray.

The risks of a Pavlik harness include:

○ Failure (5%): requiring surgical treatment
○ Avascular necrosis of femoral head
○ Interference with bonding

INCREASED RISK OF DEVELOPMENTAL DYSPLASIA OF THE HIP IS ASSOCIATED WITH

○ Females
○ Oligohydramnios
○ Breech
○ First born
○ Torticollis
○ Moulding
○ Talipes

FAMILY HISTORY IS IMPORTANT

○ 1 parent and 1 sib = 1 in 3 chance
○ 1 parent (female child) = 1 in 6 chance
○ 1 parent (male child) = 1 in 9 chance
○ 1 sib = next female child has a 1 in 9 chance

12.2.5 Hypermobility

Many people have a few hypermobile joints. Generalised joint hypermobility can be defined in terms of the Beighton score (see Box).

BEIGHTON SCORE

1. Touch palms on the floor with soles flat and a straight leg (spine hypermobility) – 1 point
2. Extend 5th metacarpophalangeal joint more than 90 degrees (1 point for each side)
3. Oppose thumb to forearm (1 point for each side)
4. Extend elbow more than 10 degrees beyond neutral (1 point for each side)
5. Extend knee more than 10 degrees beyond vertical (1 point for each side)

This gives a total of 9 potential points. A score of more than 4 is suggestive of generalised hypermobility.

Presentation

Hypermobility can present with the following symptoms

○ Arthralgia: most commonly anterior knee pain. Pain is typically felt most when starting or stopping exercise. If knee is involved then walking downstairs may cause symptoms. Treatment involves strengthening muscles surrounding the joint (swimming is good) and avoiding exercises that cause additional stretch on joint ligaments. Attention should be paid to appropriate foot wear and awareness of posture to prevent the development of chronic pain
○ Difficulty with gripping – may have difficulty grasping pens/pencils, causing problems with schoolwork/handwriting (wider pencils are easier to grip)
○ Delayed walking and history of being clumsy in early childhood

Joint hypermobility can influence the choice of careers and hobbies and if severe this should be addressed with patients and parents. In general high-level ballet and high-level contact sports should be avoided. Playing musical instruments at a high level can also cause persistent joint pain and damage.

Ehlers–Danlos syndrome

Group of conditions with different clinical presentation to general joint hypermobility primarily because of the following:

○ Paper-like scars (tissue fragility with easy bruising): most prominent on forehead and lower limbs
○ Skin hyperelasticity (snaps back into place when stretched)
○ More extreme joint hypermobility

Ten different types exist – key ones to know are:

○ Type 1: severe form, associated with premature rupture of membranes and preterm birth. Patients have a normal life expectancy and may have mitral valve prolapse
○ Type 3: mainly hypermobility. Other findings are less obvious and can be difficult to distinguish from generalised joint hypermobility
○ Type 4 (vascular form): spontaneous rupture of arteries can be seen

Suggested approach to examination of hypermobile joints

Instructions to candidate

This child has joint hypermobility, examine him.

General

■ Note body habitus (Marfanoid)
■ Look for evidence that hypermobility is affecting function (orthoses)
■ Comment on posture (sitting or standing in a way that places strain on joint ligaments)

Hands

■ Arachnodactyly (finger and thumb encircling wrist)
■ Ask child to extend 5th metacarpophalangeal joint and oppose thumb to forearm (Beighton score)

Arms

■ Look for scars/bruises
■ Assess brachial pulse character (collapsing)
■ Ask patient to extend elbows (Beighton score)

Head and neck

■ High arched palate?

Chest

■ Chest wall deformity
■ Listen for mitral valve prolapse/aortic regurgitation

Spine

■ Can they touch their palms on the floor with straight legs (Beighton score – 1 point)
■ Assess for scoliosis

Legs

■ Extend knees (Beighton score)
■ Look for atrophic scars

Feet

■ Look for pes planus (flat feet) – normal up until 6 years, beyond that it may be associated with ligamentous laxity

Gait

■ May be abnormal in severe hypermobility

Finally

■ Ehlers–Danlos and Marfan syndromes are inherited traits; you should examine parents if you suspect these conditions
■ Plot growth if you have not already done this
■ Complete cardiac and ophthalmic examination looking for evidence of Marfan syndrome
■ Measure arm span (versus height) Marfan syndrome

12.2.6 Juvenile idiopathic arthritis (JIA)

This is a very common case. Most patients attend outpatients and physiotherapy only and are rarely seen on the wards. The use of **methotrexate** has revolutionised the management of chronic arthritis. This means that children seen may have very few physical signs.

These notes are quite thorough; a good knowledge of this potentially confusing area is essential.

Epidemiology
Prevalence is 65:100 000 schoolchildren

Criteria for classification
○ Age of onset <16 years
○ Arthritis in one or more joints defined as swelling or effusion, or the presence of two or more of the following signs: limitation of range of motion, tenderness or pain on movement, and increased heat
○ Duration of disease minimum 6 weeks
○ Polyarticular: five or more joints
○ Oligoiarticular: four or fewer joints
○ Systemic disease: arthritis with intermittent fever

Systemic-onset juvenile idiopathic arthritis (formerly Still's disease)

Epidemiology
○ 20% of juvenile idiopathic arthritis
○ Onset throughout childhood (therefore can be seen in younger ages than other forms of JIA) – usually begins before 5 years of age
○ Equal sex incidence in under 5 years (but girls predominate if onset occurs later than this)
○ Systemic features may precede arthritis by months
○ Progresses to severe and long-term arthritis in one third of cases

Differential diagnosis
Differential diagnosis in this condition is important, as systemic JIA is a diagnosis of exclusion.

Main differential diagnoses are:
○ Malignancy (particularly leukaemia)
○ Systemic lupus erythematosus

O Kawasaki disease
O Rheumatic fever
O Infection/sepsis (eg TB, bacterial endocarditis, malaria)
O Reactive arthritis

CLINICAL FEATURES OF SYSTEMIC-ONSET JUVENILE IDIOPATHIC ARTHRITIS

Systemic symptoms

O Fever (>38.5°C) – needs to be present for at least 6 weeks for definitive diagnosis
O Macular, non-pruritic rash – classically a salmon pink rash, brought out by fever or heat, often fades as temperature returns to normal

Polyarticular arthritis
Other features

O Weight loss/anorexia
O Lymphadenopathy, hepatosplenomegaly
O Pericarditis, pleural effusions
O Anaemia, leukocytosis and thrombocytosis
O Rheumatoid factor (RF) and antinuclear antibody (ANA) negative
O No uveitis or sacroiliitis
O Myalgia/arthralgia

Oligoarticular juvenile idiopathic arthritis

Epidemiology
O 35%–40% of juvenile idiopathic arthritis

Presentation
O Onset during early childhood (2–5 years)
O 80% girls
O Tends to affect large joints, particularly (in order of frequency) knee, ankle, wrists
O Often joints are swollen, warm and tender but not erythematous, with mild limitation of movement (compared to child's opposite

side). The more painful the joint, the more likelihood there is of an alternative diagnosis

○ Can present with swelling but no pain

○ Hip involvement at presentation is also very rare and should prompt a search for an alternative diagnosis

○ Disease-modifying drugs such as **methotrexate** and **infliximab** have had a major impact on this condition. This means that children seen in the exam may have very few physical signs

Complications

○ **Chronic uveitis** occurs in 30%; often asymptomatic; can cause blindness. Children are seen regularly by an ophthalmologist for slit lamp examination

○ ANA positivity (90%) correlates with the risk of uveitis. Usually other blood tests (including ESR and rheumatoid factor) are normal

○ Active disease is treated with steroid eye drops and mydriatics

○ Chronic uveitis can progress to poor vision with a cloudy cornea and fixed constricted pupil

○ **Leg length discrepancy** – results from increased blood flow to the affected joint, causing that limb to grow disproportionately.

Prognosis

○ Most resolve within 6 months

○ Approximately 20% of children who initially do well will have a recurrence (most commonly within the first year)

○ Polyarthritis develops eventually in 20% cases. These children are not reclassified as having polyarticular arthritis (although their treatment is similarly aggressive) if they have four or fewer joints only involved for the first 6 months

Enthesitis-related arthritis

○ 10–15% of juvenile idiopathic arthritis

○ 90% boys

○ Onset during late childhood

○ A few large joints are involved, especially the hip girdle; sacroiliitis is common

○ Spine is commonly involved

○ Enthesitis refers to inflammation of tendon insertions; typically the Achilles tendon and plantar fascia are involved

○ Sometimes see 'sausage finger' (dactylitis)

○ Acute uveitis is seen in 10%–20% cases. ANA and RF negative

○ HLA B27 positive in 75% cases
○ Many develop ankylosing spondylitis

Polyarticular rheumatoid factor negative juvenile idiopathic arthritis

○ 20%–25% of juvenile idiopathic arthritis; 90% girls; onset at any age
○ 'Polyarticular' diagnosis requires arthritis in more than four joints in the first 6 months of disease
○ Symmetrical arthritis involving both large and small joints of upper and lower limbs but no sacroiliitis
○ Temporomandibular joint involvement (even if asymptomatic) can lead to micrognathia or limited mouth opening
○ Uveitis is rare, but more likely to occur if ANA is positive
○ RF negative, ANA positive in 25% cases
○ Prognosis: severe arthritis in 10%–15% cases. Lower likelihood of remission with younger age at diagnosis

Polyarticular rheumatoid factor positive juvenile idiopathic arthritis

○ 5%–10% of juvenile idiopathic arthritis; 80% girls; onset in late childhood
○ Resembles adult rheumatoid arthritis with symmetric polyarthritis affecting upper and lower limbs (typically hands and feet)
○ RF positive 100%; ANA 75%
    HLA DR4 suggests more aggressive course
○ No uveitis, sacroiliitis rare
○ Prognosis: severe erosive arthritis with poor functional outcome in 50% cases. Joint destruction and contractures can occur similar to adult patients unless well treated

Juvenile idiopathic arthritis – management

How to manage juvenile idiopathic arthritis is a question that is commonly asked and it is very important to give a summary answer at the outset with appropriate emphasis. This is a good opportunity to show the examiner that you appreciate the multidisciplinary management of a complex and chronic condition such as juvenile idiopathic arthritis.

You should mention

1. Non-medical therapy. This is very important and in the exam it is essential that you show to the examiner your awareness of non-medical therapies, for example physiotherapy and occupational therapy, ie hydrotherapy, passive movement, splints
2. Medical therapy. Be prepared to talk about non-steroidal anti-inflammatory drugs, local or systemic steroids, disease modifying drugs, eg **methotrexate**. Side-effects may also be discussed as these can have quite an impact on some patients

MANAGEMENT OF JUVENILE IDIOPATHIC ARTHRITIS

DRUGS

○ **Non-steroidal anti-inflammatory drugs** remain the first line, particularly **ibuprofen**. Doses are usually high and antacids are occasionally required for gastrointestinal side-effects

○ **Corticosteroid injection (triamcinolone)** – useful in oligoarticular disease. They are increasingly used early in severely inflamed joints with good results

○ **Systemic corticosteroids** in severe disease – particularly disease with systemic manifestations

○ Disease-modifying drugs such as **methotrexate** (other less used options include **ciclosporin**)

○ Anti-TNF monoclonal antibody becoming widely used (**infliximab**)

NON-DRUG TREATMENT

Physiotherapy and occupational therapy

○ Hydrotherapy
○ Passive movement
○ Gentle exercises
○ Splints

12.2.7 OTHER CONDITIONS

Psoriatic arthritis

Epidemiology
- Chronic inflammatory arthritis before 16 years of age, preceded by, accompanied by, or followed within 15 years by psoriasis
- Prevalence is expected to be 10–15 cases per 100 000
- Age at onset usually around 10 years
- F > M = 1.2 : 1

Diagnosis
- The diagnosis is clinical, according to Vancouver criteria (see Box)
- Psoriatic arthritis should be suspected in chronic arthritis with dactylitis or asymmetric involvement of large or small joints, particularly the first metatarsophalangeal or the distal interphalangeal joints
- Rheumatoid factor is absent
- ANA may be seen in 17%–50% cases (there is also a risk of uveitis)

VANCOUVER CRITERIA FOR DIAGNOSIS

DEFINITE PSORIATIC ARTHRITIS
- Arthritis with typical psoriatic rash
- Arthritis with three of the four following minor criteria
  - Dactylitis
  - Nail pitting or onycholysis
  - Psoriasis-like rash
  - Family history (first- or second-degree relatives) of psoriasis

PROBABLE PSORIATIC ARTHRITIS
- Arthritis with two of the four minor criteria

Management and prognosis
- Management is along the same lines as for juvenile idiopathic arthritis
- Many children with pauciarticular disease may progress to polyarticular disease, some requiring major reconstructive surgery of hips and other joints

○ Course may be relapsing and remitting with or without flaring of skin disease

Juvenile dermatomyositis

This is an unusual case and a rare condition in clinical practice. The following will help to increase your awareness of the condition and will be of practical use if you see a case.

○ 20% present in childhood, usually the second decade
○ Acute or sub-acute onset
○ Painful tender muscles with lethargy, skin rashes and proximal muscle weakness either shoulder girdle or lower limbs
○ Usually asymmetrical
○ Rash – characteristic – upper eyelids and upper cheeks (butterfly), rash also over elbows, hyperaemia of nail beds
○ Can get dysphagia (adults), skin calcification
○ Raised ESR and CPK
○ Confirm diagnosis with muscle biopsy
○ Treatment difficult and with long-term steroids ± other immuno-suppression

Osteogenesis imperfecta

Osteogenesis imperfecta is a disorder of connective tissue charac-terised by bone fragility. The disease encompasses a phenotypically and genetically heterogeneous group of inherited disorders that result from mutations in the genes that encode for type 1 collagen. The disorder is manifest in the tissues whose principal matrix is collagen, namely bone, sclerae and ligaments. The musculoskeletal manifesta-tions vary from perinatal lethal forms, to moderate forms with defor-mity and a propensity to fracture, to clinically silent forms with subtle osteopenia and no deformity.

Osteogenesis imperfecta type I

This is characterised by osteoporosis and excessive bone fragility, distinctly blue sclera and hearing loss. Autosomal-dominant inheri-tance, 1 in 30 000 live births. Fractures may be obvious from birth. Hearing impairment due to otosclerosis affects most patients by the fifth decade, but is rare in the first decade. Some families have dentino-genesis imperfecta – with yellow transparent teeth that are fragile. There is spontaneous improvement with puberty. X-rays show generalised osteopenia, evidence of previous fractures and callus formation at the site of new bone formation. The skull X-ray shows wormian bones.

Osteogenesis imperfecta type II

This lethal syndrome is characterised by low birth weight and typical X-ray findings of crumpled bones and beaded ribs. Autosomal-recessive inheritance in a few cases; most inheritance is by new autosomal-dominant mutations. Affects 1 in 60 000 live births; 50% are stillborn, with the remainder dying soon after birth from respiratory difficulty due to a defective thoracic cage. It is worth looking at a picture of the lethal form. X-rays show multiple fracture of the ribs, often beaded, and crumpled (accordion like) appearance of the long bones.

Osteogenesis imperfecta type III

This syndrome is characterised by severe bone fragility and multiple fractures in the newborn period which lead to progressive skeletal deformity. The sclera may be bluish at birth, but become less blue with age. Autosomal-recessive inheritance with clinical variability suggesting genetic heterogeneity. Few patients survive into adult life. X-rays show generalised osteopenia and multiple fractures, without the beading or crumpling of the ribs seen in type II.

Osteogenesis imperfecta type IV

This syndrome is characterised by osteoporosis leading to bone fragility without the other features of type I. The sclera may be bluish at birth, but become less blue as the patient matures. Autosomal-dominant inheritance. Variable age of onset and variable number of fractures; there is spontaneous improvement with puberty. X-rays show generalised osteopenia and fractures, but these are generally less than in the other forms of osteogenesis imperfecta.

Management

For osteogenesis imperfecta type II, no therapeutic intervention is helpful. For other forms, careful nursing of the newborn may prevent excessive fractures. Beyond the newborn period, aggressive orthopaedic treatment is the mainstay of treatment aimed at prompt splinting of fractures and correction of deformities. Genetic counselling is important. Reliable prenatal diagnosis is not available for all forms of osteogenesis imperfecta, although severely affected fetuses may be confidently recognised by X-rays, ultrasound screening and biochemistry.

Hemihypertrophy

This is often difficult to recognise. It may involve the whole of one side of the body, or be limited in extent, eg to just one leg. It may be congenital, in which case the tissues are structurally and functionally normal. It has been associated with mental retardation, ipsilateral paired internal organs and rarely with Wilms' tumours or adrenal carcinomas. Hemihypertrophy can be confused with regional overgrowth secondary to neurofibromatosis type I, haemangiomas and lymphangiomas. Hemihypertrophy occurs in 25% of patients with Beckwith–Wiedemann syndrome.

Miscellaneous conditions

Short neck

There are different causes of a short neck and you may come across a child in the exam with a short neck and need to be aware of the differential diagnosis.

- ○ Turner syndrome
- ○ Skeletal dysplasia
- ○ Klippel–Feil syndrome

Plagiocephaly

This is increasingly common as a phenomenon. Most plagio-cephaly is simple, does not imply a craniosynostoses and improves with follow-up. For example, in a child with a prominent left occiput who is growing and developing normally one would not consider surgery.

It is essential however to be aware of some of the more common craniosynostoses and the relevant syndromes including Crouzon's and Apert's.

Toe walking

- ○ Can be a normal finding up until age 3
- ○ Neurological disorders include cerebral palsy, Duchenne muscular dystrophy, spinal cord problems, congenital tendo-achilles shortening
- ○ Think about possible leg length discrepancy if unilateral
- ○ Habit

Foot drop

- ○ Variety of causes

○ Patient has a stepping gait and lifts the affected limb high to avoid scraping the foot on the floor. They are unable to walk on their heel
○ Possible causes
  • Lateral popliteal nerve palsy (look for signs of injury below and lateral to the affected knee)
  • Peroneal muscle atrophy (look for hereditary motor and sensory neuropathy/Charcot–Marie–Tooth disease)
  • Poliomyelitis

Orthoses

Children with neurological disorders are very prone to developing joint contractures and bony abnormalities, particularly spinal kyphoscoliosis. Orthoses are useful in helping to prevent contractures, in maintaining a good position if contractures have been repaired and in providing joint stability. They are particularly useful in aiding individual children with mobility. The type of orthosis depends on the child's individual needs, eg they may be ankle–foot orthoses if there is just ankle and foot involvement, extending to the knee if the knee is involved. Should there be a scoliosis, thoracolumbar orthoses are available. Wrist orthoses are also commonly used.

Talipes

○ Two types – positional and non-positional
○ Positional talipes occurs due to the in-utero position, and requires, at most, some parental physiotherapy
○ Non-positional talipes or clubfoot is a multifactorial deformity of primarily genetic origin; 30%–50% require casting only to recover, the cast being applied within the first week. The casts are changed weekly. Surgery is reserved for those not responding to casting. If surgery is required, usually at 6–9 months, it involves lengthening the tight tendons and releasing tight joints with pinning and casting – usually with good results. There is a 3% recurrence risk in future children.

Perthes' disease

○ Arises from disturbance of the upper femoral epiphysis secondary to ischaemic necrosis of unknown aetiology
○ Onset commonly between 4 and 9 years. Bilateral in 15% cases
○ Earliest sign is a limp, usually accompanied by pain. Initial symptoms may be intermittent, causing diagnostic confusion, especially if the initial X-rays are normal

○ X-rays should be AP and frog-leg lateral. Initially the ossified portion of the femoral head appears smaller compared to its normal counterpart, together with a widened articular cartilage space. Following this the ossific nucleus becomes more radio-opaque, then the epiphysis develops a fragmented appearance. This is followed by a gradual return to normal with new bone formation

○ Differential diagnosis is inflammatory – septic arthritis, osteomyelitis, transient synovitis, post-traumatic, fracture, neoplasia, slipped upper femoral capital epiphysis

○ The short-term aim of treatment is to reduce pain and hip stiffness

○ The disease is a self-limiting process and may last from 2 to 4 years

○ Restriction of activity helps to relieve the pain; occasionally pain may be so severe as to warrant non-weight-bearing with crutches and bed-rest

○ The long-term goal is to reduce residual deformity. Controversy exists as to the best way of doing this. The important principle is femoral head containment so that re-ossification produces a spherical femoral head. This can be achieved by non-operative bracing in abduction, or by operative means

○ Treatment method depends on the age of the child, severity of involvement of the femoral head and the expertise of the local orthopaedic surgeon

○ Prognosis is best for young children, with full recovery and no disability – the remainder are left with a degree of residual disability of varying severity

YOUR NOTES

12.3 DERMATOLOGY

12.3.1 Introduction

Skin problems may be seen in the 'Other' Station, often as part of a systemic condition such as café-au-lait spots in a child with neurofibromatosis. Remember that the stations are 9 min long so a 'spot diagnosis' of a lesion in a child with no other signs is going to be unlikely. Therefore a thorough examination of the skin is worth practising and it is well worth attending a paediatric dermatology clinic, not only to recognise common lesions but also to get used to discussing their management. The candidate is also advised to review the appearance of common skin lesions in a dermatology atlas. Specific skin conditions are discussed in this chapter in note form to complement this revision.

12.3.2 Clinical examination

Brief scheme for examination of the skin

This is difficult and it is not possible to have a scheme that is always applicable. Like any system examination remember to include a comment about the general appearance of the child before you go on to assess the skin, hair, nails and mucous membranes.

- Aim for good exposure
- Look at the hands, nails, hair and mucous membranes
- Expose other areas and don't forget axillae and soles of feet
- If desperate ask if there is a rash and where it is
- If you think a lesion is part of a systemic condition ask to examine the relevant systems. Look for lymphadenopathy, hepatosplenomegaly and at the joints if appropriate
- Mention Wood's lamp examination if applicable; this will highlight areas of altered pigmentation such as vitiligo and certain types of fungal infection. It is also used to look for the depigmented patches associated with tuberous sclerosis

Notes on skin examination

When you have noticed a lesion you will need to describe the appearance of the skin in the appropriate language:

- **Type of lesion:** macule, papule, nodule, vesicle, etc
- **Shape of individual lesions:** round, oval, linear, annular, etc
- **Distribution:** examine palms, soles, mouth, scalp
- **Extent of involvement:** circumscribed, regional, generalised
- **Pattern:** symmetry, sun-exposed area, sites of pressure, etc
- **Characteristic location:** flexural, extensor surface, palms and soles, etc
- **Colour:** red, brown, white, etc and whether blanches on pressure
- **Consistency of lesion:** infiltrated, firm, soft, doughy, etc

Macule: flat lesion that differs from surrounding because of its colour; may have any size, shape

Papule: small, solid, elevated (palpable) generally, < 1 cm in diameter

Nodule: palpable, solid, round or ellipsoid lesion larger than papule (> 1cm in diameter)

Plaque: elevation occupying large surface area formed by confluence of papules, eg psoriasis

Petechiae: pinpoint (< 2 mm in diameter) haemorrhage in the skin, does not blanch with pressure

Purpura: larger than petechiae, does not blanch with pressure

Vesicle: circumscribed, elevated lesion containing clear fluid that is < 0.5cm in diameter

Bullae: vesicles >0.5 cm diameter

Pustule: circumscribed, raised lesion containing pus

Cyst: sac containing liquid, semi-solid material

Weal: rounded, flat-topped papule or plaque that is evanescent, disappearing within hours

Scale: abnormal shedding or accumulation of stratum corneum in flakes, eg psoriasis

Crust: hardened deposits resulting from drying of exudates

Ulcer: defect in skin due to destruction of epidermis and part of dermis

Erosion: moist, circumscribed, depressed lesion due to loss of all or portion of viable epidermis

Scar: ulcer heals with scar

Atrophy: diminution in the size of cell, tissue, organ or part of the body

Table 12.1: Useful definitions

12.3.3 Skin conditions commonly seen in the exam

Note that some of these conditions will not be the only problem a patient may have; there are 9 min per station and these cannot be filled by talking about a Mongolian blue spot!

○ Eczema
○ Psoriasis
○ Mongolian blue spot
○ Strawberry naevus
○ Sebaceous naevus
○ Vitiligo
○ Lipodystrophies
○ Molluscum contagiosum
○ Epidermolysis bullosa
○ Ectodermal dysplasia
○ Erythema multiforme

Discussed in other chapters:

○ Capillary haemangioma (Sturge Weber) – see Section 11.5
○ Café-au-lait spots (neurofibromatosis) – see Section 11.5

Eczema

Eczema is a chronic, recurrent, genetically influenced skin disorder of early infancy, childhood and adult life. Cases are common and there is much to talk about; children are used for both the Clinical Station and the History Taking/Management Planning Station. The distribution and morphology of lesions are diagnostic.

○ Common problem – prevalence 15% between birth and 12 years
○ Multifactorial and associated with asthma/hay fever. Family history of atopy in 70%
○ Slight female preponderance
○ 70% cases begin <2 years and 65% have long-term remission by 16 years
○ Early-onset, severe disease carries bad prognosis.

There are characteristic pattern of evolution:

○ **Infantile phase** begins at between 1 and 6 months and lasts for 2–3 years. Rash composed of red, itchy papules and plaques, many of which ooze and crust. Symmetrically distributed over the cheeks, forehead, scalp, trunk and extensor surfaces. Nappy area usually spared.

○ **Childhood phase** between 4 and 10 years. Symmetrical distribution over wrists, ankles, flexural surfaces of arms, legs. Circumscribed, erythematous, scaly, lichenified plaques. May get secondarily infected.

○ **Adult phase** mainly involves flexural creases of arms, legs, neck and hands/feet.

This is an illness that can have a huge impact. In many cases chronic pruritus leads to sleep loss and emotional upset for the child and also the family. Eczema can also be secondarily infected with staphylococci, streptococci and Herpes simplex (eczema herpeticum). Children can become systemically unwell and require urgent treatment, especially if they have eczema herpeticum, which is life threatening.

Treatment

See Section 3.10 in History Taking/Management Planning.

○ Avoidance of exacerbating factors and allergens
○ Nail care – keep nails short to lessen trauma from scratching
○ Emollients – emulsifying ointment, creams, bath oil
○ Topical steroid preparations (the minimum potency to achieve the desired effect), wet wraps
○ Antihistamines as antipruritic/sedative agent
○ Tacrolimus
○ Antibiotics for secondary infection

Differential diagnosis

You may be asked about this (see Box).

DIFFERENTIAL DIAGNOSIS OF ECZEMA

○ **Contact dermatitis** – often clearly demarcated and linked to a known irritant
○ **Hyper IgE (Job's) syndrome** – levels of IgE extremely high: over 2000 IU/ml. Patients have recurrent boils, chest infections and sinusitis
○ **Wiskott–Aldrich syndrome** – X-linked recessive condition with thrombocytopenia and recurrent infections
○ **Seborrheic dermatitis** – infant usually <3 months with yellow scales on scalp, forehead, nappy area

Psoriasis

○ Common disorder, prevalence 1%–3%. Around 20% of patients develop rash before 20 years of age. Characterised by red, well-demarcated plaques with a dry, thick, silvery scale
○ Multi-factorial – both hereditary and environmental factors involved
○ Family history in one-third of cases
○ Distribution: scalp, sacrum and extensor surfaces of extremities; 50% children have large plaques over knees, elbows
○ Guttate psoriasis – drop-like lesions scattered all over the body including the face, trunk, and extremities in one-third of cases
○ Persistent nappy area dermatitis in infancy
○ Other variants – erythrodermic and pustular psoriasis
○ Arthritis seen in 10% cases
○ Koebner phenomenon – lesions induced in areas of local injury
○ Auspitz sign – removal of scale causes multiple, small bleeding points

The diagnosis is clinical but can be confirmed on skin biopsy. The course is chronic and unpredictable.

Treatment: this can involve topical tar, keratolytics and cortico-steroids. Chronic lesions may require psoralen plus ultraviolet A (PUVA) regime

Mongolian blue spot

You may be asked to comment on purplish pigmentation over the lower back of a baby either after a full skin examination or as part of another examination. The differential is bruising and the possibility of non-accidental injury may have been raised.

○ Bluish-black macules over lumbosacral area and buttocks of many Afro-Caribbean and Asian babies
○ Due to concentrated collection of melanocytes deep in the dermis; fade away gradually and are rarely seen in children over 4 years of age
○ Mistaken for bruising/non-accidental injury – so it is important to document them on baby/check notes if a child has been assessed in hospital for any reason. Otherwise they are of no clinical significance

Strawberry naevus

Instructions to candidate

Examine this girl's skin and tell me what you find.

Case

> *Leanne is a 3-month-old who looks well and is comfortable in her mother's arms...*
>
> **You systematically examine skin as previously described**
>
> *...on full examination of her skin she has a prominent, bright red, protuberant lesion on the upper abdomen. It is well demarcated; I would like to measure it.*
>
> *I think this is a strawberry naevus.*

Questions
Will it get bigger?
Will it disappear?
What are the potential complications?

Notes on strawberry naevus

- Common abnormality that can cause much anxiety
- It is a capillary haemangioma, although this terminology is now seldom used (capillary refers to superficial and cavernous refers to deep)
- Bright red, protuberant, compressible and sharply demarcated
- Usually not present at birth but appears within 2 months
- More common in females than males, and in ex-premature than in term babies
- Common sites – face, scalp, back, anterior chest – may be multiple
- Develops in phases – rapid expansion (during first year), stationary (6–12 months) and spontaneous involution (develops blanched, pale, grey areas)
- 60% involute by 5 years, 90% by 9 years
- Involution does not correlate with the size or site of the lesion, except for lip lesions which usually persist

○ In general no treatment is required and the parents are reassured in view of good outcome
○ Complications – ulceration, infection, haemorrhage, platelet consumption. May interfere with vision (interfering with the development of binocular vision), urination (urethra), airway (tracheo-bronchial). Visceral involvement (especially of the liver) can be fatal if untreated
○ Treatment is sometimes needed for very large lesions or lesions in which complications have arisen – options include excision, laser (much better when used for flat capillary haemangioma), corti-costeroid/interferon

You may be asked about the **Kasabach–Merritt syndrome**, which describes rapidly enlarging haemangiomas and leads to consumption of platelets (thrombocytopenia), clotting factors (coagulopathy) and red blood cells (microangiopathic haemolytic anaemia).

Sebaceous naevus

Again you may be asked to comment on this at the end of another case:

○ Solitary, oval or linear, yellow-orange, warty lesion on the scalp
○ Circumscribed area of hair loss
○ Treatment – surgical excision
○ Risk of neoplastic change (basal cell carcinoma) in 10%–15% cases after puberty

Lipodystrophy

Lipodystrophy is a loss of subcutaneous fat. You may see a child with either generalised or partial lipodystrophy. The clue is the prominent muscles with reduced subcutaneous fat particularly over the face. It is important to have some knowledge of the causes and types of lipody-strophy.

Generalised lipodystrophy
○ Congenital (autosomal recessive) or acquired (sporadic)
○ Tall children, advanced skeletal maturation, prominent muscles, enlargement of penis/clitoris, abundant curly scalp hair
○ Acanthosis nigricans, hirsutism, hepatomegaly, insulin-resistant diabetes

○ May have renal, cardiac, neurological abnormality, seizures, developmental delay, carbohydrate intolerance, hyperinsulinaemia, hypertriglyceridaemia
○ Growth hormone low despite tall stature

Partial lipodystrophy
○ Females>males (4:1)
○ Develops over a few months to several years
○ Symmetrical subcutaneous fat loss initially over the face, upper trunks and arms – leads to disproportion between the upper and lower limbs
○ Chronic glomerulonephritis associated in 25% of cases with low C3 complement due to activation of alternative pathway
○ No treatment, prognosis is guarded

Tip

Remember that in **diabetes** lipoatrophy and lipohypertrophy can occur at injection sites

---

Vitiligo
○ Symmetrical, ivory-white depigmented patches
○ Common problem; higher incidence in pigmented population. Half present under 20 years of age
○ Associated with autoimmune diseases (thyroid, diabetes, pernicious anaemia, Addison's disease)
○ Slow progression, static after variable period of time
○ Spontaneous repigmentation in 10%–20% cases
○ Caucasians usually require only camouflage make-up

Molluscum contagiosum
○ Smooth, pearly papules with characteristic central punctum
○ Caused by pox virus
○ Occurs in crops, spreads by auto-inoculation
○ Mostly no treatment is offered and the condition improves over 12–18 months
○ Cryotherapy with liquid nitrogen and curettage has been used

Ichthyosis

Ichthyosis implies dry and thick skin of varying severity. It is separate from eczema in which inflammatory change plays a key role. There are various specific syndromes. Group of inherited disorders of keratinisation with dry, thickened skin of varying severity.

Types

○ Ichthyosis vulgaris – autosomal dominant (most common, 1 in 250 and least severe)
○ X-linked recessive ichthyosis
○ Lameller ichthyosis – autosomal dominant or recessive
○ Bullous ichthyosiform erythroderma – autosomal dominant
○ Non-bullous ichthyosiform erythroderma – autosomal recessive

These are all lifelong disorders with little spontaneous remission. Lamellar and ichthyosiform erythroderma both present at birth as a 'collodion baby' (encased at birth in shiny, tight membrane); other types present within 3 months of birth.

Severe problems from the outset: thick scales, corneal dystrophy, ectropion, fever and faltering growth. Treatment is with emollients, keratolytics, oral retinoids (ichthyosiform erythrodermas), antibiotics for secondary infection.

Multiple associated syndromes; for example, Netherton syndrome (autosomal recessive).

Ectodermal dysplasia

Instructions to candidate

Comment on this child's general appearance.

Case

> Simon is a well-looking child with coarse wispy hair and sparse eyebrows and eyelashes. His skin appears to be dry. He has peri-orbital hyperpigmentation. He has pegged teeth (or false teeth).
>
> This would fit in with ectodermal dysplasia.

Notes on ectodermal dysplasia

○ Heterogeneous group of inherited conditions with primary defect in one or more of teeth, nails, hair, sweat gland function and other ectodermal tissue, eg eyes, ears, oral/nasal mucosa, melanocytes and central nervous system. There are multiple gene defects. The most common form is X-linked.

On examination (diverse features):

○ Nails – thick, dystrophic and fragile
○ Skin – atrophic, dry, wrinkled; requires emollients
○ Scalp hair very sparse; wigs are often worn
○ Facies – thick lips, saddle nose, frontal bossing, maxillary hypoplasia, abnormal ears
○ Eye – dry eyes, hypoplasia of nasolacrimal duct may lead to corneal ulcers
○ Reduced number of conical teeth, need for early use of prostheses
○ Mucosa – dry mouth, thick nasal secretions, atrophic rhinitis

Mucosal involvement also leads to recurrent chest infections, dysphagia, urethral stones and carcinomas. Asthma an association.

One life-threatening complication is hypohidrosis leading to hyperthermia; advice on cooling, activity, clothing, even relocation to cooler areas is important.

Management
○ Precautions/advice re potential for hyperthermia
○ Early dental treatment
○ Artificial tears
○ Wig
○ Regular follow-up indicated for mucosal leukoplakia and blood dysplasias as well as for above problems. Psychological input may be needed

Epidermolysis bullosa

○ Mixed group of hereditary, bullous diseases characterised by the development (in response to trauma) of vesicles, bullae or erosions.
○ Over 15 types based on inheritance, clinical features, electron microscopic identification of cleavage plane of blister:
  • Epidermolytic – within epidermis

* Junctional – at the dermoepidermal junction in the lamina lucida
* Dermatolytic – upper dermis

Best described in three categories:

○ Epidermolysis bullosa simplex (EBS) – there is a non-scarring (autosomal dominant) form that presents at birth, and mucous membranes may be involved. Feet and hand lesions are common but may be generalised. Usually improves with time. There is also a localised type of EBS – also autosomal dominant and confined to hands/feet. Usually presents in the first 2 years of life. May be confused with friction blister

○ Junctional epidermolysis bullosa – autosomal recessive, presents at birth or shortly thereafter, often progressive. There are lethal and non-lethal types. Nails are lost, teeth are dysplastic. Large granulomatous ulcers are seen in the perioral area. Mucosal involvement may lead to oesophageal strictures. Anaemia and secondary infection are common complications

○ Dystrophic epidermolysis bullosa – autosomal dominant and autosomal recessive. Recessive form is the most severe, with devastating effects. Usually present at birth. Entire skin may be affected by minor trauma. Scarring, milia formation and nail loss occur. Oral involvement with scarring of tongue and oesophageal stricture seen. Mitten-like hands/feet, contracture of large joints often result. Complications: infection, anaemia, growth retardation, amyloidosis, skin cancer (squamous carcinoma), etc. Carries a poor prognosis

Management

○ Supportive – nutrition, transfusion, gentle handling to minimise trauma, dressing of lesions, antibiotics for infection, appropriate clothing and footwear
○ Multidisciplinary involvement

Erythema multiforme

This is an acute disorder, which starts off as red papules that may blister. They then form target lesions, so called because the appearance of a bruise in the centre gives them a target-like appearance.

If there is a patient with such a condition on the ward or who has been recently discharged, they may be on a shortlist of reserve patients to cover a potential shortfall in cases. This is a condition that is frequently seen in paediatric assessment/ambulatory units.

You will be asked about causes:

○ Infections – Herpes simplex, *Mycoplasma*, Epstein–Barr virus, among others
○ Drugs – penicillins
○ Malignancy
○ Systemic lupus erythematosus

Management
○ Treat underlying cause
○ Review if any signs of Stevens–Johnson syndrome, the severest end of the spectrum of this illness

Stevens–Johnson syndrome
There is often a prodromal illness. Patients develop severe erosions of at least two mucosal surfaces. Look for genital involvement, areas of skin necrosis (often on lips and mouth leading to difficulties taking oral fluids), conjunctivitis. Patients can be very unwell and exudative fluid losses are high, much the same as in extensive burns. Patients need to be managed in a high dependency unit setting.

YOUR NOTES

12.4 ENDOCRINOLOGY AND GROWTH

12.4.1 Introduction

Remember that an assessment of/comment on growth is crucial in the exam in almost all of the short cases. During the short cases if you think a child is tall or short you should say so and say that you would plot them on a growth chart. Children with tall stature and those with short stature are both frequently seen in the exam (see Table 13.2) and approach to the assessment and knowledge of the common conditions seen is required.

Familial short stature

Familial tall stature

Turner/Noonan syndrome

Achondroplasia

Systemic disease affecting growth (eg cystic fibrosis)

Storage disorders (eg Hurler syndrome)

Marfan syndrome

Klinefelter syndrome

Homocystinuria

Goitre

Cushingoid children

Table 12.2: Conditions that are seen commonly in the exam

12.4.2 Assessment of growth

Growth charts

General practice is to correct for prematurity until aged 24 months.

The mid-parental centile can be calculated by using the following formula:

> Boy   [father's height in cm + (mother's height in cm + 12.5 cm)]/2
> Girl   [(father's height in cm −12.5 cm) + mother's height in cm]/2

Expected adult height centile falls within the target centile range which is 2 centiles above and 2 centiles below the mid-parental centile. This only applies if the parents have had a normal growth pattern themselves.

Specialist growth charts exist for some children (eg Down syndrome, Turner syndrome) – make sure you mention the specific chart if you make any of these diagnoses.

Look for any evidence of pubertal growth on the chart. Early (precocious) pubertal growth spurts tend to result in shorter than expected final adult height depending on how early it occurred and whether any treatment was given.

Bone age

This involves a left wrist X-ray, which is interpreted based on which growth plates have fused. Interpretation of bone age is summarised in Table 12.3.

Delayed bone age	Advanced bone age	Normal
Increased cortisol	Increased androgens	Familial short stature
Emotional deprivation	or oestrogens	Increased growth hormone
Decreased androgens	(precocious puberty)	Obesity
Poor nutrition	Hyperthyroidism	
Growth hormone deficiency	Cerebral gigantism	
Chronic disease	(Sotos syndrome)	
Turner syndrome		
Constitutional growth delay		

Table 12.3: Interpretation of bone age from left wrist X-ray

12.4.3 Tall stature

Suggested approach to tall stature examination

General approach

- Look for growth charts in the room. Comment on the pattern of growth as well as the current centiles. Make a decision on whether the growth pattern appears 'within normal limits' or is 'not a normal growth pattern'. Remember that 1 in 250 normal children will fall outside the 0.4th and 99.6th percentiles
- Specifically look for the mid-parental centile (MPC) and make a decision about whether the child's growth is 'tall for family size'
- Look at the parents – do they look short/ tall/ dysmorphic? Comment on any obvious findings
- If a diagnosis becomes clear (for example, obvious thyroid eye disease), direct examination towards confirming diagnosis and looking for complications

Instructions to candidate

This child has tall stature. What do you think is the cause of this?
Look at this child and tell me what you observe?

Initial procedure

- Introduce yourself as described previously

General observations

- Ill or well?
- Growth observations: height, weight, head circumference (offer to plot on growth chart)
- Obvious dysmorphic features, eg Marfanoid (direct further examination towards this)
- Any obvious thyroid signs (direct examination towards this)

Arms

- Hands: hyperthyroid features (tremor/sweatiness), arachnodactyly, ligamentous laxity
- Measure arm span and compare to height if possible
- Brachial pulses: compare the two sides. Assess character (aortic root dilatation), rate/rhythm (hyperthyroid)
- Blood pressure

Head and neck

- Mouth: high arched palate, dental crowding
- Thyroid eye signs
- Look for goitre or scar from surgery
- Listen for thyroid bruit
- Palpate neck for goitre

Chest

- Breast development in boys (obesity/Kleinfelter)
- Signs of puberty (precocious puberty)
- Pectus excavatum, scars from surgery
- Café-au-lait spots (Marfan syndrome), any neurocutaneous markings (precocious puberty)
- Perform the cardiovascular exam now (if Marfan syndrome suspected)

Spine

- Examine for scoliosis (shoes off, pelvis straight, correct for postural elements, look for curvature standing and bending over) – a feature of Marfan syndrome but also seen in tall pubertal children
- Look from the side for kyphosis
- Look for ligamentous laxity, eg touch palms of hands to the floor while keeping legs straight

Also...

- Always mention need to plot parental height/MPC
- Direct final examination towards most likely cause:
  - Mention cardiovascular exam/fundoscopy/arm span versus height if you suspect Marfan syndrome
  - Remember reflexes if thyroid signs are identified
  - Remember development/fundoscopy if homocystinuria is suspected
  - Mention genitalia/pubertal staging if Kleinfelter syndrome is suspected

If asked for investigations you should mention:

- Bone age
- Karyotype
- Thyroid function
- Any others suggested by examination findings

SOME CAUSES OF TALL STATURE

○ Familial
○ Obesity
○ Syndromes:
  • Marfan
  • Homocystinuria
  • Sotos syndrome
  • Kleinfelter syndrome
  • Beckwith–Wiedemann (normal final height)
○ Endocrine
  • Hyperthyroidism
  • Precocious puberty (often final height decreased)

12.4.4 Conditions and cases associated with tall stature

Marfan syndrome

Marfan syndrome commonly comes up in the exam and the clinical signs and management need to be thoroughly known. Marfan syndrome occurs in 1:10 000 and is inherited as an autosomal-dominant trait (defect in the fibrillin gene on chromosome 15). The diagnosis is a clinical one. In Marfan syndrome the lower segment of the body is longer than the upper segment and the arm span is greater than the height. Long-term complications are aortic dissection/regurgitation, kyphoscoliosis and lens dislocation. Children with Marfan syndrome will need yearly echocardiograms to compare their aortic root dimensions against centile charts, and regular ophthalmologic assessment. In the paediatric clinic it is important to monitor blood pressure regularly.

Examination findings
○ Tall for family size
○ Long thin face, high arched palate, dental crowding
○ Arachnodactyly – long slender fingers (ask the patient to encircle opposite wrist with thumb and little finger)
○ Sternberg's sign – thumb adducts across palm
○ Ligamentous laxity – can place palms on the floor when the legs are straight
○ Arm span greater than height
○ Pectus excavatum or carinatum

○ Scoliosis
○ Aortic root dilatation – examine brachial pulse character (compare both sides), praecordium for heave/thrill, apex beat character, presence of diastolic murmur
○ Mitral valve prolapse (late systolic murmur at apex)
○ Lens dislocation – up and in
○ Pes planus

Case – Marfan syndrome

I examined Jake, who is a teenager who appears to be tall for his age, although I would like to plot his height and weight on a centile chart. He has features of Marfan syndrome. In particular he has evidence of ligamentous laxity, his arm span is greater than his height and he has a high arched palate with some dental crowding. There is no evidence of scoliosis and his heart sounds and praecordial examination were normal. I would like to complete my examination by measuring his blood pressure in both arms, and looking at his eyes with an ophthalmoscope. I would also like to plot his mid-parental height on a centile chart.

Homocystinuria

An autosomal-recessive condition. Classic type typically presents with failure to thrive and developmental delay in infancy. Children later develop mental retardation, ocular lens subluxation and psychiatric morbidity in 50%. They are also at risk of thromboembolic disease, which can result in seizures, optic atrophy, hypertension secondary to renal infarcts and cor pulmonale. Examination findings are similar to those in Marfan syndrome. Children are tall and thin with elongated limbs, arachnodactyly, high arched palate and dental overcrowding. They are at risk of scoliosis and chest wall deformity. They have genu valgum and pes cavum.

It is essential to know the difference between Marfan syndrome and homocystinuria (Table 12.4).

	Marfan	Homocystinuria
Joints	Hyperextensible	Contractures
Lens dislocation	Up and in	Down
Facies	Long	Ruddy complexion
Intelligence	Normal	Below average
Cardiac	Aortic root dilation	Normal
Bones	Normal	Osteoporosis
Urine	Normal	Excessive homocystine

Table 12.4: Differentiating between Marfan syndrome and homocystinuria

Klinefelter syndrome (47XXY)

Individuals are tall with long limbs. Rare to have any physical signs before puberty except for tall stature. It usually presents as delayed puberty with small testicles, rarely exceeding 2 ml volume, and poor growth of pubic and facial hair. Gynaecomastia is present in 40% at puberty. Intelligence is below average for the family but usually within normal limits and behavioural problems are common.

XYY syndrome

Children present with above average height, and intelligence within normal limits but an increased incidence of behavioural difficulties. They have normal genitalia and pubertal development.

Sotos syndrome (cerebral gigantism)

Presents at birth as macrosomia and unusual facial features: prominent forehead and chin, large head circumference (which is in proportion to length) and hypertelorism. Hands, feet, ears, nose and genitalia can be large. Skeletal development is usually advanced so final adult height is usually normal.

12.4.5 Short stature

Suggested approach to short stature examination

Instructions to candidate

Examine this child who is being investigated for short stature.
Look at this child. Tell me what you see.

Initial procedure

Initial general observations are vital to targeting your examination. You should begin by...

- Introducing yourself as previously described
- Looking for growth charts (and looking at them as soon as you see them)
- Deciding whether the child is short for family size or not
- Ill or well?
- Any dysmorphic features?
- Underweight or overweight?
- Limb spine/disproportion?

The remainder of the examination can be targeted based on the observations above.

Short underweight or ill child

Examination directed towards finding an underlying chronic disease process that may have impaired growth, for example:

- Cystic fibrosis/bronchiectasis
- Coeliac disease (wasted buttocks)
- Inflammatory bowel disease (mouth ulcers, nasogastric tube)
- Insulin-dependent diabetes mellitus (IDDM; look for lipoatrophy, lipohyper-trophy) – will impair growth if poorly controlled

Short, well and normal or overweight child

Look at growth pattern if growth chart available. Look for any evidence of an endocrine disorder:

- Cushingoid?
- Hypothyroidism? (examine for goitre)
- Hypopituitarism/growth hormone deficiency? (classically associated with central obesity and characteristic midfacial crowding – not always obvious)

Finally

Finish examination by offering to plot parental height and calculate mid-parental centile (MPC).

■ Be prepared to discuss further investigations. These could be directed at looking for chronic disease (sweat test, coeliac screen, urine dip, etc) or endocrinopathy (thyroid function tests, urinary free cortisol excretion, insulin-like growth factor-1). Bone age is helpful in some circumstances.

Short dysmorphic child

Examination should be directed to noticing patterns of dysmorphic features that might aid in diagnosing the reason for the short stature. If a 'spot diagnosis' is obvious or strongly suspected (eg achondroplasia/Turner syndrome) then direct examination towards identifying the associated physical characteristics and looking for complications. If there is no obvious diagnosis then direct examination towards accurately describing what you see.

Growth

■ Offer to measure height (including sitting height if you suspect a skeletal dysplasia), weight, head circumference and if appropriate subscapular/triceps skinfold thickness and pubertal stage and plot on appropriate centile charts

■ You may be asked to plot growth velocity on the relevant chart – practise this in clinic and be quick, accurate and efficient in doing so

■ Clearly if a short child is obviously post pubertal it is relevant and should be stated

Is the child obviously dysmorphic?

■ For example Turner syndrome, Noonan syndrome, Russell–Silver dwarfism, Prader–Willi syndrome, Cornelia de Lange syndrome, Rubenstein–Taybi, Aarskog syndrome, mucopolysaccharidoses. If so then direct the examination towards that problem. Physical signs for the more commonly seen of these conditions can be found in 'Notes' section (page 413–417).

Limb/spine proportions (see Box)

■ Extend arms down lateral side: consider limb shortening if they do not reach the mid pelvis in infancy or the upper thigh after infancy. Consider spine shortening if arms extend well down upper thigh

■ Examine arms for rhizomelic (proximal), mesomelic (distal) or symmetrical shortening. A useful way to do this is to fully flex the arm at the elbow and compare the upper arm with the lower arm

■ Extend arm and examine carrying angle (cubitus valgus in Turner syndrome)

- Examine hands for hypoplastic, hyperconvex nails (Turner syndrome), short 5th metacarpal (Turner syndrome and pseudohypoparathyroidism)
- Look at spine for kyphosis/scoliosis. Take off their shoes and look from the side as well as from behind. Ask the child to bend over as part of the scoliosis examination. Look for any evidence of spinal surgery/back braces, etc
- Look at limbs for joint contractures/scars
- Head circumference

Also I would like to...

- Look at parents' size (?dysmorphism/limb disproportion) and think about mid-parental centile/offering to plot parents' heights
- Where relevant don't forget development
- If dysmorphic features are found remember that other systems, particularly cardiac, may be relevant
- Be prepared to discuss investigations. Chromosomes, white cell enzymes, bone age, skeletal survey are all useful for diagnosis depending on examination findings. Remember cardiac investigations, renal ultrasound, audiology, ophthalmology if looking for associated anomalies

CAUSES OF LIMB/SPINE DISPROPORTION

- ○ Rhizomelic shortening: achondroplasia (frontal bossing, lordosis, etc), rhizomelic chondrodysplasia punctata (like achondroplasia with less severe craniofacial features)
- ○ Mesomelic shortening: mesomelic dysplasia, Ellis–van Creveld syndrome (natal teeth, hypoplastic nails, polydactyly, cardiac anomalies)
- ○ Non-rhizomelic/mesomelic short arms and trunk: spondyloepiphyseal dysplasia, hypochondroplasia (milder cranial features of achondroplasia), mucopolysaccharidoses (coarse facies and hepatosplenomegaly), GM1 (cherry red spot)
- ○ Asymmetrical limbs: chondrodysplasia punctata, hemihypertrophy, for example in Russell–Silver
- ○ Short spine only: spinal irradiation

Notes on short stature

Short stature is a common reason for children to be referred to paediatricians. This is considered abnormal if a child is short for family size or if there is an abnormal growth pattern such as crossing two centiles downwards. Normal growth requires adequate nutrition, normal endocrine system, the absence of chronic disease and normal bone metabolism.

In infancy growth is primarily driven by nutrition.

Growth hormone becomes important in the prepubertal years and growth hormone deficiency will begin to show itself by slowed height velocity after infancy.

During puberty growth hormone shares influence with the sex steroids. A correctly timed pubertal growth spurt is necessary for normal adult height. If this occurs too early, for example in precocious puberty, the final adult height will be decreased. In constitutional delay, the onset of puberty is delayed and the child will appear to cross downwards through the centiles. There is often a family history of late puberty. However, once puberty has started, growth continues and the final adult height will not be compromised.

CAUSES OF SHORT STATURE

- ○ Familial
- ○ Chronic disease process (short and thin)
- ○ Endocrine (short and overweight): hypopituitarism (growth hormone deficiency), Cushing's, hypothyroidism, precocious puberty (shortened final height)
- ○ Syndromic: Turner syndrome, Noonan syndrome, Russell–Silver dwarfism, Prader–Willi syndrome, Cornelia de Lange syndrome, Rubenstein–Taybi syndomre, Aarskog syndrome, mucopolysaccharidoses (many others)
- ○ Skeletal dysplasia: achondroplasia, spondyloepiphyseal dysplasia, chondrodysplasia punctata, osteogenesis imperfecta (many others)
- ○ Constitutional delay
- ○ Emotional deprivation/neglect

Growth hormone

Growth hormone is given by subcutaneous injection (daily). Recommendations for use have been endorsed by the National Institute for Health and Clinical Excellence (www.nice.org.uk).

Licensed uses in children

○ Growth hormone deficiency
○ Turner syndrome
○ Chronic renal insufficiency
○ Prader–Willi syndrome (has an influence on body composition as well as height)

Other conditions (unlicensed)

Children who are short and have no biochemical evidence of growth hormone deficiency will gain 2–3 cm in final height if treated. This does not justify its widespread use. There is no effect on constitutionally delayed puberty, or on children with in-utero growth retardation. There are no long-term data on children with Down syndrome, skeletal dysplasias or Noonan syndrome. Some children with Russell–Silver dwarfism have a true growth hormone deficiency and will respond to replacement therapy.

Once on growth hormone, height velocity and IGF-1 are monitored, in order to assess compliance with treatment, response to therapy and to guide decisions about dosage. There is a potential benefit in continuing treatment into adulthood in those with proven growth hormone deficiency as it may have protective cardiovascular effects.

Adverse effects of growth hormone therapy

These include scoliosis and diabetes. Both of these conditions are felt to become clinically obvious sooner because of the effects of growth hormone treatment, in children who were likely to develop them eventually anyway. There is no evidence that growth hormone increases the risk of cancer.

12.4.6 Conditions and cases related to short stature

Turner syndrome

Occurs in 1:2000 female births. 50% are due to 45XO, 15% due to mosaic 45XO/46XX. Other mosaics make up the rest. Risk does not increase with maternal age. Can present antenatally (causes increased nuchal fold thickness on 12 week ultrasound). Mosaicism means that not all girls show the classic phenotype. The diagnosis should therefore be considered in all girls with growth or pubertal failure.

Cardiac lesions most commonly consist of a coarctation with a non-obstructive bicuspid aortic valve. Other possibilities include aortic stenosis and total anomalous pulmonary venous drainage. The ovaries degenerate into streaks in 90% by 10 years of age. Puberty rarely occurs though 10% may have breast enlargement. Levels of plasma gonadotrophins are markedly elevated.

30% of patients have renal anomalies, also including pelvic kidney and pelviureteric junction obstruction. Glue ear is common as is sensori-neural hearing deficit. Learning difficulties are usually mild.

○ Remember the associations with autoimmune disease such as autoimmune thyroiditis and inflammatory bowel disease.

Management involves regular follow up including

1. Screening for congenital anomalies (including cardiac/renal)
2. Oestrogen/progesterone replacement in adolescence
3. Growth hormone replacement therapy
4. Monitoring for complications including, hypothyroidism, hearing loss, hypertension, scoliosis, insulin resistance, neurodevelopmental difficulties, amblyopia.

Suggested examination structure for Turner syndrome

General

▓ Plot growth (remember Turner syndrome growth chart)

Arms

▓ Oedema of hands and feet in neonate
▓ Hypoplastic and hyperconvex nails
▓ Short 4th/5th metacarpals

- Examine peripheral pulses
- Widened carrying angle (cubitus valgus)

Head

- Low posterior hairline
- Prominent ears
- Neck webbing
- High arched palate
- Look in ears (glue ear)

Chest

- Shield chest
- Widely spaced nipples
- Scars from cardiac surgery
- Excessive naevi
- Breast development (think about pubertal stages and hormone supplements)
- Axillary hair

Also need to examine

- Thyroid status (autoimmune hypothyroidism?)
- Cardiovascular system (in particular four-limb blood pressure)
- Abdomen (horseshoe kidney)
- Formal audiology
- Pubertal staging

Case – Turner syndrome

> Sarah is a well-looking girl who appears short for her age and I would like to plot her height and weight on a centile chart. Examination reveals webbing of her neck and cubitus valgus. She has a short 5th metacarpal and dysplastic nails. The most likely diagnosis is Turner syndrome. I would like to examine her cardiovascular system and stage pubertal development.

Noonan syndrome

A sporadic condition mapped to chromosome 12. Autosomal-dominant inheritance. Mild mental retardation in 30%. Coagulation defects in 30% (eg von Willebrand disease, thrombocytopenia, clotting factor abnormalities).

Examination findings
○ Short stature
○ Typical facies – hypertelorism, anti-mongoloid slant, epicanthic folds, ptosis, micrognathia, low-set ears, short/webbed neck
○ Widely spaced nipples, cubitus valgus, short stature and pubertal delay
○ Classic cardiac lesion is pulmonary valve stenosis. Could also have branch pulmonary stenosis, atrial septal defect, hypertrophic cardiomyopathy
○ Cryptorchidism, hernias

Case – Noonan syndrome

*Jason is a short boy. I would like to plot his height and weight on the appropriate charts. He has hypertelorism, ptosis, micrognathia, epicanthic folds and low-set ears. Examination of his chest reveals widely spaced nipples and an ejection systolic murmur grade 3/6 loudest in the pulmonary area. It does not radiate to his carotid arteries. The most likely diagnosis is **Noonan syndrome**. His murmur is likely to be due to pulmonary stenosis. I would also like to examine his genitals for cryptorchidism and stage his puberty.*

Russell–Silver dwarfism

This is a difficult clinical diagnosis but a diagnosis that should be considered in an appropriate child.

Features
○ Growth failure
○ Triangular facies and frontal bossing
○ Micrognathia
○ Clinodactyly
○ Café-au-lait spots
○ Hemi-hypertrophy
○ Hypopituitarism

Mucopolysaccharidoses

Knowledge of the mucopolysaccharidoses and similar syndromes is important and a summary of the various conditions is listed.

Suggested examination structure for Hurler and Hunter syndromes

General observations

▓ Growth
▓ Describe coarse facial features
▓ Thickened lips
▓ Large head with frontal bossing
▓ Flat midface
▓ Prominent sutures
▓ Broad flat nose
▓ Comment on evidence of developmental problems (eg wheelchair)
▓ Look at dorsum of wrist for carpal tunnel surgery correction scar (common)

Head

▓ Examine corneas for clouding (appears after 1 year and not present in Hunter's)
▓ Examine fundi for cherry red spot (present in GM1, which is a differential)
▓ Comment on nasal discharge (common and persistent)
▓ Listen for upper airway obstruction

Cardiovascular system

▓ Examine cardiovascular system for evidence of congestive cardiac failure

Abdomen

▓ Note umbilical hernia
▓ Examine for hepatosplenomegaly

Finally

▓ Note joint stiffness and contractures
▓ Examine spine for exaggerated kyphosis (usually present), gibbus (the hump seen due to a deformed spine), scoliosis and cervical rod surgery (common in Maroteaux–Lamy and Morquio)
▓ Offer to perform developmental examination, and expect it to be delayed

Case – Mucopolysaccharidosis

> *I examined Jenny, who is a 5–year-old girl with some dysmorphic features. She has short stature as evidenced by her growth chart. She also has macrocephaly and a short neck. There is some coarsening of her facial features; in particular she has thickened lips and some frontal bossing. She has very noisy breathing suggesting a degree of upper airways obstruction. I suspect she has a mucopolysaccharidosis disorder. I would like to look in her eyes for corneal clouding and examine her abdomen for hernias and hepatosplenomegaly. I would also like to examine her cardiovascular system and her development including hearing.*

Difference between **Hunter** and **Hurler syndromes**

	Hunter	Hurler
Inheritance	X-linked	Autosomal dominant
Corneal clouding	No	Yes
Severity	Less	More
Nodules over scapulae	Yes	No

Table 12.5: Difference between Hunter and Hurler syndromes

Differential diagnosis

Other mucopolysaccharidoses:

○ Morquio syndrome – very severe physical features identical to Hurler syndrome, but normal intelligence. Will have had cervical stabilisation surgery
○ Maroteaux–Lamy syndrome – phenotypically similar to Morquio syndrome
○ Sanfilippo syndrome – less severe physical features, but profound mental retardation

Other differentials:

○ Multiple sulfatase deficiency (ichthyosis, more profound neurological deterioration)
○ GM1 gangliosidosis (pseudo-Hurler)
○ Mannosidosis (clinically like Hurler without urinary findings)
○ Fucosidosis (clinically like Hurler without urinary findings)
○ Mucolipidoses

Skeletal dysplasia

○ Around 200 disorders
○ Include osteodysplasias (eg osteogenesis imperfecta) and chondrodysplasias
○ Chondrodysplasias are characterised by disproportionality of areas affected, eg mainly affecting limbs or mainly affecting trunk
○ Diagnosis is based on skeletal survey and family history/genetics
○ Some skeletal dysplasias have non-skeletal-associated anomalies (eg Ellis–van Creveld)

Case – skeletal dysplasia

> *Sarah is a well-looking girl who appears to be short for her age as evidenced by her growth chart. She is post pubertal. There is no obvious limb disproportion but she has a marked kyphosis. I note that her mother has a similar body shape. I suspect she has a skeletal dysplasia and I would like to measure her sitting height.*

Achondroplasia

Incidence 1:20 000, autosomal dominant, 4p; 50% of cases are new mutations. Patients can expect to have a normal life span, but sudden death can occur due to cervical cord compression because of a small foramen magnum. Can also have hydrocephalus.

Special height, weight, head circumference and development charts exist for the condition. Spirometry should be performed as all patients have reduced lung capacity.

A key radiological finding is decreasing interpeduncular distances in lumbar spine (distinguishes this from hypochondrodysplasia).

Suggested examination structure for achondroplasia

If you are faced with a short child who obviously has achondroplasia, this is an approach to take in your examination.

General

▨ Growth

- Describe the facial features to the examiner: frontal bossing, flat nasal bridge, large head circumference, mandibular prognathism when older
- Look at parents and comment on whether they have achondroplasia

Limbs

- Hands are short and broad with a trident appearance
- Laxity of the ligaments
- Limbs show a rhizomelic (humerus/femur) shortening

Spine

- Examine spine for gibbus in infancy followed by lumbar lordosis and scoliosis in adolescence

Finally

- Examine the cardiovascular system for evidence of pulmonary hypertension, secondary to recurrent sleep apnoea
- Offer to examine ears for chronic serous otitis media and teeth for dental malocclusion, which is common
- Offer to plot head circumference, height and weight on special achondroplasia charts (hydrocephalus can be an early complication), and to grade development

12.4.7 Cushing syndrome

Causes of cushingoid features

Primary causes (more common in infancy):

○ Adrenocortical tumour (usually malignant)
○ McCune–Albright syndrome
○ Primary pigmented nodular adrenocortical disease

Secondary causes (more common in >7-year-olds):

○ Bilateral adrenal hyperplasia (secondary to ACTH-secreting pituitary adenoma)
○ Exogenous steroids – most common
○ Ectopic adrenocorticotropin hormone (ACTH) (eg Wilms' tumour)

Suggested examination schema for cushingoid children

General observations

▨ Growth: offer to plot weight and height, comment on truncal obesity if present
▨ Ill or well?
▨ Look for any sign of disease process potentially requiring steroid treatment – for example, allergic bronchopulmonary aspergillosis (ABPA) in children with cystic fibrosis, severe asthma (?evidence of atopy), rheumatic conditions

Arms

▨ Check blood pressure
▨ Look for proximal myopathy (both muscle weakness and wasting)
▨ Thinning of skin

Other

▨ Moon face
▨ Buffalo hump
▨ Evidence of adrenal virilism (acne, axillary hair, pubic hair, can also cause clitoromegaly and precocious puberty)

Abdomen

▨ Striae
▨ Palpate for masses

▓ Look for scars (think about adrenal surgery, gastrointestinal disease requiring steroids)

Also...

▓ Mention pubertal staging
▓ Fundoscopy (for pituitary tumour causing optic nerve pressure), visual field examination (for process affecting optic chiasm)
▓ Suggest full systems examination if systemic disease requiring exogenous steroids is suspected
▓ Don't use the term Cushing syndrome unless ACTH-secreting tumour or adrenocortical tumour suspected; if unsure refer to findings as 'cushingoid'

12.4.8 Thyroid gland

Suggested structure for examination of the thyroid gland
Instructions to candidate

Examine this child's neck
Look at this child's neck and tell me what you see

Initial procedure

Introduction as previously described
Ensure that there is a glass of water (may be beside the bed)

General observations

■ Growth
■ Ill or well
■ Obvious thyroid signs, eg eye signs, cold intolerance, etc

Inspection

■ From the front with the neck extended for enlargement of the thyroid gland and hearing aid (Pendred syndrome)
■ Is the enlargement uniform or unilateral, are there any scars?
■ If a scar is present check voice for hoarseness
■ Ask the child to take a drink; a thyroid swelling should move upwards with swallowing
■ Ask the child to stick their tongue out (if it rises during manoeuvre then it is a thyroglossal cyst)

Palpation

■ Palpate the gland whilst standing behind the child
■ Assess size, shape, consistency and surface of the mass (single diffusely enlarged thyroid, a single enlarged cyst or a multinodular goitre?)
■ Again ask to drink whilst palpating

Further examination

■ Examine tongue for high thyroglossal cyst (originates at foramen caecum)
■ Palpate for lymphadenopathy
■ Percuss sternum for retro-sternal extension
■ Auscultate mass for bruits

To say at end of neck examination

▦ I would now routinely proceed to assess the thyroid status. If you do not say this you will probably be asked to do so by the examiner – save time

Suggested structure for examination of thyroid status

Instructions to candidate

Assess this child's thyroid status.
This child is hyperthyroid; assess her thyroid status. What medications would you expect her to be on?

Hands

▦ Look for clubbing
▦ Feel for a raised temperature
▦ Ask the child to hold out their hands and feel for fine tremor
▦ Pulse rate and rhythm

Blood pressure

▦ Wide pulse pressure in hyperthyroidism

Eyes

▦ Lid oedema
▦ Exophthalmos/proptosis (examine from above)
▦ Lid retraction (able to see white of sclera above iris)
▦ Lid lag (when following examiner's finger in rapid downward gaze, the lids lag behind the iris)
▦ External ophthalmoplegia
▦ Conjunctival injection and oedema

Dentition

▦ Delayed in hypothyroidism

Neck examination (as above)

▦ If not already done

Reflexes

▦ Slow relaxation in hypothyroidism

Myopathy

▤ Occasionally get proximal myopathy in hyperthyroidism

Also

▤ Offer to plot growth (always comment on this as part of thyroid examination)
▤ Mention need for pubertal staging
▤ Comment on positive signs and commit yourself to saying whether a patient is clinically euthyroid or clinically hyper/hypothyroid. Remember a patient can have eye signs of Graves' disease but be treated and therefore clinically euthyroid
▤ Be prepared to discuss investigations and treatment (see below)

Questions to ask to help assess thyroid status

▤ Energy levels
▤ Schoolwork (usually well behaved if hypothyroid)
▤ Heat tolerance/sweatiness
▤ Constipation/diarrhoea
▤ Appetite and weight loss
▤ Muscle weakness

Hyperthyroidism

Usually Graves' disease, an autoimmune disease caused by production of thyroid-stimulating antibodies. Peak incidence is in adolescent girls. Family history is common, and there is an association with HLA DR3/B8

Presentation

○ Often insidious
○ Emotional disturbance and motor hyperactivity
○ Sweatiness and increased appetite
○ Weight loss/gain
○ Heat intolerance
○ Deterioration in school work

Investigations

○ Thyroid-stimulating hormone (TSH) low, thyroxine (T4) high
○ Thyroid-stimulating antibodies (TSH-receptor-stimulating antibodies) present and disappear on remission

○ Bone age advanced
○ Investigate first-degree relatives

Treatment

Almost half of childhood cases will remit spontaneously within 2–4 years. Many will progress to become clinically hypothyroid. Medical treatment is with **carbimazole** and **propranolol** (the latter to control acute symptoms).

'Block replacement' means that both carbimazole and **thyroxine** are used.

Definitive treatment (favoured by many) is either by **subtotal thyroidectomy** or the use of **radioactive iodine**. Severe eye disease may require treatment with **prednisolone**.

Symptoms of hyperthyroidism

○ Anxiety
○ Poor sleep
○ Sweating
○ Heat intolerance
○ Palpitations

Signs of hyperthyroidism

○ Warm sweaty hands
○ Fine tremor on holding arms outstretched
○ Tachycardia
○ Wide pulse pressure and high systolic pressure
○ Hyperactive precordium
○ Exophthalmos
○ Lid lag
○ External ophthalmoplegia
○ Thyroid bruit
○ Goitre
○ Proximal myopathy
○ Tall for family height
○ Can cause precocious puberty

Case – Graves' disease

> Sarah is a well-looking girl who appears appropriately grown for her age. I would like to plot her height and weight on a centile chart. There is an obvious goitre which moves with swallowing. It is diffusely enlarged, non-tender and firm. There is no lymphadenopathy or retrosternal extension. She has a normal pulse rate and rhythm. Sarah has proptosis. My impression is that she has **Graves' disease** but she is currently clinically euthyroid. I would like to check her blood pressure and her pubertal staging.

Thyroid eye disease

Thyroid eye disease is caused by antibodies against antigens shared by the thyroid and eye muscles. Retro-orbital inflammation and oedema of the extra-ocular muscles cause exophthalmos (synonymous with proptosis) and limited eye movements. The proptosis can be permanent. Eye changes are present bilaterally but often asymmetrically and commonly persist when euthyroid, and can worsen if rendered hypothyroid. The most concerning complications are exposure keratopathy (secondary to reduced blinking and being unable to fully close the eye) and optic atrophy (secondary to pressure effects behind the eye). An uncommon complication in childhood is external ophthalmoplegia, which is caused by lymphocytic infiltration and glycosaminoglycan deposition in the medial and inferior rectus muscles.

Signs of thyroid eye disease
- Lid oedema
- Exophthalmos/proptosis
- Lid lag (eyelid lags behind eyeball on rapid down gaze)
- Conjunctival injection and oedema
- External ophthalmoplegia

Hypothyroidism

Congenital hypothyroidism

Incidence 1:4000, usually asymptomatic until 6–12 weeks of age due to transplacental passage of maternal thyroid hormone.

Presentation
- Raised TSH on the Guthrie card
- Poor feeding
- Hoarse cry

○ Constipation
○ Lethargy
○ Jaundice
○ Wide fontanelles
○ Macroglossia
○ Umbilical hernia
○ Developmental delay
○ Later…typical facies if untreated

Aetiology
○ Thyroid dysgenesis (90%) (one-third aplasia, two-thirds ectopic)
○ Dyshormonogenesis
○ TSH/TRH (thyroid-releasing hormone) deficiency – look for associated midline defects
○ Transplacental anti-thyroid drugs

Treatment
This is with lifelong thyroid hormone replacement with **thyroxine** monitored with regular thyroid function tests. There is the occasional case of transient hypothyroidism and so usually a trial off therapy is carried out in older children, If the TSH becomes elevated during this trial then thyroxine replacement is restarted.

Outcome
Early treatment results in improved intelligence. Factors of relevance are compliance and the severity of thyroid dysfunction at diagnosis (particularly the TSH).

Juvenile (acquired) hypothyroidism

Aetiology – depends on whether a goitre is present
Goitre present:
○ Autoimmune thyroiditis (commonest)
○ Dyshormonogenesis
○ Endemic iodine deficiency
○ Goitrogen exposure
○ Infiltration

No goitre:
○ Hypoplastic or ectopic thyroid
○ Hypothalamo-hypopituitary hypothyroidism, eg post irradiation
○ Thyroidectomy

Autoimmune thyroiditis

More common in girls (5:1); onset is after 6 years, peaking in adolescence. A family history is common.

Presentation
○ Goitre and growth delay commonest
○ Thyroid diffusely enlarged in two-thirds
○ Most clinically euthyroid
○ Can be hypothyroid or even hyperthyroid

Associations
○ Trisomy 21, 45XO, Noonan syndrome
○ Polyglandular autoimmune disease type I
  • Autoimmune thyroiditis
  • Addison's disease
  • Mucocutaneous candidiasis
  • Hypoparathyroidism
○ Polyglandular autoimmune disease type II
  • Addison's disease
  • Insulin-dependent diabetes mellitus (IDDM)
  • Thyroiditis
○ Pernicious anaemia, vitiligo, alopecia

Diagnosis
T4 low and TSH high but may be clinically euthyroid at diagnosis. Thyroid peroxidase antibodies usually positive.

Treatment
○ T4 replacement if hypothyroid
○ Warn parents that school performance and behaviour deteriorate after starting treatment but will gradually settle down
○ Monitor T4 and TSH; modest elevations of TSH are common in the treated group and this is related to undertreatment. A high TSH and normal T4 may indicate erratic medication and improved compliance just before the clinic appointment
○ Arrange a trial without treatment at some stage (usually when growth is complete) to rule out transient hypothyroidism

Symptoms of hypothyroidism
○ Low energy levels
○ Good schoolwork (quiet attentive pupils whose work deteriorates after treatment)

○ Constipation
○ Delayed puberty (a small proportion have precocious puberty)
○ Delayed tooth eruption
○ Increased tendency to sleep
○ Cold intolerance

Signs of hypothyroidism

○ Cold hands
○ Thick skin
○ Bradycardia
○ Slow relaxing tendon reflexes
○ Short for family height
○ May be overweight

12.4.9 Neck lumps

At some stage during the clinical examination stations you may be asked to examine a neck lump. This is most likely to occur in the 'Other' station, which will not give you a clue as to the cause. The following scheme should help you to distinguish between a goitre and another cause of a neck lump.

Suggested structure for examination of the anterior neck

General

- Ill or well
- Any obvious features of thyroid disease (eg thyroid eye disease)
- Comment on growth and say you would like to plot this on a growth chart
- Follow a 'look, feel, listen, move' approach to remainder of the examination

Inspection

- Neck lumps (comment on any obvious lumps and say you are going to assess them further before moving on to palpation). See below for a description of potential causes of a neck swelling
- Scars
- Asymmetry of posture
- Obvious deformity (eg Klippel–Feil syndrome – examine the spine for scoliosis/spina bifida/restricted movement – remember potential for associated cardiac or renal anomalies, cleft palate and hearing problems)

Palpation

- Comment on size, shape, consistency, relation to surrounding structures (muscle, lymph nodes, trachea, overlying skin), tenderness
- Palpate along all easily identifiable structures (sternocleidomastoid muscle, carotid pulses, trachea)

Auscultation

- Need to listen for thyroid bruit (if goitre present)

Movements

- Ask patient to swallow/stick out their tongue and note any associated movements of the neck swelling (particularly for midline swellings)

Finally

- If relevant say that you would go on to examine thyroid status
- Lymphadenopathy should prompt an examination of axillary and groin lymph nodes, as well as abdominal examination (?hepatosplenomegaly). If an infective cause is suspected then look for local inflammation (teeth/gums/scalp/ears) or signs of infection elsewhere (Epstein–Barr virus/tuberculosis, etc.)
- Always look in the mouth

CAUSES OF GOITRE

- ○ Autoimmune thyroiditis
- ○ Graves' disease
- ○ Colloid/simple – normal thyroid function and no antibodies
- ○ Hyperplasia
- ○ Diffuse nodular non-toxic
  - Sub-acute thyroiditis (inflamed gland)
  - Carcinoma
  - Infiltration (Langerhan's cell histiocytosis)

Euthyroid causes of goitre

The commonest cause of goitre worldwide is dietary deficiency of iodine, usually seen in developing countries. This results in compensatory hypertrophy. You are very unlikely to see this in the examination.

More common in the developed world is a **child with autoimmune thyroiditis who is euthyroid**. Thyroid antibodies are usually present.

Simple or colloid goitres present as diffusely enlarged goitres in peripubertal girls. There are no thyroid antibodies. Multinodular goitres are rare and if seen malignancy needs to be excluded.

Other causes of neck lumps

Remember other things can be seen on examination of the anterior neck.

It is important to have a list of causes to hand as this is a very common exam scenario:

- ○ Thyroglossal cyst
- ○ Cystic hygroma

○ Haemangioma
○ Sternomastoid tumour
○ Lymphadenopathy
○ Branchial cyst

There are some infectious causes of chronic cervical lymphadenopathy:

○ Reactive lymphadenopathy following oral cavity infection or inflammation: can persist for many months after original inflammatory process has gone
○ If a list of other infections is required the following are rare causes that could be considered
  • Atypical TB
  • Infectious mononucleosis
  • Cytomegalovirus
  • *Bartonella* (cat scratch disease)
  • Toxoplasmosis
  • AIDS

Thyroglossal cyst

This is a cyst located in the midline of the neck in the route of descent of the thyroid gland from the foramen caecum. They typically rise when the tongue is protruded. They must be differentiated from an undescended lingual thyroid by radionuclide scanning as removal of ectopic thyroid tissue may render an individual hypothyroid.

Case – neck swelling

> Samuel is a well-looking boy who appears appropriately grown. He has an obvious midline swelling of his neck. This is seen to rise on sticking out his tongue but not on swallowing. The mass is smooth and firm. There is no local lymphadenopathy. The most likely diagnosis is a **thyroglossal cyst**.

12.4.10 Puberty

In boys the first sign of puberty is growth of the testicles to 4 ml and beyond (estimated with an orchidometer). This is followed 2 years later by the rapid growth phase and breaking of the voice; by this time testicular enlargement and genital development are usually well advanced.

In girls the changes of puberty are approximately 2 years earlier than those for boys, and the first feature is usually breast enlargement. This is followed by pubic hair development and menstruation is relatively late, occurring after the growth spurt.

In both sexes the pubic hair is mostly caused by androgen secretion from the adrenal glands, so-called adrenarche. The sex steroids control the other sexual characteristics and are responsible for eventual fusion of the epiphyses and cessation of growth.

It is unlikely that you will be asked to stage puberty in the examination, but you will need to be familiar with the various stages and be able to describe them (Table 12.6). Remember in boys to think about separate staging of genitalia (penis and scrotum) and axillary hair. In addition to this measuring testicular volume with an orchidometer gives valuable information. In girls separate staging exists for breast development, axillary hair and pubic hair. These are well covered in most paediatric text books and should be revised.

Tanner stages – pubic hair (male and female)	
P1	No pubic hair
P2	Small amount of long downy (fine) hair
P3	Adult type hair (coarse, curly) extending more laterally
P4	Adult type distribution – not extending onto thighs
P5	Hair extends to medial thighs
Tanner stages – axillary hair (male and female)	
A1	No axillary hair
A2	Hair present but not adult amount
A3	Adult
Tanner stages – breast development	
B1	Prepubertal
B2	Breast budding
B3	Development of breast mound
B4	Areola projects at an angle to breast mound
B5	Adult
Tanner stages – male genitalia development	
G1	Prepubertal penis (unstretched length 2.5–6 cm) scrotum and testis
G2	Scrotal laxity – no penile enlargement (normally testicular volume ≥ 4 ml)
G3	Penile lengthening, scrotal texture more adult
G4	Penile lengthening and broadening (normally testicular volume 10–12 ml), more prominent glans, darkening of scrotum
G5	Adult genitalia (testicular volume 15–25 ml)

Table 12.6: Pubertal staging

Precocious sexual development

Remember that changes in growth are closely linked to abnormalities in the pubertal process. True precocious puberty has features of normal puberty, but occurs early. The age of 8 in girls and 9 in boys is regarded as abnormally early.

True precocious puberty is commoner in girls than in boys and is idiopathic in the majority of cases. True precocious puberty in boys is uncommon and usually pathological; over half will have some form of intracranial pathology. The psychological problems are significant. Most will initially be tall but will end up with a reduced final height due to premature fusion of the epiphyses.

If the full picture of puberty does not develop it is not likely to be true precocious puberty. Girls may get breast enlargement (premature thelarche) or isolated pubic hair development (adrenarche) due to increased adrenal androgens.

In boys, if the testes are enlarged then it is likely to be true precocious puberty; if there is isolated pubic hair/penile development then the source of androgen is not testicular and is most likely adrenal.

Delayed puberty

This is present if there are no signs of puberty at age 13 years in girls and 14 years in boys. In the great majority it is physiological and when the testes enlarge or the breasts develop, all can be reassured. In girls in whom there is no breast development, Turner syndrome needs to be excluded.

When to mention pubertal staging in short case

Any disease that affects growth is likely to affect timing of puberty. This is particular important if steroids are required for treatment. Any endocrine disease is likely to affect puberty. Raised levels of TSH can stimulate gonads and cause precocious puberty. Excessive steroids can delay puberty. Some syndromes have important effects on puberty such as McCune–Albright syndrome (precocious) and Turner syndrome (delayed). Some neurological diagnoses are associated with abnormal puberty, for example tuberous sclerosis or severe cerebral palsy.

McCune–Albright syndrome

Also known as polyostotic fibrous dysplasia. Consists of abnormalities of endocrine function and skin pigmentation with characteristic fibrous dysplasia of the skeletal system. Caused by abnormality in G protein involved in cAMP formation. Cell surface receptors (eg for TSH/ACTH/luteinising hormone/follicle-stimulating hormone) are activated abnormally. The mutation leading to the abnormal gene protein is somatic, so that different tissues will have different expression of the abnormal protein. This leads to variable manifestations of the condition, with differing combinations of endocrinopathy and bone disease between patients.

Examination findings

○ Abnormal growth: may be tall or short depending on combination of endocrine disturbance/bone disease
○ Large areas of increased pigmentation with ragged 'Coast of Maine' outline
○ May have evidence of precocious puberty
○ Need to examine for signs of hyperthyroidism or cushingoid features
○ Look for evidence of bone disease: deformity from repeated fractures/evidence of surgery; can have cranial nerve compression
○ May have evidence of osteomalacia/rickets because of increased renal phosphate loss

YOUR NOTES

12.5 NEPHROLOGY

12.5.1 Introduction

Renal cases may be used in the 'Other' Station or in the Abdominal Station, eg renal mass palpable on abdominal examination.

The commonest scenarios you are likely to come across are:

○ **Child with a renal mass.** The key thing is to differentiate the renal mass from a mass due to other causes, eg spleen, faeces; this is covered in Chapter 9. Polycystic renal disease is the most likely cause although a full differential diagnosis should be known. **Palpate for a bladder:** a large bladder would be due either to bladder outlet obstruction or a neuropathic bladder. Remember a palpable megarectum may appear to be the bladder but will indent. Prune belly syndrome may also be seen (undescended testis, abdominal wall muscle defect and muscle deficiency in the urinary system with dilation).

○ **Child with nephrotic syndrome.** This is one of the commonest renal cases seen in the exam as such children are often used for a Clinical Examination session and a History Taking/Management Planning session on the same day if they are amenable. It definitely pays to know nephrotic syndrome well. The physical signs to elicit can be either those of nephrosis or those of **steroid toxicity** and both should be learnt.

Other renal cases are unusual:

○ You may see a child with **chronic renal failure** with signs of chronic disease including short stature, nutritional impairment and pallor, and who may have either a peritoneal dialysis catheter or fistula for dialysis. Children are also sometimes seen post renal transplant. It is important in them to look for the side-effects of immunosuppression and to remember that there may be nephrectomy scars if the diseased kidneys have been removed. **The transplanted kidney is likely to be in the iliac fossa and is superficial and therefore palpable.**

○ Child with loin scars. It is important to be aware that loin scars are often seen following nephrectomy for poorly functioning dysplastic or non-functioning renal tissue in childhood. The reason for the nephrectomy is the risk of sepsis if there is ongoing reflux to the poorly functioning moiety and the risk of hypertension long term.

Tip

If you see a renal patient it must be stressed here that measurement of blood pressure is very important. The correct **technique** is covered in Chapter 8, however the underlying **cause** in childhood is often renal

12.5.2 Renal masses

Case

> *Carly is a thin-looking 16-year-old girl with bilateral and ballotable loin masses. I cannot get above them, they are resonant to percussion and I have not seen them move with respiration.*
>
> *I think these masses are renal.*
>
> *She is otherwise well and has a normal blood pressure for her age.*

Supplementary questions

What is the most likely diagnosis? (Autosomal dominant polycystic renal disease as bilateral, otherwise well)

What is the differential diagnosis of a renal mass? (See below)

What is the initial investigation of choice? (Renal ultrasound)

Differential diagnosis of a renal mass

- ◯ Autosomal-dominant polycystic renal disease
- ◯ Hydronephrosis
- ◯ Cyst
- ◯ Multicystic dysplastic kidney
- ◯ Wilms' tumour
- ◯ Neuroblastoma
- ◯ Compensatory hypertrophy in unilateral renal agenesis
- ◯ Renal vein thrombosis
- ◯ Storage disorder
- ◯ Beckwith–Wiedemann syndrome
- ◯ Sepsis/abscess

Notes on polycystic renal disease

Autosomal-dominant ('adult') polycystic renal disease

Of adults with chronic renal failure, 8% have autosomal-dominant polycystic renal disease which is due to mutations in genes PKD1, 2 and 3. The cysts are actually grossly dilated nephrons, which compress surrounding parenchyma rendering it ischaemic. It commonly presents either with an asymptomatic renal mass in late childhood or with mass plus complications in early adult life.

Complications

○ Abdominal pain
○ Haematuria
○ Proteinuria
○ Hypertension
○ Chronic renal failure

Treatment is supportive.

Autosomal-recessive polycystic renal disease

This is much less common (1 in 40 000) and is due to mutations in the PKHD1 gene on chromosome 6. Presents in the neonatal period with bilateral renal masses and often respiratory distress due to the pulmonary hypoplasia which developed in utero. Hepatic cysts are common and portal hypertension can develop. The prognosis is poor; a number survive several years but inevitably progress to dialysis and transplantation.

12.5.3 Nephrotic syndrome

This is a likely case. The child may have few signs and the examiner may give you a lead into the diagnosis (see below)

Instructions to candidate

Examine this 4-year-old boy with nephrotic syndrome.

Case

> John is 4 years old. He looks small for his age; I would like to plot him on a growth chart. On inspection he appears pale and oedematous with a swollen abdomen. He also has bilateral ankle and leg swelling.
>
> He is well perfused peripherally and centrally, and is well hydrated.
>
> His pulse is 96 beats per minute. I cannot measure his JVP because of the oedema. Heart sounds are normal with no added sounds. He is not in respiratory distress and his chest is clear with no clinical signs of pleural effusions. His abdomen is distended. There are no scars or spider naevi. There is no organomegaly. I was able to elicit shifting dullness.
>
> I would also go on to assess his genitalia.
>
> I would like to take his blood pressure, dip his urine and assess him for signs of steroid toxicity.

Supplementary questions

How would you confirm your diagnosis?

I would check a urine dipstix in the first instance. I would confirm the diagnosis by confirming proteinuria (early morning protein:creatinine ratio > 200) and hypoalbuminaemia (< 25 g/l) in an oedematous child.

If he presented with abdominal pain, how would you assess him?

I would take this sign very seriously. Abdominal pain is a common symptom due to splanchnic vasoconstriction as a consequence of intravascular depletion. The other cause of abdominal pain in children with nephrotic syndrome is peritonitis. I would clinically assess circulating volume and consider sepsis, then treat accordingly.

What is the differential diagnosis?

Notes on nephrotic syndrome

A good knowledge of nephrotic syndrome is required for all parts of the exam as stressed before. More detailed notes and a thorough management plan can be found in Part I, History Taking and Management Planning. The candidate should also access recent review articles on the subject.

Physical signs of acute nephrotic syndrome

○ Oedema
○ Pallor
○ Tachypnoea and dyspnoea if there is pulmonary congestion
○ Pleural effusions and ascites
○ Peripheral, including scrotal or vulval, oedema
○ Hypertension
○ Evidence of poor circulating volume (see Box)

CLINICAL ASSESSMENT OF THE CIRCULATING VOLUME

○ Blood pressure and pulse (rate and volume)
○ Jugular venous pressure (difficult if oedematous or uncooperative child)
○ Core–peripheral temperature difference
○ Capillary return

Complications of nephrotic syndrome

○ Hypertension
○ Acute renal failure/chronic renal failure
○ Infection
○ Thrombosis
○ Malnutrition
○ Hyperlipidaemia

Management of nephrotic syndrome – summary of main points

○ Attention to fluid balance and judicious use of isotonic saline if hypovolaemic

○ Use of 20% human albumin solution for ongoing hypovolaemia or severe symptomatic oedema or ascites (discuss with renal team)
○ Steroid therapy – **prednisolone** 60 mg/m^2 until remission followed by 40 mg/m^2 on alternate days then stop
○ Treat relapses with further prednisolone and consider **cyclophosphamide** or **ciclosporin** for steroid-dependent or steroid-resistant cases

Consider referral for renal biopsy if

○ Steroid resistant, ie does not go into remission by 28 days
○ Age <12 months or >12 years
○ Persistent haematuria
○ Hypertension not secondary to circulatory problems
○ Renal failure

Differential diagnosis of nephrotic syndrome

○ Minimal change disease – most common
○ Focal segmental glomerulosclerosis
○ Mesangiocapillary glomerulonephritis (also known as membranoproliferative)
○ Membranous nephropathy
○ Henoch–Schönlein purpura with renal involvement
○ Systemic lupus erythematosus
○ Congenital nephrotic syndrome – first 6 months

12.5.4 Steroid toxicity

Instructions to candidate

Examine this boy and tell me what your findings suggest.

Case

> Jason is a 12-year-old boy who appears short and obese and I would like to plot him on a centile chart. On general examination he has a moon face and buffalo hump. There is distension of his abdomen with striae and bruising, and he has poor muscle bulk. Jason has hirsutism and hypertrichosis, there is a central line and a nasogastric tube in situ and a scar on his abdomen in the right groin with a palpable mass underneath it.
>
> These findings suggest that Jason has **iatrogenic Cushing's syndrome** secondary to steroid-induced immunosuppression following a renal transplant. Hypertrichosis suggests he is also taking ciclosporin.
>
> I would like to measure his blood pressure and dipstick his urine for glucose

Notes on steroid-induced toxicity

The clinical features of steroid toxicity (Cushing's syndrome)

General
○ Growth retardation with truncal obesity
○ Oedema
○ Hirsutism

Face and eyes
○ 'Moon face'
○ Acne
○ Cataracts

Trunk
○ Buffalo hump (centralised fat distribution)
○ Abdominal striae and bruising

Limbs

- ○ Poor muscle bulk
- ○ Proximal myopathy

Tip

Other side-effects of steroids are osteopenia, glycosuria and psychosis

---

Aetiology

There are various scenarios that can lead to steroid-induced toxicity that you may meet in the exam. Examples include:

- ○ Asthma
- ○ Juvenile chronic arthritis
- ○ Cystic fibrosis
- ○ Dermatomyositis
- ○ Crohn's disease
- ○ Post renal/cardiac transplant (look for relevant scars)
- ○ Nephrotic syndrome.
- ○ Primary Cushing's disease (extremely rare)

12.5.5 Beckwith–Wiedemann syndrome

Instructions to candidate

Examine this girl who presented in the neonatal period with profound hypoglycaemia

Case

> *Zoe looks large for her age – she is 2 years old. I would like to plot her height and weight on a centile chart. On inspection of her face she has transverse ear lobe creases and macroglossia.*
>
> *On abdominal examination I notice she has a scar adjacent to her umbilicus. There is no organomegaly.*
>
> *There is no obvious hemihypertrophy on examination of her limbs.*
>
> *The diagnosis is **Beckwith–Wiedemann** syndrome and her scar is from surgery on her exomphalos in the early neonatal period.*

Notes on Beckwith–Wiedemann syndrome

This is a rare fetal overgrowth syndrome (around 1 in 14 000 live births) associated with gene locus 11p15.5. Most cases are sporadic although there have been clusters of cases within families.

Clinically, there are major and minor features.
The diagnosis is based on either:

1. Three major features, or
2. Two major **plus** three or more minor features

Major clinical features

○ Pre- and/or post-natal overgrowth (>90th centile)
○ Macroglossia
○ Abdominal wall defects

Minor clinical features

○ Characteristic ear signs – ear lobe creases or posterior helical pits
○ Facial naevus flammus
○ Hypoglycaemia
○ Organomegaly
○ Hemihypertrophy

Natural history of disease

Infants are more likely to be delivered prematurely, 35% before 35 weeks. Exomphalos occurs in 50% of cases and hypoglycaemia is common, which is usually mild and transient, requiring frequent feeding only. However, some babies have severe hypoglycaemia requiring diazoxide. Deaths from Beckwith–Wiedemann syndrome mainly occur in infancy and are usually caused by problems related to prematurity or associated congenital cardiac disease (< 10%).

During **childhood**, the dysmorphic features become less apparent, although the macroglossia may cause feeding problems, problems with speech (requiring speech therapy) and occasionally with obstructive apnoea. Surgical tongue reduction may be required in severe cases. Overgrowth is most marked in the first few years and is associated with an advanced bone age. It tends to slow down in late childhood, and most adults are <97th centile. Hemihypertrophy occurs in 25% of cases and visceromegaly is common.

Neoplasias occur in 5%, most commonly with Wilms' tumour followed by adrenocortical carcinoma, hepatoblastoma and neuroblastoma. Children with hemihypertrophy are most at risk.

Some children have severe learning difficulties, which are thought mainly to be from neural damage secondary to neonatal hypoglycaemia rather than congenital central nervous system malformations.

By **adolescence**, the majority lead a normal life as long as there are no sequelae of neonatal hypoglycaemia.

There is controversy about abdominal tumour screening, which some centres advocate should be by regular abdominal palpation and others by regular ultrasound examination or both. Wilms' tumours can present rapidly in this group and mean size at presentation is reduced significantly if the child has 3- to 4-monthly screening. Hence many centres err on the side of caution as small tumours can be removed with preservation of renal function.

The risk factors for Wilms' tumour are important (see Box) and should be known as the association may arise as a supplementary question in a short case.

RISK FACTORS FOR THE DEVELOPMENT OF WILMS' TUMOUR

○ (Beckwith–Wiedemann syndrome)
○ Hemihypertrophy
○ Aniridia
○ DRASH syndrome

NB DRASH syndrome = ambiguous genitalia, nephropathy, Wilms' tumour

YOUR NOTES

13

CHILD DEVELOPMENT

CONTENTS

13.1   Introduction
13.2   Suggested scheme for developmental examination – infant
13.3   Developmental milestones – infant
13.4   Suggested scheme for development examination – older child
13.5   Developmental milestones – older child
13.6   Visual assessment
13.7   Assessment of hearing
13.8   Specific scenarios
        Bottom shuffling
        Handedness
        Child with severe global developmental delay
        Tired/uncooperative child
        Autism
        Down syndrome

13.1 INTRODUCTION

The development station can be a very challenging section of the exam and each candidate should have a well-practised approach to avoid nerves and fear affecting their performance. We advise that you team up with a colleague and start with as many normal healthy children as you can. Be observed and timed. The college guidance says you will most likely be asked to assess one area, eg fine motor or gross motor, and be prepared to assess others/comment on others. In practice many candidates are simply told 'assess this child's development' and are expected to make a comment about all areas. Most candidates find that they are given a child to examine who is delayed in at least one area, though you should also be prepared to be asked to examine a child who has no developmental delay whatsoever. Be mindful of the Anchor Statements provided by the College while you are preparing. You are being assessed on your ability to give clear instructions to the child, to ask about parental concerns and to use history taking where appropriate. You should not ask questions about milestones which can be directly observed as part of your examination. You are also being assessed on your ability to give a clear summary of your relevant findings, and to suggest the next step in examination or investigation/referral.

The following are some practical points about how your style and approach can reassure the examiner and the parents that you know what you are doing, and help you to maximise your performance in this station.

○ **Structured systematic approach** (start at just below estimated age and work up until just above expectations)
○ Keep to the examiners' instructions
○ Ask questions. Asking questions is OK but keep to the bare minimum to accomplish the task. As a general rule you will be able to ask questions but not where clinical exam will suffice. The examiner will want to know that you have chosen your questions carefully and in a structured way. When preparing by practising your examination technique, try to rank your questions in order of importance and see if your colleagues agree with your choice. The most important questions relate to your ability to conduct an examination and interpret the results; if giving instructions to a child you need to be sure they understand them (what is their first language? can they hear? can they see?). Other questions

relate to fine tuning your assessment of their development by incorporating things you can't assess there and then (eg toileting/climbing stairs), or checking their medical/developmental history to get a clearer understanding of their difficulties (were they premature? age of first words/walking?, etc)

○ All **equipment** is provided (don't bring your own)

○ Start by getting down to the child's height and begin playing with the child and observing/commenting. **Opportunistic observations and comments** are the key to a well rounded performance. Your attempts to engage the child can then be very targeted

○ If introducing a new activity, comment on what the child does when not being directed, eg if introducing bricks comment on what they do initially before trying to get them to build a tower. Similarly if producing pen and paper, **watch what they do and comment before directing them** to draw a circle. When directing them to an activity, start with easy tasks and progress to more difficult ones. Demonstrate what you expect them to do (makes instructions easier for them to understand)

○ Make sure you give **clear instructions** to the child. Similar to any other examination of systems, if you say to a small child 'would you like to?' and they say 'no' your structured approach will fall apart. You need to ask a child to do something in a way that sounds polite and natural, is comfortable for you and does not provide them with an option to refuse. Just as in clinical practice, with very young children, physical examinations are done with the parent's not the child's consent. Having said that, if the child is uncomfortable or uncooperative the examination will be hampered, so skilled persuasion and distraction should be practised. Above all, be nice to the child and their parent!

○ Find something the child can do and something they can't do, so that you have a **minimum and a maximum age**. Aim is to assess developmental age to within 2–3 months up to 2 years, and within 4–6 months for 2- to 5-year-olds

○ Watch your **choice of language**. The examiners will be very mindful of how you are coming across to the child's parents. Practise using phrases such as '*today the child did not demonstrate...*' rather than '*he cannot...*'

○ The aim of your examination is to **identify any developmental problems**. Be wary of over-interpreting a good performance in one area or you may find yourself in the uncomfortable position of proclaiming that a child must be either a child prodigy or a much older child with a growth problem

CONDITIONS COMMONLY SEEN IN THE EXAM

Autism/autistic spectrum
Down syndrome
Non-mobile toddler
Global delay
Hypotonia
Hemiplegia/diplegia
Normal children

13.2 SUGGESTED SCHEME FOR DEVELOPMENTAL EXAMINATION – INFANT

General observations

- Ill or well?
- Growth?
- Any obvious dysmorphic features?
- Any equipment that gives hint of delay, for example nasogastric tube, special chair

Which area of development you then concentrate on will be governed by the examiners' instructions and the position and cooperation of the infant. In general you should always start by looking and commenting on as much as possible.

Gross motor examination (posture and movement)

Remember muscle control progresses from the head down. Suggested system for a baby could be:

- Lie the child supine and assess their general tone/limb positions and movements (you could comment on vision at this stage)
- Pull on the hands or arms until the baby is in sitting position (for 3- to 6-month-old children): look for head lag, assess straightness of spine, upper limb and truncal tone, grasp reflex
- Hold the child in ventral suspension: comment on truncal tone, head lifting, position of limbs
- Place the child prone and observe their ability to lift their head/torso/roll over or crawl away
- Finish by assessing the presence of primitive reflexes (see Box)

PRIMITIVE REFLEXES

○ **Asymmetric tonic reflex:** disappears around 4 months (or child will not be able to roll). Abnormal if fixed in one position, to one side, or if lingering at 6 months

○ **Grasp:** disappears around 4–6 months (prior to child crawling). Child develops the ability to grasp voluntarily as the reflex disappears

○ **Moro:** becomes less dramatic then disappears by 3–6 months. If present look for symmetry of response. Needs to disappear or the child will not be able to roll normally

○ **Stepping:** disappears by 2–3 months, reappears as child starts walking at 10–15 months (voluntarily)

○ **Downward parachute:** protective responsive, develops around 4–6 months

○ **Forward parachute response** (7–10 months)

Mobile infants (rolling/pulling to stand/cruising) will not cooperate with this approach and are best assessed by just observing how they move about.

Fine motor (vision and manipulation)

▪ In a baby, try to ascertain whether the baby can fix and follow. Remember you must be silent when you are doing this as babies will turn their heads to sound and this can be misleading

▪ Use a toy or interesting object and watch how the baby grasps and explores the object

▪ Look for passing from one hand to another and mouthing. Ensure that both hands can grasp equally well. In older infants could comment on their ability to let go of a toy, and object permanence

▪ Use something small (eg tiny piece of paper) to assess pincer grip

▪ Comment on pointing

Speech

▪ Comment on any vocalisation you hear

Hearing

▪ Normal practice would be to ask the parents whether they have any concerns about a baby's hearing; the examiner may be happy for you to do this. Make sure you have commented on what you can see and hear first. If the baby clearly startles to a loud noise then comment on it!

- There are other key questions that provide evidence of hearing development; for example, recognising their own name/Mama and Dada sounds, etc. Be familiar with these so you can ask them if you are given the opportunity

Social

- Watch the infant's interactions with you and with its parent
- Comment on smiling; comment on what games the parent plays with their child and how the child responds
- Look for the presence or absence of stranger awareness
- Make sure the child and parent are comfortable with you before you try waving/clapping/playing peek-a-boo, etc

And finally

- Have some questions prepared in case the examiner lets you ask them. If allowed then concentrate on social and hearing questions as these are difficult to assess fully in an exam environment
- Be prepared to order your findings in a logical sequence; this will put the examiner at ease!
- Think about the next investigation or referral if any abnormality is found.

Case – Normal 6-month-old boy

Jake demonstrated rolling from front to back. When prone he lifted his torso off the couch on his hands. When pulled to a sitting position he had a straight back and good head control. He sits briefly unsupported and bears weight on his legs. He has no Moro reflex. He is not crawling and does not attempt to pull to stand. This gives him a developmental age of 6 months for gross motor function.

Jake demonstrated fixing and following past the midline. He has no obvious squint. He can grasp with an immature grasp, in both hands and can bring a brick into the midline and into his mouth. He does not appear to have object permanence. He has a developmental age of 6 months for fine motor function.

He is babbling and his mother has no concerns about his hearing; she does not feel that he responds to his own name but he does recognise familiar voices. This gives him a developmental age of 6 months for hearing and speech.

Jake is not obviously upset by strangers and laughs when playing peek-a-boo. His mother reports that he is not yet able to indicate what he wants. For social development this gives him a developmental age of 6 months.

Jake has normal development for a 6-month-old child in all areas.

13.3 DEVELOPMENTAL MILESTONES – INFANT

Note – age ranges are to be used as a guide. You will notice different texts have slightly different quoted ranges. Development occurs in a logical sequence and this is more important than the age range for each milestone. You should carry in your head a general idea about the variation in ages at which different milestones are reached, but be very clear about the ordered progression of development and which key milestones carry age-specific warning signs.

Infant milestones

Infant milestones are listed in Tables 13.1–13.4.

Time	Milestones
6 weeks	• Turns head to one side when supine • Asymmetric tonic reflex present • Jerky arm movements • Some head lag/incomplete head control • In ventral suspension head held in same plane as body momentarily, hips extended • Chin intermittently lifted off couch when prone • Moro present
3 months	• No head lag when pulled to sit • Strong kick • Bears weight on forearms and partly lifts torso off floor when prone; head to 45° and looking around • In ventral suspension: head held above rest of body, looking around
6 months	• Spontaneously elevates head when supine • Lifts head when about to be pulled up to sitting position • Sits with straight back – if not unsupported then may show righting reflexes • Sits unsupported (5–7 months) • Rolling (2–6 months) • Lifts entire torso off floor when prone, bearing weight on hands (arms extended); head to 90° • Bears weight on legs, when held in standing position (3–7 months) • Can reach for toy
9 months	• Sits unsupported • Crawling (6–9 months) • Pulling to stand

Table 13.1: Infant milestones: motor *(continued overleaf)*

Time	Milestones
12 months	• Gets to sitting from lying position (6–11 months) • Pulls to stand and lets him/herself down (6–10 months) • Cruising (walks holding onto furniture) (7–13 months) • Stands alone (11–14 months) • Walks independently (10–15 months)

Table 13.1: Infant milestones: motor *continued*

Time	Milestone
Birth to 9 months	• Stares (at birth) • Follow side to side (6 weeks) • Reaches to grasp (palmar grasp) (3–6 months) • Mouthing (from 4½ months) • Grasps, brings to midline then mouths (6 months) • Transfers hand to hand (6 months) • Fixes on small objects (5–8 months) • Follows fallen toys (4½–8 months) (object permanence)
9–12 months	• Throws (9–15 months) • Pincer grasp (9–14 months) • Bangs bricks together (7–13 months) • Points with index finger (12 months) • Scribbles (12–24 months)

Table 13.2: Infant milestones: fine motor

Milestone	Time
● Comment on noises/vocalisation	
● Startled by sudden noise/quietens to human voice	6 weeks
● Turns to sound	3–6 months
● Turns to mothers voice/laughs/babbles	6 months
● Imitates speech sounds	From 4 to 9 months
● Mamma/ dadda sounds (used non-specifically)/ combining syllables	6–9 months
● Responds to own name/understands simple commands	12 months
● Uses mamma/dadda appropriately	7–13 months
● First word (not mamma or dadda)	11–15 months

Table 13.3: Infant milestones: hearing and speech

Milestone	Time
● Smiles	6 weeks
● Looks at faces	6 weeks
● Stranger awareness	6–8 months
● Plays peek-a-boo	5–10 months
● Waving	8–13 months
● Indicates wants (not by crying)	10–15 months
● Casting	9–12 months
● Clapping	9–12 months

Table 13.4: Infant milestones: social

13.4 SUGGESTED SCHEME FOR DEVELOPMENTAL EXAMINATION – OLDER CHILD

Instructions to candidate

Assess this child's development

This child has Down syndrome. Assess his fine motor development.

Assess this child's speech and language development by talking to her and her mother.

Assess this 3-year-old's gross motor development.

Initial procedures

Introduce yourself to the parents and child.

If not already told, ask whether you can ask the parent some questions.

Some key questions

- Do you speak English at home? (If seems relevant!)
- Have you any concerns about your child's vision or hearing? (Important if you are going to be asking a child to copy or follow instructions)
- Has your child got any pain anywhere?
- Was your child born at term or were they premature?

Note: if there is some time after the clinical assessment, or if the child is completely uncooperative, you may get an opportunity to ask a developmental history, so have some questions in mind.

General observations

Where relevant, make a comment on the following

- Growth
- Ill or well

If there are no obvious things to comment on in the following areas, save time by not mentioning them!

- Equipment (wheelchairs, nasogastric tubes, hearing aids, etc)
- Obvious dysmorphic features
- Obvious neurocutaneous stigmata

Gross motor examination (posture and movement)

What is the child doing now?

Observe and comment in less cooperative or less directable children. Think about:

- Gait
- Running
- Climbing

For older children think about asking them to:

- Jump up high
- Stand on one foot
- Kick a ball
- Bounce and catch a ball
- Ride a tricycle
- Climb stairs if stairs available!

There will be equipment provided to assess gross motor function in older children, so look for tricycles and balls when you get into the room and don't forget to use them if they are appropriate.

Remember to join in and look like you are having fun no matter how stressed you are. Be enthusiastic and congratulate them loudly! Often this is best left towards the end of the examination as once you have encouraged them to run about and kick a ball they may not want to stop and do something that requires more focus.

If you get a chance to ask the parents a question then, 'how does your child go up and down stairs' is an excellent way to be very specific about which milestones have been reached.

Fine motor and vision

This is an excellent place to start your examination, particularly if the child is focused on a 'sitting down' activity when you arrive in the room.

Always start by watching and commenting before directing the child towards more specific activities. A suggested sequence is as follows:

1. Picture book
   - This is better suited for younger toddlers
   - Look out for pointing, recognising pictures and turning pages
   - Remember to comment on vocabulary and speech as this can often be assessed using the pictures in the book

2. Drawing (if pen and paper handy) – *'Are you good at drawing? Can you draw'*
   - Be careful to note whether the child can imitate (child watches as you draw a shape) or copy (paper covered and the child cannot see what you are drawing until you are finished). As a general rule, imitating comes approximately 2 months before copying. Make sure you use the right terminology when reporting findings
   - If you are in the middle of a full developmental assessment you may well be able to get all the information you need to comment on developmental stage with this activity alone. You could then quickly move on to other areas. If you have only been asked to assess fine motor and vision then spend some more time on this activity and definitely include drawing a person if you are assessing an older child
3. Building blocks – *'Let's do some building – can you do this?'*
   - Remember the difference between copying and imitating as described above.
4. Other activities – you may have been supplied with equipment to assess
   - Threading beads
   - Using scissors
   - Matching colours

Hearing and speech

- Pointing to body parts
- Ask about name, age, boy or girl, counting, birthday
- Comment on vocabulary and how easy the child is to understand

Social

For toddlers (you may need to ask the parents for most of these) the questions are all to do with self-care/independence. Remember that most preschools are funded to accept children from 30 months and require them to be out of nappies.

- Dressing
- Toileting
- Eating and drinking

For older children, ask about activities and friends at school or preschool.

Finally

Keep the presentation of developmental stage confined to categories. Be systematic.

First comment on 'developmental age' for each area of development you have assessed.

In the area of gross motor skills, he has a developmental age of..., because he can..., but today he did not demonstrate.... In the area of fine motor and vision...'

Next comment on whether you feel this is appropriate to the child's chronological age, or whether you feel it is delayed. Also comment on whether the delay is isolated to one area of development or concerns several areas. Be aware of the limitations, as well as the significance of your findings.

Suggest a next examination based on what you have noted, eg neurological exam of lower limbs/spine, assessment of child's vision, etc.

If the child has some delay be prepared to discuss investigations/referral.

13.5 DEVELOPMENTAL MILESTONES – OLDER CHILD

Age or activity	Milestone
18 months	• Running, bending over
	• Walks carrying toy
	• Pushes/pulls
	• Climbs onto a chair
2 years	• Stands on tip toe
	• Squats and stands up
	• Jumps up (in place)
3 years	• Walks on tip toes
	• Briefly stands on one foot (for 1 s)
	• Jumps with both feet together (30 months)
	• Runs fast
	• Rides a tricycle – pushing pedals (there may be a tricycle in the room!)
4 years	• Hops
	• Stands on one foot for 3–5 s
	• Ask mother if child can climb a ladder
Gait	• Broad based – 15 months
	• 18 months – purposeful and confident gait
Ball skills	• Kicks ball (15–24 months)
	• Can run to kick a ball (4 years)
	• Bounces and catches ball (5 years)
Stairs	• Crawls upstairs – from 15 months
	• With help (holding onto adults hand) 21 months
	• Climbs with 2 feet per step holding onto rail – 2 years
	• Climbs with 1 foot per step – 3 years
	• Descends with 2 feet per step – 3 years
	• Up and down stairs in normal 'adult' fashion/ running upstairs – 4 years

Table 13.5: Milestones for the older child: motor

Task		Time
● Grasp – delicate pincer grasp		10–18 months
● Enjoys simple picture books		12–18 months
● Turning pages		18 months
● Removes wrappers from sweets		2–2½ years
● Cutting paper		3 years
● Threads large beads onto shoelace		3 years
● Matches two to three primary colours		3 years
Drawing	● Horizontal scribble	12–24 months
	● Circular scribble	2–2½ years
	● Imitates vertical line	2½ years
	● Copies circle	2½–3 years
	● Copies cross/square	4 years
	● Draws a recognisable house	4 years
	● Copies triangle	5 years
	● Draws a person with a head	3 years
	● Draws with head plus three other parts (two arms = one part)	4 years
Building Tower:		
	● Two bricks	15 months
	● Three to four bricks	16 to 24 months
	● Seven bricks	2 years
	● Nine bricks	3 years
	Imitates bridge of three bricks	4 years
	Copies 3 steps from six bricks	5 years

Table 13.6: Milestones for the older child: fine motor (vision and manipulation)

Time (years)	Milestone
1–2	<ul><li>At least three words (12–18 months)</li><li>Often constantly babbling (18 months)</li><li>Naming body parts– *'can you point to your...'* (18 months)</li><li>Pointing to pictures (18–24 months)</li></ul>
2	<ul><li>Plurals (find two of something and say 'what are these?')</li><li>Gives name</li><li>Large vocabulary (definitely greater than 20 words)</li><li>Puts two words together</li></ul>
3	<ul><li>Prepositions? (*'Where is the...?'*)</li><li>Are you a boy or a girl?</li><li>How old are you?</li><li>What colour is the...?</li><li>Uses sentences of four words</li><li>Speech is understandable to strangers</li></ul>
4	<ul><li>*'Let's do some counting...'* (up to 10 = 4 years)</li><li>Speech is grammatical</li><li>Knows several nursery rhymes</li></ul>
5	<ul><li>Fluent and clear speech</li><li>Knows birthday</li></ul>

Table 13.7: Milestones for the older child: hearing and speech

Task	Milestone and normal time of achievement
Dressing	• Tries to help with dressing (eg arms into coat) (12–15 months)
	• Takes off shoes and socks (13–20 months)
	• Can get dressed with a little help/supervision (2½–3½ years)
	• Dresses without help (3½–5½ years)
Toileting	• Indicates toilet needs (from 18 months)
	• Dry during the day (ie out of nappies) (2½–3 years)
	• Uses toilet alone/washes and dries hands (3 years)
Eating/drinking	• Uses spoon (makes a mess, but can get food to mouth) (14–18 months)
	• Uses spoon skilfully (18 months)
	• Drinks from cup (10–16 months)
	• Eats with spoon and fork (2½ years)
	• Eats with knife and fork (4 years)
Play/behaviour	• Explores environment (13–20 months)
	• Tantrums when frustrated (2 years)
	• Imitates adult activities (2 years)
	• Plays alone (2–2½ years)
	• Likes to help adults (3 years)
	• Shares toys (4 years)
	• Understands taking turns (4 years)
	• Dramatic make believe (4 years)
	• Chooses own friends (5 years)

Table 13.8: Milestones for the older child: social

Classic 'warning signs' of developmental delay

Fine motor/vision

○ Fixed squint at any age
○ Hand preference before **18 months** (usually not established until third year)
○ Not staring/no visual fixation or following at **6 weeks**
○ Immature grip at **18 months**
○ Still casting at **18 months**

Speech/hearing

○ Failure to respond to sound at any age
○ Inability to understand simple commands at **18 months**
○ Not babbling at **12 months**
○ No spontaneous vocalisation at **18 months**
○ Unable to speak in short sentences at **2½ years**
○ Unable to understand speech at **2½ years**
○ Poor articulation making speech difficult to understand at **4 years**

Always remember to mention audiology referral if you notice delay in this area of development (and be aware of how hearing is tested in different age groups, see below).

Gross motor

○ Asymmetrical neonatal reflexes – up to **6 weeks**
○ Excessive head lag past **6 weeks**
○ Persistence of primitive reflexes (eg Moro/asymmetric tonic reflex at **6 months**)
○ Unable to sit or weight bear, absence of saving reactions at **12 months**
○ Not standing at **18 months**
  • In boys: think about Duchenne muscular dystrophy
  • If upper body gross motor development is normal (sitting with straight back, reaching for toys, normal head control): think about problems with hips or spine

Social/behavioural

○ Failure to smile: average age is 5 weeks, should be concerned if not smiling at **6 weeks**

Notes for the development station

> ## Some key investigations for unexplained developmental delay
>
> - Chromosomes
> - Fragile X
> - Thyroid function tests
> - Creatine phosphokinase (CPK)
> - Metabolic screen
> - X-rays (hips/spine)
> - Neuroimaging

Multidisciplinary assessment

Paediatricians are seldom the only professionals to assess a child where there is concern about developmental delay. Remember the other key professionals involved (see Box).

> ## KEY PROFESSIONALS INVOLVED IN CHILD ASSESSMENT
>
> - Paediatrician
> - Physiotherapist
> - Occupational therapist
> - Speech and language therapist
> - Portage worker
> - Educational psychologist (if a child is likely to have special educational needs or benefit from specialised school or nursery placement)
> - Audiology
> - Ophthalmology/orthoptics
> - Orthotics
> - Orthopaedic surgeon
> - Neurologist
> - Geneticist
> - GP
> - Health visitor
> - Nursery/school teacher

13.6 VISUAL ASSESSMENT

Chapter 11, on neurology, contains a description of how to examine the eyes. It is essential to watch experts assess vision. These are some additional notes on the assessment of visual acuity.

Assessing visual acuity

Most of the time this is fulfilled by observation. Observe the ability to fix and follow and then later to pick up small objects at the peripheries of the visual field in the younger child. In the older child use a picture book or the written word. Remember to test both eyes. It is of crucial importance to stay quiet when assessing vision so as not to use voice as the stimulus. The examiner will look for this. Numerous candidates slip up on this.

It is also essential to have some background knowledge that relates to the more sophisticated assessment of visual acuity:

○ Minimum observable tests where you attempt to establish the smallest object the child can see, eg hundreds and thousands, silver sweets, Smarties®, cubes or the STYCAR graded balls

○ Minimum separable tests measuring the ability to separate visual stimuli are the most precise method, eg Snellen charts (not under 3 years), STYCAR letter tests, STYCAR toy tests, Sonksen Silver test, silhouettes, Ladybird pictures, forced-choice preferential looking acuity card procedure

○ Whichever method is used, each eye should be tested separately. This is well tolerated <8 months and >2 years but not in between. The eye should be covered with the parent's hand, a patch or a blackened lens. Most children will cooperate with both eyes open up to the age of 3 years, but will not cooperate with covering the eye until about 4 years

○ Electrophysiological techniques are useful in the investigation of some visual disorders, particularly the inherited retinal disorders, cerebral storage diseases and demyelinating diseases

○ Electroretinogram (ERG) is derived from the outer or superficial layers of the retina and may be normal when there is complete optic atrophy, or completely abnormal when there is retinitis pigmentosa long before a clinical defect becomes apparent

○ Visual evoked responses represent the electrophysiological activity generated when the nerve impulses travel from the eye to the cortex, and are used to assess the integrity of the visual pathways. They are useful when used in conjunction with the ERG

13.7 ASSESSMENT OF HEARING

It is essential to attend an audiology clinic to learn about the assessment of hearing. The information in this section is intended as helpful notes and should be read in conjunction with standard texts and practical experience gained in the clinic setting.

○ 0.5–1 newborn/1000 live births have permanent, moderate to severe, bilateral sensorineural hearing loss. In addition children become deaf throughout childhood for various reasons, and the estimated prevalence of permanent, bilateral hearing loss of moderate to severe degree increases to 1.5 – 2/1000 children under the age of 6 years

○ Important as a screening procedure: hearing tests are performed in all children at some stage, as deafness can have a major impact on the development of the child. The earlier the defect is picked up the better the prognosis

○ Until children reach the developmental age of 3–4 years, they cannot be expected to respond to a pure tone audiogram, so different methods of assessment must be employed

○ You should not be asked to perform a hearing test in the exam as you will soon learn that examination rooms (which contain a lot of children) have a background noise level far above that acceptable for a hearing test. You may be asked to talk the examiner through one of the general principles

○ There are two types of hearing tests: those used for the diagnosis of hearing loss, and those used as screening procedures

○ A good history from the parents is the first step in a hearing assessment – parental suspicion of hearing loss, family history, high risk factors, failed screening test, symptoms of middle ear disease or behavioural problems

Evoked otoacoustic emissions

○ Method used by the universal newborn hearing screening programme in UK

○ Sound stimulus produces an acoustic emission from the cochlea that can be detected by a small microphone placed within the ear canal, analysed and displayed; the child needs to be calm and still

○ Any hearing defect, even a minor conductive defect, abolishes this, and hence this is a very good test both for screening and diagnosis

○ It does not however establish the degree of hearing loss

Distraction testing

By 6–9 months, children have learnt to control their sitting balance and head posture and can turn to sound either above or behind them, hence they can take part in a distraction test:

○ Explain the test to the mother/carer
○ Position the baby carefully
○ The distracter sits in front of the baby and gains their attention by any appropriate means
○ This activity is then suddenly stopped; the baby waits for the reintroduction of play and the tester, who is standing behind the baby and out of their visual field, presents a sound stimulus
○ When the baby turns to look for the sound source they are rewarded with praise. If they do not respond, the tester raises the intensity of the sound stimulus until the baby responds
○ Sounds are presented to each side

Pitfalls: the baby becomes too interested in the examiner or the baby responds to visual stimulus after play has ceased and becomes used to the test.

Distraction with visual reinforcement: audiology rooms are equipped with loud speakers through which a variety of electronically controlled signals can be played in a sophisticated version of the distraction test.

Cooperative tests

Distraction testing becomes more difficult after 15 months as the child develops object permanence and becomes more engrossed in play (they are unlikely to turn to even loud noises in the distraction test). From this stage onwards it is usually possible to use cooperative tests, although the age range at which children will cooperate is wide. Here you use either the child's ability to discriminate speech or tasks that demand a response to certain sounds. One of each should usually be performed. It is difficult to assess each ear separately, but to a certain extent this is academic as the immediate aim is to assess functional hearing and the ability to develop language.

Speech discrimination tests

○ The McCormick toy test is the most widely used. Here a set of toys is placed in front of the child. Generally toys are paired, with each pair having similar sounding names, eg key and tree, cup and duck, horse and house, spoon and shoe, etc. Having involved the child in play with these toys, the examiner covers their mouth (to stop the child lip reading), and lowers the level of their voice intensity and asks the child to identify one of the objects on the table

○ The voice should be at a level of 30–40 dB

Performance tests

In these tests the child is asked to perform a particular task when they hear a certain sound (eg placing a brick in a basket)

○ The child must not be able to see the examiner making the test noise
○ The sound stimulus may be warble tones or narrow band noise at varying levels of intensity
○ The child must be familiar with the game first

Pure tone audiometry

A pure tone audiogram is a reliable method of testing children in each ear and can be consistently used in the normal child from 5 years onwards, sometimes earlier:

○ Headphones are placed on the child and the test starts with an easily audible tone, gradually reducing until the tone can no longer be heard
○ Each ear is tested in turn
○ Pitfalls: uncooperative children, unintentional visual clues by the tester or the parent
○ Anxious children may not respond to the sound even at high levels
○ This should be cross-checked with formal or informal speech tests

Electrical response audiometry

These tests are based on the fact that a few milliseconds after sound reaches the ear, action potentials are propagated in the cochlea, along the auditory pathways to the brainstem and cortex. It is possible to detect these potentials and use them to find the child's threshold for hearing.

Brainstem auditory evoked responses (BSER)

The BSER is recorded from three surface electrodes (usually scalp, mastoid and forehead). It represents transmission of the auditory signal from the cochlea to the brainstem. The child can be awake (if very relaxed), asleep or under anaesthetic. The complex waveform is demonstrated by computer analysis of the EEG. It is particularly useful for children who are autistic, blind or severely learning disabled and is widely used as a screening test in high-risk neonates.

Electrocochleography

A needle electrode is inserted through the tympanic membrane, on to the promontory of the middle ear, and the action potentials of the cochlea are recorded. The stimulus is normally a train of clicks. A general anaesthetic is usually required and this invasive test is rarely used.

Screening for hearing loss

The need for early detection of hearing defects is clear and screening for hearing loss is carried out in all infants in the UK. The traditional way of performing this used to be the distraction test at 6–9 months, usually carried out by health visitors. The test is satisfactory and reliable but the level of continued training and supervision required is high. Its value as a screening test for the hearing loss associated with secretory otitis media is also limited as this condition evolves throughout childhood. For children who do not have the strength to turn their heads it cannot be used.

The newborn hearing screening programme has replaced the distraction hearing test as the primary screening tool for congenital hearing loss (see www.hearing.screening.nhs.uk).

A high degree of vigilance by professionals dealing with children and parents is an additional and excellent screening test. The newborn screening test will not necessarily pick up mild hearing loss. In addition, there are many causes of acquired hearing loss (the most common being secretory otitis media) which need monitoring and occasionally intervention.

After the newborn screen the next routine test of hearing is at school entry. Children undergo a hearing test in the form of a simplified PTA (pure tone audiogram) at a fixed intensity, usually 20–25 dB. Any children failing the assessment are referred to an audiology clinic.

13.8 SPECIFIC SCENARIOS

Bottom shuffling

This runs in families and tends to delay walking; bottom shufflers are often not walking until 18–24 months. There is no evidence that bottom shuffling itself delays development in any other way; hence, it is important to establish the locomotor skills of a child who is over 18 months old and not walking but bottom shuffling. Bottom shuffle is usually an isolated event and such children will eventually walk, although a careful look is required as hemiplegic children often bottom shuffle.

> ### LOCOMOTOR PROBLEMS THAT COULD AFFECT THE LOWER LIMBS DISPROPORTIONATELY (MIMICKING SIMPLE BOTTOM SHUFFLING)
>
> Spine problem, eg spina bifida
> Neuromuscular problem: muscular dystrophy, spastic diplegia
> Bone/joint problem: developmental dysplasia of the hip, osteogenesis imperfecta
> Hypotonia

If you notice bottom shuffling and the rest of the developmental exam is normal be sure to mention that you would proceed to a neurological examination and an examination of the hips and spine. You could also ask about a family history of bottom shuffling or late walking.

Handedness

Normally appears in third year.

Be aware of abnormal causes of hand preference before this age – these could include:

- Lower motor neurone lesions, eg brachial plexus injury (from birth trauma)
- Upper motor neurone lesions, eg hemiplegia

○ Visual field problems
○ Congenital abnormalities/musculoskeletal problems/trauma
Mention a more detailed neurological examination and assessment of vision as part of your summing up. Could also ask parents about when they first noticed a hand preference, or past medical history including birth history.

Child with severe global developmental delay

Children with severe delay have a lot of input to achieve developmental milestones but the targets are the same as those for children who develop normally. They need to be able to move about, look around, explore the world with their senses, see, hear and communicate. They also need to develop independence with day-to-day activities, to play and to interact with people. Look for evidence of how they are being encouraged to do these things and it will give clues to their developmental stage and abilities.

○ Don't be thrown – remember your structure. Comment on as much as you can observe and then ask if you are allowed to talk to the parents about the rest
○ **Gross motor** – try a 'head to toe' approach, thinking about head control, sitting independently, rolling, weight bearing, cruising and walking. Don't forget that reaching for things is a gross motor skill. Comment on any obvious aids to gross motor function – wheelchair or specially adapted chair, walking aids
○ **Fine motor/ vision** – comment on obvious squints/glasses/eye contact. Do they reach/grasp/bring objects to the midline? Are they using both hands equally? Are they able to open their hands? Are they able to release objects they have grasped? Can they point?
○ **Speech/hearing** – look for hearing aids. Describe the character/quality of their vocalisation. Ask whether they recognise familiar voices, respond to their own name, follow commands
○ **Social** – think about toileting (are they in nappies?), eating and drinking (gastrostomy/nasogastric tube?). Do they help with dressing? Look for a social smile. Do they play with toys/explore their environment? How do they indicate what they want? Do they have tantrums?

In your summing up, comment on whether the child is more delayed in one area than another and anything you have noticed that is being done to improve or aid their development. Try to assign a developmental age for each area. Make a comment on the limitations of your assessment; for example, if they are strapped into a wheelchair you may be unable to fully assess their locomotor function, or if they are not positioned upright with their head in the midline you may not be able to properly assess their fine motor function/vision.

Tired/unco-operative child

Be prepared for this. The examiner is looking for a sympathetic approach and intelligent observations. The parents will be stressed. If the parents are not trying to distract the child out of their tantrum then it may be a sign that you will not be able to either. Don't try for too long. Comment on as much as you can observe. Be structured in your approach. Say *'can I ask the child's mother some questions?'* and have a structured plan for which questions to ask.

Case – Unco-operative toddler

Maya was upset throughout the examination and I had difficulty engaging her in any activities that would help me to assess her fine motor and communication skills in particular.

In the area of social development she demonstrated some stranger anxiety when I entered the room. She appeared to be having a tantrum which is a normal developmental milestone for a 2 year old. Her mother reports that she enjoys imitative play but does not understand sharing her toys. I note that she is wearing nappies and her mother reports that she is not yet dry by day. This gives her a social developmental age of 2 years.

She demonstrated running and climbing. She refused to try to kick a ball and her mother reports that she has never pedalled a tricycle and she uses two feet per step when climbing stairs. Her gross motor skills have a developmental age of 2 years.

Maya does not have an obvious squint and her mother has no concerns about her vision. I was not able to assess her fine motor skills today but her mother reports that she can scribble, that she enjoys looking at picture books and can turn pages. She does not yet know any colours. This gives her a fine motor and visual developmental age of at least 2 years.

Maya refused to answer me when I asked her questions about naming body parts today. Her mother reports that she would normally be able to do this. She also knows her name and age but not her address. Her family understands her but her speech is often intelligible to strangers. Her mother has no concerns about Maya's hearing. She has a developmental age of 2 years for speech and hearing.

Based on a developmental history from her mother, Maya has normal development across all areas. However, it was difficult to demonstrate this today due to her unwillingness to cooperate.

Autism

Affects 2:100 000–5:100 000 children
Boys:girls = 3:1.

Affects three main areas of functioning, namely the classic triad of social interaction, communication (verbal and non-verbal) and behaviour.

Social interaction

- Qualitative impairment of social interaction
- Difficulty with or inability to respond to social cues or to appreciate the feelings of others
- Can seem aloof and indifferent, although most show attachment to parents and carers
- Passive and in their own world until interrupted
- Social contacts with others are approached in a repetitive way
- In young children: may not want to be kissed or cuddled
- Slow to distinguish between parents and other adults

Communication (verbal and non-verbal)

- Limited content of speech, pedantic and concrete interpretation of language
- Limited use of gesture or facial expression as a means of communication
- May avoid eye contact during communication
- Do not point to indicate their needs as young children
- May develop ways of meeting their needs which do not involve communication
- Echolalia is common
- Speech without intonation

Behaviour

- Reduced imagination, lack of pretend play
- Restrictive and repetitive range of behaviours and play
- Inflexible
- Rigidity is imposed on day-to-day functioning
- Upset by minor changes in environment or routine
- Rituals are common
- Some imaginative play activities may be copied, eg from the television, and performed exactly the same repeatedly
- Narrow range of interest

○ Specific behaviours which may be seen
- Twirling, rocking, head banging
- Wetting and soiling
- Impulsivity, tantrums, over- or under-activity

A range of other problems may be found. For example, changes in cognitive function, dislike of loud noises or crowded places. Abnormalities usually become evident before the age of 3 years. Autistic spectrum describes abnormalities of these areas that do not fit neatly into the syndromes described by Kanner or Asperger.

Suggested scheme for examination of the child with autism

Children with autism are commonly seen in the developmental section of the exam. You need to have a structured approach which assesses their development but also looks for key features that point to an autistic spectrum disorder.

Initial procedures

Introduce yourself to the parents and child

Keep to the examiners' instructions. If asked to 'assess this child's development' then start with gross motor and fine motor, which should not be impaired in classic autism. This will give you time to watch their play and social interactions. If asked for just social or speech/hearing then start by saying as many things as you can observe that are relevant to these areas. If asked to assess whether a child has any autistic features then combine what you see with key questions for the parents.

Examination

Social

- Lack of stranger awareness
- Inability to direct child towards an activity
- Lack of eye contact
- You may not be able to get their attention at all
- Look for evidence of pretend play: how are they using the objects in the room and does it show imagination?
- Are they in nappies?

Communication

- Are they using words (if so, you can ask about name/age/body parts/colours, etc)?

▧   Are they using facial expressions/gestures to communicate?
▧   How does their parent communicate with them?

Questions to ask

If you get an opportunity to ask questions then think about what you are trying to assess. Chances are you will not be expected to make a diagnosis of autism (a process that can sometimes take highly experienced people many hours of observation). You are trying to show a discrepancy in development between gross and fine motor skills and social/communication skills, and that the quality of social interaction and communication is not normal. You will need to demonstrate to the examiner that you have an understanding of what is normal development by the questions you ask. I would suggest including these:

1. Do you have any concerns about hearing or vision? (There may be a good reason why you can't get their attention)
2. Ask about toileting skills, dressing and eating
3. Ask about pretend play, sharing and friendships (in an older-looking preschool child)
4. Ask about language (vocabulary, putting words together, understanding commands/prepositions)
5. Ask how they indicate what they want; for example, whether they point, use facial expressions, eye contact and gestures

These are crucial to making a sensible statement about your developmental examination. The following would be icing on the cake if you have time to spare.

1. Ask about past medical history, family history
2. Ask about more specific 'autism' symptoms: rituals/repetitive behaviours/rigidity (remember that most normal toddlers feel safer with set routines and can have a tantrum when these are altered – is this child's behaviour more extreme than what you would normally expect?)

Finally

When summing up, order your findings in a structured way as described above. Make sure you compare delay in one area of development with the other areas and include some comment on the severity and the limitations of your assessment. Be sensitive.

Case – Is autism assessment appropriate for this child?

Andrew is a 3-year-old boy with a family history of autism. On entering the room the most striking observation was that he did not appear to notice that we were there and did not react with any stranger anxiety such as is commonly seen in 3-year-old boys. He did not establish eye contact with anyone in the room including his mother. He was constantly exploring his environment but did not play with the toys which are here and I could not engage him in any play activity. I notice that he is wearing nappies. These features suggest marked delay in social skills.

He was vocalising but did not have any easily recognisable words and his mother reports that he indicates what he wants by taking her hand and putting it on the object he is interested in, such as the fridge or the television. He had very little facial expression. This suggests a delay in communication skills.

The delay in social and communication skills was out of proportion to his gross motor and fine motor development although I was unable to engage him in any formal assessment of these today. These features would be in keeping with a diagnosis of **autism**. *In addition to this his mother describes some behavioural traits that are typical of autistic children. In particular he has several rituals around dressing and washing which appear to be autistic in nature. He becomes very anxious and has tantrums when there are small deviations from these rituals. Based on these findings I would agree that a referral for an autism assessment is warranted.*

Down syndrome

The common misconception is that Down syndrome children are grossly developmentally delayed. There is a complete spectrum of disabilities of Down syndrome and the disability tends to be a learning disability rather than a physical disability. In the first few years development can often be normal, with learning problems becoming apparent at 3–4 years. In view of this their educational placement should depend on their ability rather than their diagnosis – some Down syndrome children enjoy integration into mainstream education, although most will eventually require some form of more specialised provision. When faced with a Down syndrome child for a developmental assessment, do not be put off; the developmental examination is just the same, and they may fall within the normal range for motor development.

YOUR NOTES

YOUR NOTES

INDEX

abdominal examination 159–60
abdominal pain
  functional 38, 136
  recurrent 35–9
abdominal scars 202–3
abducens nerve 274
accessory nerve 271
accommodation 279
achondroplasia 418–19
adrenaline 246
Alagille's syndrome 231–2
allergic bronchopulmonary
    aspergillosis 15
allergies
  egg protein 133
  peanuts 133
alpha-1 antitrypsin deficiency 232
alternate cover test 283–4
ambiguous genitalia 128
anaemia 342–4
ankle clonus 292
anorexia 136
antalgic gait 295
antibiotics in cystic fibrosis 18
anti-epileptics 131–2
aortic stenosis 177–9
  subaortic 177
  subvalvular 177
  supravalvular 167, 177
  valvular 177
apex beat 155
ascites 219

asthma 20–7, 240–3
  acute 25, 242
  delivery devices 242–3
  differential diagnosis 241
  drug therapy 24, 242
  epidemiology 241
  long-term treatment 25
  management 241
  poor response to therapy 26
ataxia 46, 314
ataxia telangiectasia 315–16
ataxic gait 294
atheosis 46
athetoid cerebral palsy 302
athetosis 297
atrial septal defect 174–5
atrioventricular septal defect 162
audit cycle 105–8
auditory nerve 274
auricular nerve 271
auscultation 156, 173
autism 480–3
autoimmune thyroiditis 427
autonomy 100–1

Barlow test 371
Becker's muscular dystrophy 310
Beckwith-Wiedemann syndrome
    201, 447–9
Beighton score 373
Bell's palsy 275–6
beneficence 101

biliary atresia
  extrahepatic   77–8
  extra-hepatic   230–2
  intra-hepatic   231–2
Blalock-Taussig shunt   186
blindness in one eye   272
blood pressure   152–4
blood transfusion
  consent for   109–13
  Jehovah's witnesses   113
  risks of   112–13
bone age   402
bottom shuffling   476
bradycardia   136
brainstem auditory evoked
    responses   474–5
breaking bad news   84, 88–95
breast milk   114–17
bronchiectasis   253–4
bronchiolitis   31, 244–6
  discharge   246
  high-risk groups   246
  management   245–6
bulbar palsy   276
Burkholderia cepacia   18

café-au-lait spots   320
cannula insertion   126
capacity   111
carbamazepine   132
cardiology   147–97
  see also individual conditions
cardiomyopathy   187–8
cardiopulmonary shunt   163
cardiovascular examination
    151–60
cataracts   287
ceftazidime   18
central nervous system   291–305
cerebellar ataxia   303
cerebellar examination   296
cerebral palsy   40–8, 301–3
  diagnosis   44
  investigation   46–7
  malnutrition   209
  treatment   47–8
CHARGE association   192

cherry red spot   286
chest wall scars   154–5
child development   451–84
  developmental delay   33–4,
    469–70
  developmental milestones in
    infants   459–61
  developmental milestones in
    older children   465–8
  examination of infants   455–8
  examination of older children
    462–5
  hearing assessment   472–5
  multidisciplinary assessment
    470
  unco-operative children   478–9
  visual assessment   471
chorea   297
choreoathetosis   46
chronic conditions   83–4, 118–21
chronic fatigue syndrome   75–6
chronic lung disease of infancy
    257–9
ciprofloxacin   18
cirrhosis   227–9
clinical trials   125
clubbing   151, 200, 237
  causes of   237
coarctation of aorta   179–82
coeliac disease   57, 215–17
coloboma   289
conduct of interview   4
confidentiality   102–3
congenital heart disease   165
  malnutrition   208
  surgery   194–7
conjunctival pallor   154
consent   83
  blood transfusion   109–13
  intercostal drain   126
  umbilical arterial catheter
    insertion   126
constipation   66–7, 217–18
contraception   129–30
cooperative tests   473
corneal clouding   287
corneal reflections   282

cor pulmonale 15–16
cover/uncover test 283
cranial nerves 269–74
  infants 271–4
  older children 270–1
  see also individual nerves
Crohn's disease 69–70, 213–14
Cushing syndrome 420–1
  steroid toxicity 445–6
cyanosis 154, 182–4
cyanotic congenital heart disease
  161
cystic fibrosis 11–19, 211–12,
  247–52
  antibiotics 18
  blood spot testing 94
  breaking bad news 88–95
  clinical problems 250–1
  co-existing conditions 18–19
  complications 18–19
  diagnosis 94–5, 249–50
  DNase 18
  endocrine problems 16
  gastrointestinal/hepatic problems
    16
  gene therapy 19
  genetics 249
  genitourinary problems 17
  hospital admission 129
  malnutrition 209
  management 251–2
  metabolic problems 16
  nutrition 17, 251
  pancreatic enzyme supplements
    18
  physiotherapy 17, 251
  respiratory problems 15–16
cytomegalovirus, transmission in
  breast milk 117

dermatology 388–99
developmental delay 33–4, 469–70
developmental hip dysplasia 136
developmental milestones
  infants 459–61
  older children 465–8
dextrocardia 170

diabetes mellitus
  and cystic fibrosis 16
  diagnosis 127–8
  hyperglycaemia 58–9
  insulin regimes 132–3
  non-compliance 118–21
  transfer to adult services 129
diarrhoea 68, 136
di George syndrome 192
diplegia 45
Disability Living Allowance 43
distal intestinal obstruction
  syndrome 16
distraction testing 473
DNase, in cystic fibrosis 18
double outlet right ventricle 183
Down syndrome 64–5, 127, 130–1,
  162, 190, 201, 484
Duane syndrome 289
Duchenne muscular dystrophy
  308–9
dysdiadochokinesis 296
dystonia 297

ectodermal dysplasia 396–7
eczema 73–4, 390–1
education, audit cycle 105–8
Edwards' syndrome 193
egg allergy 133
Ehlers-Danlos syndrome 193,
  374
Eisenmenger's syndrome 162, 172,
  186–7
electrical response audiometry 474
electrocochleography 475
Emergency Protection Order 111
endocarditis, infective 188–9
  prophylaxis 189
endocrinology 401–36
epidermolysis bullosa 397–8
epilepsy 131
  contraceptive choices 129–30
  see also seizures
EpiPens 133
Erb's palsy 366
erythema multiforme 398–9
ethical framework 100–1

ethical issues   85
    care of very preterm infants   124
    disclosure of HIV status   96–104
evoked otoacoustic emissions   472
eye examination   277
eye movements   270, 282
eye signs in systemic conditions
    288

facial nerve   271, 274
    palsy   274–5
facioscapulohumeral muscular
    dystrophy   310
failure to thrive   62–3
Fallot's tetralogy   184–6
Fanconi anaemia   344
fetal alcohol syndrome   193
floppy infant   310–11
flucloxacillin   74
foot drop   294, 384–5
Friedreich's ataxia   308, 315
fundoscopy   279

gait examination   293–5
gastroenterology   199–232
    see also individual conditions
gastrostomy tube feeding   209–10
Gaucher's disease   223
gene therapy in cystic fibrosis   19
Giardia lamblia   68
Gillick competence   111
glasses   278
global developmental delay
    477–8
glossopharyngeal nerve   271, 274
glycogen storage disease   222–3
goitre   431
Gower's sign   294, 306
Graves' disease   424–6
growth   401–36
growth charts   402
growth hormone   411–12
Guillain-Barré syndrome   307
Guthrie test   250

haematology   333–56
haemophilia   354–5, 369

Haemophilus spp.   18
Haemophilus influenzae   54
handedness   476–7
Haroteaux-Lamy syndrome   417
Harrison's sulcus   238
headaches   71–2
hearing assessment   472–5
hearing problems   33
    screening for   475
heart murmurs   129, 157–9
    grading of   159
    innocent   164, 169–70
heart rate, normal ranges   152
heart sounds   156–7
hemianopia
    bitemporal   272
    homonymous   272
hemihypertrophy   384
hemiplegia   45
Henoch-Schönlein purpura
    339–40
hepatic fibrosis, congenital   226
hepatology   199–232
    see also individual conditions
hepatomegaly   219, 220–2
hepatosplenomegaly   220
history taking   4–5
HIV
    disclosure of status   96–104
    transmission through breast milk
        117
homocystinuria   406–7
Horner's syndrome   280–1
Hunter syndrome   416–17
Hurler syndrome   416–17
hyperexpansion   237–8
hyperglycaemia   58–9
hypermobility   373–5
hypersplenism   334
hyperthyroidism   424–6
hypoglossal nerve   271, 274
hypoglycaemia   135
hypomelanosis of Ito   325–6
hyposplenism   334
hypothyroidism   426–9
    juvenile (acquired)   427
hypovolaemia   53

icthyosis 396
idiopathic thrombocytopenic
    purpura 340–1
immune function 137
incontinentia pigmenti 325–6
infant feeds, concentration of 207
infantile spinal muscular atrophy
    type I 312–13
infants
  failure to thrive 62–3
  heart murmurs 129
  intercostal drain insertion 126
  premature *see* premature infants
infection in nephrotic syndrome
    54
inflammatory bowel disease 69–70
inhalers 242–3
insulin regimes 132–3
intercostal drain 126
interpretation 5–6
intravenous fluids 136
intraventricular haemorrhage in
    premature infant 128
ipratropium bromide 31, 245
iron deficiency anaemia 343

jaundice, neonatal 134
Jehovah's witnesses 113
juglar venous pressure 168–9
justice 101
juvenile dermatomyositis 382
juvenile idiopathic arthritis 368,
    376
  enthesitis-related 378–9
  management 379–80
  oligoarticular 377–8
  polyarticular rheumatoid factor
      negative 379
  polyarticular rheumatoid factor
      positive 379
  systemic-onset 376–7

Kartagener's syndrome 155, 255–6
Kasabach-Merritt syndrome 394
Kawasaki disease 134
Kayser-Fleischer rings 232

Klinefelter syndrome 407
Kocher's incision 203
koilonychia 200
Kugelberg-Welander disease 306
kyphoscoliosis 260–1

lamotrigine 132
laparotomy scar 202
laryngomalacia 262–3
learning difficulties 33–4
leg length discrepancy 378
lens dislocation 287
LEOPARD syndrome 193
leukotriene receptor antagonists
    25
limb girdle muscular dystrophy
    310
limp 295
lipodystrophy 394–5
liver transplantation 227–30
lung disease
  chronic 32
    malnutrition in 208
lymphadenopathy 337–8

McCune-Albright syndrome 435–6
malnutrition 206
  cases 208–9
management planning 5–8
Marfan syndrome 193, 287, 405–6
meconium ileus 16
median nerve
  injury 370
  palsy 366
medical errors 84–5, 114–17, 126
meropenem 18
metabolic syndrome 211
migraine 71–2
  abdominal 38
Moebius syndrome 289
molluscum contagiosum 395
Mongolian blue spot 392
monoplegia 301
montelukast 25
Morquio syndrome 417
movement abnormalities 296–7
MRSA in premature infants 127

mucopolysaccharidoses   416–17
myotomes   300
myotonia   297
myotonic dystrophy (dystrophica
    myotonica)   313
  congenital   313

neck lumps   430–2
neonatal hip examination   371–2
neonatal jaundice   134
nephrology   438–49
nephrotic syndrome   49–54, 438,
    442–4
  complications   443
  differential diagnosis   444
  general management   53, 443–4
  investigations   52
  parental education   54
  steroid management   53
neurocutaneous syndromes   319
neurodevelopmental assessment
    291
neurofibromatosis
  type I   319–20
  type II   321–2
neurology   267–326
neuromuscular disease   304–18
  differential diagnosis   305
non-maleficience   101
Noonan syndrome   191, 414–15
nutrition
  cystic fibrosis   17
  premature infants   32–3
nutritional status   205–6
nutritional supplementation
    206–8
nystagmus   285

obesity   210–11
obstructive airway disease   237–8
oculomotor nerve   273
olfactory nerve   270, 272
optic nerve   270, 272
orthoses   385
Ortolani test   371
osteogenesis imperfecta   369–70,
    382–3

palivizumab   246
palpation   155, 173
pancreatic enzyme supplements
    18
papilloedema   286
Patau syndrome   193
patent ductus arteriosus   32
peanut allergy   133
performance tests for hearing   474
peripheral nervous system
    291–305
periventricular haemorrhage   33
periventricular leukomalacia   33
peroneal muscular atrophy   308
Perthes' disease   385–6
physiotherapy, cystic fibrosis   17
Pierre-Robin sequence   264–5
piperacillin   18
plagiocephaly   384
plantar reflexes   292
pneumothorax, spontaneous   126
polycystic renal disease
  autosomal dominant   440–1
  autosomal recessive   441
portal hypertension   224–7
portal vein obstruction   226
port wine stain   324
postural abnormalities   296–7
Prader-Willi syndrome   130
premature infants
  breast milk   114–17
  ethics of offering care   124
  intraventricular haemorrhage
    128
  MRSA   127
  nutrition   32–3
  risks for   134–5
  wheeze   28–34
primary ciliary dyskinesia   255–6
primitive reflexes   292, 456
pseudobulbar palsy   43, 276
Pseudomonas spp.   18
psoriasis   392
psoriatic arthritis   368–9, 381–2
ptosis   280–1
puberty   433–6
  delayed   435

precocious 435
Tanner stages 434
pulmonary atresia 182–3
pulmonary stenosis 175–7
pupil response 279
pure tone audiometry 474
purpura 339–41

quadriplegia 45

radial nerve palsy 366
rectal prolapse 16
reflexes, primitive 292, 456
renal mass 438, 440
respiratory distress 246
respiratory distress syndrome 31,
    126
respiratory medicine 233–65
    see also individual conditions
reticuloendothelial system 333
retinopathy of prematurity 33
rheumatology 358–86
ribavirin 246
Romberg's sign 294, 296
Russell-Silver dwarfism 415

salbutamol 31
salmeterol 25
Sanfilippo syndrome 417
scoliosis 45
scotoma 272
sebaceous naevus 394
seizures 60–1, 131–2
    see also epilepsy
sensory examination 296
short case preparation 141–5
short neck 384
short stature 408–12
Shprintzen syndrome 192
sickle cell disease 350–3
sickle crisis 135, 352
skeletal dysplasia 418
skin lesions 389
sodium valproate 132
Sotos syndrome (cerebral gigantism)
    407
spastic gait 294

spastic quadriplegia 302
speech discrimination tests 473–4
spherocytosis, hereditary 345–6
spina bifida 317–18
spinal muscular atrophy type III
    306
spirometry 238–9
splenomegaly 219, 224–7
squint 282–4
    non-paralytic 284
Staphylococcus spp. 18
Statement of Special Educational
    Needs 43
steatorrhoea 16
steroids
    inhaled 128–9
    nephrotic syndrome 53
steroid toxicity 445–6
Stevens-Johnson syndrome 399
strawberry naevus 393–4
stridor 262–3
Sturge Weber syndrome 324–5
surgery, congenital heart disease
    194–7

tacrolimus 74
talipes 385
tall stature 403–5
tendon reflexes 292
thalassaemia 347–9
thrombocytopenia, absent radius
    (TAR) syndrome 341
thrombosis 54
thyroglossal cyst 432
thyroid eye disease 426
thyroid gland 422–3
thyroid status 423–4
tics 297
toe walking 384
topiramate 132
total anomalous pulmonary venous
    drainage 183
total parenteral nutrition 32–3
tracheostomy 264
transposition of great arteries 183
tremor 297
Trendelenburg gait 295, 359

trigeminal nerve   271, 273–4
trisomy   13 *see* Patau syndrome
trisomy   18 *see* Edwards' syndrome
trisomy   21 *see* Down syndrome
trochlear nerve   273
truncus arteriosus   183
tuberous sclerosis   322–4
Turner syndrome   191, 413–14

ulnar nerve palsy   366
umbilical arterial catheter insertion
    126
umbilical hernia   218
univentricular heart   183–4
unlicensed medications   125
uveitis   289, 378

VACTERL association   192
vagal nerve   271, 274
ventricular septal defect   166,
    171–4

visual acuity   270, 278, 471
visual assessment   471
vitiligo   395
von Gierke's disease   222–3
von Willebrand's disease   355–6

waddling gait   294
Werdnig-Hoffman disease
    312–13
wheeze, in infants   28–34
Williams syndrome   167, 191
Wilms' tumour   448–9
Wilson's disease   232
windswept hip deformity   45
Wiskott-Aldrich syndrome   341
withdrawal of treatment   123
work-related problems   124–5

XYY syndrome   407